D0160477

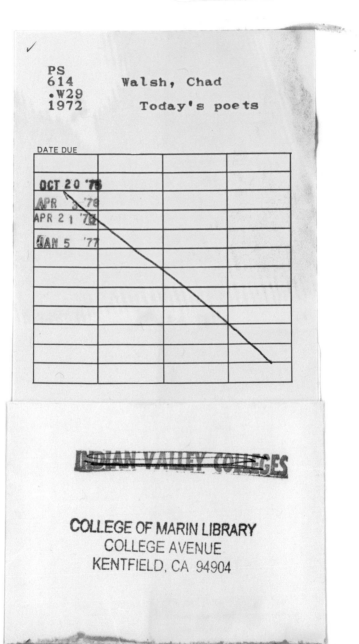

TODAY'S POETS

AMERICAN AND BRITISH POETRY
SINCE THE 1930's

SECOND EDITION

REVISED AND ENLARGED

TODAY'S POETS

AMERICAN AND BRITISH POETRY

SINCE THE 1930'S

EDITED WITH AN INTRODUCTION BY

CHAD WALSH BELOIT COLLEGE

SECOND EDITION
REVISED AND ENLARGED

CHARLES SCRIBNER'S SONS
NEW YORK

A-1.72[V]

PRINTED IN THE UNITED STATES OF AMERICA
LIBRARY OF CONGRESS CATALOG CARD NUMBER 76-162784
SBN 684-12701-6

ACKNOWLEDGMENTS

Grateful acknowledgment is made to the following authors, publishers, agents,
and individuals for their permission to reprint the poems in this anthology:

GEORGE ALLEN & UNWIN LTD. For rights in Great Britain and the Common-
wealth to Brian Patten, "Now We Will Either Sleep, Lie Still, or Dress Again,"
"The Prophet's Good Idea," "Through the Tall Grass in Your Head," and "Sad
Adam" from *Notes to the Hurrying Man*. For "Little Johnny's Confession" and
"Little Johnny Takes a Trip to Another Planet" from *Little Johnny's Confession*.

THE ALTERNATIVE PRESS. For Allen Ginsberg, "Rain-wet Asphalt Heat, Garbage
Curbed Cans Overflowing" from *broadside*.

ATHENEUM PUBLISHERS, NEW YORK. For rights in the United States for George
MacBeth, "The Blood Woman" from *The Colour of Blood*, copyright © 1965,
1966, 1967 by George MacBeth. For "Marshall" from *The Night of Stones*,
copyright © 1968 by George MacBeth.

JOHN BENNETT. For John Bennett, "#2," "#4," "#7," and "#29" from *The
Zoo Manuscript*, published by Sydon Press, 1968. For "Episode: Father and
Small Son" and "Elegy for Anne Jones" from *Griefs and Exultations*, published by
St. Norbert College Press, 1970.

BLACK SPARROW PRESS. For Diane Wakoski, "In Place of a Phone Call to
Arabia," "The Magician," and "The Magellanic Clouds" from *The Magellanic
Clouds*, copyright © 1970 by Diane Wakoski.

CARL BODE. For Carl Bode, "Beginnings," "Sonnet: The Window," "Variation
on a Theme by Dylan Thomas," "The Planet," "Smorgasbord," and "Nocturne."

BROADSIDE PRESS. For Don L. Lee, "The Self-Hatred of Don L. Lee" from
Black Pride, copyright © 1968 by Don L. Lee. For "But He Was Cool," "com-
munication in whi-te," "Malcolm Spoke/who listened?," "Black Sketches," and "A
Message All Blackpeople Can Dig" from *Don't Cry Scream*, copyright © 1969
by Don L. Lee.

CALDER & BOYARS LTD. For rights in Great Britain and the Commonwealth for

Robert Creeley, "The Immoral Proposition," "The Operation," "The Whip," "A Wicker Basket," "She Went to Stay," "Ballad of the Despairing Husband," "The Door," "Jack's Blues," "The Name," "The Rose," and "The Wife" from *For Love*.

JONATHAN CAPE LTD. For rights in Great Britain and the Commonwealth for Derek Walcott, "A Far Cry from Africa," "Ruins of a Great House," "Parang," "A Letter from Brooklyn," "The Polish Rider," and "Bronze" from *In a Green Night*. For "The Gulf" from *The Gulf*.

UNIVERSITY OF CHICAGO PRESS. For rights in the United States for Thom Gunn, "Innocence," "Flying Above California," and "My Sad Captains" from *My Sad Captains*. For "The Goddess" and "Touch" from *Touch*.

CITY LIGHTS BOOKS. For Allen Ginsberg, "In the Baggage Room at Greyhound" from *Howl and Other Poems*, copyright © 1956, 1959 by Allen Ginsberg. For Part IV of "Kaddish" from *Kaddish and Other Poems*, copyright © 1961 by Allen Ginsberg. For "Kral Majales" and "Wales Visitation" from *Planet News*, copyright © 1968 by Allen Ginsberg.

JOHN CUSHMAN ASSOCIATES, INC. For rights in the United States for John Wain, "This Above All Is Precious and Remarkable," "Anniversary," "Apology for Understatement," "Brooklyn Heights," and "A Song About Major Eatherly" from *Weep Before God*, copyright © 1961 by John Wain.

J. M. DENT & SONS LTD. AND THE TRUSTEES FOR THE COPYRIGHTS OF THE LATE DYLAN THOMAS. For rights, exclusive of U.S., for Dylan Thomas, "Especially When the October Wind," "Do You Not Father Me," "Altarwise by Owl-Light," "When All My Five and Country Senses See," "A Refusal to Mourn the Death, by Fire, of a Child in London," "Poem in October," "The Hunchback in the Park," "Do Not Go Gentle into that Good Night," "Fern Hill," and "In the White Giant's Thigh" from *Collected Poems*.

UNIVERSITY OF DETROIT PRESS. For Brother Antoninus, "Hospice of the Word" and "A Canticle to the Christ in the Holy Eucharist" from *The Crooked Lines of God*.

ANDRE DEUTSCH LIMITED. For Roy Fuller, "The Pure Poet," "Epitaph on a Bombing Victim," "Y.M.C.A. Writing Room," "The Tribes," "Crustaceans," "Rhetoric of a Journey," "The Image," "On Reading a Soviet Novel," "The Day," and "Versions of Love" from *Collected Poems 1936–1961*.

For Laurie Lee, "Bombay Arrival," "The Edge of Day," "Sunken Evening," "Home from Abroad," "Scot in the Desert," and "Long Summer" from *My Many Coated Man*.

DOUBLEDAY AND COMPANY, INC. For Brother Antoninus, "A Siege of Silence," copyright © 1958 by Brother Antoninus. For "What Birds Were There" and "In All These Acts" from *Hazards of Holiness*, copyright © 1962 by Brother Antoninus. For "The Rose of Solitude," copyright © 1962 by Brother Antoninus; and "The Way of Life and the Way of Death," copyright © 1967 by Brother Antoninus, from *The Rose of Solitude*.

For rights in the United States and Canada for James Dickey, "Giving a Son to the Sea" (Part II of "Messages"), copyright © 1969 by James Dickey; and "In the Pocket," copyright © 1970 by James Dickey, from *The Eyebeaters, Blood, Victory, Madness, Buckhead and Mercy*. "Giving a Son to the Sea" was first published by *The New Yorker*.

For rights in the United States and Canada for Theodore Roethke, "The Cycle," copyright 1941 by *The Virginia Quarterly Review*; "The Far Field," copyright © 1962 by Beatrice Roethke, Administratrix of the Estate of Theodore Roethe; "A Field of Light," copyright 1948 by *The Tiger's Eye*; "I Knew a Woman," copyright 1954 by Theodore Roethke; "Light Listened," copyright © 1964 by Beatrice Roethke, Administratrix of the Estate of Theodore Roethke, "Otto," copyright © 1963 by Beatrice Roethke, Administratrix of the Estate of Theodore Roethke; "Praise to the End!," copyright 1950 by Theodore Roethke; "The Waking," copyright 1948 by Theodore Roethke; and "In a Dark Time," copyright © 1960 by Beatrice Roethke, Administratrix of the Estate of Theodore Roethke; from *Collected Poems of Theodore Roethke*. "In a Dark Time" was first published by *The New Yorker*. "Otto" was first published by *Partisan Review*.

For Diane Wakoski, "The Night a Sailor Came to Me in a Dream" and "The Hermit" (from "From the Tarot Deck") from *Inside the Blood Factory*, copyright © 1968 by Diane Wakoski.

DUFOUR EDITIONS, INC., CHESTER SPRINGS, PENNSYLVANIA. For Patricia Beer, "Lemmings," "Brunhild," "Head of a Snowdrop," "Young Widow," "A Dream of Hanging," and "A Visit to Little Gidding."

For Roy Fuller, "Those of Pure Origins" and the epigraph at the beginning of *New Poems*.

E. P. DUTTON & CO., INC. For rights in the United States for Carl Bode's poems "Who Calls the English Cold?" "Covent Garden Market," "Personal Letter to the Ephesians," "The Bad Children," "Requiem," "The Burial of Terror," and "Sonnet: Head Next to Mine" from *The Man Behind You*, copyright © 1959 by Carl Bode.

For rights in the United States for Lawrence Durrell's poems "Conon in Exile," "Alexandria," "On First Looking into Loeb's Horace," "The Lost Cities," and "The Critics" from *Collected Poems*, copyright © 1956, 1960 by Lawrence Durrell. For rights in the United States and Canada to "Troy" and "A Persian Lady," from *The Ikons and Other Poems*, copyright © 1961, 1963, 1964, 1965, 1966 by Lawrence Durrell.

FABER AND FABER LTD. For rights in Great Britain and the Commonwealth for George Barker, "Secular Elegies," "Summer Song I," "Summer Song II," "Channel Crossing," and "Stanzas on a Visit to Longleat House in Wiltshire, October 1953" from *Collected Poems 1930–1955*. For "A Little Song in Assisi" from *The View from a Blind I*.

For British rights for John Berryman, "I've Found Out Why, That Day That Suicide," "Great Citadels Whereon the Gold Sun Falls," "For You Am I Collared O To Quit My Dear," and "All We Were Going Strong Last Night This Time" from *Berryman's Sonnets*. For "Henry's Guilt" (371 of *The Dream Songs*) from *The Dream Songs*. For "Crisis" and Part I of "Eleven Addresses to the Lord" from *Love and Fame*.

For rights in Great Britain and the Commonwealth for Lawrence Durrell, "Conon in Exile," "Alexandria," "On First Looking into Loeb's Horace," "The Lost Cities," "The Critics," "Troy," and "A Persian Lady" from *Collected Poems*.

For rights in Great Britain and the Commonwealth for the three lines quoted in the Introduction from T. S. Eliot's poem "The Love Song of J. Alfred Prufrock" from *Collected Poems 1909–1962*.

For Thom Gunn, "The Beach Head" from *Fighting Terms*. For "On the Move," "The Silver Age," and "The Corridor" from *The Sense of Movement*. For rights in Great Britain and the Commonwealth to "Innocence," "Flying Above California," and "My Sad Captains" from *My Sad Captains*. For "The Goddess" and "Touch" from *Touch*.

For rights in Great Britain and the Commonwealth to Ted Hughes, "Dick Straightup" from *Lupercal*. For "Wodwo" and "New Moon in January" from *Wodwo*. For "Lineage," "Crow and Mama," and "Examination at the Womb-Door" from *Crow*. For British rights to "The Hawk in the Rain," "Secretary," "The Jaguar," "Law in the Country of the Cats," and "Childbirth" from *The Hawk in the Rain*.

For Philip Larkin, "One Man Walking a Deserted Platform" and "Heaviest of Flowers, the Head" from *The North Ship*. For British rights to "Here" and "Home Is So Sad" from *The Whitsun Weddings*.

For British rights for Robert Lowell, "The Holy Innocents," "Christmas in Black Rock," "The Quaker Graveyard in Nantucket," "Winter in Dunbarton," "Salem," "Children of Light," "Mr. Edwards and the Spider," "The Dead in Europe," and "Falling Asleep over the Aeneid" from *Poems 1938–1949*. For "Robert Frost" and "The Pacification of Columbia" from *Notebook*.

For Richard Murphy, "Droit de Seigneur" from *Sailing to an Island*. For British rights to "After the Noose, and the Black Diary Deeds" (from "The Battle of Aughrim") and "The God Who Eats Corn" from *The Battle of Aughrim*.

For British rights to Theodore Roethke, "The Cycle," "A Field of Light," "Praise to the End!," "The Waking," "I Knew a Woman," "The Far Field," "Light Listened," "Otto," and "In a Dark Time" from *Collected Poems of Theodore Roethke*.

For British rights to Richard Wilbur, "The Pardon," "Still, Citizen Sparrow," "Love Calls Us to Things of This World," "A Voice from under the Table," "Beasts," and "A Baroque Wall-Fountain in the Villa Sciarra" from *Poems 1943–1956*. For "Advice to a Prophet," "She," and "In the Smoking-Car" from *Advice to a Prophet*. For "Fern-Beds in Hampshire County" from *Walking to Sleep*.

FARRAR, STRAUS & GIROUX, INC. For rights in the United States and Canada to John Berryman, "I've Found Out Why, That Day That Suicide," "Great Citadels Whereon the Gold Sun Falls," "For You Am I Collared O To Quit My Dear," and "All We Were Going Strong Last Night This Time" from *Berryman's Sonnets*, copyright © 1952, 1967 by John Berryman. For "Henry's Guilt" (371 of *The Dream Songs*), copyright © 1959, 1962, 1963, 1964, 1965, 1966, 1967, 1968, 1969 by John Berryman. For "Crisis" and Part I of "Eleven Addresses to the Lord," from *Love and Fame*, copyright © 1970 by John Berryman.

For Robert Lowell, "Inauguration Day: January 1953," "Grandparents," and "Memories of West Street and Lepke" from *Life Studies*, copyright © 1956, 1959 by Robert Lowell. For rights in the United States and Canada for "Robert Frost" and "The Pacification of Columbia" from *Notebook*, copyright © 1967, 1968, 1969, 1970 by Robert Lowell.

For rights in the United States for Derek Walcott, "A Far Cry from Africa," "Ruins of a Great House," "Parang," "A Letter from Brooklyn," "The Polish Rider," and "Bronze" from *Selected Poems*, copyright © 1962, 1963, 1964 by Derek Walcott. For "The Gulf" from *The Gulf*, copyright © 1963, 1964, 1965, 1969, 1970 by Derek Walcott.

FULCRUM PRESS. For rights in Great Britain and the Commonwealth for Gary Snyder, "January" (from "Six Years"), and "Beneath My Hand and Eye the Distant Hills, Your Body" from *The Back Country*.

GRANADA PUBLISHING LIMITED. For rights in Great Britain and the Commonwealth for George Barker, "No Other Tiger Walked That Way That Night" and "Epitaph: On the Suicide of the Painter John Minton" from *Collected Poems*, published by MacGibbon and Kee.

For R. S. Thomas, "A Labourer," "A Peasant," "Song," "The Airy Tomb," "Saint Antony," "In a Country Church," "Chapel Deacon," "Age," "Poetry for Supper," "Anniversary," and "A Welsh Testament" published by Rupert Hart-Davis.

HARCOURT BRACE JOVANOVICH, INC. For rights in the United States for the three lines quoted in the Introduction from T. S. Eliot's "The Love Song of J. Alfred Prufrock" from *Collected Poems 1909–1962*, copyright © 1963, 1964, by T. S. Eliot.

For rights in the United States and Canada for Robert Lowell, "The Holy Innocents," "Christmas in Black Rock," "The Quaker Graveyard in Nantucket," "Winter in Dunbarton," "Salem," "Children of Light," "Mr. Edwards and the Spider," and "The Dead in Europe" from *Lord Weary's Castle*, copyright 1944, 1946 by Robert Lowell. For "Falling Asleep over the Aeneid" from *The Mills of the Kavanaughs*, copyright 1948 by Robert Lowell.

For Bink Noll, "The Picador Bit," copyright © 1962 by Bink Noll; " 'All My Pretty Ones? Did You Say All?' " copyright © 1960 by Bink Noll; "Air Tunnel, Monticello," copyright © 1961 by Bink Noll; "Lunch on Omaha Beach," copyright © 1962 by Bink Noll; "For Jane Kane, Whom We Knew in Our Young Marriages," copyright © 1962 by Bink Noll; and "The Rented Garden," copyright © 1958 by Bink Noll; from *The Center of the Circle*. For "The Hunchback's Bath" and "To the God Morpheus" from *The Feast*, copyright © 1967 by Bink Noll.

For rights in the United States and Canada for Richard Wilbur, "Love Calls Us to the Things of This World," "A Voice from under the Table," and "Baroque Wall-Fountain in the Villa Sciarra" from *Things of This World*, copyright © 1956 by Richard Wilbur. For "Beasts" from *Things of This World*, copyright 1955 by Pantheon Books. For "Advice to a Prophet," copyright © 1959 by Richard Wilbur; "She," copyright © 1958 by Richard Wilbur; and "In the Smoking-Car," copyright © 1960 by Richard Wilbur; from *Advice to a Prophet and Other Poems*. For "Fern-Beds in Hampshire County" from *Walking to Sleep: New Poems and Translations*, copyright © 1967 by Richard Wilbur. For "The Pardon" and "Still, Citizen Sparrow" from *Ceremony and Other Poems*, copyright 1948, 1949, 1950 by Richard Wilbur.

HARPER & ROW, PUBLISHERS, INC., For rights in the United States and Canada for Ted Hughes, "The Hawk in the Rain," "Secretary," "The Jaguar," "Law in the Country of the Cats," and "Childbirth" from *The Hawk in the Rain*, copyright © 1957 by Ted Hughes. For rights in the United States to "Dick Straightup" from *Lupercal*, copyright © 1959 by Ted Hughes. For "Lineage," "Crow and Mama," and "Examination at the Womb-Door" from *Crow*, copyright © 1971 by Ted Hughes. For "Wodwo" and "New Moon in January" from *Wodwo*, copyright © 1962 by Ted Hughes. "Crow and Mama" was first published in *The New Yorker*.

For rights in the United States for Sylvia Plath, "Daddy," "Lady Lazarus," and "Contusion" from *Ariel*, copyright ©1963 by Ted Hughes.

For W. D. Snodgrass's poem "Vampire's Aubade" from *After Experience*, copyright © 1968 by W. D. Snodgrass.

WILLIAM HEINEMANN LTD. For rights in Great Britain and the Commonwealth for Carl Bode, "Who Calls the English Cold?" "Covent Garden Market," "Personal Letter to the Ephesians," "The Bad Children," "Requiem," "The Burial of Terror," and "Sonnet: Head Next to Mine" from *The Man Behind You*.

HILL AND WANG, INC. For rights in the United States for Brian Patten, "Now We Will Either Sleep, Lie Still, or Dress Again," "The Prophet's Good Idea," "Through the Tall Grass in Your Head," and "Sad Adam" from *Notes to the Hurrying Man*, copyright © 1969 by Brian Patten. For "Little Johnny's Confession" and "Little Johnny Takes a Trip to Another Planet," from *Little Johnny's Confession*, copyright © 1967 by Brian Patten.

THE HOGARTH PRESS LTD. For Laurie Lee, "First Love" and "Field of Autumn" from *The Sun My Monument*.

THE HOLLINS CRITIC. For Carl Bode's poem "Smorgasbord."

HOUGHTON MIFFLIN COMPANY. For Anne Sexton, "Some Foreign Letters" from *To Bedlam and Part Way Back*. For rights in the United States and Canada to "The Truth the Dead Know," "In the Deep Museum," and "The Fortress" from *All My Pretty Ones*. For "For My Lover, Returning to His Wife" and "You All Know the Story of the Other Woman" from *Love Poems*.

OLWYN HUGHES. For Ted Hughes, "Dark Women" and "Encounter," copyright © 1971 by Ted Hughes.

For British rights for Sylvia Plath, "Daddy," "Lady Lazarus," and "Contusion" from *Ariel*, copyright © 1965 by Ted Hughes. For "Two Views of a Cadaver Room" and "Colossus" from *The Colossus and Other Poems*, copyright © 1961 by Sylvia Plath; all published by Faber and Faber Ltd.

MARGOT JOHNSON AGENCY. For Howard Nemerov, "Runes" and Brainstorm" from *New and Selected Poems*, copyright © 1960 by the University of Chicago Press. For "Beyond the Pleasure Principle" from *The Blue Swallows*, copyright © 1967 by Howard Nemerov. For "A Spell Before Winter," "Human Things," "De Anima," and "The Dial Tone" from *The Next Room of the Dream*, copyright © 1962 by Howard Nemerov.

ALFRED A. KNOPF, INC. For rights in the United States for Richard Murphy, "After the Noose, and the Black Diary Deeds" (Part IV of "Now") and "The God Who Eats Corn" from *The Battle of Aughrim*, copyright © 1968 by Richard Murphy.

For rights in the United States for Sylvia Plath, "Two Views of a Cadaver Room," copyright © 1960 by Sylvia Plath; and "The Colossus," copyright © 1961 by Sylvia Plath; from *The Colossus and Other Poems*.

For W. D. Snodgrass, "Orpheus" and "These Trees Stand," copyright ©

1956 by W. D. Snodgrass; "The Marsh," copyright © 1957 by W. D. Snodgrass; "The Campus on the Hill," copyright © 1958 by W. D. Snodgrass; and "September in the Park" and "The Operation," copyright © 1959 by W. D. Snodgrass; from *Heart's Needle*.

DENISE LEVERTOV. For Denise Levertov, "The Gypsy's Window" and "Laying the Dust" from *Here and Now*, copyright © 1957 by Denise Levertov.

LITTLE, BROWN AND COMPANY. For the lines by Emily Dickinson quoted in the Introduction, from *The Complete Poems of Emily Dickinson*, edited by Thomas H. Johnson.

LONGMAN GROUP LTD. For Patricia Beer, "Ghost" and "Rome Twelve O'clock" from *Loss of the Magyar and Other Poems*. For "Love Song" from *The Survivors*.

THE STERLING LORD AGENCY. For British rights for Anne Sexton's "The Truth the Dead Know," "In the Deep Museum," and "The Fortress" from *All My Pretty Ones*, copyright © 1961, 1962 by Anne Sexton. For "For My Lover, Returning to His Wife" and "You All Know the Story of the Other Woman" from *Love Poems*, copyright © 1967, 1968, 1969 by Anne Sexton.

MACGIBBON & KEE LTD. For British rights for Lawrence Ferlinghetti, "Just as I used to say . . ." (#2 from "Pictures of the Gone World"), "In Golden Gate Park that day . . ." (#8 from "A Coney Island of the Mind"), "Constantly risking absurdity . . ." (#15 from "A Coney Island of the Mind"), "Dove sta amore . . ." (#28 from "A Coney Island of the Mind"), and "Dog" (from "Oral Messages"), from *A Coney Island of the Mind*.

THE MACMILLAN COMPANY. For rights in the United States for the quotation from *The Autobiography of William Butler Yeats* that appears in the Introduction.

THE MACMILLAN COMPANY OF CANADA AND MACMILLAN LONDON AND BASINGSTOKE. For George MacBeth, "Ode on a Grecian Urn" and the accompanying note from *The Burning Cone*. For rights in Great Britain and the Commonwealth for "The Blood-Woman" from *The Colour of Blood*. For "Marshall" from *The Night of Stones*.

For rights in Great Britain and the Commonwealth for John Wain "This Above All Is Precious and Remarkable," "Anniversary," "Apology for Understatement," "Brooklyn Heights," and "A Song About Major Eatherley" from *Weep Before God*.

For rights in Great Britain and the Commonwealth for the quotation from *The Autobiography of William Butler Yeats* that appears in the Introduction.

THE MARVELL PRESS, ENGLAND. For Philip Larkin, "Lines on a Young Lady's Photograph Album," "Wedding-Wind," "Reasons for Attendance," "Going," "Maiden Name," "Wires," "Church Going," "Poetry of Departures," and "If, My Darling" from *The Less Deceived*, copyright © 1955, 1972 by The Marvell Press.

UNIVERSITY OF MISSOURI PRESS, COLUMBIA, MISSOURI. For John Bennett, "Bulkington: Musing at the Helm, Midnight," "Ishmael: The Pod," "Ahab: His Vision of the Kraken," and "Ahab: At His Cabin Window, Midnight" from *The Struck Leviathan/Poems on Moby Dick*, copyright © 1970 by John Bennett.

NEW DIRECTIONS PUBLISHING CORPORATION. For William Everson (Brother Antoninus), "August" and "The Stranger" from *The Residual Years*, copyright 1948 by New Directions Publishing Corporation.

For rights in the United States and Canada for Lawrence Ferlinghetti, "Just as I used to say . . ." (#2 from "Pictures of the Gone World"), "In Golden Gate Park that day . . ." (#8 from "A Coney Island of the Mind"), "Constantly risking absurdity . . ." (#15 from "A Coney Island of the Mind"), "Dove sta amore . . ." (#28 from "A Coney Island of the Mind"), and "Dog" (from "Oral Messages") from *A Coney Island of the Mind*, copyright 1955, ©1958 by Lawrence Ferlinghetti. For "The Great Chinese Dragon" from *Starting from San Francisco*, copyright © 1961 by Lawrence Ferlinghetti. For "O Man in Saffron," "O Listen," "Sunlight casts its leaves," "Time a Traveler," and "Passing By" from *Back Roads to Far Places*, copyright © 1970, 1971 by Lawrence Ferlinghetti.

For rights in the United States and Canada for Denise Levertov, "Merritt Parkway," "Illustrious Ancestors," "A Map of the Western Part of the County of Essex in England," "Resting Figure," "The Jacob's Ladder," and "Matins" from *The Jacob's Ladder*, copyright © 1958, 1960, 1961 by Denise Levertov Goodman. For "With Eyes at the Back of Our Heads," "The Quarry Pool," and "To the Snake" from *With Eyes at the Back of Our Heads*, copyright © 1958, 1959 by Denise Levertov Goodman. For rights in the United States and Canada for "The Heart" from *Relearning the Alphabet*, copyright © 1966 by Denise Levertov Goodman. "A Map in the Western Part of the County of Essex in England" and "To the Snake" were first published in *Poetry*.

For Kenneth Patchen, "At the New Year," "The Carts of the Wee Blind Lass," "Now I Went Down to the Ringside and Little Henry Armstrong Was There," "Christ! Christ! Christ! That the World," "For Miriam," and "An Easy Decision" from *Collected Poems*, copyright 1939 by New Directions Publishing Corporation, 1943, 1946, 1952 by Kenneth Patchen. For "Where?" from *Doubleheader*, copyright © 1958 by Kenneth Patchen. For "Because He Liked to Be at Home" and "Because My Hands Hear the Flowers Thinking" from *Because It Is*, copyright © 1960 by New Directions Publishing Corporation. For "The New Being," "O When I Take My Love Out Walking," "In a Crumbling," and for rights in the United States and Canada for "Do I Not Deal with Angels," "The Great Sled-Makers," and "O Now the Drenched Land Wakes" from *Collected Poems*, copyright 1942, 1949, 1954, © 1957 by New Directions Publishing Corporation.

For rights in the United States and Canada for Gary Synder, "January" (from "Six Years") and "Beneath My Hand and Eye the Distant Hills, Your Body" from *The Back Country*, copyright © 1965, 1966 by Gary Snyder. For "Wave," "Kyoto Born in Spring Song," "Burning Island," "Revolution in the Revolution in the Revolution," and "What You Should Know to Be a Poet" from *Regarding Wave*, copyright © 1968, 1970 by Gary Snyder. "Wave" and "Kyoto Born in Spring Song" were first published in *Poetry*.

For rights in the United States for Dylan Thomas, "Especially When the October Wind," "Do You Not Father Me," "Altarwise by Owl-Light," "When All My Five and Country Senses See," "A Refusal to Mourn the Death, by Fire, of a Child in London," "Poem in October," "The Hunchback in the Park," "Do Not Go Gentle into that Good Night," "Fern Hill," and "In the White Giant's Thigh" all from *Collected Poems*, copyright 1938, 1939, 1943, 1946 by New Directions Publishing Corporation, 1952 by Dylan Thomas.

THE NEW YORKER MAGAZINE, INC. For Bink Noll, "Angel," copyright © 1969 by the New Yorker Magazine, Inc.

THE NEW YORK TIMES. For John Bennett, "Jennifer in the Children's Zoo" (#2 of *The Zoo Manuscript*), copyright © 1967 by The New York Times Company.

OCTOBER HOUSE INC. For rights in the United States for George Barker, "Secular Elegies I–VI," "Summer Song I," "Summer Song II," "Channel Crossing," "Stanzas on a Visit to Longleat House in Wiltshire, October 1953," and "A Little Song in Assisi" from *Collected Poems 1930–1965*, copyright © 1957, 1962, 1965 by George Granville Barker. For rights in the United States and Canada to "No Other Tiger Walked That Way That Night" and "Epitaph: On the Suicide of the Painter John Minton" from *Collected Poems 1930–1965*, copyright © 1957, 1962, 1965 by George Granville Barker.

For Robert Hayden, "Sphinx," "The Dream," "Zeus Over Redeye," and "El-Hajj Malik El-Shabazz" from *Words in the Mourning Time*, copyright © 1970 by Robert Hayden. For "Night, Death, Mississippi" and "Mourning Poem for the Queen of Sunday" from *Collected Poems*, copyright © 1966 by Robert Hayden.

LAWRENCE POLLINGER LTD. For British rights for Denise Levertov, "Merritt Parkway," "Illustrious Ancestors," "A Map of the Western Part of the County of Essex in England," "Resting Figure," "The Jacob's Ladder," and "Matins" from *The Jacob's Ladder*.

For British rights for Kenneth Patchen, "Do I Not Deal with Angels," "The Great Sled-Makers," and "O Now the Drenched Land Wakes."

THERON RAINES. For British rights for James Dickey, "Giving a Son to the Sea" (Part II of "Messages"), copyright © 1969 by James Dickey; and "In the Pocket," copyright © 1970 by James Dickey; from *The Eyebeaters, Blood, Victory, Madness, Buckhead and Mercy*.

RANDOM HOUSE, INC. For the three lines quoted in the Introduction from W. H. Auden's poem "In Memory of W. B. Yeats," from *Collected Shorter Poems 1927–1957*, copyright © 1964 by W. H. Auden.

For rights in the United States for Philip Larkin, "Here" and "Home Is So Sad" from *The Whitsun Weddings*, copyright © 1965 by Philip Larkin.

For Karl Shapiro's poems "Elegy for a Dead Soldier," copyright 1944 by Karl Shapiro; "Love for a Hand," copyright 1952 by Karl Shapiro; "The Recognition of Eve" (Part II of "Adam and Eve"), copyright 1951 by Karl Shapiro; and "University," copyright 1940, © 1968 by Karl Shapiro; from *Poems 1940–1953*. For "August Saturday Night on the Negro Street" from *The Bourgeois Poet*, copyright © 1962 by Karl Shapiro. For "I Swore to Stab the Sonnet" and "How Beautifully You Clothe Your Body" from *White-Haired Lover*, copyright © 1967 by Karl Shapiro. "I Swore to Stab the Sonnet" and "How Beautifully You Clothe Your Body" were first published in *Poetry*.

RAPP & WHITING. For British rights for James Dickey, "In the Lupanar at Pompeii," "The Heaven of the Animals," and "In the Tree House at Night" from *Poems 1957–1967*.

For British rights for James Wright, "The Minneapolis Poem," "In Terror of Hospital Bills," "Outside Fargo, North Dakota," "Two Postures Beside a Fire," "The Frontier," "The Lights in the Hallway," and "In Response to a Rumor that the Oldest Whorehouse in Wheeling, West Virginia, Has Been Condemned" from *Shall We Gather at the River*.

ROUTLEDGE & KEGAN PAUL LTD. For rights in Great Britain and the Commonwealth for John Wain, "Reason for not Writing Orthodox Nature Poetry" from *Words Carved on a Sill*.

RUTGERS UNIVERSITY PRESS. For John Ciardi, "Elegy," "To Judith Asleep," "A Thanks That Flesh Is Sad," "Palaver's No Prayer," "In Place of a Curse," "After Sunday Dinner We Uncles Snooze," "An Island Galaxy," "Credibility," "Vodka," "English A," "Suburban Homecoming," and "Was a Man."

ST. MARTIN'S PRESS, INC. For rights in the United States for John Wain, "Reason for not Writing Orthodox Nature Poetry" from *Words Carved on a Sill*.

SCORPION PRESS. For George MacBeth, "Report to the Director" from *The Broken Places*, copyright © 1963 by Scorpion Press.

CHARLES SCRIBNER'S SONS. For Robert Creeley, "The Moon" and "The Boy" from *Pieces*, copyright © 1969 by Robert Creeley. For rights in the United States and Canada for "The Immoral Proposition," "The Operation," "The Whip," "A Wicker Basket," "She Went to Stay," "Ballad of the Despairing Husband," "The Door," "Jack's Blues," "The Name," "The Rose," and "The Wife," from *For Love*, copyright © 1962 by Robert Creeley.

THE SWALLOW PRESS, CHICAGO. For Chad Walsh "Ode on a Plastic Stapes," "Ode on the First Ape That Became a Man," "The Archaic Hours," "Water Lilies," and "Poverty" from *The End of Nature*, copyright © 1969 by Chad Walsh.

TOTEM PRESS. For Gary Snyder, "The Ancient Forests of China Logged" and "Maudgalyâyana saw hell" from *Myths and Texts*, copyright © 1960 by Gary Snyder.

JOHN WAIN. For John Wain, "Sestina for Khasan Israelov" from *Wildtrack*.

DIANE WAKOSKI. For Diane Wakoski, "Sleep" and "Winter Apples" from *Discrepancies and Apparitions*.

CHAD WALSH. For Chad Walsh, "Ode to the Finnish Dead," "A Gentleness," and "Rejoice in the Basements of Memory."

WESLEYAN UNIVERSITY PRESS. For James Dickey, "The Dusk of Horses," "The Scarred Girl," and "The Poisoned Man" from *Poems 1957–1967*, copyright © 1961, 1962, 1963 by James Dickey. For rights in the United States and Canada for "In the Lupanar at Pompeii," "The Heaven of Animals," and "In the Tree House at Night," all from *Poems 1957–1967*, copyright © 1961, 1962, 1963 by James Dickey. "The Heaven of Animals," "In the Tree House at Night," "The Dusk of Horses," "The Scarred Girl," and "The Poisoned Man" were first published in *The New Yorker*.

For Vassar Miller, "Adam's Footprint," "Fantasy on the Resurrection," "The Final Hunger," "No Return," "Ballad of the Unmiraculous Miracle," "Song for a Marriage," "In Consolation," "Return," "For Instruction," "From an Old Maid," "Protest," and "Love's Eschatology" from *My Bones Being Wiser*, copyright © 1960, 1963, 1968 by Vassar Miller. For "Sloth" and "Remembering Aunt Helen" from *Onions and Roses*, copyright © 1960, 1963, 1968 by Vassar Miller.

For James Wright, "A Blessing" and "On Minding One's Own Business" from *Collected Poems*, copyright © 1958, 1960, 1961, 1964, 1966, 1967, 1968 by James Wright. For rights in the United States and Canada to "The Minneapolis Poem," "In Terror of Hospital Bills," "Outside Fargo, North Dakota," "The Frontier," "The Lights in the Hallway," "Two Postures Beside a Fire," and

"In Response to a Rumor that the Oldest Whorehouse in Wheeling, West Virginia, Has Been Condemned" from *Collected Poems*, copyright © 1958, 1960, 1961, 1964, 1966, 1968 by James Wright. "A Blessing," "Outside Fargo, North Dakota," and "The Lights in the Hallway" were first published in *Poetry*.

MR. M. B. YEATS. For rights in Great Britain and the Commonwealth for the quotation from *The Autobiography of William Butler Yeats* that appears in the Introduction.

FOR DAVID AND MARION STOCKING
COLLEAGUES · FELLOW
EDITORS OF "THE BELOIT
POETRY JOURNAL" · OLD
FRIENDS

CONTENTS

EDITOR'S PREFACE

to the second edition

Toward a Redefinition of "MODERN POETRY"

Like all anthologies of contemporary poetry, *Today's Poets* was beginning to be out of date less than a decade after publication. Hence this second edition, revised and enlarged. The general principles of the anthology, as described below, remain unaltered, but the book has been thoroughly updated. A few of the original poets are omitted; more than a dozen have been added, including several very young and promising newcomers. In many cases, the poets retained from the first edition are now represented by more recent work.

"Modern poetry" is a slippery and relative term. In the first decades of the century it made sense to begin anthologies with Walt Whitman (1819–92), Emily Dickinson (1830–86), Thomas Hardy (1840–1928), or Gerard Manley Hopkins (1844–89). What made sense then has become a senseless tradition. Anthologies of modern poetry grow bigger and bigger until they resemble two-volume encyclopedias. Even so, the real moderns usually get short shrift, often being represented by only a few pages.

One might defend the traditional starting points by saying that Whitman, Dickinson, Hardy, and Hopkins are pioneers who prepared the way for the poets now alive and writing. Granted. But the same is true of John Donne (1573–1631) and the anonymous author of *Beowulf*. Contemporary poetry is what it is partly because of all the major and some of the minor poets who have preceded it.

The only practical expedient is to fix arbitrarily on a date, and let it be the dividing line between "modern poetry" and what has gone before. In the process, a new set of labels will be needed. From Walt Whitman to, say, W. H. Auden, one might speak of the *early moderns* or the *transitional poets*. That period has a certain integrity. During that time occurred most of the poetic mutations that still largely shape the poetry of today. The great technical experiments were made; striking shifts in poetic sensibility took place. Though some of the major figures of the transitional period are alive and very much alive, they already securely belong to literary history, and have earned their place in general anthologies of English-language verse "from Beowulf to W. H. Auden." The term "modern poetry" can now be conveniently limited to the still newer generations of poets. For purposes of the present anthology, Auden (1907–) is considered the last of the transitional "old masters," and Theodore Roethke (born a year later) leads the procession of the "real moderns." Arbitrary as lines of demarcation are, it is not totally fanciful to think of Auden as a culmination of trends pointing back to Eliot and Pound, and Roethke as pointing forward to much that is now happening in British and American poetry.

Today's Poets is therefore a collection of forty-odd poets, British and American, who have come to the fore in the last three or four decades. Each has sufficient space so that some balanced idea can be formed of his scope and achievement.

The primary criterion has been quality. It would be absurd to assert that these are *the* forty-two best, but I would simply maintain that all of them are interesting and that a fair number will make their way into the permanent corpus of English-language poetry.

The second criterion has been variety. The whole spectrum, from the wildly experimental to the traditional, is on display here. Many of the poets blessedly refuse to fit into any critical pigeonhole. Nor are all of them well-known figures. I am happy to include certain poets who are among the most interesting but who too rarely or never have been anthologized: John Bennett, Derek Walcott, Carl Bode, R. S. Thomas, to name a few.

Today's Poets should be of particular use in universities and colleges. It brings within one set of covers a substantial representation of the "real moderns," British and American. It provides sufficient material for a course in contemporary poetry or can serve to supplement the traditional anthologies in those courses that begin around Whitman and come down to the present.

The section "Notes on the Poets" gives basic biographical and bibliographical information. It is followed by an alphabetical "Index of Authors and Titles" for quick reference. Untitled poems are given under the first line, enclosed in square brackets.

I owe thanks to many more persons than I can mention by name. First of all, my gratitude to many of the poets themselves who not only cooperated by giving permission but frequently suggested particular poems for inclusion or provided me with previously unpublished poems. My thanks also to a great number of scholars, editors, poets, critics, and students in Great Britain and the United States who counseled with me and sometimes called my attention to poets whose work I might otherwise have overlooked. Special thanks to the following: Wilbur F. Scott, Philip Durham, Carl Bode, Howard Sergeant, George MacBeth, Peter Stitt, Loretta Larvick, David Stocking, Marion Kingston Stocking, Aspasia Kolis, and my daughter Alison.

Chad Walsh

Beloit College
June 1971

TODAY'S POETS

INTRODUCTION

A *Sampling of Moderns*

It is intriguing to imagine what the most respected Victorian poets would make of the poetry written in Britain and America during the past thirty or forty years. One suspects that if, by some time-warp or other device of science fiction, Tennyson and Longfellow could wander unobserved through the modern poetry collection in the Harvard Lamont Library or turn through the pages of this present anthology, their initial reaction would be a mixture of recognition, surprise, bewilderment, indignation, and excitement. Here are the opening lines from seven poems of our times.[1]

with your eyes of appendix operation
with your eyes of abortion
with your eyes of ovaries removed
with your eyes of shock
with your eyes of lobotomy

FROM "Kaddish," by Allen Ginsberg

I've taken a trip to another planet
And I'll be away for a while,
so don't send the Escaped Children Squad after me
The Universe is too wild.

FROM "Little Johnny Takes a Trip to
Another Planet," by Brian Patten

[1] For the poems in their entirety, see Index of Authors and Titles.

My wife asleep, her soft face turned from me,
My children sleeping in their rooms as well,
I get up, drawn to the window, to see what I must see:
Silver, and black and silver. There is almost a
    silver smell.

FROM "Sonnet: The Window," by Carl Bode

From what I am, to be what I am not,
To be what once I was, from plan and plot
To learn to take no thought,
I go, my God, to Thee.

FROM "Return," by Vassar Miller

animals come in all colors.
dark meat will roast as fast as whi-te meat
especially in
the unitedstatesofamerica's
new
self-cleaning ovens.

FROM "Malcolm Spoke/who listened?" by Don L. Lee

Animal Henry sat reading the *Times Literary Supplement*
with a large Jameson & a worse hangover.

FROM "The Dream Songs," by John Berryman

A spider in the bath. The image noted:
Significant maybe but surely cryptic.
A creature motionless and rather bloated,
The barriers shining, vertical and white:
Passing concern, and pity mixed with spite.

FROM "The Image," by Roy Fuller

FAMILIAR AND STRANGE

There is much in the seven poems that would seem perfectly familiar and natural to Tennyson and Longfellow. They would note that poets still write about religious experience and love of a woman. And poets still write sonnets—sometimes.

Not everything is strange, but much is. A typical Victorian poet would find Roy Fuller's spider distasteful and would regret that Allen Ginsberg chose to list so many surgical operations. Patten's poem would suggest, at best, whimsical verse for children (which it is not intended to be), and Don L. Lee's poem requires a knowledge of post-Victorian history in order to make sense.

In short, modern poetry has enough continuity with Victorian poetry so that Longfellow and Tennyson would find themselves partially at home. At the same time, they would feel they had stepped in a treacherous and bizarre landscape, where old landmarks were scattered amid new and ominous sights.

Continuity and change—these are the two key concepts to be kept in mind when reading the poetry of our times and comparing it with that of earlier centuries.

THE LINEAGE OF REVOLUTION

No period has a monopoly on poetic innovations. When old English alliterative and accentual verse yielded to rhymed and metrical stanzas, it was a revolution. The introduction of blank verse in the sixteenth century was another revolution. The seventeenth century saw John Donne and the other Metaphysicals writing a poetry in which the sacred and the profane, the lovely and the grotesque, were combined into a violent dislocation of what the Elizabethans had called poetry. With the coming of Romanticism, Keats and Wordsworth were berated by the reviewers as though their names were Pound and Eliot; they were accused of willful obscurity, lines that did not scan, and substituting sound for sense.

If poetry, while maintaining its continuity in a long and living tradition, is always in process of mutating into new forms and new sensibilities, the late nineteenth and early twentieth centuries cannot claim to be unique. All the period can reasonably assert, with substantial evidence, is that the mutations have been unusually frequent and violent, so that Longfellow might have more trouble reading John Berryman than Alexander Pope would have had reading Longfellow.

LONGFELLOW AND ROBERT LOWELL

Everything one can say about "Modern Poetry" may be disproved by singling out this poem or that, but certain generalizations *can* be made, in a broad, almost statistical way. For example, it is extremely unlikely that any modern poet would write a poem like

Longfellow's "The Jewish Cemetery at Newport," and it is equally
unlikely that any Victorian (with the possible exception of Hopkins)
would have written Robert Lowell's "The Quaker Graveyard in
Nantucket." The opening sections of the two poems are as follows:

THE JEWISH CEMETERY AT NEWPORT

How strange it seems! These Hebrews in their graves,
    Close by the street of this fair seaport town,
Silent beside the never-silent waves,
    At rest in all this moving up and down!

The trees are white with dust, that o'er their sleep
    Wave their broad curtains in the southwind's breath,
While underneath these leafy tents they keep
    The long, mysterious Exodus of Death.

And these sepulchral stones, so old and brown,
    That pave with level flags their burial-place,
Seem like the tablets of the Law, thrown down
    And broken by Moses at the mountain's base.

The very names recorded here are strange,
    Of foreign accent, and of different climes;
Alvares and Rivera interchange
    With Abraham and Jacob of old times.

THE QUAKER GRAVEYARD IN NANTUCKET

A brackish reach of shoal off Madaket,—
The sea was still breaking violently and night
Had steamed into our North Atlantic Fleet,
When the drowned sailor clutched the drag-net. Light
Flashed from his matted head and marble feet,
He grappled at the net
With the coiled, hurdling muscles of his thighs:
The corpse was bloodless, a botch of reds and whites,
Its open, staring eyes
Were lustreless dead-lights
Or cabin-windows on a stranded hulk
Heavy with sand. We weight the body, close

Its eyes and heave it seaward whence it came,
Where the heel-headed dogfish barks its nose
On Ahab's void and forehead; and the name
Is blocked in yellow chalk.
Sailors, who pitch this portent at the sea
Where dreadnaughts shall confess
Its hell-bent deity,
When you are powerless
To sand-bag this Atlantic bulwark, faced
By the earth-shaker, green, unwearied, chaste
In his steel scales: ask for no Orphean lute
To pluck life back. The guns of the steeled fleet
Recoil and then repeat
The hoarse salute.

Even on a first reading, some of the differences are obvious. One is the relatively superficial fact that Longfellow shows traces of a standardized "poetic diction" (*o'er, climes*), whereas Lowell's language is that of normal but intense prose. More importantly, Longfellow tells the reader from the beginning how he should respond: "How strange is seems!" Lowell gradually evokes the reader's response by indirect means as the poem goes along. Longfellow's poem is very regular in its form—lines of iambic pentameter, rhyming *abab*. Lowell's rhythm is basically iambic pentameter, but filled with deliberate irregularities and rough combinations of syllables. The line length varies, perhaps according to some pattern, but if so the pattern is not transparent. Longfellow uses straight rhyme. Lowell employs a series of modulations between pure rhyme and various sorts of half rhyme (*Madaket, night, Fleet, lute*, etc., which have in common the same terminal consonant, *t*).

"The Jewish Cemetery at Newport" pictures the fact of death in broad, general, gentle strokes. "The Quaker Graveyard" has the realism of a medical student's first experience in anatomy laboratory ("a botch of reds and whites,/Its open, staring eyes"). The figurative language of Longfellow's poem is readily grasped and seems merely an extra ornament rather than an essential part of the poem. For instance, "Exodus of Death" is a striking phrase and might have been expanded so as to create the structure of the entire poem; but Longfellow simply uses it for its momentary beauty and then drops it. The allusion to *Moby Dick* in Lowell's phrase, "Ahab's void and forehead," is not an incidental adornment; it is further developed as the poem progresses and is a structural part of the whole work.

Longfellow's poem is much more relaxed; he is in no hurry, and has no compulsion to make every word work hard. A line can say very little but say it pleasantly—"At rest in all this moving up and down!" where the words after "rest" add little to the thought or mental picture, since the previous line with its phrase "never-silent waves" has already implied the up and down motion. Lowell's poem is more compressed, having scarcely a word that could be blue-penciled without destroying some essential fact, idea, or image.

Finally, Longfellow pretty much says it straight. His poem is like an essay written in verse. Lowell's poem is devious and would be extremely difficult to convert into a prose paraphrase.

Lowell is far from being the most "modern" of the moderns in his way of writing. And Longfellow is not a straw man. He is a considerably better poet than most recent critics have granted, and "The Jewish Cemetery" is one of his best poems. The two are discussed here not to encourage that self-congratulation in which every literary period likes to indulge, but simply to set in contrast a good poem, typical of the nineteenth century, and a good poem, typical of the present.

Mutations

Poetry has undergone a series of mutations, some of which produced brief-lived monsters, while others were so successful that they succeeded in the Darwinian struggle for poetic survival. It remains to look at a few of the poets in whom these mutations are evident. There is no space here to discuss any poet in detail. The most that can be attempted is a brief listing of the particular ways in which certain poets broke ground for the future.

POE AS PIONEER

For present purposes, Edgar Allan Poe (1809–49) will serve as a beginning. The first American poet who was also a major literary critic, Poe's example in his verse and perhaps still more in the impact of his critical theories make him a living influence still. He is, for one thing, a great-great-grandfather of the New Criticism and its more recent developments. He insisted that a poem is a thing in its own right, an esthetic construct. It is not designed to make men good or happy. This craftsman's eye view of poetry naturally involved an extreme and highly technical interest in technique itself. Along with this, in Poe's poetry as well as his criticism, was a strong psychological bent, the desire to present feelings and emotions in a chemically pure state.

Poe profoundly excited the French poet Baudelaire, and through him the influence of Poe passed into the mainstream of French symbolism, to suffer various sea-changes there and be re-exported later to the English-speaking countries, via Eliot and Pound among others. Poe is thus, indirectly at least, one of the many reasons that "The Jewish Cemetery," excellent as it is, could scarcely be written by any poet living today.

THE MANY WHITMANS

Walt Whitman (1819–92) is the next revolutionary. It is important to distinguish among the various Whitmans. Subsequent poets have picked and chosen among the protean aspects of his poetry. Some have been mainly attracted by the strutting pose of the poet himself, who shortened his name from Walter to Walt and wrote anonymous reviews of his own work in which he hinted at his devilish lustfulness.

Whitman the two hundred per cent male—in his poetry if not in his real life—is the least significant Whitman. To any American poet he offered something more important: America itself as the subject matter of poetry—not merely the new world, but the new humanity—vital, democratic, advancing toward an ultimate brotherhood.

To American poets, Whitman offered the real America. To all poets he offered a subject matter in which plain people and ordinary experiences are as worthy of the poet's attention as the limited range of "poetic subjects" hitherto acceptable.

He was a later and more radical Wordsworth in his expansion of subject matter; he was also a Wordsworth when he set out to free himself from a stylized "poetic diction," and raise the language or ordinary speech to the intensity of poetry. Like Wordsworth, he partially succeeded and partially failed. He floundered about amid colloquialisms and a linguistic hodgepodge of words grabbed wherever he could find them—"These from me, O Democracy, to serve you, ma femme!"—and he constantly slipped back into the hackneyed language of the poetasters—"Then dearest child, mournest thou only for Jupiter?", "O Threat! O throbbing heart!" At his best, however, he did for daily language what he did also for daily life, revealing the poetry in both.

Whitman also set about to liberate himself from conventional scansion. He was a pioneer in free verse. This term was subsequently to be abused and cheapened by a great horde of poets, particularly around the time of World War I, who took the term to mean that anything goes: Prose chopped up into lines of varying length becomes, by some alchemy of the printer, poetry. Whitman's free verse was not merely a negative thing, a declaration of independence against anapests and dactyls; rather, it was an effort to discover other rhythms—the cadence of breath groups, the natural rhythm that thought and feeling produce when they are purified and raised to the excitement of poetry. The lasting legacy of Whitman's experiments in free verse is that the poet has a bigger tool kit. He may choose—many do choose—not to use the tools that Whitman proposed, but at least they are there. Just as Whitman expanded the scope of poetry, he expanded and diversified the devices that make for rhythm and the sense of poetic form.

One part of Whitman's legacy has only just begun to be recognized clearly. Many readers have been puzzled at Whitman's colossal egotism combined with his consuming passion for the masses and the grasses. The key seems to be that Whitman was, before everything else, a mystic. Perhaps a Taoist would understand his poetry better than a Thomist would. In his creedless perception of whatever is ultimate, Whitman was constantly reworking some primal and intensely personal experience—the direct awareness of the unity of all things. Thus the egoistic "I" is no longer mere egotism; "I" and America are one; America and mankind are one; mankind and a blade of grass are one.

DICKINSON

One other American poet calls for attention at this point, Emily Dickinson (1830–86). At its worst her poetry can be offensively cute. But at its best, it is—and this may be claiming too little—the greatest poetry written by any American woman.

From a technical viewpoint, Dickinson's stanza forms seem at first to present little that is new. Most of her poems could be sung to the hymn tunes that were intoned weekly in Amherst. On a more careful reading, the freedom of rhythm within the traditional patterns becomes evident; she could vary and "rough up" her meters in as boldly modern a way as Robert Lowell.

Important aspects of Dickinson's poetry point toward the modern rediscovery of the "Metaphysical" poets of the seventeenth century. There is in Dickinson the same willingness to see unsuspected resemblances between things usually put in different conceptual pigeonholes.

> Bring me the sunset in a cup,
> Reckon the morning's flagons up,
>   And say how many dew;
> Tell me how far the morning leaps,
> Tell me what time the weaver sleeps
>   Who spun the breadths of blue!

Most of all, her poetry anticipates the sensibility that crystalized in the Imagist movement around the time of World War I. Dickinson hates to say abstract things abstractly; she suggests them obliquely by quick phrases that bring up an evocative sensory image:

> Inebriate of air am I,
> And debauchee of dew,
> Reeling, through endless summer days,
> From inns of molten blue.

If nineteenth-century poetry tended to be long-winded and patiently explicit, Dickinson represents the revolt toward compressed, indirect statement. She was willing to communicate, but only on her own terms, which meant that the reader would have to throw off his easy assumptions about the nature of poetry and re-educate himself by reading her work, one poem at a time. This stubborn determination not to spoon-feed the reader lies back of much "modern obscurity."

HOPKINS AND TODAY'S POETRY

The next great source of poetic mutations is the English Jesuit priest Gerard Manley Hopkins (1844–89), whose influence, like that of Dickinson, was posthumous. A younger contemporary of Tennyson's, Hopkins was in some curious ways the poetic cousin of

Whitman. For one thing, he loosened the traditional patterns of meter. This he did not by free verse but by evolving what he called "sprung rhythm." The number of stressed syllables in a line creates the beat; the unstressed syllables may vary in number and position. For example, the opening stanza of "Hurrahing in Harvest" has five heavy stresses to each line, but no ingenuity of scansion can torture the lines into iambic pentameter or any other standard meter:

> Summer ends now; now, barbarous in beauty, the stooks arise
>   Around; up above, what wind-walks! what lovely behaviour
>   Of silk-sack clouds! has wilder, willful-wavier
> Meal-drift moulded ever and melted across skies?

Like Whitman also—and like Dickinson in her more elusive way—Hopkins had a vision. An orthodox Catholic Christian, he interpreted the vision in the terms of traditional theology, seeing the splendor of all things as a reflection or manifestation of God the Creator—"The world is charged with the grandeur of God. / It will flame out, like shining from shook foil." His poetic concern is to behold, to glorify in words, to give thanks. In giving thanks, he pushes and compresses language to the point where it seems it will break under the weight of glory. Great clusters of vividly expressive words are created: "stallion stalwart," "very-violet-sweet," "the dappled-with-damson west," "daylight's Dauphin, dapple-dawn-drawn Falcon, in his riding / Of the rolling level underneath him steady air. . . ."

Hopkins' technical experiments live on in the resources available to any modern poet; his spirit, so far as it can be recaptured, is visible in much of the work of such poets as Brother Antoninus and Ned O'Gorman.

OUT OF IRELAND

The Irish poet William Butler Yeats (1865–1939) is in himself almost a history of late nineteenth- and early twentieth-century poetry, for he evolved from the dreamy, Celtic-twilight softness of his earlier verse to the leaner, more intellectual, and exceedingly complex poetry of his later period.

Yeats was not a great technical innovator. His rhythms, his stanza forms are not too different from those of the Victorian period during which he was born and wrote his first poems. Nor is his greatest contribution the use he made of Irish folklore in his early poetry. His importance is first of all that he was one of the poets to fall strongly under the spell of the French Symbolists. This is a catch-all term that commonly includes Baudelaire, Verlaine, Laforgue, Rimbaud, Mallarmé, and the Belgian Maeterlinck. With all their diversity, they had a certain approach in common. They aimed at indirect suggestion rather than explicit statement; they sought symbols that would evoke a particular emotion or perception by a sudden flash of empathy and insight on the reader's part. Their poetry tended away from formal, logical presentation toward a teasing ambiguity, a mysterious vagueness of surface. Sometimes they have been compared in their complexity and deviousness to the English Metaphysicals, but the latter had in addition a passionate cerebral quality. Later, in the work of T. S. Eliot, the influence of the French Symbolists was to combine with that of the Metaphysicals and jointly contribute a large share of the obscurity for which modern poetry has been roundly damned.

Yeats was also one of the first poets to face the characteristic dilemma of the modern poet—what frame of reference to use when society as a whole has no universal and coherent set of beliefs. The nineteenth century clung to the fiction that society was Christian, but by the time of Yeats' maturity it was evident that Christianity is simply one alternative among many that the individual may choose in order to make sense of his experience. It is not a poet's proper job to create a pattern of beliefs and values, but he needs one inside of which he can write poetry. Much of the poetry of this century has been a desperate quest for something to believe, even if the belief can sometimes be only "as if it were true."

Certain poets have experienced a conversion or reconversion to some established faith—Eliot and Auden who turned to orthodox Christianity, the Marxist converts of the 1930's, etc. In doing so, they have found themselves with a frame of reference. Others have felt as Yeats did in his famous autobiographical statement:

> I was unlike others of my generation in one thing only. I am very religious, and deprived by Huxley and Tyndall, whom I detested, of the simple-minded religion of my childhood, I had made a new religion, almost an infallible church of poetic tradition, of a fardel of stories, and of personages, and of emotions, inseparable from their first expression, passed on from gen-

eration to generation by poets and painters with some help from philosophers and theologians. . . . I had even created a dogma: "Because those imaginary people are created out of the deepest instinct of man, to be his measure and his norm, whatever I can imagine those mouths speaking may be the nearest I can go to truth." [1]

Yeats' "as if" faith was a strange and wonderful composite, but it made possible some of the greatest poems of the century. At the same time it set an example. The poet without a traditional faith is emboldened to ransack other times and cultures, take what he likes, add any contributions from his own imagination, and thus create a substitute faith.

THE QUESTION OF FROST

The next poet presents a problem. Robert Frost (1874–1963) is unquestionably a major poet but is he a seminal poet? Does his poetry represent a mutation and therefore an influence on later poets? The scholars and critics have been slow in getting around to Frost. The lovable but deceptive mask of the well-adjusted, normal, rustic American that he wore deceived them for a time into thinking his poetry was simple. The man was not simple; neither is the poetry.

One strand of Frost's verse has a kinship with Ralph Waldo Emerson (1803–82). [2] This comes out in his quietly meditative poems, particularly those with a country setting, where the facts of nature serve as a kind of allegory or commentary on human affairs. But—despite Frost's jibes about free verse—there is a strain of the Whitman in him. Whitman aimed at being the poet of the common man, writing in the common language. He only partially succeeded in both attempts; his common men remain curiously generalized and abstract, and his language of common speech is a *mélange* that no common man ever spoke. Whether or not Frost was in any way influenced by Whitman, he achieved in large measure what Whitman had set out to do. In poem after poem he presents ordinary people, sharply individualized, and presents them as though

[1] *The Autobiography of William Butler Yeats*, The Macmillan Company, New York, 1953, pp. 101–2.

[2] In a longer introduction, one would need to say more about Emerson, whose pervasive influence—in ideas and stance more than technique—affected poets as diverse as Whitman, Dickinson, Robinson, and Frost. See Hyatt H. Waggoner, *American Poets from the Puritans to the Present*, 1968.

he identifies himself with them. Better than either Wordsworth or Whitman, he coaxes everyday language into yielding its poetry. In these ways, and in his ability to make a fragment of narrative serve as a moral or philosophic parable, he has offered a model to poets whose inclinations are *not* toward French symbolism and its Anglo-Saxon derivatives. One suspects—it is very difficult to pin it down—that Frost has quietly influenced a number of later poets, including Louis Coxe, Richard Wilbur, and Richard Eberhart, and that it may eventually be found that he has infiltrated the poetic tradition and shaped it as surely as Eliot, Pound, and the other poets most frequently mentioned. Perhaps the evident movement in recent poetry back to relative clarity and apparent simplicity owes a great but largely unrecognized debt to Frost.

OUT OF IDAHO

Next, out of Hailey, Idaho, came Ezra Pound (1885–) who was to be the impresario of the "new poetry." Armed with a lofty view of his own gifts and the poet's role as cultural savior, he arrived in England in 1908 and soon was correcting Yeats' manuscripts, as later he was to blue-pencil the rough draft of Eliot's *The Waste Land*.

At the time of Pound's arrival, English poetry was tending toward a kind of verse later called Georgian, from the anthologies issued between 1912–22. The term embraced poets as diverse as John Masefield, W. H. Davies, Harold Monro, James Stephens, and Robert Graves; but—for a time at any rate—they seemed to have in common a quiet lyricism, a love of nature, a bias in favor of rustic settings.

Pound had not crossed the Atlantic to become a dutiful Georgian. The English soon recognized in him a dynamo of ideas and energy and the ability to organize a literary campaign as though it were the capture of a military bridgehead. Such a campaign was the Imagist Movement, whose first anthology was issued in 1914 under Pound's impetus. The credo of Imagism finally crystalized to include the language of common speech, the *exact* word, the free use of new rhythms when suitable, absolute freedom in choice of subject, the use of imagistic instead of generalized or abstract language, concentration. These principles scarcely appear revolutionary now, but at their time, against the Georgian backdrop, they were.

Poetry: A Magazine of Verse was established in Chicago by Harriet Monroe in 1912, and it proved a convenient American outlet. Meanwhile, Pound soon quarreled with his transatlantic assistant, Amy Lowell, and in pique pulled out of the organized movement, leaving its leadership to her.

There is no time here to trace the later career of Pound and the movements and controversies in which he has been involved. His most obvious importance is simply that for years he kept things stirred up. He was always discovering new poets, finding publishers for them, issuing manifestoes, and challenging the poetic assumptions of the past.

His own career as a poet is curiously broken and fragmentary. After a brilliant start he yielded more and more to poetic and personal eccentricities, powerfully aided and abetted by his later infatuation with Mussolini's doctrines. The *Cantos* are a magnificent series of fragments, a hodgepodge of doggerel, smart aleck verse, intellectual pretentiousness, crudity, and soaring bits of poetry, all held together by the force of certain key ideas of social philosophy and further given form by the poetic convention that all times and cultures exist simultaneously for the poet; a Chinese philosopher can discuss usury with Thomas Jefferson.

Pound was yet another transmission belt for the influence of the nineteenth-century French Symbolists. In general, he has been an all-purpose literary middleman, with his translations and adaptations from Old English, Provençal, Latin, Chinese, Italian, and French poetry. He represents cultural eclecticism, an outlook powerful in all the modern arts.

Commonly Pound is grouped with Eliot and Yeats as an ancestor of the modern tradition of highly learned and cerebral verse. It might also be argued that he stands partly in the Whitman tradition and has broadened it and passed it along, much modified, one grants. In the *Cantos* he uses colloquial rhythms as freely as Whitman, and puts on the same mantle of bard and prophet. At any rate, Pound's achievements have been so varied that his example points in half a dozen different directions at once. Almost every later poet has felt the direct or indirect influence of one Pound or the other.

Finally, Pound is the clearest example of the lover's quarrel between poet and society. This has been more a rule than an exception since the Romantic Movement. One of the recurrent themes of poetry is, "Where does poetry—and the poet—fit in?" Some poets, like Pound, have seriously elected themselves the legislators of the world and have turned bitter and destructive when society did not ratify the election. Others have merely lamented their isolation or wittily satirized the establishment; some have holed up in their privacy and written poetry for other poets to read in *their* privacy.

POET AND CRITIC

Another American arrived in England in 1914 and remained there to become a British subject. He was a gentleman already from his upper-class New England background, though by accident of history he had been born in St. Louis. T. S. Eliot (1888–1965) scarcely needs detailed discussion. Not only has his literary criticism been the greatest modern fountainhead for thinking about poetry, but his poetic example has been the single largest influence in shaping the contemporary poetic tradition. Even the poets now in rebellion against "grandfather" find their rebellion shaped and colored by the inescapable fact of Eliot and the Eliot influence.

Afflicted from the start with a brooding horror of the meaninglessness of life in the depersonalized world of the modern wasteland, Eliot sought and found in certain strands of French Symbolism the poetic tools that would enable him to capture, express, and thereby transcend the emptiness of futility. Later his quest, essentially religious as well as esthetic, was to lead him to Classicism, Crown, and Church; but in the earlier poetry, such as *Prufrock*, one finds the horror, the sense of paralysis, and unreality in its purest state. One sees also the characteristic Eliot devices that were to become part of the tool kit of contemporary verse. There is the free use of historical, literary, and mythological allusions from all periods to throw light on the present moment. There is the tendency to organize a poem not by some logical progression, but by psychological states or free association—in *Prufrock* the reader is never sure just what happens when or whether it all happens in the mind of Prufrock—but what he does know is the contents of Prufrock's mind. With Eliot the strong tendency of poetry to be psychological becomes stronger.

One item of Eliot's critical theory is of particular importance: the doctrine of the "objective correlative," which he defines as "a set of objects, a situation, a chain of events which shall be the formula of that particular emotion; such that, when the external facts, which must terminate in sensory experience, are given, the emotion is immediately evoked." Prufrock does not say, "I have wasted my life in trivial experiences"; he says, "I have measured out my life with coffee spoons." He does not say, "I wish I could live purely by instinct"; he says, "I should have been a pair of ragged claws / Scuttling across the floors of silent seas," evoking a picture of primitive, mindless savagery.

Eliot was also one of the great rediscoverers of the English metaphysical tradition, supremely John Donne, with its serious punning, its refusal to be over-solemn, its oblique and frequently bizarre comparisons, in general its insistence that poetry is not concerned only with the obviously "beautiful" but can create its effects by the skillful juxtaposition of wildly assorted elements of experience and observation.

THE 'THIRTIES

One could almost end at this point and say that Eliot was the last great source of poetic mutations and there remains only a series of minor adaptations of a rich and varied tradition. Almost, but not quite. Deeply as W. H. Auden shows the influence of Eliot, he is an innovator and influence in his own right—the seminal poet of the 1930's, a period when politics and international relations pressed so inescapably on the consciousness of everyone that poetry itself was inevitably drawn to social themes.

Auden is a member and chief theoretician of a so-called group (sometimes styled the "Pylon Poets") consisting of himself, Louis MacNeice, C. Day Lewis, and Stephen Spender. Because they partially overlapped at Oxford, the journalists invested them with a cohesion they never possessed. (The four never sat together in the same room till one day after World War II, Mr. Auden assures me.) In Auden's early poetry there is a mixture of Freud and Marx that seemed to offer a modern substitute for the vanished Christian certainties of an earlier time; later he was to return to the Church as an Anglo-Catholic *cum* Kierkegaard, though this return was not to mark any loss of the sharp eye for the social scene.

As versatile a poet as Dryden, Auden is from a technical view-point the great eclectic and experimenter. He can turn out a ballad or mimic the rhythms of music hall tunes; from the sonnet and the sestina to the alliterative verse of the Old English period he is completely the master. But his versatility goes beyond mere technique. He is the peculiarly modern man, finding images and implications in the detective story, exploring Dante's territory in a New York bar, impartially writing elegies for Marx, Freud, and Yeats. In him the poetic buffoon and the prophet are inseparably united; he cavorts and in cavorting says some of the more profound and compelling things that the verse of this century has uttered.

Innovation and Achievement

We have been looking not at the poets represented in this anthology, but at their immediate predecessors. The quest was for seminal figures whose work embodies the "mutations" that unmistakably separate twentieth-century poetry from that of the nineteenth century. The poets singled out were those who broke new ground and bequeathed models, techniques, or attitudes that continue to be profoundly influential in the work of most current poets.

Innovation is not of course an invariable or only criterion of excellence. It is doubtful that E. A. Robinson or Robert Graves can be called important innovators, but they are important poets. Nor has this survey attempted even to list all the major pathfinders. It seems odd indeed to have reached this point without at least a passing mention of William Carlos Williams, Wallace Stevens, or e. e. cummings, who have all left poetry something different from what they found it. But at least enough has been said to indicate some of the striking mutations that have taken place during the past hundred years, setting the stage for the poets here anthologized.

STUBBORN INDIVIDUALITY

It is, of course, merely a handy figure of speech to talk of poetry as though it evolves like some species of reptile. Every poet is a bundle of personal mutations, no matter how much he may be influenced by the poetic climate bequeathed him by the poets before him, and the example of his contemporaries. Nor are the only influences those of poetry itself. Two poets could have identical talents, temperaments, and sensibilities, but if they lived in different periods of time, or different parts of the world, their poetry would be different. A poet responds to the world around him—its sights, problems, unspoken assumptions, the great events that are taking place. The outer world not merely gives subject matter but colors the poet's responses. On the other hand, two poets living in the same period and experiencing the same historical events may respond in utterly different ways to the world around them. Take the fact of the industrial revolution. Auden made poetry out of abandoned mine pits and rusty sidings; Frost chose to be a lone striker and settle for the certainties of the rural world.

POET AND PUBLIC

Looking backward now at the changes in poetry from the mid-nineteenth century up to the 'thirties, the total impression is twofold: enlargement and eclecticism. The poet has been liberated to use or create any form or type of language; he can write free verse or sestinas; he can be as psychological as an analyst or as theological as a Thomist; he can ransack exotic literatures, mythologies, and anthropological journals for his purposes; he can create a private faith or adopt a public one; he can be as obscure as he wishes or appoint himself a public bard.

The price of this immense liberty was for a time the partial loss of a public. The pace of poetic mutation proved too fast for the ordinary man and even for many men with more than average intelligence and education. As early as the Romantic Movement, relations between poet and public began to be strained and touchy, and the poet (or any artist) as alienated figure became a staple of literature as well as of sociological observation.

Nonetheless, the separation between poet and public has at no time been absolute. Some nineteenth-century poets—Tennyson, Longfellow, even the "difficult" Browning—succeeded in winning substantial publics. In our own century, Robert Frost became an uncrowned laureate. Other poets strove desperately to meet the public halfway but failed; such was Vachel Lindsay who eventually drank the Lysol of defeat. Still other poets have written for them-selves, for other poets, for a handful of passionate poetry lovers, and have not sought a vast audience.

The frequent and till recently accelerating alienation of poets is matched by the alienation of other artists, and in every case it seems to date from the late eighteenth or early nineteenth century, when the factory chimneys began to belch, a new social class rose to dominance, and literature and the arts entered into their "Ro-mantic" phase. The poet, who had sometimes been on easy terms with his aristocratic patron, discovered that the ascetic capitalists of Birmingham and Manchester—often rising from a culturally im-poverished background—had less interest in the "frivolities of life." Still, they encouraged literacy and a great potential reading public was created, which collectively became the new patron of the writers.[1] This public, recently introduced to literature, wanted books that were moralistic, comforting, and easy to understand. Some poets and novelists adapted and flourished. Others went their own way, offending by frankness, obscurity, newfangled ways of writing, dangerous ideas. The tradition was established that the poet who wants to be true to himself is likely to be at odds with society. This assumption in time became an almost unquestioned truth. Only in recent decades, as we shall see, has poetry begun to create anew a substantial and growing public.[2]

POETRY AND LITERARY CRITICISM

One other factor in the evolution of modern verse deserves mention. This is the rise of literary criticism. The "New Criticism," now venerable but still influential, includes such names as T. S. Eliot, I. A. Richards, John Crowe Ransom, and Allen Tate. It has produced a body of probing and highly technical analyses of poetry that has no parallel in any earlier period. Its specialty is the *ex-plication de texte*: the minute examination of a poem line by line, word by word, to see how the poem functions as an autonomous work of art. It is an approach strong on levels of meaning, ambiguity, poetic texture. This kind of criticism has interested many poets, and

[1] Here, as in several other places in this Introduction, I am indebted to my good friend, Professor Wilbur S. Scott, for certain lines of thought.

[2] During the "poetic renaissance" about the time of World War I and for a few years afterwards, there was also a considerable flurry of interest in poetry.

in a number of cases poet and critic are contained inside one skin. The study of literary criticism has undoubtedly influenced some poets, leading them consciously to seek the subtle effects analyzed by the critics. The results can be enrichment or an inhibiting self-consciousness, depending on the poet.

The Polarization of American Poetry

Coming at last to the poets represented in this collection and beginning with the Americans, it is possible to make a few generalizations, always with suitable escape clauses for the exceptions.

Up to the 1950's, and for several decades previously, the Eliot-Pound-Yeats tradition of modernism, as modified by Auden and others of the next generation, and sometimes with a dash of Frost, was the standard point of departure for many beginning poets. They basked in the sunshine of official approval; they were the poets most often honored with Guggenheims and other awards, and published in the better literary quarterlies. Indeed, a kind of loosely organized literary establishment evolved, an interlocking directorate of poets, professors, critics, and publishers, with one person often wearing more than one hat.

It would be wrong, however, to think of poets in this tradition as mechanically writing in the manner of the great transitional poets. That tradition had become progressively modified, toned down, domesticated. The result was a kind of poetry less startling than the early work of Eliot or Pound, tastefully modern, exquisitely competent in technique, often immensely erudite, sometimes too civilized to be quite human.

The poets carrying on the generalized but progressively modified heritage of the great poetic revolutionaries were found increasingly on campuses. A typical life cycle might be college, a summer at a writer's workshop, very likely a master's degree but more rarely a Ph.D., a first book of poetry, perhaps a Lamont or a Guggenheim, eventually a position teaching poetry, criticism, and creative writing on some campus, more books of poetry, occasional readings on other campuses, often an editorial connection with a literary periodical.

THE UNDERGROUND THAT CAME ABOVE GROUND

Meanwhile, an underground current of poetry survived in America and eventually came to the surface with notoriety and fanfare. This current includes among its poetic ancestors Whitman, certain aspects of Pound, W. C. Williams, Lindsay, Sandburg, and frequently a strong seasoning of Zen. The underground survived during its lean years in experimental (and now defunct) Black Mountain College (North Carolina), in San Francisco, among certain poets in New York and others scattered over the country—all united by kindred ideals, tiny magazines, and tinier presses.

The turning point came in the mid-'fifties, when the media discovered the "Beats," [1] thanks first of all to the authorities in San Francisco who, unsuccessfully, brought charges against poet Ginsberg and publisher Ferlinghetti for the four-letter words in Ginsberg's *Howl*. The Beats were a poetic movement as well as a life style; and though the poets differed greatly one from another, they had many things in common—in general, a preoccupation with what they said in their verse rather than how they said it, free verse, a Whitmanesque bardic stance, an oral or declamatory quality, an inclination to explore the subject matter and earthy language of common life.

The rise to public recognition of the Beats lifted many other Underground poets into the light of public, or at least critical, recognition. Soon there was not one poetic establishment but two, and young poets could turn to either or both for inspiration. Surprising conversions occurred along the way. Karl Shapiro, for instance—a meticulous craftsman—publicly renounced Eliot and all his works and turned to the writing of prose poetry strongly reminiscent of the Beats. With the passage of time, the conflict and competition of the two strands, dramatized in the anthologies, the "academic" *New Poets of England and America* and *The New American Poetry, 1945–1960* (the Underground, now aboveground, counterblast) gradually ameliorated as individual poets evolved in their own special directions, and new poets came to the fore. On the whole,

[1] The label *Beat* was never very precise but has been the most often applied to such poets as Allen Ginsberg, Jack Kerouac, Gregory Corso, Gary Snyder, and Philip Whalen. Not all poets of the "Underground" were Beats.

it now seems clear that the emergence of the Underground in the 'fifties was of key importance and that American poetry, though today going in all directions at once, shows a stronger impact of Ginsberg, Creeley, Snyder, etc., than of the old academic establishment—Nemerov, Wilbur, Peter Viereck, etc. Meanwhile, some of the "wild man" poets have been lured into teaching summer workshops or even year-round college courses. Perhaps the main effect of the rise of the Underground has been to enlarge the variety of current American poetry and to encourage beginning poets to explore every approach from the exquisite formalism of Richard Wilbur to the strident incantations of Allen Ginsberg.

THE BRITISH SCENE

In the British Isles the picture was, at least until recently, somewhat more sedate, with a relative shortage of poetic "wild men." It is true that in the mid-1930's Dylan Thomas rose like some elemental force of magic in Wales and produced a poetry of Dionysian magnificence, which was imitated, always with baleful results, by many beginning poets. These made the mistake of assuming that he wrote in a frenzy of spontaneity, whereas he was actually a meticulous craftsman, cold sober at his desk, writing and rewriting a poem through countless drafts, cannily using the Apollonian mind to create the cries of Dionysius.

Apart from Thomas, British poetry for a long time presented a relatively quiet scene in the post-World War II period. The influence of Eliot, Yeats, and Auden continued strong. Minor movements came and went, manifestoes briefly flared. Poetry seemed, as in America, a special interest cultivated by the poets themselves, university dons, a few readers here and there. The great training grounds for young poets continued to be Oxford and Cambridge, with occasionally a red brick university.

Since publishers and the BBC are concentrated in London, poetry tended to be more centralized in England than the United States, where geography was enough to encourage some regional centers of poetry. Whether this centralization (and we shall see that it is weakening) is good or bad is a point of debate. Poetic politicking is facilitated and can quickly become a full-time occupation. "Movements" are spawned overnight, dissected in the press, buried before the leaves fall. At any rate, during the decade after the end of World War II there existed in Britain something that—to an outsider's eyes—looked suspiciously like a poetic establishment, an interlocking network of poets, publishers, journalists, and teachers, plus the essential BBC.

"THE MOVEMENT"

The 1940's saw a brief-lived Apocalyptic Movement, complete with the inevitable anthology. It was neo-Romantic in tone; there were touches of surrealism and large chunks of half-digested Dylan Thomas. The movement proved a poetic dead end. Its main importance was the negative one of helping prepare the way for what curiously came to be called simply "The Movement," and which was a revolt against many strands of twentieth-century poetry, including the Apocalyptic.

The Movement, whose anthology, *New Lines*, appeared in 1956, was the doing of young poets from Oxford and Cambridge, the majority of whom were academics by profession. Some were influenced by the austere intellectual quality of Empson's poetry, but still more they were swayed by their antipathies. They were in revolt against the dream magnificence and frenzy of Dylan Thomas, the chaos and obscurity of the Apocalyptics, even against the old masters, Eliot, Pound, and Auden. In rejecting Eliot as a poetic father many turned to a substitute, Robert Graves, who was a loner gradually emerging into critical esteem. They argued that poetry should speak to the ordinary intelligent reader: It should not be too private, too queer, too personal, too loaded down with esoteric symbols. In their theories they were latterday Alexander Popes, trying to reclaim for poetry a substantial role in the lives of reasonably cultivated citizens. They were strong on poetic discipline and form; in particular the Italian stanza *terza rima* became a necessary rite of passage for many young poets. Implied as much as expressed in their stance was a "little England" orientation, the feeling that the bloodstream of English poetry had become contaminated by foreign influences: Eliot and Pound, the seductive lures of French Symbolism. The Movement was thus in many ways a back-to-native-roots crusade.

New Lines contained the work of nine poets—Elizabeth Jennings, John Holloway, Philip Larkin, Thom Gunn, Kingsley Amis, D. J. Enright, Donald Davie, Robert Conquest, and John Wain. Of these, Larkin has remained truest to the original purposes of the Movement, and his poetry demonstrates the impressive though limited achievements possible with such a concept of poetry.

The Movement involved a lowering of sights, a more modest view of what poetry ought to do. It was a wholesome clean-up operation, banishing a great deal of fuzzy romanticism and un-inspired symbol-chasing and cosmic muttering; but its inhibitions soon became evident, even to most of the poets involved. It was too matter-of-fact, too commonsensical, too completely British. There was something anachronistic about the way it turned aside from the broader poetic currents swirling in many other parts of the world. It was insular.

THE MAVERICKS AND OTHER FACTIONS

New Lines was promptly followed by a counterattack, a rival anthology, *Mavericks* (1957), including the work of J. C. Hall, David Wright, Vernon Scannell, Dannie Abse, Michael Hamburger, John Smith, Anthony Cronin, W. Price Turner, and Jon Silkin. The foreword attacked the Movement as fundamentally anti-poetic and argued for more spontaneity, for the Dionysian and the Romantic.

A longer-lived influence was "the Group," an informal poets' workshop, founded originally by Philip Hobsbaum in the mid-'fifties and subsequently continued under the leadership of Edward Lucie-Smith. Poems by members are distributed in advance and analyzed at each meeting. A joint anthology resulted as early as 1963. Among the distinguished poets of the Group are Ted Hughes and George MacBeth. The Group has functioned more as a bardic school than a clearly defined literary movement, though certain attitudes tend to be dominant: an emphasis on clarity and naturalism, suspicion of Pound and Eliot; favorable regard for D. H. Lawrence and Wilfred Owen.

In the late 1950's it appeared that the newest thing in Britain was a kind of neo-classicism, as manifested in *New Lines*, whereas the seething novelty in America was the Beats and similar groups who were exploring the wild and woolly possibilities of poetry. Thus the two English-speaking worlds seemed to be going at a fast clip in opposite directions. This has now changed.

For one thing, an "Underground" poetic movement, at first clearly influenced and shaped by Ginsberg, Ferlinghetti, etc., gradually rose in England. For a time it led a very marginal life on the fringes of the established literary world. It was kept alive by a handful of dedicated poets and organizers, most notably Mike Horovitz, publisher of *New Departures*. Gradually the Underground came above ground; there were appearances on BBC, poetry readings in increasingly public places, climaxing in a reading at Albert Hall in 1965. Seven thousand attended to hear many British and European poets plus Ginsberg, Corso, and Ferlinghetti. The British Underground today is very much visible.

At any rate, in both America and Britain a poet today is surrounded by so many conflicting, though sometimes converging, tendencies that he is almost compelled to find his own particular way in the creative and teeming jungles of movements, anthologies, trends and counter-trends. Words like "establishment" lose their meaning when the rebel movement of yesterday becomes the alternative establishment of today. This is confusing for literary historians but perhaps fortunate for poets.

Transatlantic Tendencies

The foregoing impressions of the recent and current American and British scenes are very sketchy and need to be supplemented by a grabbag of observations on assorted tendencies that prevail to some extent in one world or both.

DECENTRALIZATION

In America, the production and consumption of poetry have never been concentrated too heavily in one spot. Neither Boston nor even New York has ever been as much the all-encompassing literary center as London. The "poetic renaissance" during and immediately after World War I had a strong midwest branch (Masters, Lindsay, Sandburg), firm roots in New England (Frost, Robinson), as well as a big New York base. When the American Underground rose to public attention in the 1950's, it was at San Francisco. The tendency in the United States has been for decentralization to increase in recent years, with many campuses becoming regional poetry centers. The wandering habits of poets—living a year or two here and then finding another base a thousand miles away—plus the readings many of them periodically give from coast to coast counteract any strong tendency toward the development of clearly defined regional styles, though occasionally there is a poet whose region is integral to his work: William Stafford and Gary Snyder on the west coast, for example.

By contrast, London has until recently dominated the evolution of British poetry. True, an occasional figure on the geographical fringes went his quiet and stubborn way and was finally discovered by London and BBC. An instance is the Welsh parson R. S. Thomas, who published his work for many years in obscure places until he was discovered by BBC and given the imprimatur of a London house, complete with a laudatory introduction by John Betjeman. Another is the West Indian Derek Walcott, who indeed has lived in England but has his permanent home in Trinidad.

More recently, the magnetism and grip of London seem to have diminished. Richard Murphy, living on the west coast of Ireland, has grown steadily in recognition. Various regional centers of young poets—Birmingham, Liverpool, Newcastle—have arisen, often with a strong emphasis on poetry as an oral art or allied with music. The publishing houses are still mostly in London, but when they search for new talent and titles, they are increasingly compelled to explore the hinterlands.

THE PROJECTIVIST THEORY

Recent decades have seen various manifestoes by individual poets setting forth theories of the nature of poetry and how one best goes about creating it. Most of these have been fragmentary and impressionistic, revealing more about the habits of the particular poet than the universals of the art. The one statement that continues to be widely studied is Charles Olson's "Projective Verse," published in 1950 in *Poetry New York*. Written in gnomic language, it lends itself to varied interpretations, depending on the needs of the poet or critic mediating upon it. In general, the essay represents an approach strongly influenced by Ezra Pound and William Carlos Williams and a move away from any preoccupation with form for the sake of form. Poetry writing is depicted as a dynamic activity, more like an athletic event than the weaving of a rug. The underlying principle is an aphorism Olson quotes from Robert Creeley: "Form is never more than an extension of content." The line of verse is described not as a set number of syllables or feet, but as a unit shaped by the poet's breathing and pauses. In many ways Olson's essay codifies the intuitions of that generation of American poets who broke away from the formalism of the academics in the 1950's. A number of American poets show, in their highly varied ways, similar attitudes, among them Creeley, Robert Duncan, Paul Blackburn, and Denise Levertov. In Britain, Charles Tomlinson and Donald Davie have acknowledged Olson's influence.

CONCRETE POETRY

George Herbert and other seventeenth-century poets occasionally shaped a poem to match its contents: A poem about the crucifixion would be put together of short and long lines forming a cross on the printed page. The modern Concrete Poetry Movement represents a much more complex and sophisticated experimentation with devising poems so as to achieve a kind of graphic art. The arrangement of words on the page, the kinds of typefaces, the use of blank spaces—all these are employed to create a visual design which may be either representational or abstract. The immediate ancestors of the Concrete Movement probably include earlier experiments in Futurism and Dadaism, as well as certain poems of e. e. cummings. The movement itself is an international one and has the appeal that (in its visual aspects) it transcends the barriers of language. So far, Concrete poetry is much more evident in the British Isles (especially Scotland) than in the United States. By general consent, Ian Hamilton Finlay is the most notable British practitioner of this hybrid art.

I confess that so far I have not been unduly impressed by the artistic possibilities of Concrete verse as anything more than a charming and mostly light-hearted game, and therefore have not attempted to represent it in this anthology. The continuing evolution of the form may very well prove me mistaken, as anthology editors generally are.

POETRY AS CONFESSION

The type of poetry dominant in the late 'forties and early 'fifties tended, as we have seen, to be intellectually complex, often devious and obscure. The personality and life of the poet were not exactly canceled out but shrouded with various layers of ambiguity. He seldom stripped the flesh from his chest to say, "Look at my beating heart."

A move toward emotional and psychological directness has been evident in recent decades. Increasingly poets have written verse as candid as if they were upon the couch and confessing all to the analyst. Robert Lowell, whose early poetry has a formal massiveness that denies the reader a direct look at the poet's heart, suddenly mutated in *Life Studies* (1959) into a confessional poet, directly speaking of the most intimate recesses of his life. A younger poet, W. D. Snodgrass, in the same year published *Heart's Needle*, a poignant and intensely personal cycle of poems about his divorce and his relation with his young daughter. Other poets who display an equal or greater candor are Anne Sexton, John Berryman, and Allen Ginsberg. Perhaps the most extreme example is the late Sylvia Plath, whose posthumous *Ariel* carries self-revelation to the point where the reader shares the ultimate reaches and depths of madness.

In the most recent years, there seems to have been a slight waning of the urge to confess, as more and more poets become politically and socially committed and find themselves grappling with public themes.

THE RISE OF A POETRY PUBLIC

There has always been a steady, but often quite small, public for poetry in its printed form. At times that market has consisted of little more than libraries, other poets, English professors, a handful of miscellaneous poetry lovers. As recently as twenty years ago an American publisher would be reasonably pleased if he sold a thousand copies of a first book of verse.

Except for a few poets enjoying intense vogues, the sale of poetry books is still modest, though better than formerly. The really significant growth in a public has been in verse presented orally. Many poets, famous or obscure, have become troubadours wandering from campus to campus and occasionally pausing at other places willing to sponsor a public reading. On the campuses, and to some extent elsewhere, poetry in its oral presentation is becoming more an accepted and enjoyed part of life than it has been for a long time;

one suspects that for one student who will sit down with a book of poetry there are ten who will eagerly attend a reading and linger with the poet afterwards to get acquainted. It appears that a widely based poetry public is gradually evolving, similar to the music public that developed when L.P.'s became available. The miracles of the electronic age also play a role in the case of poetry now that so many poets are available on record, tape, or cassette. These tendencies are strongly in evidence on both sides of the Atlantic.

BLACK POETRY

The public role of poetry is especially evident among blacks. Indeed, this represents a long tradition, straight from the early spirituals (whose words are often magnificent folk poetry) through jazz lyrics, on to the present when poetry is becoming one of the principal means by which black consciousness is expressed and experienced. By the beginning of the 'seventies the young black poet, Don L. Lee, had sold more than 80,000 copies of his paperbacks. Older poets, like Robert Hayden, gradually emerged as major figures not merely in the expression of black consciousness but of mankind's universal condition. In view of the creative ferment among blacks today it seems a safe prophecy to suggest that black poets will play a major role both in the expression of the consciousness of their people and in the total development of American poetry. Because of the strong folk roots of their verse, they may provide models for other poets attempting a type of poetry which abolishes the distinction between the high, middle, and low brow.

THE POET AS UNACKNOWLEDGED LEGISLATOR

Recent years have seen American, and to some extent British, poets on the front line of political and social protests. In the United States the Indo-Chinese War, dragging on endlessly, was the major goad, though other causes were also important: racial injustice, the status of the poor, ecology, a vaguely defined but powerful sense of malaise in regard to the "system."

One thinks of the poetry read-ins organized by Robert Bly in protest against war; of Robert Lowell joining in the storming of the Pentagon; of that anti-war senator, Eugene McCarthy, turning poet in the midst of a political campaign. Whole anthologies have been published in protest of war. Some poets have deliberately crossed the obscure line dividing legal demonstration from conscientious violation of law and accepted jail as the price.

These public activities have not been separated from the day-by-day writing of poetry. The poet who takes part in a demonstration is likely to record the event and its meaning in verse, and verse in turn inspires others to follow his example. As compared to the late 'forties and early 'fifties, poets seem to have a stronger social and political awareness. To a large extent they are setting themselves the task of speaking as the consciousness and conscience of a nation.

White House and Pentagon perhaps lose no sleep over the threat thus posed. And to support their serenity they could quote W. H. Auden:

> For poetry makes nothing happen: it survives
> In the valley of its making where executives
> Would never want to tamper . . .[1]

It may be that a poet wishing to influence governmental decisions would do better to ring doorbells, distribute prose leaflets, get out the vote . . . rather than to write poems on the sorrows and horrors of the age. Perhaps, however, in a longer run the poets will prove to be not exactly the unacknowledged legislators of the world, but at least one of the many forces shaping the sensibility and consciousness of the future. If, as many keen observers suggest, a new consciousness is gradually shaping up, particularly among the young, then this in the long run will have political and social consequences, because the decisions men make are conditioned by the pair of spectacles through which they view the world. The poets, musicians, artists, and film-makers may thus indirectly play an important long-range social and political role.

THE FUTURES OF POETRY

If one assumes that some kind of psychological and spiritual mutation is actually taking place, especially but not exclusively among the young, and that a new respect for intuition, imagination, and feeling is one part of the outcome, it seems likely that poetry will become more, rather than less, important. Being an art that uses words, it can deal with explicit ideas; and at the same time it can

[1] W. H. Auden, "In Memory of W. B. Yeats," from *Collected Shorter Poems 1927–1957*, Random House, 1964, p. 142.

reverberate with emotion, sudden insight, transcendence of the ordinary moment. Instead of being an optional luxury and refinement, poetry may become much more the bread of ordinary life.

It seems likely that poetry will split into several separate arts. One will be the sort of book poetry already familiar. There will always be poets who prefer to be experienced silently on the printed page, and a public that likes it that way. For intellectually complex poetry that cannot be taken in during one quick hearing the printed text remains essential.

Then there will be poetry which moves toward an alliance with the visual arts. Concrete poetry is an early example of what may lie ahead. Further experiments will be made, and some Michelangelo of language-and-shape may at last reveal possibilities that most readers, including this one, have not been able to visualize.

My own bias is that the major evolution of poetry will be toward various kinds of alliances with the arts of movement: music, dance, drama. Already this is happening, especially with music. The poet-composer-performer is returning and functioning much as he did in the Elizabethan period. One does not talk of Bob Dylan, Leonard Cohen, or the Beatles without speaking both of poetry and music.

Poetry readings are showing a tendency to take on touches of drama: Some poets chant their poems, make use of musical instruments, achieve special effects in dialogue with tape recorders. It would not be a very long evolution for a small corps of performers, aided perhaps by electronics and dancers, to develop a style of poetry reading that would be basically dramatic and perhaps akin to the early stages of Greek drama. The poetic drama, which has rarely been admitted through the front door of the theater in recent centuries, may find its way back via an expanded type of poetry reading.

Concluding Reflections on the Present Poets

I have confessed to my optimism about the future of poetry. But what about the achievements of the present and last couple of decades? Are we perhaps living in a time of epigones? The great figures that loomed from Yeats to Auden are gone or old. Will their successors leave as big a mark on literary history?

Who knows? It is hard to follow on the heels of giants. But it is comforting to know that not all the giants were recognized for their size at first sight. Until late in his life Robert Frost was treated with benign condescension by most of the critics. If there are giants among the poets in the book, they have not yet been officially labeled as such in most cases.

It could prove to be true that the present is an interim period when the ground is being prepared for another period of major poetry. Perhaps most of the poets now living are doomed to be listed as forerunners of something more important. I doubt myself that this is so. Talk of periods and influences—and this Introduction has been guilty—obscures the stubborn individuality of writers, and the way that a supremely gifted writer can transcend the limitations of a particular period. Some, a few, of these present poets will some day stand as obviously major figures and the literary historians of that time will wonder that we did not instantly recognize them. It may be that already we can dimly discern a few of the giants: probably Roethke; possibly Lowell; almost certainly (I would say) Derek Walcott, though so far he has not been extensively examined by the literary critics.

I see that I have slipped into a way of speaking that I cordially deplore. To talk about poets as though they were competing racehorses is to miss half the sustenance and delight they can give. It is far better to forget the critical pecking orders and to enjoy each poet, each poem, unique and one at a time. Let the future (which means literary historians of the future) say which are giants and which are merely tall for their times. Meanwhile, one fact is clear. Few periods of American or British poetry have produced a larger number of poems so varied and excellent that it would gravely diminish mankind's patrimony if they were allowed to lie forgotten in magazines and slender volumes of verse. This anthology is merely a sample of the poetic riches created in the past three or four decades. It demonstrates that those poets who rightly bear the title of modern are faithful but not slavish heirs of a great tradition. They are adding new and unique wealth, year by year, to the heritage.

C.W.
Beloit College

THEODORE ROETHKE
(1908–63)

The Cycle

Dark water, underground,
Beneath the rock and clay,
Beneath the roots of trees,
Moved into common day,
Rose from a mossy mound
In mist that sun could seize.

The fine rain coiled in a cloud
Turned by revolving air
Far from that colder source
Where elements cohere
Dense in the central stone.
The air grew loose and loud.

Then, with diminished force,
The full rain fell straight down,
Tunneled with lapsing sound
Under even the rock-shut ground,
Under a river's source,
Under primeval stone.

A *Field of Light*

1

Came to lakes; came to dead water,
Ponds with moss and leaves floating,
Planks sunk in the sand.

A log turned at the touch of a foot;
A long weed floated upward;
An eye tilted.

> Small winds made
> A chilly noise;
> The softest cove
> Cried for sound.

> Reached for a grape
> And the leaves changed;
> A stone's shape
> Became a clam.

> A fine rain fell
> On fat leaves;
> I was there alone
> In a watery drowse.

2

Angel within me, I asked,
Did I ever curse the sun?
Speak and abide.

> Under, under the sheaves,
> Under the blackened leaves,
> Behind the green viscid trellis,
> In the deep grass at the edge of a field,
> Along the low ground dry only in August,—

Was it dust I was kissing?
A sigh came far.

Alone, I kissed the skin of a stone;
Marrow-soft, danced in the sand.

3

The dirt left my hand, visitor.
I could feel the mare's nose.
A path went walking.
The sun glittered on a small rapids.
Some morning thing came, beating its wings.
The great elm filled with birds.

Listen, love,
The fat lark sang in the field;
I touched the ground, the ground warmed by the killdeer,
The salt laughed and the stones;
The ferns had their ways, and the pulsing lizards,
And the new plants, still awkward in their soil,
The lovely diminutives.

I could watch! I could watch!
I saw the separateness of all things!
My heart lifted up with the great grasses;
The weeds believed me, and the nesting birds.
There were clouds making a rout of shapes crossing a windbreak of
            cedars,
And a bee shaking drops from a rain-soaked honeysuckle.
The worms were delighted as wrens.
And I walked, I walked through the light air;
I moved with the morning.

Praise to the End!

1

It's dark in this wood, soft mocker.
For whom have I swelled like a seed?
What a bone-ache I have.
Father of tensions, I'm down to my skin at last.

It's a great day for the mice.
Prickle-me, tickle-me, close stems.
Bumpkin, he can dance alone.
Ooh, ooh, I'm a duke of eels.

    Arch my back, pretty-bones, I'm dead at both ends.
    Softly softly, you'll wake the clams.
    I'll feed the ghost alone.
    Father, forgive my hands.

The rings have gone from the pond.
The river's alone with its water.
All risings
Fall.

2

Where are you now, my bonny beating gristle,
My blue original dandy, numb with sugar?
Once I fished from the banks, leaf-light and happy:
On the rocks south of quiet, in the close regions of kissing,
I romped, lithe as a child, down the summery streets of my veins,
Strict as a seed, nippy and twiggy.
Now the water's low. The weeds exceed me.
It's necessary, among the flies and bananas, to keep a constant vigil,
For the attacks of false humility take sudden turns for the worse.
Lacking the candor of dogs, I kiss the departing air;
I'm untrue to my own excesses.

Rock me to sleep, the weather's wrong.
Speak to me, frosty beard.
Sing to me, sweet.

    Mips and ma the mooly moo,
    The likes of him is biting who,
    A cow's a care and who's a coo?—
    What footie does is final.

    My dearest dear my fairest fair,
    Your father tossed a cat in air,

Though neither you nor I was there,—
What footie does is final.

Be large as an owl, be slick as a frog,
Be good as a goose, be big as a dog,
Be sleek as a heifer, be long as a hog,—
What footie will do will be final.

I conclude! I conclude!
My dearest dust, I can't stay here.
I'm undone by the flip-flap of odious pillows.
An exact fall of waters has rendered me impotent
I've been asleep in a bower of dead skin.
It's a piece of a prince I ate.
This salt can't warm a stone.
These lazy ashes.

3

The stones were sharp,
The wind came at my back;
Walked along the highway,
Mincing like a cat.

The sun came out;
The lake turned green;
Romped upon the goldy grass,
Aged thirteen.

The sky cracked open
The world I knew;
Lay like the cats do
Sniffing the dew.

I dreamt I was all bones;
The dead slept in my sleeve;
Sweet Jesus tossed me back:
I wore the sun with ease.

The several sounds were low;
The river ebbed and flowed:
Desire was winter-calm,
A moon away.

Such owly pleasures! Fish come first, sweet bird.
Skin's the least of me. Kiss this.
Is the eternal near, fondling?
I hear the sound of hands.

Can the bones breathe? This grave has an ear.
It's still enough for the knock of a worm.

I feel more than a fish.
Ghost, come closer.

4

Arch of air, my heart's original knock,
I'm awake all over:
I've crawled from the mire, alert as a saint or a dog;
I know the back-stream's joy, and the stone's eternal pulseless longing.
Felicity I cannot hoard.
My friend, the rat in the wall, brings me the clearest messages;
I bask in the bower of change;
The plants wave me in, and the summer apples;
My palm-sweat flashes gold;
Many astounds before, I lost my identity to a pebble;
The minnows love me, and the humped and spitting creatures.

I believe! I believe!—
In the sparrow, happy on gravel;
In the winter-wasp, pulsing its wings in the sunlight;
I have been somewhere else; I remember the sea-faced uncles.
I hear, clearly, the heart of another singing,
Lighter than bells,
Softer than water.

Wherefore, O birds and small fish, surround me.
Lave me, ultimate waters.
The dark showed me a face.
My ghosts are all gay.
The light becomes me.

The Waking

I wake to sleep, and take my waking slow.
I feel my fate in what I cannot fear.
I learn by going where I have to go.

We think by feeling. What is there to know?
I hear my being dance from ear to ear.
I wake to sleep, and take my waking slow.

Of those so close beside me, which are you?
God bless the Ground! I shall walk softly there,
And learn by going where I have to go.

Light takes the Tree; but who can tell us how?
The lowly worm climbs up a winding stair;
I wake to sleep, and take my waking slow.

Great Nature has another thing to do
To you and me; so take the lively air,
And, lovely, learn by going where to go.

This shaking keeps me steady. I should know.
What falls away is always. And is near.
I wake to sleep, and take my waking slow.
I learn by going where I have to go.

I Knew a Woman

I knew a woman, lovely in her bones,
When small birds sighed, she would sigh back at them:

Ah, when she moved, she moved more ways than one:
The shapes a bright container can contain!
Of her choice virtues only gods should speak,
Or English poets who grew up on Greek
(I'd have them sing in chorus, cheek to cheek).

How well her wishes went! She stroked my chin,
She taught me Turn, and Counter-turn, and Stand;
She taught me Touch, that undulant white skin;
I nibbled meekly from her proffered hand;
She was the sickle; I, poor I, the rake,
Coming behind her for her pretty sake
(But what prodigious mowing we did make).

Love likes a gander, and adores a goose:
Her full lips pursed, the errant note to seize;
She played it quick, she played it light and loose;
My eyes, they dazzled at her flowing knees;
Her several parts could keep a pure repose,
Or one hip quiver with a mobile nose
(She moved in circles, and those circles moved).

Let seed be grass, and grass turn into hay:
I'm martyr to a motion not my own;
What's freedom for? To know eternity.
I swear she cast a shadow white as stone.
But who would count eternity in days?
These old bones live to learn her wanton ways:
(I measure time by how a body sways).

The Far Field

I

I dream of journeys repeatedly:
Of flying like a bat deep into a narrowing tunnel,
Of driving alone, without luggage, out a long peninsula,

The road lined with snow-laden second growth,
A fine dry snow ticking the windshield,
Alternate snow and sleet, no on-coming traffic,
And no lights behind, in the blurred side-mirror,
The road changing from glazed tarface to a rubble of stone,
Ending at last in a hopeless sand-rut,
Where the car stalls,
Churning in a snowdrift
Until the headlights darken.

II

At the field's end, in the corner missed by the mower,
Where the turf drops off into a grass-hidden culvert,
Haunt of the cat-bird, nesting-place of the field-mouse,
Not too far away from the ever-changing flower-dump,
Among the tin cans, tires, rusted pipes, broken machinery,—
One learned of the eternal;
And in the shrunken face of a dead rat, eaten by rain and ground-
    beetles
(I found it lying among the rubble of an old coal bin)
And the tom-cat, caught near the pheasant-run,
Its entrails strewn over the half-grown flowers,
Blasted to death by the night watchman.

I suffered for birds, for young rabbits caught in the mower,
My grief was not excessive.
For to come upon warblers in early May
Was to forget time and death:
How they filled the oriole's elm, a twittering restless cloud, all one
    morning,
And I watched and watched till my eyes blurred from the bird shapes,—
Cape May, Blackburnian, Cerulean,—
Moving, elusive as fish, fearless,
Hanging, bunched like young fruit, bending the end branches,
Still for a moment,
Then pitching away in half-flight,
Lighter than finches,
While the wrens bickered and sang in the half-green hedgerows,
And the flicker drummed from his dead tree in the chicken-yard.

—Or to lie naked in sand,
In the silted shallows of a slow river,
Fingering a shell,
Thinking:
Once I was something like this, mindless,
Or perhaps with another mind, less peculiar;
Or to sink down to the hips in a mossy quagmire;
Or, with skinny knees, to sit astride a wet log,
Believing:
I'll return again,
As a snake or a raucous bird,
Or, with luck, as a lion.

I learned not to fear infinity,
The far field, the windy cliffs of forever,
The dying of time in the white light of tomorrow,
The wheel turning away from itself,
The sprawl of the wave,
The on-coming water.

III

The river turns on itself,
The tree retreats into its own shadow.
I feel a weightless change, a moving forward
As of water quickening before a narrowing channel
When banks converge, and the wide river whitens;
Or when two rivers combine, the blue glacial torrent
And the yellowish-green from the mountainy upland,—
At first a swift rippling between rocks,
Then a long running over flat stones
Before descending to the alluvial plain,
To the clay banks, and the wild grapes hanging from the elmtrees,
The slightly trembling water
Dropping a fine yellow silt where the sun stays;
And the crabs bask near the edge,
The weedy edge, alive with small snakes and bloodsuckers,—

I have come to a still, but not a deep center,
A point outside the glittering current;

My eyes stare at the bottom of a river,
At the irregular stones, iridescent sandgrains,
My mind moves in more than one place,
In a country half-land, half-water.

I am renewed by death, thought of my death,
The dry scent of a dying garden in September,
The wind fanning the ash of a low fire.
What I love is near at hand,
Always, in earth and air.

IV

The lost self changes,
Turning toward the sea,
A sea-shape turning around,—
An old man with his feet before the fire,
In robes of green, in garments of adieu.

A man faced with his own immensity
Wakes all the waves, all their loose wandering fire.
The murmur of the absolute, the why
Of being born fails on his naked ears.
His spirit moves like monumental wind
That gentles on a sunny blue plateau.
He is the end of things, the final man.

All finite things reveal infinitude:
The mountain with its singular bright shade
Like the blue shine on freshly frozen snow,
The after-light upon ice-burdened pines;
Odor of basswood on a mountain-slope,
A scent beloved of bees;
Silence of water above a sunken tree:
The pure serene of memory in one man,—
A ripple widening from a single stone
Winding around the waters of the world.

Light Listened

O what could be more nice
Than her ways with a man?
She kissed me more than twice
Once we were left alone.
Who'd look when he could feel?
She'd more sides than a seal.

The close air faintly stirred.
Light deepened to a bell,
The love-beat of a bird.
She kept her body still
And watched the weather flow.
We live by what we do.

All's known, all, all around:
The shape of things to be;
A green thing loves the green
And loves the living ground.
The deep shade gathers night;
She changed with changing light.

We met to leave again
The time we broke from time;
A cold air brought its rain,
The singing of a stem.
She sang a final song;
Light listened when she sang.

Otto

I

He was the youngest son of a strange brood,
A Prussian who learned early to be rude

To fools and frauds: He does not put on airs
Who lived above a potting shed for years.
I think of him, and I think of his men,
As close to him as any kith or kin.
Max Laurisch had the greenest thumb of all.
A florist does not woo the beautiful:
He potted plants as if he hated them.
What root of his ever denied its stem?
When flowers grew, their bloom extended him.

II

His hand could fit into a woman's glove,
And in a wood he knew whatever moved;
Once when he saw two poachers on his land,
He threw his rifle over with one hand;
Dry bark flew in their faces from his shot,—
He always knew what he was aiming at.
They stood there with their guns; he walked toward,
Without his rifle, and slapped each one hard;
It was no random act, for those two men
Had slaughtered game, and cut young fir trees down.
I was no more than seven at the time.

III

A house for flowers! House upon house they built,
Whether for love or out of obscure guilt
For ancestors who loved a warlike show,
Or Frenchmen killed a hundred years ago,
And yet still violent men, whose stacked-up guns
Killed every cat that neared their pheasant runs;
When Hattie Wright's angora died as well,
My father took it to her, by the tail.
Who loves the small can be both saint and boor,
(And some grow out of shape, their seed impure;)
The Indians loved him, and the Polish poor.

IV

In my mind's eye I see those fields of glass,
As I looked out at them from the high house,
Riding beneath the moon, hid from the moon,
Then slowly breaking whiter in the dawn;
When George the watchman's lantern dropped from sight
The long pipes knocked: it was the end of night.
I'd stand upon my bed, a sleepless child
Watching the waking of my father's world,—
O world so far away! O my lost world!

In a Dark Time

In a dark time, the eye begins to see.
I meet my shadow in the deepening shade;
I hear my echo in the echoing wood—
A lord of nature weeping to a tree.
I live between the heron and the wren,
Beasts of the hill and serpents of the den.

What's madness but nobility of soul
At odds with circumstance? The day's on fire!
I know the purity of pure despair,
My shadow pinned against a sweating wall.
That place among the rocks—is it a cave,
Or winding path? The edge is what I have.

A steady storm of correspondences!
A night flowing with birds, a ragged moon,
And in broad day the midnight comes again!
A man goes far to find out what he is—

Death of the self in a long, tearless night,
All natural shapes blazing unnatural light.

Dark, dark my light, and darker my desire.
My soul, like some heat-maddened summer fly,
Keeps buzzing at the sill. Which I is *I*?
A fallen man, I climb out of my fear.
The mind enters itself, and God the mind,
And one is One, free in the tearing wind.

CARL BODE

(1911–)

from "LONDON SONNETS"

VI: *Who Calls the English Cold?*

Who calls the English cold? Eros is
Everywhere: lying on Hyde Park's summer lawn
The couples of young London touch; beyond
The bole of every tree there peeps the faun.

Canes tap on the gravelled walk, old ladies
Pass close by, skiffs skim the Serpentine
Yet there is only mouth on mouth
And a quickening as arms entwine.

Alone the visitor keeps the bench, having
Briskly walked nowhere; head back and eyes aslant
He regards the guttering day and hears the
Words of love as Hyde Park orators' rant.

Seizing his cane or skiff, louring at the faun,
He strides the swelling lawn up to the road above
Where his orator proclaims
Universal love.

XV: *Covent Garden Market*

By God I hate to grow old.
Resignation, pushcart philosophy,
White dry film, geraniums drowned in tea;
Each hair lost or greyed turns me cold,
Lines scored on my face do not need to bleed;
Beyond the Covent Gardener hawking fruit,
Black apples, melons, berries, turned to suit
The epicure, who feeds on maggots as the maggots feed.

What can deceive me? The mind itself, the very soul,
Wears through; the peddler falls across his cart,
Yellow and limp, soon for someone else to push
    Away—no tipping at the Burning Bush—
    Stand and deliver at the crumbling hole!
Let no black-coated fool dare take my part
And mumble over me that everything that stops must start.

Personal Letter to the Ephesians

Breaking through the sandy soil
The bony finger rises, then
Grows into an arm;
And all can see the bony mouth
Fixed on the word Alarm.

But none can taste the salt
Of terror, not having died
Themselves, not having known
The smothering grave nor
The crushing weight of stone.

But these bones of John the Baptist
Will flower into flesh
And he will walk anointed
With oils of fragrant hawthorn,
Bright bleeding-heart and pointed

Valentine. There is no life
Without a death, perhaps no
Peace without a terror.
Beware of crying out the truth
Unless, O men of Ephesus,
You also speak in error.

The Bad Children

The children of light—mongoloid,
Hydrocephalic, crazed, awry—
Will build their glass houses
Out of shards of pale sky
Or brittle splinters of causes.

Their names will be biblical,
Esther, Naomi, Levi, Moses,
Or else cheap blue plastic,
Charlene, Joni, Sondra, Elvis.
Their minds will be lame or spastic,

Their hearts futile. While they
Play with their impossible toys
Their parents, aching, will stand
And watch them. Outside, the healthy noise
Of other children, playing Pretend,

Joyously aping the children of light,
Will meet the ears of the wordless
Parents. And they will stop and ponder

The rich health of the children of darkness,
Who deny God. And they will wonder

(The fathers turning to the mothers),
They will wonder as they try to measure
Sure causes against clumsy effects,
Which is worse, God's displeasure
In this world or the next?

Requiem

So. They and I are back from the outside.
Sitting in the cold sunlight of the parlour
We agree, with no pride,
That we never saw so many lovely flowers.
Petals still lie on the rug; the heavy scent has not died.

There is not much else for us to talk
About really—not much to say or do,
Except to get up and walk
Around in the cold, scented sunlight; so I sit
Looking down, and pull into strands a piece of flower stalk.

I think, of course, of that night last year
When I dreamt that you need not have died, so that my
Mind was filled with a dull, queer
Kind of loneliness which would not go away for
A long while; I remember it well as I sit here.

And I well remember those flowers,
Thick leaves with dust on them, coarse hairy stems
Forced by late summer showers.
The blooms were large and had a flat, metallic
Odour. They were bouquets of love, they were ours.

The Burial of Terror

How green the green at Salem is,
The lawn below the sea,
So lay a lace upon the face,
The face no longer his
Nor like to be,

A gauze upon the curious gaze
And then in sea-green fear
At the trees bent over the lawn
Let him go his curious ways,
Or far or near,

To the richness of the water. Why,
Peace has never been here.
Yet who can say where it has gone?
Who has seen it disappear?

Sonnet: Head Next to Mine

Head next to mine but turned aside, you lie
As if you had to listen to make love—
As if the central sense were sound, not touch,
As if a brittle word were an impatient shove;

But too as if the smallest sigh came from
The finger lightly laid upon your hair;
Or from a tense embrace, wave after wave
Of subtle resonance along the air.

What do you hear? Brows knit, eyes anxiously
Intent, your face shows that the oncoming sound
Must be austere or shrill; and I myself
No longer feel—or hear—my pulses pound;

Until I feel your mouth answer my seeking—
And then I know lips were not made for speaking.

Sonnet: The Window

My wife asleep, her soft face turned from me,
My children sleeping in their rooms as well,
I get up, drawn to the window, to see what I must see:
Silver, and black and silver. There is almost a silver smell.

The moon on this burnished California hill,
The stars with their sober silver spark.
I know. And the savor of the night through the patch of dill.
If I could drink aromatics or take eucalyptus bark,

If I could drink sense and have its glow to keep,
Or even if I could bathe the folded shapes of words
With any light of mine this once, then I could sleep.
Straining, I stand and can hear no sound, no wind, no birds . . .

But all at once there comes the howl of a far-off hound
And all that I want to say is said in that single sound.

Variation on a Theme by Dylan Thomas

Why, everyone speaks Welsh; the stipple sheen;
Of pink. Black stitching through the opal floor;
You ask aghast, what do those people mean
And each brick-bombast wall becomes a door.

Before that, though, the empyrean opens up,
Tongues of angels tickled at their tips,
Coal miners filing down the valleys for to sup
Never even swipe their blackened lips.

And earlier still, the public wife has stood
Where billows beat against the robbing line.
What she has done was for the public good—
Water for arid Wales, surcease at the mine.

And earliest of all, the lush green lay,
The loving, easy land where no one went away.

The Planet

The solid ocean and the liquid land:
On both—free from my cage of ribs, dressed
In my Sunday best—I steadfast stand
Or sailing sing hosannas which call me blest.

Onward the ritual winds, the vestments sway.
Through the church windows the rain shines down
In lucent drops upon the sunny day.
And I—I die indefinitely of brown.

I rise; to ponder puzzles or to peer
At the prettiest girls in church. I sit;
And stare at the blonde one kneeling near.
I kneel; and undress her lovingly, bit by bit.

Until at last, the benediction done,
I bolt; and see you beckoning in the sun.

The Nocturne

Why the hell do you use all that black
In your painting, my neighbor asks across the fence.
I thumb my canvases, the oboes going slack,
Flutes elegantly wailing, the colors colors of elegance.

Of course the concert stops; the composer done,
He wipes his hands upon a greasy rag of fire
Replying flatly that he was only having fun
And who the hell are you, may I inquire?

I crane my neck upon the latest night.
It shapes and opens up into arcades
And avenues and pergolas of light.
My eye, now leading its battalions on, invades
The widening valleys, the martial music bright
With scimitars; and everywhere the neighbors lean on spades.

Smorgasbord

I think of Captain Cook and the merry Polynesians
Who Clubbed him down
And not long afterward feasted on rump steak
Done brown.

On Livingston in Africa, stripped of his spectacles
And dumped into the melting pot.
Native informants, still alert, report he made a toughish dish
Even when hot.

The female Captain Kyd (rumored as weighing a succulent
Three hundred pounds),
Basted with her bra and panties on, ended in thick-lipped
Smacking sounds.

The table spread before me has trays and bellied pots
And fulfilled tureens of food
For the crewcut Army couple on vacation with their
Crewcut brood.

Pastrami cheek by herring, boiled beef with bullion
Butts, cadwallador in slices (rare),
Pimientoes strewn on salad, swordfish with its sword, and
Hot jugged hare.

The fat salesman from New Jersey, his raunchy Edna wife,
The blue-haired sisters from Seattle,
The old farmer with his flock of cawing children—
All do battle.

Elbowing one another, they eat even as they heap their plate
And I think of how Cook and Livingston and flab
Annie helped the heathen to celebrate.

Beginnings

Was the Word.
The first time you touch a girl, the very flesh
In a suave rise of orient sun,
Soft, firm, tender curve.
The first time you walk stiffly
Among the temporary dead,
Deaf to their crying or crowing.
Beneath your boot the small bones snap
As they never will again.
The first time, transfixed, you see from far off
The windy plains of Troy, the vast steppes of Astrakhan,
Illimitable snow, and then the mind of God Itself.

Beginnings are good. But terminals? . . .
How do you get rid of a girl?
How do you tell her that,
The curve descending, the lumen gone,
You have finished? Even leaving
A prostitute, do you shake hands and say
God be with you?

And how do you leave Green-Lawn?
The entrance beckons, bold and arched,
The iron grillwork painted gold,
The road gravelled and the pathways plumed.
But you wander bewildered through
The tall stones and low mounds. The embedded lawns

Rise toward the horizon—but no horizon happens.
Look high as you can, there is never an exit marked.
Earth shows no rim; the sky lacks edges.
Panting you sink back to the bottom of
A vast concave. Eternity is a white circle, surely,
Slowly revolving, cooling, chilling.
Yet who can see a conclusion?
Who can see a conclusion?

KENNETH PATCHEN

(1911–)

At the New Year

In the shape of this night, in the still fall
     of snow, Father
In all that is cold and tiny, these little birds
     and children
In everything that moves tonight, the trolleys
     and the lovers, Father
In the great hush of country, in the ugly noise
     of our cities
In this deep throw of stars, in those trenches
     where the dead are, Father
In all the wide waiting, and in the liners
     out on the black water
In all that has been said bravely, in all that is
     mean anywhere in the world, Father
In all that is good and lovely, in every house
     where sham and hatred are
In the name of those who wait, in the sound
     of angry voices, Father
Before the bells ring, before this point little in time
     has rushed us on
Before this clean moment has gone, before this night
     turns to face tomorrow, Father
There is this high singing in the air

Forever this sorrowful human face in eternity's window
And there are other bells that we would ring, Father
Other bells that we would ring.

'Do I Not Deal with Angels'

Do I not deal with angels
When her lips I touch

So gentle, *so warm and sweet*—falsity
Has no sight of her
O the world is a place of veils and roses
When she is there

I am come to her wonder
Like a boy finding a star in a haymow
And there is nothing cruel or mad or evil
Anywhere

'The Carts of the Wee Blind Lass'

The carts of the wee blind lass
Were covered with silvery wool
That shone on the road
Like sheep walking with God.
Her hair was caught in a fine knot
At the toe of her brain, and her eyes
Had been painted over by imps of heaven.
She held her name in a little dish,
And always at crossings she cried it.

The carts were pulled by horses
Fashioned of mountain-bones
And the anger of yellow eagles.
Their wheels rolled on a single track
That led a little above the air.

And what sell ye, my pretty?
It is nothing I sell, true sir.

Then what do ye bring? lassie say . . .
It is apples I bring. Yet none for you.

Now tell me short the name of this good lad
That I may send him spinning . . .
Then spin the devil, my happy wit;
For my apples are for him.
O take my pretty apples, Mr. Dark!

O all my juicy ripe apples are for thee!

Now I Went Down to the Ringside and Little Henry Armstrong Was There

They've got some pretty horses up in the long dark mountains.
Get him, boy!

They've got some nifty riders away yonder on that big sad road.
Get him, boy!

They've got some tall talk off in that damn fine garden.
Get him, boy!

When you can't use your left, then let the right go.
When your arms get tired, hit him with a wing.
When you can't see very good, smell where he is.

They've got some juicy steaks in that nice sweet by-and-by.
Get him, boy!

They've got a lot of poor black lads in that crummy old jailhouse.
Get him, boy!

O they've got a lot of clean bunks up in their big wide blue sky.
That's his number, boy!

'Christ! Christ! Christ! That the World'

Christ! Christ! Christ! that the world
Should be so dark and desolate for so many!
That there should be hungry and sick and homeless
In every land on earth!

Brothers who are without light and hope—
For whom Death is a friend, whose hand will save them!

This should rot the hearts of men!
Instead—instead—
O you dirty filthy swine!

'O When I Take My Love Out Walking'

O when I take my love out walking
In the soft frosted stillness of this summer moon

Then are the mysteries all around us
O what can I say!
   the ever-known, the ever-new
   like her they seem
O lully, lullay ʼ
   only this little moment is real
Here at the edge of the world
   and the throne. The rest's a lie
   which shadows scheme.

Now gentle flowers are awash on the sleeping hill
And as I bend to kiss her opened lips
O then do the wonders and the sparklings seem
A shabby tinsel show for my dear queen.

The New Being

They'd make you believe that your problem is one of sex,
That men and women have mysteriously become
Strange and fearful to one another—sick, diseased, cold—
And that is true. But no loss of a father-image or of
Any other image, did this. Why don't you face the truth for once?
You have accepted the whole filthy, murderous swindle without
A word of protest, hated whomever you were told to hate,
Slaughtered whomever you were told to slaughter; you've lied,
Cheated, made the earth stink with your very presence—Why
Shouldn't you despise and hate one another? Why shouldn't
Your flesh crawl everytime you touch one another?
Why should you expect to make 'love' in a bed fouled with corpses?

Oh, you poor, weak little frauds, sucking around
Frantically for something to ease your guilt—
Why don't you face it?
Your birthright, liferight,
Deathright, and now your
Sexright, you've lost. What
Did you expect? How
Else could it be? You've
Made property and money your only gods—
        Well, this is their rule,
        This is what you wanted.
        And now they'll wipe you out.
        Why don't you face it?
        Stop sucking around.
        Your pet witch-doctors can't help you,
        They're all sick from the same thing.
        Your pompous intellectuals can't help you,
        They're all sick from the same thing.
        Your sly, vicious statesmen can't help you,
        They're all sick from the same thing.
        Why don't you face it?
        No, your problem is not one of sex—
        Your problem is that you have betrayed your animal

Into hands as cruel and bloody as your own.
Man is dead.
I don't know what kind of thing you are.

For Miriam

As beautiful as the hands
Of a winter tree
And as holy
Base are they beside thee

As dross beside thee

O green birds
That sing the earth to wakefulness
As tides the sea
Drab are they beside thee

As tinsel beside thee

O pure
And fair as the clouds
Wandering
Over a summer field
They are crass beside thee
The hands
Move through the starhair

As tawdry beside thee

An Easy Decision

I had finished my dinner
Gone for a walk.

It was fine
Out and I started whistling.
It wasn't long before
I met a
Man and his wife riding on
A warbond with a clatter of
Skeletons running along after them.

I nodded ugh and
Went on.
Pretty soon I met another
Couple
This time with nineteen
Kids and all of them
Riding on
A big smiling whatthehellisit

I invited them home

n a Crumbling

Majesty of horns sweeps in the stagtide . . .

After such glory . . . the glory of that vast frosty wood there
. . O the belling of that glory bringing a face to each of night's cold
indows—this defeat, this death, this petty corruption . . . He stum-
ed to his knees, and the proud forehead of his running broke upon
e sand like an egg.

(Ah, the angry, lung-colored stain that flowered at his bridle, that
illed like a cottony cheese over his withers and harness-buckling
. . that raged like a tattering doom of flags above the chariot there
. . that rose like the grim pale frost of an agony above the decaying
linter of wheels . . .)

The stain widens, briefly . . . hesitates . . . then drains back without trace.

The Great Sled-Makers

They get drunk, these Great Sled-Makers. Their copper mugs, around which their fingers easily circle once, and once again, hold what's called a "quart handsome" (about five and ⅜s gallons mirke-measure).

The Great Sled-Makers get drunk like other people do hopeless. An hour or two old they demand whisky, and poor slap–hoppy brute the mother who'd not lay them lovely on . . . all pink-fuzzy, ah, happy little belchers, rest ye well in between the worlds, as you might say.

Seven sees most married. Typically they live above saloons, their sole furniture a firehouse pole.

For, you must understand, it doesn't take a few hours or even a few days to make a Great-Sled; it takes closer to a thousand years.

Eleven have been built so far, not counting of course those which slip away from time to time (no doubt you've heard of tidal waves and earthquakes). Each is heavier than all the mountains placed together on a table having proper equipment for weighing of this sort; each requires a highway of at least a million lanes . . . at the very least. In other words, the Great-Sleds are not small. Just picture them! with their runners of molten silver, their golden bodies painted a screaming red under a zigzag of yellow and buff stripes. The effect is quite nice Only so far, you've probably guessed by now, nobody's bought nary a one.—*Whh-isky, bo-oy!*

Where?

There's a place the man always say
Come in here, child

No cause you should weep
Wolf never catch the rabbit
Golden hair never turn white with grief
Come in here, child
No cause you should moan
Brother never hurt his brother
Nobody here ever wander without a home
There must be some such place somewhere
But I never heard of it

'O Now the Drenched Land Wakes'

O now the drenched land wakes;
Birds from their sleep call
Fitfully, and are still.
Clouds like milky wounds
Float across the moon.

O love, none may
Turn away long
From this white grove
Where all nouns grieve.

Because He Liked to Be at Home

He usually managed to be there when
He arrived. A horse, his name was
Hunry Fencewaver Walkins—he'd sometimes
Be almost too tired to make it;
Because, since he also hated being alone,
He was always on the alert to pop forth
At a full run whenever the door opened.
Then one day it happened—
He didn't get there in time!
Of course he couldn't risk opening the door—

So, panting, he just stood there in the hall—
And listened to the terrible sound of himself weeping
In that room he could never, never enter again.

Because My Hands Hear the Flowers Thinking

I scooped up the moon's footprints but
The ground climbed past with a sky
And a dove and a bent vapor.
The other half of cling together wove by
In the breath of the willows: O fall in
Fall in! sang eagle ox ferret elm and riverbank . . .
And we, O we too must learn to live here!
To usefully use what we are! O fall in
Fall in beside our brothers! For only in giving
Love may we achieve trust and true community. O
Of these wondrous likenesses, none, O none at all
Can we know unless we take the giving of love
As our pledge and only law! O in this lion-leaf,
This glory of a son's unseeking belief that soars
Over every road where his mother walks in the
Splendor and mystery of birth-death . . . O there!
In that known unknown country . . . O there may we
See with the eyes of grass; hear our own voices
In the speaking of the trees; and touch our lives
With hands of rock and hurrying mountains . . . O on
The floor of the seas, and at the back of this dead
Bird's radiant face, our lives are watching us—
I think they are not lived in this world

WILLIAM EVERSON
(BROTHER ANTONINUS)
(1912–)

August

Smoke color:
Haze thinly over the hills, low hanging,
But the sky steel, the sky shiny as steel, and the sun shouting.
The vineyard: in August the green-deep and heat-loving vines
Without motion grow heavy with grapes.
And he in the shining, on the turned earth, loose-lying,
The muscles clean and the limbs golden, turns to the sun the
    lips and the eyes;
As the virgin yields, impersonally passionate,
From the bone core and the aching flesh, the offering.

He has found the power and come to the glory.
He has turned clean-hearted to the last god, the symbolic sun.
With earth on his hands, bearing shoulder and arm the light's
    touch, he has come.
And having seen, the mind loosens, the nerve lengthens,
All the haunting abstractions slip free and are gone;
And the peace is enormous.

The Stranger

Pity this girl.
At callow sixteen,

Glib in the press of rapt companions,
She bruits her smatter,
Her bed-lore brag.
She prattles the lip-learned, light-love list.
In the new itch and squirm of sex,
How can she foresee?

How can she foresee the thick stranger,
Over the hills from Omaha,
Who will break her across a hired bed,
Open the loins,
Rive the breach,
And set the foetus wailing within the womb,
To hunch toward the knowledge of its disease,
And shamble down time to doomsday?

Hospice of the Word

Maurin House, Fifth & Washington, Oakland

In the ventless room,
Over the beds at the hour of rising,
Hangs now the smother and stench of the crude flesh;
And at the grimed sink
We fill the basin of our mutual use,
Where our forty faces, rinsed daily,
Leaves each its common trace,

Is it then in this?
In this alone, then, that we find our oneness?
Who never in cleanliness, never in purity
Have ever truly met?

O my brothers! Each brings his sin-deforméd face
To the greasy pan! Is it not a terrible thing
To come upon our lives, here in each other?
In the inalienable commonality of our grosser selves?

And found there, that sign and testimonial
Of our secret hearts! Could it not have been other?
A true revealment of the soul's intent,
A freer gift, welcomed, and most dear?

Far off, in clefted rocks and dells, the springwater
Throbs out the faultless pulse of earth,
A lucent flow.

And God's sheer daylight
Pours through our shafted sky
To proffer again
The still occasion of His grace
Where we might meet each other.

I I

But the stain remains, ubiquitous, under the thumb,
In the crease of the knuckle or about the wrist,
Or there where the lice-suck leaves its tracing along the rib.
As I too, at night undressing, my body, its odor
Lifts like a sigh of the utter flesh:
The common breath of the poor.

"Could it not have been other?"
Moan of the scrupulous self,
Wrung outcry of the oppressed heart
Thrown back to God.

But how else and where?
Not in the urbane apartments, surely,
The suburban mansions,
Nor the luxurious hotels.

For in the crucible of revulsion
Love is made whole. St. Francis
Ran on gooseflesh toward the leper's sore:
He saw His God. Improbable and rare,
Most priceless ingredient,

It lurks behind the stubble beards;
And night after night, under the hovering breath of hundreds,
It is there; and morning after morning,
In the innominate faces soused at the shallow pan,
That in this has become like that makeshift dish
Seized up in haste without foreknowledge
That April afternoon, toward three,
When the oblique lance, upthrust,
Unloosed the floodgates of the Redemption—
How many faces, rinsed there,
Might rise, like mine, from the Bloodbath,
Almost whole? The bowl where Pilate
Damped his mincing fingers and the immortal Dish
Under the crossbeam, merge here, where the Christ-gaze
Focusses and holds. Of love, tortured and serene,
It stares from the visage of all men,
Unsanctioning, its immense pity and its terrible grief!
Or there on the nail above the sink
Where the townswoman's culled linen, smutched,
Gives back the Divine Face!
How many times each day is not that impetuous brow
Thrusted into my sight, saying always:
"Not these but *this*. Look! It is I!"

O Lord and Sacrificer! I turn to meet,
But the dead sin of the inordinate self
Tentacles my heart! Take now my wrong!

And very fast, a movement
Shifting forthright through the nimbus
Of a veiled withholdance, His look
Lances, and His unbelievable mouth,
Torrent of joy, pressed home,
Shudders the rapt heart.

Gustate, et videte quoniam suavis est Dominus!

A Canticle to the Christ in the Holy Eucharist

Written on the Feast of St. Therese of the Child Jesus, Virgin and Contemplative, 1953

And the many days and the many nights that I lay as one barren,
As the barren doe lies on in the laurel under the slope of Mt. Tamalpais.
The fallow doe in the deep madrone, in the tall grove of the redwoods,
Curling her knees on the moist earth where the spring died out of the mountain.
Her udder is dry. Her dugs are dry as the fallen leaves of the laurel,
Where she keeps her bed in the laurel clump on the slope of Tamalpais.

Sudden as wind that breaks east out of dawn this morning you struck,
As wind that poured from the wound of dawn in the valley of my beginning.
Your look rang like the strident quail, like the buck that stamps in the thicket.
Your face was the flame. Your mouth was the rinse of wine. Your tongue, the torrent.

I fed on that terror as hunger is stanched on meat, the taste and the trembling.
In the pang of my dread you smiled and swept to my heart.
As the eagle eats so I ate, as the hawk takes flesh from his talon,
As the mountain lion clings and kills, I clung and was killed.

This kill was thy name. In the wound of my heart thy voice was the cling,
Like honey out of the broken rock thy name and the stroke of thy kiss.
The heart wound and the hovering kiss they looked to each other,
As the lovers gaze in their clasp, the grave embrace of love.

This name and the wound of my heart partook of each other.
They had no use but to feed, the grazing of love.
Thy name and the gaze of my heart they made one wound together.
This wound-made-one was their thought, the means of their knowledge.

There is nothing known like this wound, this knowledge of love.
In what love? In which wounds, such words? In what touch? In whose
    coming?
You gazed. Like the voice of the quail. Like the buck that stamps in
    the thicket.
You gave. You found the gulf, the goal. On my tongue you were meek.

In my heart you were might. And thy word was the running of rain
That rinses October. And the sweetwater spring in the rock. And the
    brook in the crevice.
Thy word in my heart was the start of the buck that is sourced in the
    doe.
Thy word was the milk that will be in her dugs, the stir of new life in
    them.
You gazed. I stood barren for days, lay fallow for nights.
Thy look was the movement of life, the milk in the young breasts of
    mothers.

My mouth was the babe's. You had stamped like the buck in the man-
    zanita.
My heart was dry as the dugs of the doe in the fall of the year on
    Tamalpais.
I sucked thy wound as the fawn sucks milk from the crowning breast
    of its mother.
The flow of thy voice in my shrunken heart was the cling of wild
    honey,
The honey that bled from the broken comb in the cleft of Tamalpais.

The quick of thy kiss lives on in my heart with the strike, the wound
    you inflicted,
Like the print of the hind feet of the buck in the earth of Tamalpais.
You left thy look like a blaze on my heart, the sudden gash in the
    granite,
The blow that broke the honeycomb in the rock of Tamalpais.

And the blaze of the buck is left in the doe, his seal that none may
    have her.
She is bred. She takes his sign to the laurel clump, and will not be seen.
She will lie under laurel and never be seen. She will keep his secret.

She will guard in her womb his planted pang. She will prove her token.
She will hold the sign that set her trust, the seal of her communion.

I will feed thy kiss: as the doe seeks out the laurel clump and feeds her
    treasure.
I will nurse in my heart the wound you made, the gash of thy delivery.
I will bear that blaze in my struck soul, in my body bring it.
It keeps in me now as the sign in the doe, the new life in the mother.

For each in that wound is each, and quick is quick, and we gaze,
A look that lives unslaked in the wound that it inflicted.
My gaze and thine, thy gaze and mine, in these the troth is taken.
The double gaze and the double name in the sign of the quenchless
    wound,
The wound that throbs like wakening milk in the winter dugs of the
    doe,
Like honey out of the broken comb in the rock of Tamalpais.

Thou art gone. I will keep thy wound till you show. I will wait in the
    laurel.
I know as the knowledge is of the doe where she lies on Tamalpais.
In the deep madrone. In the oak. In the tall grove of the redwoods.
Where she lies in laurel and proves the wound on the slope of Mt.
    Tamalpais.

A Siege of Silence

A siege of silence? Thy meaning-moving voice
Hushed in the heart's crypt, thine eye
Shut in unreckoning slumber—
God? God? What storms of the dredgèd deep
Your absence lets, the rock-croppage mind,
Kelp-girthed, sunken under swell,
All seas of the unislanded soul
Typhooned, hurricaned to hell!

God! God! A place of eels and octopuses
Opens down under! Hell-stench

Sulphurs the waters, the drench of madness
Gags my plunged head! Death's belly rips!
The Devil's ruptured fundament,
Fawning with reechy kisses,
Strokes my lips!

God, to purge the memory pure
What cautery is needful?
To ease the soul of rancor,
Quench its hate?
God, God of the paradisal heart
I wait!

What Birds Were There

Wheresoever the body is, thither will the eagles be gathered together.

—SAINT LUKE'S GOSPEL

I dream that I am leaving the scene of an execution. Night has fallen, and I am walking slowly through deserted country. The execution has been awesome rather than terrifying, and as I meditate on what has happened, it is as if I can see about me, in the night-shapes of bushes, the dark figures of various great birds, which, as I pass between them, settle into the contours of human heads. I become aware that these are the faces of the executioners, hardening as they transform into abstract and hieratic projections, without personality, serving to represent fixation points of human nature, utterly inflexible in their particular constellations of consciousness, and I know they will never relent. I think how sad it is that nature cannot reject the logic of its own determinism. Then I come out upon a clearing, and notice on my left a hill of graves, and an owl, like that of Minerva, perched upon a stone. Looking west I see the moon, with the face of a diseased woman, sinking into the sea.

Two magpies under the cypresses.
And what birds were there then I wonder,
To make a graveness in the afternoon
When the nailing was done to the cross hilt,
The man-act centered on the heart of God, irrevocable?
Sparrows, to be sure, scratching about in the street offal,

Yes, curb-brawlers, common as fleas,
Picking right and left for barley seed in the horse manure.
Doubtless a meadowlark off on a fence,
V-breasted, his splendor-drenched throat
Reaved on the spontaneous uprush
Of a rapture unremarked.
Or perhaps that treetop dandy the oriole,
Spinner of gestures, withdrawn now deep in his solitary covert,
His dulcet song, like rich contralto,
Unnoticed on that air.
Say rather, and more to the point,
Two gyrfalcons for outriders sweeping the cross quarter,
Circling, kleeing their strict sabbatical cries,
Imprecational and severe as executioners,
A curse on all triflers. Say further,
The mountain raven, malevolent prophet,
Utterer of virulent indictive oaths,
Imperious from the lodgepole pine,
Damnation drawn down out of the black beak inexorable.
Say too the appalled roadrunner,
Off in a fright scandalized over the stubble patch,
The town curs yelping after. Say most significantly
That grim gliding keeper of appointments, that dark
Ceremonial purist the vulture, a frown on the sky,
Methodical as an undertaker, adaptative
And deferential as the old woman of griefs
Who wraps up the dead.

But this does not mean, small birds of a feather,
That you, in your earnest beneficent presences,
Were somehow inapposite: linnets and speckled finches,
Fleet swallows, sheer swifts of the chimney;
Nor may it impeach your own most consonant
Purling evocative condolence, rain doves of the roof.
Better than those who thumbed sharp iron and plaited thorn!
Better than those who rattled dice for a stranger's shirt
And sponged galled water! Better than those
Who palmed hard silver to close a deal and slunk off after,

Too guilty to haggle! Oh, better by far
Than any of these were you, were you, flit messengers,
Arrived at that place all unbeknownst of what was toward,
But quietly there, not come but *sent*, keeping a tryst
After friend and foe had all alike gone over the hill,
Back down to man's dearth, man's glib and man's madness,
Nor left any light, the owl only upon the slab
To mourn the ruse when the moon sagged out, exhausted,
Her face demented, her jaw half gone,
Till the fierce star of morning
Pierced like the inner eye of God that scorning cloud,
Birthmarked that dawn!

In All These Acts

Cleave the wood and thou shalt find Me, lift the rock and I am there!

—THE GOSPEL ACCORDING TO THOMAS

Dawn cried out: the brutal voice of a bird
Flattened the seaglaze. Treading that surf
Hunch-headed fishers toed small agates,
Their delicate legs, iridescent, stilting the ripples.
Suddenly the cloud closed. They heard big wind
Boom back on the cliff, crunch timber over along the ridge.
They shook up their wings, crying; terror flustered their pinions.
Then hemlock, tall, torn by the roots, went crazily down,
The staggering gyrations of splintered kindling.
Flung out of bracken, fleet mule deer bolted;
But the great elk, caught midway between two scissoring logs,
Arched belly-up and died, the snapped spine
Half torn out of his peeled back, his hind legs
Jerking that gasped convulsion, the kick of spasmed life,
Paunch plowed open, purple entrails
Disgorged from the basketwork ribs
Erupting out, splashed sideways, wrapping him,
Gouted in blood, flecked with the brittle silver of bone.
Frenzied, the terrible head

Thrashed off its antlered fuzz in that rubble
And then fell still, the great tongue
That had bugled in rut, calling the cow-elk up from the glades,
Thrust agonized out, the maimed member
Bloodily stiff in the stone-smashed teeth . . .

                                                    Far down below,
The mountain torrent, that once having started
Could never be stopped, scooped up that avalanchial wrack
And strung it along, a riddle of bubble and littered duff
Spun down its thread. At the gorged river mouth
The sea plunged violently in, gasping its potholes,
Sucked and panted, answering itself in its spume.
The river, spent at last, beating driftwood up and down
In a frenzy of capitulation, pumped out its life,
Destroying itself in the mother sea,
There where the mammoth sea-grown salmon
Lurk immemorial, roe in their hulls, about to begin.
They will beat that barbarous beauty out
On those high-stacked shallows, those headwater claims,
Back where they were born. Along that upward-racing trek
Time springs through all its loops and flanges,
The many-faced splendor and the music of the leaf,
The copulation of beasts and the watery laughter of drakes,
Too few the grave witnesses, the wakeful, vengeful beauty,
Devolving itself of its whole constraint,
Erupting as it goes.

                    In all these acts
Christ crouches and seethes, pitched forward
On the crucifying stroke, juvescent, that will spring Him
Out of the germ, out of the belly of the dying buck,
Out of the father-phallus and the torn-up root.
These are the modes of His forth-showing,
His serene agonization. In the clicking teeth of otters
Over and over He dies and is born,
Shaping the weasel's jaw in His leap
And the staggering rush of the bass.

from "THE WAY OF LIFE AND ·THE WAY OF DEATH"

I

> Mexico: and a wind on the mesa
> Blowing its way out of sluggish centers,
> Coaxing a tropical fragrance,
> The moist rains of December.
>
> Mangoes and rum, the bright
> Blades of poinsettias.
>
> A soft call of birds in the forest,
> A sound of women dipping water at wells,
> The taunting of little children.
>
> I think of poinsettias out of the earth,
> Red as a rose in the teeth of a woman,
> Black as the hair of the virgin of Guadalupe,
> As shaken with passion as the spilled Blood of Christ.
>
> I split my heart on the blood of Mexico.
> I have nailed myself to the Mexican cross.

The Rose of Solitude

> Her heart a bruise on the Christ-flesh suffered out of locked
> agonies of rebirth.
> Her soul fierced inward upon the extravagant passion of woman
> cut between somber and radiant choices.
> Her lips panting the Name of God as she thrusts out the tip
> of her tongue for one more drop of his nerving grace.
>
> Solitary Rose! What wall could entomb her? She is all polish
> and ecstasy.

She is all passion, all fire and devotion. She is all woman, in
    love of God bitten by the rapture of God.
She sounds through my mind thirsting the inconceivable excel-
    lence of Christ.
I hear her feet like rain-clashes run the flat streets to do His will.

All ache. Her heart the glorified Wound. Her soul curls back
    on its pang as the toes of the Christ clutched back on that
    Nail.
In the stigmata of His gaze her love coils like the flesh on its
    iron, the love-ache of the opening.
When she utters the Holy Name you could never doubt God
    died for the love of man.

Solitary Rose! Unspeakable primacy! The masked and dangerous
    glint of implication!
The gleam of death in the knives of her desire! The crescendos
    thirsted in the strings of her passion!
I have seen in her eyes destinies expand and race out beyond the
    apogees of perfection!

She catches them all! Birds beak for her! In the click of her
    teeth she bites little pieces!
Dance! Dance! Never stint that torrential heart, girl and mother,
    holy immolation,
Free as none else of the vice of the self: that narrow hoard of
    unbroachable stinkings!
In the lift of her head earth glints and sparkles! The seethe of
    her voice is pure as the ecstasy of fire in ice!

Solitary Rose! The Spanish pride! The Aztec death! The Mexican
    passion! The American hope!
Woman of the Christ-hurt aching in moan! God-thirster!
    Beautiful inviolable well-deep of passion!
In the fiercest extravagant love is the tangible source of all
    wisdom!
In the sprint of your exquisite flesh is evinced the awesome
    recklessness of God's mercy!

LAWRENCE DURRELL

(1912–)

Conon in Exile

I

Three women have slept with my books,
Penelope among admirers of the ballads,
Let down her hair over my exercises
But was hardly aware of me; an author
Of tunes which made men like performing dogs;
She did not die but left me for a singer in a wig.

II

Later Ariadne read of *The Universe*,
Made a journey under the islands from her own
Green home, husband, house with olive trees.
She lay with my words and let me breathe
Upon her face; later fell like a gull from the
Great ledge in Scio. Relations touched her body
Warm and rosy from the oil like a scented loaf,
Not human any more—but not divine as they had hoped.

III

You who pass the islands will perhaps remember
The lovely Ion, harmless, patient and in love.
Our quarrels disturbed the swallows in the eaves,
The wild bees could not work in the vine;

83

Shaken and ill, one of true love's experiments,
It was she who lay in the stone bath dry-eyed,
Having the impression that her body had become
A huge tear about to drop from the eye of the world.
We never learned that marriage is a kind of architecture,
The nursery virtues were missing, all of them,
So nobody could tell us why we suffered.

I V

It would be untrue to say that *The Art of Marriage*
And the others: *Of Peace in the Self* and *Of Love*
Brought me no women; I remember bodies, arms, faces,
But I have forgotten their names.

V

Finally I am here. Conon in exile on Andros
Like a spider in a bottle writing the immortal
Of Love and Death, through the bodies of those
Who slept with my words but did not know me.
An old man with a skinful of wine
Living from pillow to poke under a vine.

At night the sea roars under the cliffs.
The past harms no one who lies close to the Gods.
Even in these notes upon myself I see
I have put down women's names like some
Philosophical proposition. At last I understand
They were only forms for my own ideas,
With names and mouths and different voices.
In them I lay with myself, my style of life,
Knowing only coitus with the shadows,
By our blue Aegean which forever
Washes and pardons and brings us home.

Alexandria

To the lucky now who have lovers or friends,
Who move to their sweet undiscovered ends,

Or whom the great conspiracy deceives,
I wish these whirling autumn leaves:
Promontories splashed by the salty sea,
Groaned on in darkness by the tram
To horizons of love or good luck or more love—
As for me I now move
Through many negatives to what I am.

Here at the last cold Pharos between Greece
And all I love, the lights confide
A deeper darkness to the rubbing tide;
Doors shut, and we the living are locked inside
Between the shadows and the thoughts of peace:
And so in furnished rooms revise
The index of our lovers and our friends
From gestures possibly forgotten, but the ends
Of longings like unconnected nerves,
And in this quiet rehearsal of their acts
We dream of them and cherish them as Facts.

Now when the sea grows restless as a conscript,
Excited by fresh wind, climbs the sea-wall,
I walk by it and think about you all:
B. with his respect for the Object, and D.
Searching in sex like a great pantry for jars
Marked 'Plum and apple'; and the small, fell
Figure of Dorian ringing like a muffin-bell—
All indeed whom war or time threw up
On this littoral and tides could not move
Were objects for my study and my love.

And then turning where the last pale
Lighthouse, like a Samson blinded, stands
And turns its huge charred orbit on the sands
I think of you—indeed mostly of you,
In whom a writer would only name and lose
The dented boy's lip and the close
Archer's shoulders; but here to rediscover
By tides and faults of weather, by the rain
Which washes everything, the critic and the lover.

At the doors of Africa so many towns founded
Upon a parting could become Alexandria, like
The wife of Lot—a metaphor for tears;
And the queer student in his poky hot
Tenth floor room above the harbour hears
The sirens shaking the tree of his heart,
And shuts his books, while the most
Inexpressible longings like wounds unstitched
Stir in him some girl's unquiet ghost.

So we, learning to suffer and not condemn
Can only wish you this great pure wind
Condemned by Greece, and turning like a helm
Inland where it smokes the fires of men,
Spins weathercocks on farms or catches
The lovers at their quarrel in the sheets;
Or like a walker in the darkness might,
Knocks and disturbs the artist at his papers
Up there alone, upon the alps of night.

On First Looking into Loeb's Horace

I found your Horace with the writing in it;
Out of time and context came upon
This lover of vines and slave to quietness,
Walking like a figure of smoke here, musing
Among his high and lovely Tuscan pines.

All the small-holder's ambitions, the yield
Of wine-bearing grape, pruning and drainage
Laid out by laws, almost like the austere
Shell of his verses—a pattern of Latin thrift;
Waiting so patiently in a library for
Autumn and the drying of the apples;
The betraying hour-glass and its deathward drift.

Surely the hard blue winterset
Must have conveyed a message to him—

The premonitions that the garden heard
Shrunk in its shirt of hair beneath the stars,
How rude and feeble a tenant was the self,
An Empire, the body with its members dying—
And unwhistling now the vanished Roman bird?

The fruit-trees dropping apples; he counted them;
The soft bounding fruit on leafy terraces,
And turned to the consoling winter rooms
Where, facing south, began the great prayer,
With his reed laid upon the margins
Of the dead, his stainless authors,
Upright, severe on an uncomfortable chair.

Here, where your clear hand marked up
'The hated cypress' I added 'Because it grew
On tombs, revealed his fear of autumn and the urns',
Depicting a solitary at an upper window
Revising metaphors for the winter sea: 'O
Dark head of storm-tossed curls'; or silently
Watching the North Star which like a fever burns

Away the envy and neglect of the common,
Shining on this terrace, lifting up in recreation
The sad heart of Horace who must have seen it only
As a metaphor for the self and its perfection—
A burning heart quite constant in its station.

Easy to be patient in the summer,
The light running like fishes among the leaves,
Easy in August with its cones of blue
Sky uninvaded from the north; but winter
With its bareness pared his words to points
Like stars, leaving them pure but very few.

He will not know how we discerned him, disregarding
The pose of sufficiency, the landed man,
Found a suffering limb on the great Latin tree
Whose roots live in the barbarian grammar we

Use, yet based in him, his mason's tongue;
Describing clearly a bachelor, sedentary,
With a fond weakness for bronze-age conversation,
Disguising a sense of failure in a hatred for the young,

Who built in the Sabine hills this forgery
Of completeness, an orchard with a view of Rome;
Who studiously developed his sense of death
Till it was all around him, walking at the circus,
At the baths, playing dominoes in a shop—
The escape from self-knowledge with its tragic
Imperatives: *Seek, suffer, endure.* The Roman
In him feared the Law and told him where to stop.

So perfect a disguise for one who had
Exhausted death in art—yet who could guess
You would discern the liar by a line,
The suffering hidden under gentleness
And add upon the flyleaf in your tall
Clear hand: 'Fat, human and unloved,
And held from loving by a sort of wall,
Laid down his books and lovers one by one,
Indifference and success had crowned them all.'

The Lost Cities

For Paddy and Xan

One she floats as Venice might,
Bloated among her ambiguities:
What hebetude or carelessness shored up
Goths were not smart enough to capture.
The city, yes: the water: not the style.

Her dispossession now may seem to us
Idle and ridiculous, quivering
In the swollen woodwork of these
Floating carcases of the doges,

Dissolving into spires and cages of water:
Venice blown up, and turning green.

Another wears out humbly like a craft:
Red wells where the potter's thumb
Sealed his jars of guaranteed oil.
That fluent thumb which presses
On history's vibrating string,
Pressing here, there, in a wounded place.

Some have left names only: Carthage:
Where the traveller may squeeze out
A few drops of ink or salt,
On deserted promontories may think:
'No wonder. A river once turned over
In its sleep and all the cities fled.'

Now in Greece which is not yet Greece
The adversary was also strong.
Yet here the serfs have built their discontents
As spiders do their junctions, here,
This orchard, painted tables set outside
A whitewashed house,
And on a rusty nail the violin
Is hanging by one wrist, still ownerless:

Disowned by the devastator and as yet
Uncherished by its tenants in the old
Human smells of excrement and cooking:
Waiting till the spades press through to us,
To be discovered, standing in our lives,

Rhodes, death-mask of a Greek town.

The Critics

They never credit us
With being bad enough

The boys that come to edit us:
Of simply not caring when a prize,
Something for nothing, comes our way,
A wife, a mistress, or a holiday
From People living neckfast in their lies.

No: Shakespear's household bills
Could never be responsible, they say,
For all the heartbreak and the 1,000 ills
His work is heir to, poem, sonnet, play . . .
Emended readings give the real reason:
The times were out of joint, the loves, the season.

Man With A Message—how could you forget
To read your proofs, the heartache and the fret?
The copier or the printer
Must take the blame for it in all
The variants they will publish by the winter.

'By elision we quarter suffering.' Too true.
'From images and scansion can be learned.' . . .
Yet under it perhaps may be discerned
A something else afoot—a Thing
Lacking both precedent and name and gender:
An uncreated Weight which left its clue,
Making him run up bills,
Making him violent or distrait or tender:
Leaving for Stratford might have heard It say:
'Tell them I won't be back on Saturday.
My wife will understand I'm on a bender.'
And to himself muttering, muttering: 'Words
Added to words multiply the space
Between this feeling and my expressing It.
The wires get far too hot. Time smoulders
Like a burning rug. I *will* be free.' . . .

And all the time from the donkey's head
The lover is whispering: 'This is not
What I imagined as Reality.
If truth were needles surely eyes would see?

Troy

By maunding and imposture Helen came,
Eater of the white fig, the sugar-bread;
Some beauty, yes, but not more than her tribe
Lathe-made for stock embraces on a bed.
I am astonished when they talk of her,
The shattered cities, bone from human bone
Torn; defaced altars and burning hearths.
For such as she deaf impulse worked in men:
They dug up graves and ripped down scions of stone,
In act and wish unseparated then.
The test for cultures this insipid drone!
Yes, for a doll the hero, wild-eyed freak
Howled at his mother's grave, yet stopped to dry
One tear of Helen on the sarcastic cheek.

A Persian Lady

Some diplomatic mission—no such thing as 'fate'—
Brought her to the city that ripening spring.
She was much pointed out—a Lady-in-Waiting—
To some Persian noble; well, and here she was
Merry and indolent amidst fashionable abundance.
By day under a saffron parasol on royal beaches,
By night in a queer crocked tent with tassels.

He noted the perfected darkness of her beauty,
The mind recoiling as from a branding-iron:
The sea advancing and retiring at her lacquered toes;
How would one say 'to enflame' in her tongue,
He wondered, knowing it applied to female beauty?
When their eyes met he felt dis-figured
It would have been simple—three paces apart!

Disloyal time! They let the seminal instant go,
The code unbroken, the collision of ripening wishes

Abandoned to hiss on in the great syllabaries of memory.
Next day he deliberately left the musical city
To join a boring water-party on the lake,
Telling himself 'Say what you like about it,
I have been spared very much in this business.'

He meant, I think, that never should he now
Know the slow disgracing of her mind, the slow
Spiral of her beauty's deterioration, flagging desires,
The stagnant fury of the temporal yoke,
Grey temple, long slide into fat.

On the other hand neither would she build him sons
Or be a subject for verses—the famished in-bred poetry
Which was the fashion of his time and ours.
She would exist, pure, symmetrical and intact
Like the sterile hyphen which divides and joins
In a biography the year of birth and death.

ROY FULLER

(1912–)

The Pure Poet

He spoke of poetry: his lips had shrunk
To lines across the gums: he also stank.
He said that since the Greeks few had the gifts,
That syphilis and lice were perquisites.
He brought a charnel breath and spotted cloths,
The swansdown shroud was fluttered when he coughed
His postulate of the sufficient word.
I felt viridian when he launched on blood,
Perceived the surgery behind the trance,
That his long travels in pursuit of tense
Were clearly all compelled by social syntax;
And but for his unpleasant human antics
I could have pitied him for being dead.
Still he sat on and told me how he made
His money, villa, servants, the model globe,
His regular habits and the seven-faced cube.
Further I could not follow him, among
The obscure allusions to important dung,
Nor as at length he tried a final scare
And vanished through the non-existent door.

Epitaph on a Bombing Victim

Reader, could his limbs be found
Here would lie a common man:
History inflicts no wound
But explodes what it began,
And with its enormous lust
For division splits the dust.
Do not ask his nation; that
Was History's confederate.

Y. M. C. A. Writing Room

A map of the world is on the wall: its lying
Order and compression shadow these bent heads.
Here we try to preserve communications;
The map mocks us with dangerous blues and reds.

Today my friends were drafted; they are about
To be exploded, to be scattered over
That coloured square which in reality
Is a series of scenes, is boredom, cover,

Nostalgia, labour, death. They will explore
Minutely particular deserts, seas and reefs,
Invest a thousand backcloths with their moods,
And all will carry, like a cancer, grief.

In England at this moment the skies contain
Ellipses of birds within their infinite planes,
At night the ragged patterns of the stars;
And distant trees are like the branching veins

Of an anatomical chart: as menacing
As pistols the levelled twigs present their buds.

They have exchanged for this illusion of danger
The ordeal of walking in the sacred wood.

The season cannot warm them nor art console.
These words are false as the returning Spring
From which this March history has made subtraction:
The spirit has gone and left the marble thing.

The Tribes

I think of the tribes: the women prized for fatness
Immovable, and by a sympathetic
    Magic sustaining the herds,
    On whose strange humps sit birds;

And those with long dung-stiffened capes of hair,
And those that ceremonially eat their dead;
    The ornamental gashes
    Festered and raised with ashes;

The captured and dishonoured king compelled
To straddle a vertical and sharpened stake,
    Until, his legs hauled at,
    The point burst from his throat;

And all the prohibitions and the cheapness
Of life so hardly got, where it is death
    Even to touch the palace
    And poison expresses malice.

Now in the white men's towns the tribes are gathered
Among the corrugated iron and
    The refuse bins where rats
    Dispute with them for scraps.

Truly, civilisation is for them
The most elemental struggle for bread and love;

For all the tabus have gone,
It is man against man alone.

On waste plots and in the decrepit shanties
They begin to discover the individual,
   And, with the sense in time
   Of Adam, perpetuate crime.

The most horrible things you can imagine are
Happening in the towns and the most senseless:
   There are no kings or poison,
   Are laws but no more reason.

Crustaceans

Upon the beach are thousands of crabs; they are
Small, with one foreclaw curiously developed.
Against the ashen sand I see a forest
Of waving, pink, in some way human, claws.
The crabs advance or, perhaps, retreat a step
And then like Hamlet's father slowly beckon
With that flesh-coloured, yes, obscene, incisor.
These actions in the mass take on a rhythm
—The sexual display of higher beasts,
The dance of the tribe, or the enthusiasm
Of a meeting.
                        If you go closer to the crabs
You see that with their normal claws they are making
Spheres from the sand, small perfect rounds, which they,
After a little preliminary twiddling,
Produce from beneath their bodies suddenly,
Like jugglers, and deposit by their holes.
While this goes on, that monstrous foreclaw, that
Button hole, is motionless. And all around
The shafts sunk by these creatures lie the eggs
Of sand, so patiently, endlessly evolved.
At last I stretch and wave my hand: the crabs
Instantly bolt down their holes and pull a sphere,

A trap door, after them, and in a second
The beach is still.
                    While I was watching them
My eyes unfocused with the effort, or
Maybe it was the whole activity
Which like an idea detached itself from its
Frame, background: and I thought, are these that I
Regard with such pity, disgust, absorption, crabs?

Rhetoric of a Journey

Train takes me away from the northern valleys
Where I lived my youth and where my youth lives on
In the person of my parent and the stone walls,
The dialect of love I understand
But scarcely speak, the mills and illnesses.

In Trollope's novel open on my knee
The characters are worried about money:
The action revolves round the right to a necklace.
I have only to bend my head and immediately
I am lost in this other reality, the world
Of art, where something is always missing.
In *The Eustace Diamonds* life is made tolerable
By standing away from time and refusing to write
Of the hours that link the official biography.

I think of the poem I wrote on another visit—
A list of the poet's hoarded perceptions:
The net of walls thrown over waves of green,
The valleys clogged with villages, the cattle
Pink against smoking mills—and only now
Experience what was delayed and omitted.
For those were rooms in which we dared not look
At each other's load of emotion: it was there
Our past had to die: and where we acknowledged
With pain and surprise our ties with the disregarded.

I would like to renounce the waking rational life,
The neat completed work, as being quite
Absurd and cowardly; and leave to posterity
The words on book-marks, enigmatic notes,
Thoughts before sleep, the vague unwritten verse
On people, on the city to which I travel.
I would like to resolve to live fully
In the barbarous world of sympathy and fear.

Says his life to the poet: 'Can you make verse of this?'
And the poet answers: 'Yes, it is your limitations
That enable me to get you down at all.'
The diamonds glitter on his paper and
His sons sail unloved to the Antipodes.
Those whom a lack of creativeness condemns
To truth see magazines in the hands of the patient
And realise that the serial will go on
After death; but the artist becomes ill himself.
For only the fully-committed participate
In the revolution of living, the coming to power
Of death: the others have always some excuse
To be absent from the shooting, to be at home
Curled up with a book or at the dentist's.

Sometimes I find it possible to feign
The accent of the past, the vulgar speech
Which snobbery and art have iced; but feel no longer
The compulsion of hills, the eternal interests
Which made my fathers understand each other.
That mockery of solidarity
Some of the civilised always experience,
Waiting half hopefully for the dreaded barbarians,
Sick of their culture, traitors to the division
Of toil and sensibility. Yet really
I can speak easily only to myself.
The tears meant for others are wept in front of the glass;
The confession is never posted; and the eye
Slides away from the proffered hand and discovers
An interesting view from the window.

The ridiculous mottled faces pass in stiff
Procession: relations, friends and chance encounters.
And the asinine minds that lie behind the gestures
Of goodness I can never reciprocate
Repel me with their inability
To escape from the grossest errors. Is it weakness
That sometimes imagines these shaped as heroes?
That cannot conceive of happiness as other
Than the apotheosis of the simple and kind?
That refuses to see how the century rises, pale,
From the death of its dream, ignoring the gains
Of the cruel, the different wishes of slaves?

The train removes me to another set
Of evasions. The valleys disappear. The train
Bolts through the central plain. I shall discover
Whether Lizzie Eustace retained her diamonds,
How far the hordes are from the city,
And my end will make significant for me
A casual place and date. My own child
Will grow from the generous warmth of his youth and perhaps
Discover, like me, that the solemn moments of life
Require their unbearable gaucheness translated to art.
For the guilt of being alive must be appeased
By the telling observation, and even feeling
Can only be borne retrospectively.
Bending over to kiss, the sensitive see with alarm
That their selves are still upright: the instant of death is announced
By a rattle of tin in the corridor. Meaning is given
These disparate happenings, our love is only
Revealed, by conventions: 'Dear Mother, I hope you are better.'
Or 'Lizzie resolved that she would have her revenge.'

The lilac will last a fortnight if the rain
Arrives, the sparrows will always turn to let
Their lime drop over the gutter, the gardener
Will lift the chickweed, and the clots of nests
In the elms disappear in the whirling green of summer.

At the end of the twilit road a figure is standing
Calling us to go in, while the far-off rumours
Of terrible facts which at last may destroy
Our happiness spoil our play. In the place we go to
The kettle boils on the fire, the brasses are polished,
But people are busy with pain in another room.
One night I shall watch the city and black sky meet
In the distance, the car lights stream on the heath like tracer,
And in such moments of lonely and mild exultation
This rhetoric will be forgotten, and the life of omission go on.
Behind me will lie the sad and convulsive events
As narrative art, and as fated, immortal and false.

The Image

A spider in the bath. The image noted:
Significant maybe but surely cryptic.
A creature motionless and rather bloated,
The barriers shining, vertical and white:
Passing concern, and pity mixed with spite.

Next day with some surprise one finds it there.
It seems to have moved an inch or two, perhaps.
It starts to take on that familiar air
Of prisoners for whom time is erratic:
The filthy aunt forgotten in the attic.

Quite obviously it came up through the waste,
Rejects through ignorance or apathy
That passage back. The problem must be faced;
And life go on though strange intruders stir
Among its ordinary furniture.

One jibs at murder, so a sheet of paper
Is slipped beneath the accommodating legs.
The bathroom window shows for the escaper
The lighted lanterns of laburnum hung
In copper beeches—on which scene it's flung.

We certainly would like thus easily
To cast out of the house all suffering things.
But sadness and responsibility
For our own kind lives in the image noted:
A half-loved creature, motionless and bloated.

On Reading a Soviet Novel

Will not the Local Party Secretary
Prove that his love of men's not innocent:
The heroine at last be blown off course
By some base, gusty, female element:
And the grave hero be eventually torn
By a disgraceful infantile event?

No, in this world the good works out its course
Unhindered by the real, irrelevant flaw.
Our guilty eyes glaze over with ennui
At so much honest purpose, rigid law.
This is not life, we say, who ask that art
Show mainly what the partial butler saw.

And yet with what disquiet we leave the tale!
The mere appearance of the descending Goth,
So frightful to a sedentary race,
Made him invincible. It is not wrath
That breaks up cultures but the virtues of
The stupid elephant, the piddling moth.

The threatened empire dreads its rival's arms
Less than the qualities at which it sneers—
The slave morality promoted to
A way of life: naïve, old-fashioned tears
Which once it shed itself by bucketsful
In nascent, optimistic, long-dead years.

The Day

At the time it seemed unimportant: he was lying
In bed, off work, with a sudden pain,
And she was haloed by the morning sun,
Enquiring if he'd like the daily paper.

So idle Byzantium scarcely felt at first
The presence in her remoter provinces
Of the destructive followers of the Crescent.

But in retrospect that day of moderate health
Stood fired in solid and delightful hues,
The last of joy, the first of something else—
An inconceivable time when sex could be
Grasped for the asking with gigantic limbs,
When interest still was keen in the disasters
Of others—accident, uprising, drouth—
And the sharp mind perceived the poignancy
Of the ridiculous thoughts of dissolution.

A day remembered by a shrivelled empire
Nursed by hermaphrodites and unsustained
By tepid fluids poured in its crying mouth.

Versions of Love

'My love for you has faded'—thus the Bad
Quarto, the earliest text, whose midget page
Derived from the imperfect memories
Of red-nosed, small-part actors
Or the atrocious shorthand of the age.

However, the far superior Folio had
'My love for you was fated'—thus implying
Illicit passion, a tragic final act.
And this was printed from the poet's own

Foul papers, it was reckoned;
Supported by the reading of the Second
Quarto, which had those sombre words exact.

Such evidence was shaken when collation
Showed that the Folio copied slavishly
The literals of that supposedly
Independent Quarto. Thus one had to go
Back to the first text of all.

'My love for you has faded'—quite impossible.
Scholars produced at last the emendation:
'My love for you fast endured.'
Our author's ancient hand that must have been
Ambiguous and intellectual
Foxed the compositors of a certainty.
And so the critical editions gave
Love the sound status that she ought to have
In poetry so revered.

But this conjecture cannot quite destroy
The question of what the poet really wrote
In the glum middle reaches of his life:
Too sage, too bald, too fearful of fiasco
To hope beyond his wife,
Yet aching almost as promptly as a boy.

Those of Pure Origin

Ein Räthsel ist Reinentsprunges. Auch
Der Gesang kaum darf es enthüllen. Denn
Wie du anfiengst, wirst du bleiben

—HÖLDERLIN

A mystery are those of pure origin.
Even song may hardly unveil it.
For as you began, so you will remain.

—TRANSLATION BY MICHAEL HAMBURGER

After a throbbing night, the house still dark, pull
Back the curtains, see the cherry standing there—
Grain of the paper under wash of rain-clouds.

No, our disguises are not intended to
Deceive. On the contrary. And could you name
Us we shouldn't be compelled to appear so
Confusingly—smothered in white stars, whistling
Hymn tunes, putting out scaly paws to attract
Attention. Under comic aliases—
Even the specific for insomnia:
Peppermint, lime blossom, betony, scullcap—
We entice you into our dissident realms.
The staggering plots you invent in hours
Abbreviated by anxiety are
Hatched by our logic. Just as when you try to
Talk with the girl of fifteen we tilt her shoe
Inward to imply her different order.

For it's *your* world we're expounding. Don't mistake
Our endeavours. We can't tell you where you're from.
Indeed, despite our immanence we're the last
Who could reveal more than is there already.

Let alone where you're going! Darwin's infant
Enquired about his friend's father: 'Where does
He do his barnacles?'—assumption of a
Universal preoccupation no more
Naive than yours, whether of indifference or
Concern. It's quite plausible that the concept
Of outside disappears outside—in that place
Where nebulae no longer have to awake
And pretend to be happy.
                              Our advice is:
Prefer the less likely explanation.
Different evenings, the evening star appearing
In different corners of the pane—conceive
No senseless revolution in the heavens
But a lucky change of erotic fortune;
A goddess steeped not in urine but in love.
And then so often you've been wrong why shouldn't
You be wrong about the extinction of man?

It's true we tend to avoid you, fatal as
You are in general to our fragility.
But sometimes one of us, whom you knew in flight
And particularly admired for his looks,
Lies down and allows the wind to blow the wrong way
His once glossy pinions. Look into his eye.
It regards you still, though fixed as well on worlds
More real than at that moment you can bear.
Of course, you'll soon take your spade and among
Pebbles, lapis worms, inter the eye from sight.

'Considering my present condition,
I can neither concentrate on poetry
Nor enjoy poetry.' That final letter
May seem a defeat after a lifetime of
Assuming the reality of the art.
Not to us, though it's we are the defeated.
For we boast of our patience—coral *croissants*
Anchored at last to just too-heavy hill-tops;
Laboratories of finches; Galapagos
Of revelation awaiting an observer.
And you, even in the children's puzzle, are
You certain you've seen all the hidden objects?
Yes, there's the extrusion of the wall in
A clawed hump, and a grey frayed rope-end blown round
And round a bough. But what are the abstract shapes
As enigmatic in significance as
Those painters find incised from oceans by arcs
Of a parasol or enclosed from a beach
By the severe bay of a young throat and jaw?

That countenance whose eyes are as pale as if
The flesh had been clipped out to show the ash sky
Behind it . . . The voice that unavailingly
Says: 'Do you remember taking your laundry
To the woman with elephant legs?' . . . The past
As ambiguous as hailstones in the gales
Of Spring: the future certain—the instant when

You stop being convinced of our existence,
And meaningless that blackbirds masquerade as owls,
That also in the dusk, making free of it
For assignations, jealousies (those affairs
Of energy and waiting unwearying,
Of obsession with menstrual blood), occur
The strange pre-marital flights of humans.

What does it matter that the baptistery proves
As dusty and void as bad nuts when its doors
Provide a progression of style, the basher
Of bronze breaking out from pious platitudes
Into arcades of applied geometry,
Thronged with our perfect but realistic forms?

The mad poet called us, untranslatably:
'Those of pure origin'—left you to divine
Whether we rise from phenomena or,
Perhaps more likely, also require your presence,
As the cathedral the plague, pity the war.

But how can we pretend our hemisphere-wide
Lament, the random trickling and joining of tears
On acres of glass, is entirely for your
Predicament—as your lives, borne upon the
More and more dubiously physical, move
To regions of abnegation and concern
Whose angels we are; though, under cruel casques,
Our curls, our thick, parted lips ever youthful,
Complexions marked with still unmalignant moles
Of the actual, scabs on unfolding leaves?

GEORGE BARKER

(1913–)

Secular Elegies

I

My pig-faced kingdom with tongues of wrong
And an historical gait of trial and error,
Under whose bridges Time, faster than rivers,
Bears individual and event along
Into a past overloaded with souvenirs:

Now answer history with a marvellous golden Yes
As she steps up asking all future questions.
The historians in their tombs, sighing, will sleep
Deeper, and the sailors, who always had great visions,
Smile for the island that ceased to be an illusion.

The instinct of the bird governs its acts of war,
Who, titivating itself at crossroads, rises and rises
Singing from the destructive wheels that come roar-
ing towards it, and in the end, after the reverses,
Perches whistling on the shattered axles proudly.

The armies of Hohenzollern, brooding on loss,
Know best that the real enemy is never there
Pinned akimbo on the gun-sight, but in the cause.

O sheeted in their horoscopes like togas
Under red stars strut the catchpenny Caesars.

Heroes who ride your wishing horses over
The breakfast tables of the population,
Your beds are full of hands. And when you shiver
What stalks across your grave is a whole nation:
And when you close an eye your life is over.

But the conquerors, reddening their heels on us,
They will not ever really die, but continually
Thrash on the hotbed of their animus:
Not one of them shall die hopefully and finally,
For them the grave will also be full of us.

11

Where formerly he saw birds in bushes, now
The cyclist resting from his uphill labour
Observes the skull of Cromwell on a bough
Admonishing his half heart, and he shoulders
His way upward against the wind to the brow.

The political cartoonist in his bed
Hears voices break his sleep he does not know:
The morning papers show what the people said.
Librarians in their studies, the lights low,
Sense Milton breathing in his marble head.

The clerk hears Clive cheering in a darkness.
And from the ponds of commons, in broad day,
The effigies of great sailors rise in their starkness
With the *Hood* in their hands, and cry:
'Nevertheless we mourn also the *Bismarck!*'

There it is necessary to walk carefully
And swallows must dive wisely, for the air,
So full of poems and ghosts, is truly
Populated with more than meets the eye:
Some principles have become poltergeist there.

Where, in its sepulchres, the long past rests
Brocaded with daydreams, there the truth is known:
What makes the people happiest is best.
But the fish in its undersea caves and bird in its nest
Know that the shark and cuckoo never rest.

Sometimes the punts in summer on the rivers,
Gliding like dancers over the slovenly water
Saw as they traced their way among the shallows
Images under them pinned in a cage of shadows
Struggling to catch the eye. It was the future.

The quavering Chamberlain, trapped between disasters,
Hiding his head in an hour-glass: four kings and
The bicyclist Queen, like uprooted pilasters,
Flying across the sea: coiled in the ampersand
The hakencreutz accumulates but never masters.

And some, in silence, looking for their lives
In the lines of their hands, the merciless words saw
That turned Nebuchadnezzar into a cow:
Others, who came kissing and bringing olives,
Had a change of heart and are dead now.

Sad in his alcove of love Pascal lamented:
'My friend, my friend, you were born on the other side.'
Firstly we die because of places. O the demented
Alexander, who, eternally discontented,
Desires more, is us. Finally we die of pride.

III

Satan is on your tongue, sweet singer, with
Your eye on the income and the encomium:
Angels rhapsodise for and from their faith.
And in the studies of chromium
Lucifer seduces Orpheus with a myth.

But the principle of evil is not autonomous.
Like the Liberty Horse with a plume at a circus

Under the whipmaster it steps proud in its circles.
When I let slip one instant the whip of the will
All hell's scot free with fire at the nostril.

Thus if the crux and judgement never is
Left to our own to do with as we will,
But the decision, like a master key, lies
Wholly in the higher hands that hold all—
How can we be as innocent as this?

Everything that is profound loves the mask,
Said the Dionysian who never wore one.
Thus our damnation and our condemnation,
Wiser than Nietzsche, never taking a risk,
Wears the mask of a necessary satisfaction.

Not, Love, when we kiss do the archangels weep
For we are naked then wherever we are,
Like tigers in the night; but in our sleep
The masks go down, and the beast is bare:
It is not Love but double damnation there.

Marooned on the islands of pride, lonely
And mad on the pyramids of achievement,
Disillusioned in the cathedrals of doxology,
The sad man senses his continual bereavement:
God has just died, and now there is only

Us. The gold bull with its horns of finances
Over the sensual mountains goes gallivanting
In glory: all night and all day it dances,
Absurd and happy because nothing is wanting.
The sad man hides his grief in his five senses.

IV

Then from its labours I rest my hand on the table
And there where hitherto the poem had been,
Now, in its deadliness sleeping but capable,

Agent and gadget of destruction, the machine
Of actual damnation lies and is culpable.

Everything that we touch, sooner or later,—
The uprooted arbutus hung at the head of the bed,
The untouchable trophies in the arcanum of nature,
The dizzy stars, the testes, and the sacred
Dove—everything that we dissect for data
Dies as we finger for the heart of the matter.

O but the Doric arm tattooed with falsity
That riddles this embrace where worlds hide,
Larger than railways where they hold a country
Sleeping and waking in their iron anatomy,
Takes me to the breast where I am pacified

Under the frenzies of all sensual wonders.
What shall I say when, big at my mouth,
The Hesperidean with a worm in its splendours
Hangs like the bub of a whore? Or what truth
Find in the kiss that dazzles all my windows?

And so in circles over existential deserts
I and you wander, lost, and arm in arm;
Lost, lost. And the visions paying us visits
Lead us to mirages where, in a morning dream,
We forget the headaches and the lost Edens.

V

O Golden Fleece she is where she lies tonight
Trammelled in her sheets like midsummer on a bed,
Kisses like moths flitter over her bright
Mouth, and, as she turns her head,
All space moves over to give her beauty room.

Where her hand, like a bird on the branch of her arm,
Droops its wings over the bedside as she sleeps,
There the air perpetually stays warm

Since, nested, her hand rested there. And she keeps
Under her green thumb life like a growing poem.

My nine-tiered tigress in the cage of sex
I feed with meat that you tear from my side
Crowning your nine months with the paradox:
The love that kisses with a homicide
In robes of red generation resurrects.

The bride who rides the hymenæal waterfall
Spawning all possibles in her pools of surplus,
Whom the train rapes going into a tunnel,
The imperial multiplicator nothing can nonplus:
My mother Nature is the origin of it all.

At Pharaoh's Feast and in the family cupboard,
Gay corpse, bright skeleton, and the fly in amber,
She sits with her laws like antlers from her forehead
Enmeshing everyone, with flowers and thunder
Adorning the head that destiny never worried.

VI

Temper the whirlwind to the unborn lamb,
Mother of us all, lapped in your shawls of cause;
Large in your arms wrap our sad amalgam
That, spinning its tails among the other stars,
Mopes, lost and weeping, far, far from its home.

Cover with your pity the broken Pole
Where, like a rag, the pride of the human hangs
Dirty as dishcloths. And with summer console
Us for the equinox of our anguish.
Humour the arrogant ships that sail.

Too near the tooth of the truth and the weather,
The thinkers in their cockleshells, the captains
Sinking each other; and always permit neither
Wholly to find their ends, for they seek islands
Of Death and Truth that should always be further.

And in due season to their last bed take
The lovers who are the cause of all the trouble;
Let the manikin Adam successfully undertake
What Atlas only, bending an apish double,
Hitherto managed with the world on his back.

O temper the whirlwind to the unborn lamb!
And on the tongue of the young in its cradle
Lightly lay silver spoons. And the same
Love extend to those who groom your bridal
That they, mother of us all, suffer in your name.

Summer Song I

I looked into my heart to write
    And found a desert there.
But when I looked again I heard
Howling and proud in every word
    The hyena despair.

Great summer sun, great summer sun,
    All loss burns in trophies;
And in the cold sheet of the sky
Lifelong the fishlipped lovers lie
    Kissing catastrophes.

O loving garden where I lay
    When under the breasted tree
My son stood up behind my eyes
And groaned: Remember that the price
    Is vinegar for me.

Great summer sun, great summer sun,
    Turn back to the designer:
I would not be the one to start
The breaking day and the breaking heart
    For all the grief in China.

My one, my one, my only love,
　　Hide, hide your face in a leaf,
And let the hot tear falling burn
The stupid heart that will not learn
　　The everywhere of grief.

Great summer sun, great summer sun,
　　Turn back to the never-never
Cloud-cuckoo, happy, far-off land
Where all the love is true love, and
　　True love goes on for ever.

Summer Song II

Soft is the collied night, and cool
These regions where the dreamers rule,
As Summer, in her rose and robe,
Astride the horses of the globe,
Drags, fighting, from the midnight sky,
The mushroom at whose glance we die.

Channel Crossing

To John Lehmann

And just by crossing the short sea
To find the answer sitting there
Combing out its snaky hair
And with a smile regarding me
Because it knows only too well
That I shall never recognize
The axioms that I should prize
Or the lies that I should tell.

I saw the question in the sky
Ride like a gull to fool me, as
The squat boat butted at the seas

As grossly as through ultimates I
Churn up a frothy wake of verbs
Or stir a muddy residue
Looking for that answer who
Sanctifies where she perturbs.

The horror of the questionmark
I looked back and saw stand over
The white and open page of Dover
Huge as the horn of the scapegoat. Dark
It stood up in the English day
Interrogating Destiny
With the old lip of the sea:
"What can a dead nation say?"

As these words wailed in the air
I looked at Europe and I saw
The glittering instruments of war
Grow paler but not go from where
Like a Caesarian sunset on
The cold slab of the horizon
They lay foretelling for tomorrow
Another day of human sorrow.

But when I turned and looked into
The silent chambers of the sea
I saw the displaced fishes flee
From nowhere into nowhere through
Their continent of liberty.
O skipping porpoise of the tide
No longer shall the sailors ride
You cheering out to sea.

I thought of Britain in its cloud
Chained to the economic rocks
Dying behind me. I saw the flocks
Of great and grieving omens crowd
About the lion on the stone.

And I heard Milton's eagle mewing
Her desolation in the ruin
Of a great nation, alone.

That granite and gigantic sigh
Of the proud man beaten by
Those victories from which we die;
The gentle and defeated grief
Of the gale that groans among
Trees that are a day too strong
And, victorious by a leaf,
Show the winner he was wrong.

The continent of discontent
Rose up before me as I stood
Above the happy fish. Endued
With hotter and unhappier blood
Contented in my discontent,
I saw that every man's a soul
Caught in the glass wishing bowl:
To live at peace in discontent.

O somewhere in the seven leagues
That separate us from the stricken
Amphitheatre of the spirit,
O somewhere in that baleful sea
The answer of sad Europe lodges,
The clue that causes us to sicken
Because we cannot find and share it,
Or, finding, cannot see.

So in the sky the monstrous sun
Mocked like a punishment to be,
Extending, now, to you and me
The vision of what we have done:
And as the boat drew to the quay
I thought, by crossing the short water
I shall not find, in its place,
The answer with a silent face.

Stanzas on a Visit to Longleat House in Wiltshire, October 1953

To John Farrelly

Dead pomp sneering underground
Glares up at a horned foot of clay
Where the hog of multitude hangs around
Among these tremendous memories
That delegate to our day
The superannuated and damned glories.

A quidnunc with a shopping bag
Stops gossiping with another hag
And where immense conceptions were
Dragged shrieking from their cellars here
The ragged-arsed mechanics squat
Owning what they haven't got.

O rare rain of disinterest
Descend on this fouled public nest
And rout out all vulgarities
That, crowding through its majesties,
Gut to bare shell and bone
The grandeur of the dead and gone.

In car–park, garden and urinal
The free and ignorant, almost
As easy as at a Cup Final
Gawk through the stone-transparent ghost
Of this once noble house, now lost
In the gross error of survival.

"Come," said my proud and sulking friend,
"Four angels up to Heaven's Gate,
And looking down at Longleat
So far below, shall disappear
The human termite, leaving there
Stones and spectres hand in hand."

And from that aerial sweep of height
The valley fell through depths of pine
Down through green distances until
From glimmering water rising bright
Longleat, bird's-eyed in sunshine,
Smiled up from its own funeral.

I saw the heroic seizins fade
And hide in laurels of old trees
As brassbands of indignities
Exploded echoes to degrade
The splendours and the miseries
Of that cold illustrious shade.

A *Little Song in Assisi*

Sprightly the cockcrowing
sun from that stone bed
high in the hilly morning
where a saint lay down his head
steps gallivanting.

All small things including
bird lizard and beast
and the dayspring beginning
dance from the doors of the east
like lambs skedaddling.

There is such an alighting
tenderness in the air
like wings after hovering
that a dove might be here,
hidden but apprehending.

Peasant and priest toiling
over the patched hill side,
the acolyte at his hoeing,
see from that iron tressel
the saint's huge brother rising

until, like a lark, lifting
the valleyed Umbrian veils,
the heart of Francis, dazzling
bird in the air, reveals
the grace of that ragged man
transfiguring everywhere.

No Other Tiger Walked That Way
That Night

No other tiger walked that way that night.
She tied her hand with promises to the gate,
She gave her head in red on a golden plate,
She hung her heart out on a begging arm:
No other tiger walked that way that night.

She wound her bowels out around a tree,
She shed astrologies of tears; she bled
Till the seas choked with love unsatisfied;
She nailed her sex with negatives to the bed:
No other tiger slept between her knees.

She stood on corners till the morning came
Mesmerising her misery with another day;
She wept in public; she died when a name
Was the same, or when a lovesong was over:
No other tiger came to be her lover.

She remembered the couch-kingdomed queens
Who keep their children inside contraceptives;
She tried to lead the simplest of possible lives;
Her room was always haunted by sweet dreams;
No other tiger spoke in superlatives.

No other tiger walked that way that night—
Not when she begged on the knees where

The sabre-toothed baby wrestled in its lair
Among her memories of an amorous May:

Not when she opened her future like a gate,
No other tiger ever entered there.
No other tiger, either by night or day,
Ever ever ever walked that way.

Epitaph: On the Suicide of the Painter John Minton

Rest, Johnny, rest, rest,
Under your starry dirt;
The lifelong daymare's past.
Clawing those harpies tear
And rend your haunted heart
But you are not there
For at the lonely last
That hooked nail in the nerve
And the crisscrossrow bone
Know that you are gone.
And now that your Now is Never
At last, at last,
The three foul Furies must
Leave you alone for ever
Leave you alone, at last.

ROBERT HAYDEN
(1913–)

Night, Death, Mississippi

I.

A quavering cry. Screech-owl?
Or one of them?
The old man in his reek
and gauntness laughs—

One of them, I bet—
and turns out the kitchen lamp,
limping to the porch to listen
in the windowless night.

Be there with Boy and the rest
if I was well again.
Time was. Time was.
White robes like moonlight

In the sweetgum dark.
Unbucked that one then
and him squealing bloody Jesus
as we cut it off.

Time was. A cry?
A cry all right.
He hawks and spits,
fevered as by groinfire.

Have us a bottle,
Boy and me—
he's earned him a bottle—
when he gets home.

II.

Then we beat them, he said,
beat them till our arms was tired
and the big old chains
messy and red.

O Jesus burning on the lily cross

Christ, it was better
than hunting bear
which don't know why
you want him dead.

O night, rawhead and bloodybones night

You kids fetch Paw
some water now so's he
can wash that blood
off him, she said.

O night betrayed by darkness not its own

Mourning Poem for the Queen of Sunday

Lord's lost Him His mockingbird,
His fancy warbler;
Satan sweet-talked her,
four bullets hushed her.

Who would have thought
she'd end that way?

Four bullets hushed her. And the world a-clang with evil.
Who's going to make old hardened sinner men tremble now
and the righteous rock?
Oh who and oh who will sing Jesus down
to help with struggling and doing without and being colored
all through blue Monday?
Till way next Sunday?

All those angels
in their cretonne clouds and finery
the true believer saw
when she rared back her head and sang,
all those angels are surely weeping.
Who would have thought
she'd end that way?

Four holes in her heart. The gold works wrecked.
But she looks so natural in her big bronze coffin
among the Broken Hearts and Gates-Ajar,
it's as if any moment she'd lift her head
from its pillow of chill gardenias
and turn this quiet into shouting Sunday
and make folks forget what she did on Monday.

Oh, Satan sweet-talked her,
and four bullets hushed her.
Lord's lost Him His diva,
His fancy warbler's gone.
Who would have thought,
who would have thought she'd end that way?

Sphinx

If he could solve the riddle,
she would not leap

from those gaunt rocks to her death,
but devour him instead.

It pleasures her to hold
him captive there—
to keep him in the reach of her
blood-matted paws.

It is your fate, she has often
said, to endure
my riddling. Your fate to live
at the mercy of my

conundrum, which, in truth,
is only a kind
of psychic joke. No, you shall
not leave this place.

(Consider anyway the view from
here.) In time,
you will come to regard my questioning
with a certain pained

amusement; in time, get so
you would hardly find
it possible to live without
my joke and me.

The Dream

(1863)

That evening Sinda thought she heard the drums
and hobbled from her cabin to the yard.
The quarters now were lonely-still in willow dusk
after the morning's ragged jubilo,
when laughing crying singing the folks went off
with Marse Lincum's soldier boys.

But Sinda hiding would not follow them: those
Buckras with their ornery
     funning, cussed commands, oh they were not were not
the hosts the dream had promised her.

     and hope when these few lines reaches your hand they
     will fine you well. I am tired some but it is war you know
     and ole jeff Davis muss be ketch an hung to a sour apple
     tree like it says in the song I seen some akshun but that is
     what i listed for not to see the sights ha ha More of our
     peeples coming every day. the Kernul calls them contrybans
     and has them work aroun the Camp and learning to be
     soljurs. How is the wether home. Its warm this evening but
     theres been lots of rain

     How many times that dream had come to her—
more vision than a dream—
     the great big soldiers marching out of gunburst,
their faces those of Cal and Joe
     and Charlie sold to the ricefields oh sold away
a-many and a-many a long year ago.
     Fevered, gasping, Sinda listened, knew this was
the ending of her dream and prayed
     that death, grown fretful and impatient, nagging her,
would wait a little longer, would let her see.

     and we been marching sleeping too in cold rain and mirey
     mud a heap a times. Tell Mama Thanks for The Bible
     an not worry so. Did brother fix the roof yet like he prom-
     ised? this mus of been a real nice place befor the fighting
     uglied it all up the judas trees is blosommed out so pretty
     same as if this hurt and truble wasnt going on. Almos like
     something you mite dream about i take it for a sign The
     Lord remembers Us Theres talk we will be moving into
     Battle very soon agin

     Trembling tottering Hep me Jesus Sinda crossed
the wavering yard, reached
     a redbud tree in bloom, could go no farther, clung

to the bole and clinging fell
        to her knees. She tried to stand, could not so much
as lift her head, tried to hold
        the bannering sounds, heard only the whipoorwills
in tenuous moonlight; struggled to rise
        and make her way to the road to welcome Joe and Cal
and Charlie, fought with brittle strength to rise.

So pray for me that if the Bullit with my name rote on it
get me it will not get me in retreet i do not think them
kine of thots so much no need in Dying till you die I all
ways figger, course if the hardtack and the bullybeef do
not kill me nuthing can i guess. Tell Joe I hav shure seen
me some ficety gals down here in Dixieland & i mite jus go
ahead an jump over the broomstick with one and bring her
home, well I muss close with Love to all & hope to see you
soon Yrs Cal

Zeus Over Redeye

(*The Redstone Arsenal*)

        Enclave where new mythologies
        of power come to birth—
        where coralled energy and power breed
        like prized man-eating animals.
        Like dragon, hydra, basilisk.

        Radar corollas and Holland tulips
        the colors of Easter eggs
        form vistas for the ironist.
        Where elm, ailanthus, redbud grew
        parabola and gantry rise.

        In soaring stasis rocket missiles loom,
        the cherished weapons named for Nike
        (O headless armless Victory),
        for Zeus, Apollo, Hercules—
        eponyms of redeyed fury
        greater, lesser than their own.

Ignorant outlander, mere civilian,
not sure always of what it is
I see, I walk with you among
these totems of our fire-breathing age,
question and question you,

who are at home in terra guarded like
a sacred phallic grove.
Your partial answers reassure
me less than they appall.
I feel as though invisible fuses were

burning all around us burning all
around us. Heat-quiverings twitch
danger's hypersensitive skin.
The very sunlight here seems flammable.
And shadows give
us no relieving shade.

El-Hajj Malik El-Shabazz

(Malcolm X)

O masks and metamorphoses of Ahab, Native Son

I

The icy evil that struck his father down
and ravished his mother into madness
trapped him in violence of a punished self
struggling to break free.

As Home Boy, as Dee-troit Red,
he fled his name, became the quarry of
his own obsessed pursuit.

He conked his hair and Lindy-hopped,
zoot-suited jiver, swinging those chicks
in the hot rose and reefer glow.

His injured childhood bullied him.
He skirmished in the Upas trees
and cannibal flowers of the American Dream—

but could not hurt the enemy
powered against him there.

II

Sometimes the dark that gave his life
its cold satanic sheen would shift
a little, and he saw himself
floodlit and eloquent;

yet how could he, "Satan" in The Hole,
guess what the waking dream foretold?

Then false dawn of vision came;
he fell upon his face before
a racist Allah pledged to wrest him from
the hellward-thrusting hands of Calvin's Christ—

to free him and his kind
from Yakub's white-faced treachery.
He rose redeemed from all but prideful anger,

though adulterate attars could not cleanse
him of the odors of the pit.

III

Asalam alaikum!

He X'd his name, became his people's anger,
exhorted them to vengeance for their past;
rebuked, admonished them,

their scourger who
would shame them, drive them from
the lush ice gardens of their servitude.

Asalam alaikum!

Rejecting Ahab, he was of Ahab's tribe.
"Strike through the mask!"

IV

Time. "The martyr's time," he said.
Time and the karate killer,
knifer, gunman. Time that brought
ironic trophies as his faith

twined sparking round the bole,
the fruit of neo-Islam.
"The martyr's time."

But first, the ebb time pilgrimage
toward revelation, hejira to
his final metamorphosis;

Labbayk! Labbayk!

He fell upon his face before
Allah the raceless in whose blazing Oneness all
were one. He rose renewed renamed, became
much more than there was time for him to be.

KARL SHAPIRO

(1913–)

University

To hurt the Negro and avoid the Jew
Is the curriculum. In mid-September
The entering boys, identified by hats,
Wander in a maze of mannered brick
    Where boxwood and magnolia brood
    And columns with imperious stance
    Like rows of ante-bellum girls
      Eye them, outlanders.

In whited cells, on lawns equipped for peace,
Under the arch, and lofty banister,
Equals shake hands, unequals blankly pass;
The exemplary weather whispers, "Quiet, quiet"
    And visitors on tiptoe leave
    For the raw North, the unfinished West,
    As the young, detecting an advantage,
      Practice a face.

Where, on their separate hill, the colleges,
Like manor houses of an older law,
Gaze down embankments on a land in fee,
The Deans, dry spinsters over family plate,
    Ring out the English name like coin,

131

Humor the snob and lure the lout.
Within the precincts of this world
    Poise is a club.

But on the neighboring range, misty and high,
The past is absolute: some luckless race
Dull with inbreeding and conformity
Wears out its heart, and comes barefoot and bad
    For charity or jail. The scholar
    Sanctions their obsolete disease;
    The gentleman revolts with shame
        At his ancestor.

And the true nobleman, once a democrat,
Sleeps on his private mountain. He was one
Whose thought was shapely and whose dream was broad;
This school he held his art and epitaph.
    But now it takes from him his name,
    Falls open like a dishonest look,
    And shows us, rotted and endowed,
        Its senile pleasure.

Elegy for a Dead Soldier

I

A white sheet on the tail-gate of a truck
Becomes an altar; two small candlesticks
Sputter at each side of the crucifix
Laid round with flowers brighter than the blood,
Red as the red of our apocalypse,
Hibiscus that a marching man will pluck
To stick into his rifle or his hat,
And great blue morning-glories pale as lips
That shall no longer taste or kiss or swear.
The wind begins a low magnificat,
The chaplain chats, the palmtrees swirl their hair,
The columns come together through the mud.

II

We too are ashes as we watch and hear
The psalm, the sorrow, and the simple praise
Of one whose promised thoughts of other days
Were such as ours, but now wholly destroyed,
The service record of his youth wiped out,
His dream dispersed by shot, must disappear.
What can we feel but wonder at a loss
That seems to point at nothing but the doubt
Which flirts our sense of luck into the ditch?
Reader of Paul who prays beside this fosse,
Shall we believe our eyes or legends rich
With glory and rebirth beyond the void?

III

For this comrade is dead, dead in the war,
A young man out of millions yet to live,
One cut away from all that war can give,
Freedom of self and peace to wander free.
Who mourns in all this sober multitude
Who did not feel the bite of it before
The bullet found its aim? This worthy flesh,
This boy laid in a coffin and reviewed—
Who has not wrapped himself in this same flag,
Heard the light fall of dirt, his wound still fresh,
Felt his eyes closed, and heard the distant brag
Of the last volley of humanity?

IV

By chance I saw him die, stretched on the ground,
A tattooed arm lifted to take the blood
Of someone else sealed in a tin. I stood
During the last delirium that stays
The intelligence a tiny moment more,
And then the strangulation, the last sound.
The end was sudden, like a foolish play,
A stupid fool slamming a foolish door,
The absurd catastrophe, half-prearranged,

And all the decisive things still left to say.
So we disbanded, angrier and unchanged,
Sick with the utter silence of dispraise.

V

We ask for no statistics of the killed,
For nothing political impinges on
This single casualty, or all those gone,
Missing or healing, sinking or dispersed,
Hundreds of thousands counted, millions lost.
More than an accident and less than willed
Is every fall, and this one like the rest.
However others calculate the cost,
To us the final aggregate is *one*,
One with a name, one transferred to the blest;
And though another stoops and takes the gun,
We cannot add the second to the first.

VI

I would not speak for him who could not speak
Unless my fear were true: he was not wronged,
He knew to which decision he belonged
But let it choose itself. Ripe in instinct,
Neither the victim nor the volunteer,
He followed, and the leaders could not seek
Beyond the followers. Much of this he knew;
The journey was a detour that would steer
Into the Lincoln Highway of a land
Remorselessly improved, excited, new,
And that was what he wanted. He had planned
To earn and drive. He and the world had winked.

VII

No history deceived him, for he knew
Little of times and armies not his own;
He never felt that peace was but a loan,
Had never questioned the idea of gain.
Beyond the headlines once or twice he saw
The gathering of a power by the few

But could not tell their names; he cast his vote,
Distrusting all the elected but not law.
He laughed at socialism; *on mourrait*
Pour les industriels? He shed his coat
And not for brotherhood, but for his pay.
To him the red flag marked the sewer main.

VIII

Above all else he loathed the homily,
The slogan and the ad. He paid his bill
But not for Congressmen at Bunker Hill.
Ideals were few and those there were not made
For conversation. He belonged to church
But never spoke of God. The Christmas tree,
The Easter egg, baptism, he observed,
Never denied the preacher on his perch,
And would not sign Resolved That or Whereas.
Softness he had and hours and nights reserved
For thinking, dressing, dancing to the jazz.
His laugh was real, his manners were home made.

IX

Of all men poverty pursued him least;
He was ashamed of all the down and out,
Spurned the panhandler like an uneasy doubt,
And saw the unemployed as a vague mass
Incapable of hunger or revolt.
He hated other races, south or east,
And shoved them to the margin of his mind.
He could recall the justice of the Colt,
Take interest in a gang-war like a game.
His ancestry was somewhere far behind
And left him only his peculiar name.
Doors opened, and he recognized no class.

X

His children would have known a heritage,
Just or unjust, the richest in the world,

The quantum of all art and science curled
In the horn of plenty, bursting from the horn,
A people bathed in honey, Paris come,
Vienna transferred with the highest wage,
A World's Fair spread to Phoenix, Jacksonville,
Earth's capitol, the new Byzantium,
Kingdom of man—who knows? Hollow or firm,
No man can ever prophesy until
Out of our death some undiscovered germ,
Whole toleration or pure peace is born.

XI

The time to mourn is short that best becomes
The military dead. We lift and fold the flag,
Lay bare the coffin with its written tag,
And march away. Behind, four others wait
To lift the box, the heaviest of loads.
The anesthetic afternoon benumbs,
Sickens our senses, forces back our talk.
We know that others on tomorrow's roads
Will fall, ourselves perhaps, the man beside,
Over the world the threatened, all who walk:
And could we mark the grave of him who died
We would write this beneath his name and date:

EPITAPH

Underneath this wooden cross there lies
A Christian killed in battle. You who read,
Remember that this stranger died in pain;
And passing here, if you can lift your eyes
Upon a peace kept by a human creed,
Know that one soldier has not died in vain.

Love for a Hand

Two hands lie still, the hairy and the white,
And soon down ladders of reflected light
The sleepers climb in silence. Gradually

They separate on paths of long ago,
Each winding on his arm the unpleasant clew
That leads, live as a nerve, to memory.

But often when too steep her dream descends,
Perhaps to the grotto where her father bends
To pick her up, the husband wakes as though
He had forgotten something in the house.
Motionless he eyes the room that glows
With the little animals of light that prowl

This way and that. Soft are the beasts of light
But softer still her hand that drifts so white
Upon the whiteness. How like a water-plant
It floats upon the black canal of sleep,
Suspended upward from the distant deep
In pure achievement of its lovely want!

Quietly then he plucks it and it folds
And is again a hand, small as a child's.
He would revive it but it barely stirs
And so he carries it off a little way
And breaks it open gently. Now he can see
The sweetness of the fruit, his hand eats hers.

from A D A M   A N D   E V E

II

The Recognition of Eve

Whatever it was she had so fiercely fought
Had fled back to the sky, but still she lay
With arms outspread, awaiting its assault,
Staring up through the branches of the tree,
The fig tree. Then she drew a shuddering breath
And turned her head instinctively his way.
She had fought birth as dying men fight death.

Her sigh awakened him. He turned and saw
A body swollen, as though formed of fruits,
White as the flesh of fishes, soft and raw.
He hoped she was another of the brutes
So he crawled over and looked into her eyes,
The human wells that pool all absolutes.
It was like looking into double skies.

And when she spoke the first word (it was *thou*)
He was terror-stricken, but she raised her hand
And touched his wound where it was fading now,
For he must feel the place to understand.
Then he recalled the longing that had torn
His side, and while he watched it whitely mend,
He felt it stab him suddenly like a thorn.

And when she spoke the first word (it was *thou*)
He was terror-stricken, but she raised her hand
And touched his wound where it was fading now,
For he must feel the place to understand.
Then he recalled the longing that had torn
His side, and while he watched it whitely mend,
He felt it stab him suddenly like a thorn.

He thought the woman had hurt him. Was it she
Or the same sickness seeking to return;
Or was there any difference, the pain set free
And she who seized him now as hard as iron?
Her fingers bit his body. She looked old
And involuted, like the newly-born.
He let her hurt him till she loosed her hold.

Then she forgot him and she wearily stood
And went in search of water through the grove.
Adam could see her wandering through the wood,
Studying her footsteps as her body wove
In light and out of light. She found a pool
And there he followed shyly to observe.
She was already turning beautiful.

[August Saturday Night on the Negro Street]

August Saturday night on the Negro street the trolleys clang and break sweet dusty smoke. Cars hoot meaningless signals. The air is in a sweat of Jim Crow gaiety, shopping, milling, rubbing of flesh, five miles of laughter in white Baltimore. The second floor dance hall has a famous trumpet. You can't move on the floor, which rolls like waves and is in actual danger of giving way. The temperature adds to the frenzy. There is a no pause in the jump and scream of the jazz, heatwaves of laughter, untranslatable slang. The dancing is demotic, terpsichorean. It's like a war of pleasure. It's the joy of work. The fatigue is its own reward.

Across the street in the corner drug store where whiskey is sold and every blandishment of skin, a teeming Negress crowds at the perfume counter, big arms like haunches and bosom practically bare. She laughs with her friends above the cut-glass bottles with frenchified names and recently invented colors. She purchases a sizeable vial of some green scent, pays green dry money, unstoppers the bottle and dumps the entire load between her breasts! O glorious act of laughter in the half-serious bazaar of the Jew-store!

I Swore to Stab the Sonnet

I swore to stab the sonnet with my pen,
Squash the black widow in a grandstand play
By gunning down the sonnet form—and then
I heard you quote my schoolboy love Millay.
I went to find out what she used to say
About her tribulations and her men
And loved her poetry though I now am gray
And found out love of love poems once again.
Now I'm the one that's stabbed—son of a bitch!
With my own poisoned ballpoint pen of love
And write in *sonnet* form to make my *pitch*,
Words I no longer know the meaning of.
If I could write one honest sentence now
I'd say I love you but I don't know how.

How Beautifully You Clothe Your Body

How beautifully you clothe your body
As if to say, undress me if you can
And find how beautiful I really am.
Only a beauty dares to wear a wig
But I can cradle you and you are big
(Minus the worship of the insincere)
Or worship you without becoming slave
Or post-post-adolescent Indian-brave.
You dress burnt-orange, square-shape cotton, silk,
Nylon and Turner, Veronese, glass,
High-breasted with a Zeuxian-Keatsean ass,
Alice-in-Wonderland 16—twice 16—
As if age entered in, although it does,
Making me love you mostly in your clothes.

R. S. THOMAS

(1913-)

A Labourer

Who can tell his years, for the winds have stretched
So tight the skin on the bare racks of bone
That his face is smooth, inscrutable as stone?
And when he wades in the brown bilge of earth
Hour by hour, or stoops to pull
The reluctant swedes, who can read the look
In the colourless eye, as his back comes straight
Like an old tree lightened of the snow's weight?
Is there love there, or hope, or any thought
For the frail form broken beneath his tread,
And the sweet pregnancy that yields his bread?

A Peasant

Iago Prytherch his name, though, be it allowed,
Just an ordinary man of the bald Welsh hills,
Who pens a few sheep in a gap of cloud.
Docking mangels, chipping the green skin
From the yellow bones with a half-witted grin
Of satisfaction, or churning the crude earth
To a stiff sea of clods that glint in the wind—
So are his days spent, his spittled mirth

Rarer than the sun that cracks the cheeks
Of the gaunt sky perhaps once in a week.
And then at night see him fixed in his chair
Motionless, except when he leans to gob in the fire.
There is something frightening in the vacancy of his
    mind.
His clothes, sour with years of sweat
And animal contact, shock the refined,
But affected, sense with their stark naturalness.
Yet this is your prototype, who, season by season
Against siege of rain and the wind's attrition,
Preserves his stock, an impregnable fortress
Not to be stormed even in death's confusion.
Remember him, then, for he, too, is a winner of wars,
Enduring like a tree under the curious stars.

Song

We, who are men, how shall we know
Earth's ecstasy, who feels the plough
Probing her womb,
And after, the sweet gestation
And the year's care for her condition?
We, who have forgotten, so long ago
It happened, our own orgasm,
When the wind mixed with our limbs
And the sun had suck at our bosom;
We, who have affected the livery
Of the times' prudery,
How shall we quicken again
To the lust and thrust of the sun
And the seedling rain?

The Airy Tomb

Twm was a dunce at school, and was whipped and shaken
More than I care to say, but without avail,

For where one man can lead a horse to the pail
Twenty can't make him drink what is not to his mind,
And books and sums were poison to Tomos, he was stone
    blind
To the printer's magic; yet his grass-green eye
Missed neither swoop nor swerve of the hawk's wing
Past the high window, and the breeze could bring,
Above the babble of the room's uproar,
Songs to his ear from the sun-dusted moor,
The grey curlew's whistle and the shrill, far cry
Of circling buzzard . . . This was Twm at school,
Subject to nothing but the sky and the wind's rule.
And then at fourteen term ended and the lad was free.
Scatheless as when he entered, he could write and spell
No more than the clouds could or the dribbling rain,
That scrawled vague messages on the window pane.

And so he returned to the Bwlch to help his father
With the rough work of the farm, to ditch, and gather
The slick ewes from the hill; to milk the cow,
And coax the mare that dragged the discordant plough.
Stepping with one stride thus from boy to man,
His school books finished with, he now began
Learning what none could teach but the hill people
In that cold country, where grass and tree
Are a green heritage more rich and rare
Than a queen's emerald or an untouched maid.
It were as well to bring the tup to the wild mare,
Or put the heron and the hen to couple,
As mate a stranger from the fat plain
With that gaunt wilderness, where snow is laid
Deadly as leprosy till the first of May,
And a man counts himself lucky if All Saints' Day
Finds his oats hived in the tottering barn.
But Tomos took to the life like a hillman born;
His work was play after the dull school, and hands,
Shamed by the pen's awkwardness, toyed with the fleece
Of ewe and wether; eyes found a new peace
Tracing the poems, which the rooks wrote in the sky.

So his shadow lengthened, and the years sped by
With the wind's quickness; Twm had turned nineteen,
When his father sickened and at the week's end died,
Leaving him heir to the lean patch of land,
Pinned to the hill-top, and the cloudy acres,
Kept as a sheep-walk. At his mother's side
He stood in the graveyard, where the undertaker
Sprinkled earth rubble with a loud tattoo
On the cheap coffin; but his heart was hurt
By the gash in the ground, and too few, too few,
Were the tears that he dropped for that lonely man
Beginning his journey to annihilation.
He had seen sheep rotting in the wind and sun,
And a hawk floating in a bubbling pool,
Its weedy entrails mocking the breast
Laced with bright water; but the dead and living
Moved hand in hand on the mountain crest
In the calm circle of taking and giving.
A wide sepulchre of brisk, blue air
Was the beast's portion, but a mortal's lot
The board's strictness, and an ugly scar
On the earth's surface, till the deliberate sod
Sealed off for ever the green land he trod.

But the swift grass, that covered the unsightly wound
In the prim churchyard, healed Tomos' mind
Of its grave-sickness, and December shadows
Dwindled to nothingness in the spring meadows,
That were blowsy with orchis and the loose bog-cotton.
Then the sun strengthened and the hush of June
Settled like lichen on the thick-timbered house,
Where Twm and his mother ate face to face
At the bare table, and each tick of the clock
Was a nail knocked in the lid of the coffin
Of that pale, spent woman, who sat with death
Jogging her elbow through the hot, still days
Of July and August, or passed like a ghost
By the scurrying poultry—it was ever her boast
Not to stay one winter with the goodman cold

In his callous bed. Twm was bumpkin blind
To the vain hysteria of a woman's mind,
And prated of sheep fairs, but the first frost came
To prove how ungarnished was the truth she told.

Can you picture Tomos now in the house alone,
The room silent, and the last mourner gone
Down the hill pathway? Did he sit by the flame
Of his turf fire and watch till dawn
The slow crumbling of the world he had known?
Did he rebuild out of the ragged embers
A new life, tempered to the sting of sorrow?
Twm went to bed and woke on the grey morrow
To the usual jobbery in sty and stable;
Cleaned out the cow-house, harnessed the mare,
And went prospecting with the keen ploughshare.
Yet sometimes the day was dark, and the clouds remembered,
Herded in the bare lanes of sky, the funeral rite,
And Tomos about the house or set at table
Was aware of something for which he had no name,
Though the one tree, which dripped through the winter
        night
With a clock's constancy, tried hard to tell
The insensitive mind what the heart knew well.

But March squalls, making the windows rattle,
Blew great gaps in his thoughts, till April followed
With a new sweetness, that set the streams gossiping.
On Easter Day he heard the first warbler sing
In the quick ash by the door, and the snow made room
On the sharp turf for the first fumbling lamb.
Docking and grading now until after dark
In the green field or fold, there was too much work
For the mind to wander, though the robin wove
In the young hazel a sweet tale of love.
And what is love to an uncultured youth
In the desolate pastures, but the itch of cattle
At set times and seasons? Twm rarely went down

With his gay neighbours to the petticoat town
In a crook of the valley, and his mind was free
Of the dream pictures which lead to romance.
Hearts and arrows, scribbled at the lane's entrance,
Were a meaningless symbol, as esoteric
As his school fractions; the one language he knew
Was the shrill scream in the dark, the shadow within the
    shadow,
The glimmer of flesh, deadly as mistletoe.

Of course there was talk in the parish, girls stood at their
    doors
In November evenings, their glances busy as moths
Round that far window; and some, whom passion made
    bolder
As the buds opened, lagged in the bottom meadow
And coughed and called. But never a voice replied
From that grim house, nailed to the mountain side,
For Tomos was up with the lambs, or stealthily hoarding
The last light from the sky in his soul's crannies.
So the tongues still wagged, and Tomos became a story
To please a neighbour with, or raise the laughter
In the lewd tavern, for folk cannot abide
The inscrutable riddle, posed by their own kin.
And you, hypocrite reader, at ease in your chair,
Do not mock their conduct, for are you not also weary
Of this odd tale, preferring the usual climax?
He was not well-favoured, you think, nor gay, nor rich,
But surely it happened that one of those supple bitches
With the sly haunches angled him into her net
At the male season, or, what is perhaps more romantic,
Some lily-white maid, a clerk or a minister's daughter,
With delicate hands, and eyes brittle as flowers
Or curved sea-shells, taught him the tender airs
Of a true gallant?
          No, no, you must face the fact
Of his long life alone in that crumbling house
With winds rending the joints, and the grey rain's claws

Sharp in the thatch; of his work up on the moors
With the moon for candle, and the shrill rabble of stars
Crowding his shoulders. For Twm was true to his fate,
That wound solitary as a brook through the crimson heather,
Trodden only by sheep, where youth and age
Met in the circle of a buzzard's flight
Round the blue axle of heaven; and a fortnight gone
Was the shy soul from the festering flesh and bone
When they found him there, entombed in the lucid weather.

Saint Antony

Saint Antony in the sand saw shapes rising,
Formed by the wind, sinuous, lewd
As snakes dancing; their bitter poison
Entered the soul through his pale eyes.

Sleep came; the dances were renewed
Upon the retina, the lids not proof
Against the orgy of the spheres.
Night long he ranged the Bacchanalian dark,
Himself the prey, the hunter and the wood.

In a Country Church

To one kneeling down no word came,
Only the wind s song, saddening the lips
Of the grave saints, rigid in glass;
Or the dry whisper of unseen wings,
Bats not angels, in the high roof.

Was he balked by silence? He kneeled long,
And saw love in a dark crown
Of thorns blazing, and a winter tree
Golden with fruit of a man's body.

Chapel Deacon

Who put that crease in your soul,
Davies, ready this fine morning
For the staid chapel, where the Book's frown
Sobers the sunlight? Who taught you to pray
And scheme at once, your eyes turning
Skyward, while your swift mind weighs
Your heifer's chances in the next town's
Fair on Thursday? Are your heart's coals
Kindled for God, or is the burning
Of your lean cheeks because you sit
Too near that girl's smouldering gaze?
Tell me, Davies, for the faint breeze
From heaven freshens and I roll in it,
Who taught you your deft poise?

Age

Farmer, you were young once.
And she was there, waiting, the unique flower
That only you could find in the wild moor
Of your experience.
Gathered, she grew to the warm woman
Your hands had imagined
Fondling soil in the spring fields.

And she was fertile; four strong sons
Stood up like corn in June about you.
But, farmer, did you cherish, tend her
As your own flesh, this dry stalk
Where the past murmurs its sad tune?
Is this the harvest of your blithe sowing?

If you had spared from your long store
Of days lavished upon the land

But one for her where she lay fallow,
Drying, hardening, withering to waste.
But now—too late! You're an old tree,
Your roots groping in her in vain.

Poetry for Supper

'Listen, now, verse should be as natural
As the small tuber that feeds on muck
And grows slowly from obtuse soil
To the white flower of immortal beauty.'

'Natural, hell! What was it Chaucer
Said once about the long toil
That goes like blood to the poem's making?
Leave it to nature and the verse sprawls,
Limp as bindweed, if it break at all
Life's iron crust. Man, you must sweat
And rhyme your guts taut, if you'd build
Your verse a ladder.'
                                'You speak as though
No sunlight ever surprised the mind
Groping on its cloudy path.'

'Sunlight's a thing that needs a window
Before it enter a dark room.
Windows don't happen.'
                                So two old poets,
Hunched at their beer in the low haze
Of an inn parlour, while the talk ran
Noisily by them, glib with prose.

Anniversary

Nineteen years now
Under the same roof

Eating our bread,
Using the same air;
Sighing, if one sighs,
Meeting the other's
Words with a look
That thaws suspicion.

Nineteen years now
Sharing life's table,
And not to be first
To call the meal long
We balance it thoughtfully
On the tip of the tongue,
Careful to maintain
The strict palate.

Nineteen years now
Keeping simple house,
Opening the door
To friend and stranger;
Opening the womb
Softly to let enter
The one child
With his huge hunger.

A Welsh Testament

All right, I was Welsh. Does it matter?
I spoke the tongue that was passed on
To me in the place I happened to be,
A place huddled between grey walls
Of cloud for at least half the year.
My word for heaven was not yours.
The word for hell had a sharp edge
Put on it by the hand of the wind
Honing, honing with a shrill sound
Day and night. Nothing that Glyn Dwr

Knew was armour against the rain's
Missiles. What was descent from him?

Even God had a Welsh name:
We spoke to him in the old language;
He was to have a peculiar care
For the Welsh people. History showed us
He was too big to be nailed to the wall
Of a stone chapel, yet still we crammed him
Between the boards of a black book.

Yet men sought us despite this.
My high cheek-bones, my length of skull
Drew them as to a rare portrait
By a dead master. I saw them stare
From their long cars, as I passed knee-deep
In ewes and wethers. I saw them stand
By the thorn hedges, watching me string
The far flocks on a shrill whistle.

And always there was their eyes' strong
Pressure on me: You are Welsh, they said;
Speak to us so; keep your fields free
Of the smell of petrol, the loud roar
Of hot tractors; we must have peace
And quietness.
                        Is a museum
Peace? I asked. Am I the keeper
Of the heart's relics, blowing the dust
In my own eyes? I am a man;
I never wanted the drab rôle
Life assigned me, an actor playing
To the past's audience upon a stage
Of earth and stone; the absurd label
Of birth, of race hanging askew
About my shoulders. I was in prison
Until you came; your voice was a key
Turning in the enormous lock
Of hopelessness. Did the door open
To let me out or yourselves in?

JOHN BERRYMAN

(1914–)

[I've Found Out Why, That Day, That Suicide]

I've found out why, that day, that suicide
From the Empire State falling on someone's car
Troubled you so; and why we quarrelled. War,
Illness, an accident, I can see (you cried)
But not this: what a bastard, not spring wide! . .
I said a man, life in his teeth, could care
Not much just whom he spat it on . . and far
Beyond my laugh we argued either side.

'One has a right not to be fallen on! . .'
(Our second meeting . . yellow you were wearing.)
Voices of our resistance and desire!
Did I divine then I must shortly run
Crazy with need to fall on you, despairing?
Did you bolt so, before it caught, our fire?

154   JOHN BERRYMAN
```

## [Great Citadels Whereon the Gold Sun Falls]

Great citadels whereon the gold sun falls
Miss you O Lise sequestered to the West
Which wears you Mayday lily at its breast,
Part and not part, proper to balls and brawls,
Plains, cities, or the yellow shore, not false
Anywhere, free, native and Danishest
Profane and elegant flower,—whom suggest
Frail and not frail, blond rocks and madrigals.

Once in the car (cave of our radical love)
Your darker hair I saw than golden hair
Above your thighs whiter than white-gold hair,
And where the dashboard lit faintly your least
Enlarged scene, O the midnight bloomed . . the East
Less gorgeous, wearing you like a long white glove!

## [For You Am I Collared O to Quit My Dear]

For you am I collared O to quit my dear
My sandy-haired mild good and most beautiful
Most helpless and devoted wife? I pull
Crazy away from this; but too from her
Resistlessly I draw off, months have, far
And quarrelling—irrelation—numb and dull
Dead Sea with tiny aits . . Love at the full
Had wavered, seeing, foresuffering us here.

Unhappy all her lone strange life until
Somehow I friended it. And the Master catches
Me strongly from behind, and clucks, and tugs.
He has, has he? my heart-relucting will.
She spins on silent and the needle scratches.
—This all, Lise? and stark kisses, stealthy hugs?
```

[*All We Were Going Strong Last Night This Time,*]

All we were going strong last night this time,
the *mots* were flying & the frozen daiquiris
were downing, supine on the floor lay Lise
listening to Schubert grievous & sublime,
my head was frantic with a following rime:
it was a good evening, an evening to please,
I kissed her in the kitchen—ecstasies—
among so much good we tamped down the crime.

The weather's changing. This morning was cold,
as I made for the grove, without expectation,
some hundred Sonnets in my pocket, old,
to read her if she came. Presently the sun
yellowed the pines & my lady came not
in blue jeans & a sweater. I sat down & wrote.

from THE DREAM SONGS

1

Huffy Henry hid   the day,
unappeasable Henry sulked.
I see his point,—a trying to put things over.
It was the thought that they thought
they could *do* it made Henry wicked & away.
But he should have come out and talked.

All the world like a woolen lover
once did seem on Henry's side.
Then came a departure.
Thereafter nothing fell out as it might or ought.
I don't see how Henry, pried
open for all the world to see, survived.

What he has now to say is a long
wonder the world can bear & be.
Once in a sycamore I was glad
all at the top, and I sang.
Hard on the land wears the strong sea
and empty grows every bed.

4

Filling her compact & delicious body
with chicken páprika, she glanced at me
twice.
Fainting with interest, I hungered back
and only the fact of her husband & four other people
kept me from springing on her

or falling at her little feet and crying
'You are the hottest one for years of night
Henry's dazed eyes
have enjoyed, Brilliance.' I advanced upon
(despairing) my spumoni. —Sir Bones: is stuffed,
de world, wif feeding girls.

—Black hair, complexion Latin, jewelled eyes
downcast . . . The slob beside her   feasts . . . What wonders is
she sitting on, over there?
The restaurant buzzes. She might as well be on Mars.
Where did it all go wrong? There ought to be a law against Henry.
—Mr. Bones: there is.

66

'All virtues enter into this world:')
A Buddhist, doused in the street, serenely burned.
The Secretary of State for War,
winking it over, screwed a redhaired whore.
Monsignor Capovilla mourned. What a week.
A journalism doggy took a leak

against absconding coon ('but take one virtue,
without which a man can hardly hold his own')
the sun in the willow
shivers itself & shakes itself green-yellow
(Abba Pimen groaned, over the telephone,
when asked what that was:)

How feel a fellow then when he arrive
in fame but lost? but affable, top-shelf.
Quelle sad semaine.
He hardly know his selving. ('that a man')
Henry grew hot, got laid, felt bad, survived
('should always reproach himself'.

76

Henry's Confession

Nothin very bad happen to me lately.
How you explain that? —I explain that, Mr Bones,
terms o' your bafflin odd sobriety.
Sober as man can get, no girls, no telephones,
what could happen bad to Mr Bones?
—*If* life is a handkerchief sandwich,

in a modesty of death I join my father
who dared so long agone leave me.
A bullet on a concrete stoop
close by a smothering southern sea
spreadeagled on an island, by my knee.
—You is from hunger, Mr Bones,

I offers you this handkerchief, now set
your left foot by my right foot,
shoulder to shoulder, all that jazz,
arm in arm, by the beautiful sea,
hum a little, Mr Bones.
—I saw nobody coming, so I went instead.

351

Animal Henry sat reading the *Times Literary Supplement*
with a large Jameson & a worse hangover.
Who will his demon lover
today become, he queried. Having made a dent
in the world, he insisted on special treatment,
massage at all hours.

Love in the shadows where the animals *come*
tickled his nerves' ends. He put down *The Times*
& began a salvage operation,
killing that is the partly incoherent,
saving the mostly fine, polishing the surfaces.
Brain- & instinct-work.

On all fours he danced about his cage, poor Henry
for whom, my love, too much was never enough.
Massage me in Kyoto's air.
The Japanese women are better than the Swedes,
more rhythmical, more piercing.
                              Somewhere, everywhere
a girl is taking her clothes off.

371

Henry's Guilt

Sluggish, depressed, & with no mail to cheer,
he lies in Ireland's rains bogged down, aware
of definite mental pain.
He hasn't a friend for a thousand miles to the west
and only two in London, he counted & guessed:
ladies he might see again.

He has an interview to give in London
but the ladies have never married, frolicsomes
as long ago they were,
must he impute to him their spinsterhood
& further groan, as for the ones he stood
up & married fair?

Connection with Henry seemed to be an acre in Hell,
he crossed himself with horror. Doubtless a bell
ought to've been hung on Henry
to warn a-many lovely ladies off
before they had too much, which was enough,
and set their calves to flee.

Crisis

My offended contempt for the mental & stylistic workings of

Ruskin & Carlyle

extended to their advocate,
who also mouthed at me Wordsworth in Hamilton Hall
holding up my appreciation of that great poet

for more than eighteen months.
Later he wrote a book on E. A. Robinson,
a favourite of mine (not interesting metrically
but with the gist of it in him)

which I went into with Schadenfreude
gratified to find it insensitive & unworthy.
O I come here to a tricky old scandalous affair!
He tried to keep me from *graduating*.

I may explain that this man had come to hate me personally.
Not only did I give him hell in class:
I saw my nine friends did. With ironic questions
& all but insolent comment & actual interruptions

we made Professor Neff wish he was elsewhere
rather than in English 163.
I must further explain: I needed a B,
I didn't need an A, as in my other six courses,

but the extra credits accruing from those A's
would fail to accrue if I'd any mark under B.
The bastard knew this,
as indeed my predicament was well known

through both my major Departments. Under the risk I ran
with Neff, I took care to keep an elaborate notebook
on all the readings Romantic & Victorian
to flourish if he got funny. He got very funny,—

leaving instructions not to post his marks
till the last stated day, he sailed for Italy,
and I found myself with a C,
squarely in the middle of Hell.

Luckily the Dean was down there with me,
along with Mark & my advisor Gutmann
& the whole senior staff of the English Department,
because I *had* to graduate:

not only had they put me in Phi Beta Kappa,
they'd given me their major Fellowship
for two years in England
& the disgrace if I couldn't take it up

would be general: only embarrassing
but very that: a plague. But what could they do?
I showed my notebook around & pointed out
the Apollinaire-like implausibility of my C

considering all my A's & my magisterial notebook.
I didn't have to mention personal spite.
They held unhappy meetings for two days.
To change the mark of a colleague in his absence?

Finally, a command decision:
they'd give me a second exam, invented by themselves,
& judge it, & if my paper justified,
they'd elevate the highly irrational mark.

I took it—it was fair, hard—& I killed it.
I never knew what I got, but the course-grade
cranked upward to a B. I graduated.
In my immediate section of the Commencement line

we were mostly Phi Betes, & the normal guys would have
nothing to do with us.

I collected my first installment, more dead than alive
from over-work & poetic theory & practice & Miss Jean B—
a thousand dollars it was—and took off for Canada,
to nurse my dark wounds & prepare my psyche for Cambridge,

a still more foreign scene.

from "ELEVEN ADDRESSES TO THE LORD"

I

Master of beauty, craftsman of the snowflake,
inimitable contriver,
endower of Earth so gorgeous & different from the boring Moon,
thank you for such as it is my gift.

I have made up a morning prayer to you
containing with precision everything that most matters.
'According to Thy will' the thing begins.
It took me off & on two days. It does not aim at eloquence.

You have come to my rescue again & again
in my impassable, sometimes despairing years.
You have allowed my brilliant friends to destroy themselves
and I am still here, severely damaged, but functioning.

Unknowable, as I am unknown to my guinea pigs:
how can I 'love' you,
I only as far as gratitude & awe
confidently & absolutely go.

I have no idea whether we live again.
It doesn't seem likely
from either the scientific or the philosophical point of view
but certainly all things are possible to you,

and I believe as fixedly in the Resurrection-appearances to Peter
& to Paul
as I believe I sit in this blue chair.
Only that may have been a special case
to establish their initiatory faith.

Whatever your end may be, accept my amazement.
May I stand until death forever at attention
for any your least instruction or enlightenment.
I even feel sure you will assist me again, Master of insight &
beauty.

LAURIE LEE

(1914–)

First Love

That was her beginning, an apparition
of rose in the unbreathed airs of his love,
her heart revealed by the wash of summer
sprung from her childhood's shallow stream.

Then it was that she put up her hair,
inscribed her eyes with a look of grief,
while her limbs grew as curious as coral branches,
her breast full of secrets.

But the boy, confused in his day's desire,
was searching for herons, his fingers bathed
in the green of walnuts, or watching at night
the Great Bear spin from the maypole star.

It was then that he paused in the death of a game,
felt the hook of her hair on his swimming throat,
saw her mouth at large in the dark river
flushed like a salmon.

But he covered his face and hid his joy
in a wild-goose web of false directions,

and hunted the woods for eggs and glow-worms,
for rabbits tasteless as moss.

And she walked in fields where the crocuses
branded her feet, and mares' tails sprang
from the prancing lake, and the salty grasses
surged round her stranded body.

Field of Autumn

Slow moves the acid breath of noon
over the copper-coated hill,
slow from the wild crab's bearded breast
the palsied apples fall.

Like coloured smoke the day hangs fire,
taking the village without sound;
the vulture-headed sun lies low
chained to the violet ground.

The horse upon the rocky height
rolls all the valley in his eye,
but dares not raise his foot or move
his shoulder from the fly.

The sheep, snail-backed against the wall,
lifts her blind face but does not know
the cry her blackened tongue gives forth
is the first bleat of snow.

Each bird and stone, each roof and well,
feels the gold foot of autumn pass;
each spider binds with glittering snare
the splintered bones of grass.

Slow moves the hour that sucks our life,
slow drops the late wasp from the pear,
the rose tree's thread of scent draws thin—
and snaps upon the air.

Bombay Arrival

Slow-hooved across the carrion sea,
Smeared by the betel-spitting sun,
Like cows the Bombay islands come
Dragging the mainland into view.

The loose flank loops the rocky bone,
The light beats thin on horn and hill;
Still breeds the flesh for hawks, and still
The Hindu heart drips on a stone.

Around the wide dawn-ridden bay
The waters move their daggered wings;
The dhow upon its shadow clings—
A dark moth pinioned to the day.

False in the morning, screened with silk,
Neat as an egg the Town draws near,
False as a map her streets appear
Ambling, and odourless as milk.

Until she holds us face to face—
A crumbling mask with bullet pores,
A nakedness of jewels and sores
Clutched with our guilt in her embrace.

The Edge of Day

The dawn's precise pronouncement waits
With breath of light indrawn,
Then forms with smoky, smut-red lips
The great O of the sun.

The mouldering atoms of the dark
Blaze into morning air;
The birdlike stars droop down and die,
The starlike birds catch fire.

The thrush's tinder throat strikes up,
The sparrow chips hot sparks
From flinty tongue, and all the sky
Showers with electric larks.

And my huge eye a chaos is
Where molten worlds are born;
Where floats the eagle's flaming moon,
And crows, like clinkers, burn;

Where blackbirds scream with comet tails,
And flaring finches fall,
And starlings, aimed like meteors,
Bounce from the garden wall;

Where, from the edge of day I spring
Alive for mortal flight,
Lit by the heart's exploding sun
Bursting from night to night.

Sunken Evening

The green light floods the city square—
  A sea of fowl and feathered fish,
  Where squalls of rainbirds dive and splash
And gusty sparrows chop the air.

Submerged, the prawn-blue pigeons feed
  In sandy grottoes round the Mall,
  And crusted lobster-buses crawl
Among the fountains' silver weed.

There, like a wreck, with mast and bell,
  The torn church settles by the bow,
  While phosphorescent starlings stow
Their mussel shells along the hull.

The oyster-poet, drowned but dry,
  Rolls a black pearl between his bones;

The typist, trapped by telephones,
Gazes in bubbles at the sky.

Till, with the dark, the shallows run,
    And homeward surges tides and fret—
    The slow night trawls its heavy net
And hauls the clerk to Surbiton.

Home from Abroad

Far-fetched with tales of other worlds and ways,
My skin well-oiled with wines of the Levant,
I set my face into a filial smile
To greet the pale, domestic kiss of Kent.

But shall I never learn? That gawky girl,
Recalled so primly in my foreign thoughts,
Becomes again the green-haired queen of love
Whose wanton form dilates as it delights.

Her rolling tidal landscape floods the eye
And drowns Chianti in a dusky stream;
The flower-flecked grasses swim with simple horses,
The hedges choke with roses fat as cream.

So do I breathe the hayblown airs of home,
And watch the sea-green elms drip birds and shadows,
And as the twilight nets the plunging sun
My heart's keel slides to rest among the meadows.

Scot in the Desert

All day the sand, like golden chains,
The desert distance binds;
All day the crouching camels groan,
Whipped by the gritty winds.

The mountain, flayed by sun, reveals
Red muscles, wounds of stone,
While on its face the black goats swarm
And bite it to the bone.

Here light is death; on every rock
It stretches like a cry,
Its fever burns up every bush,
It drinks each river dry.

It cracks with thirst the creviced lip,
It fattens black the tongue,
It turns the storm cloud into dust,
The morning dew to dung.

Men were not made to flourish here,
They shroud their heads and fly—
Save one, who stares into the sun
With sky-blue British eye.

Who stares into the zenith sun
And smiles and feels no pain,
Blood-cooled by Calvin, mist and bog,
And summers in the rain.

Long Summer

Gold as an infant's humming dream,
Stamped with its timeless, tropic blush,
The steady sun stands in the air
And burns like Moses' holy bush.

And burns while nothing it consumes;
The smoking branch but greener grows,
The crackling briar, from budded lips,
A floating stream of blossom blows.

A daze of hours, a blaze of noons,
Licks my cold shadow from the ground;
A flaming trident rears each dawn
To stir the blood of earth around.

Unsinged beneath the furnace sky
The frenzied beetle runs reborn,
The ant his antic mountain moves,
The rampant ram rewinds his horn.

I see the crazy bees drop fat
From tulips ten times gorged and dry;
I see the sated swallow plunge
To drink the dazzled waterfly.

A halo flares around my head,
A sunflower flares across the sun,
While down the summer's seamless haze
Such feasts of milk and honey run

That lying with my orchid love,
Whose kiss no frost of age can sever,
I cannot doubt the cold is dead,
The gold earth turned to good—forever.

DYLAN THOMAS
(1914–53)

Especially When the October Wind

Especially when the October wind
With frosty fingers punishes my hair,
Caught by the crabbing sun I walk on fire
And cast a shadow crab upon the land,
By the sea's side, hearing the noise of birds,
Hearing the raven cough in winter sticks,
My busy heart who shudders as she talks
Sheds the syllabic blood and drains her words.

Shut, too, in a tower of words, I mark
On the horizon walking like the trees
The wordy shapes of women, and the rows
Of the star-gestured children in the park.
Some let me make you of the vowelled beeches,
Some of the oaken voices, from the roots
Of many a thorny shire tell you notes,
Some let me make you of the water's speeches.

Behind a pot of ferns the wagging clock
Tells me the hour's word, the neural meaning
Flies on the shafted disk, declaims the morning
And tells the windy weather in the cock.

Some let me make you of the meadow's signs;
The signal grass that tells me all I know
Breaks with the wormy winter through the eye.
Some let me tell you of the raven's sins.

Especially when the October wind
(Some let me make you of autumnal spells,
The spider-tongued, and the loud hill of Wales)
With fists of turnips punishes the land,
Some let me make you of the heartless words.
The heart is drained that, spelling in the scurry
Of chemic blood, warned of the coming fury.
By the sea's side hear the dark-vowelled birds.

Do You Not Father Me

Do you not father me, nor the erected arm
For my tall tower's sake cast in her stone?
Do you not mother me, nor, as I am,
The lovers' house, lie suffering my stain?
Do you not sister me, nor the erected crime
For my tall turrets carry as your sin?
Do you not brother me, nor, as you climb,
Adore my windows for their summer scene?

Am I not father, too, and the ascending boy,
The boy of woman and the wanton starer
Marking the flesh and summer in the bay?
Am I not sister, too, who is my saviour?
Am I not all of you by the directed sea
Where bird and shell are babbling in my tower?
Am I not you who front the tidy shore,
Nor roof of sand, nor yet the towering tiler?

You are all these, said she who gave me the long suck,
All these, he said who sacked the children's town,
Up rose the Abraham-man, mad for my sake,
They said, who hacked and humoured, they were mine.

I am, the tower told, felled by a timeless stroke,
Who razed my wooden folly stands aghast,
For man-begetters in the dry-as-paste,
The ringed-sea ghost, rise grimly from the wrack.

Do you not father me on the destroying sand?
You are your sisters' sire, said seaweedy,
The salt sucked dam and darlings of the land
Who play the proper gentleman and lady.
Shall I still be love's house on the widdershin earth,
Woe to the windy masons at my shelter?
Love's house, they answer, and the tower death
Lie all unknowing of the grave sin-eater.

Altarwise by Owl-Light

I

Altarwise by owl-light in the half-way house
The gentleman lay graveward with his furies;
Abaddon in the hangnail cracked from Adam,
And, from his fork, a dog among the fairies,
The atlas-eater with a jaw for news,
Bit out the mandrake with to-morrow's scream.
Then, penny-eyed, that gentleman of wounds,
Old cock from nowheres and the heaven's egg,
With bones unbuttoned to the half-way winds,
Hatched from the windy salvage on one leg,
Scraped at my cradle in a walking word
That night of time under the Christward shelter:
I am the long world's gentleman, he said,
And share my bed with Capricorn and Cancer.

II

Death is all metaphors, shape in one history;
The child that sucketh long is shooting up,
The planet-ducted pelican of circles
Weans on an artery the gender's strip;

Child of the short spark in a shapeless country
Soon sets alight a long stick from the cradle;
The horizontal cross-bones of Abaddon,
You by the cavern over the black stairs,
Rung bone and blade, the verticals of Adam,
And, manned by midnight, Jacob to the stars.
Hairs of your head, then said the hollow agent,
Are but the roots of nettles and of feathers
Over these groundworks thrusting through a pavement
And hemlock-headed in the wood of weathers.

III

First there was the lamb on knocking knees
And three dead seasons on a climbing grave
That Adam's wether in the flock of horns,
Butt of the tree-tailed worm that mounted Eve,
Horned down with skullfoot and the skull of toes
On thunderous pavements in the garden time;
Rip of the vaults, I took my marrow-ladle
Out of the wrinkled undertaker's van,
And, Rip Van Winkle from a timeless cradle,
Dipped me breast-deep in the descended bone;
The black ram, shuffling of the year, old winter,
Alone alive among his mutton fold,
We rung our weathering changes on the ladder,
Said the antipodes, and twice spring chimed.

IV

What is the metre of the dictionary?
The size of genesis? the short spark's gender?
Shade without shape? the shape of Pharaoh's echo?
(My shape of age nagging the wounded whisper).
Which sixth of wind blew out the burning gentry?
(Questions are hunchbacks to the poker marrow).
What of a bamboo man among your acres?
Corset the boneyards for a crooked boy?
Button your bodice on a hump of splinters,
My camel's eyes will needle through the shrowd.
Love's reflection of the mushroom features,
Stills snapped by night in the bread-sided field,

Once close-up smiling in the wall of pictures,
Arc-lamped thrown back upon the cutting flood.

V

And from the windy West came two-gunned Gabriel,
From Jesu's sleeve trumped up the king of spots,
The sheath-decked jacks, queen with a shuffled heart;
Said the fake gentleman in suit of spades,
Black-tongued and tipsy from salvation's bottle.
Rose my Byzantine Adam in the night.
For loss of blood I fell on Ishmael's plain,
Under the milky mushrooms slew my hunger,
A climbing sea from Asia had me down
And Jonah's Moby snatched me by the hair,
Cross-stroked salt Adam to the frozen angel
Pin-legged on pole-hills with a black medusa
By waste seas where the white bear quoted Virgil
And sirens singing from our lady's sea-straw.

VI

Cartoon of slashes on the tide-traced crater,
He in a book of water tallow-eyed
By lava's light split through the oyster vowels
And burned sea silence on a wick of words.
Pluck, cock, my sea eye, said medusa's scripture,
Lop, love, my fork tongue, said the pin-hilled nettle;
And love plucked out the stinging siren's eye,
Old cock from nowheres lopped the minstrel tongue
Till tallow I blew from the wax's tower
The fats of midnight when the salt was singing;
Adam, time's joker, on a witch of cardboard
Spelt out the seven seas, an evil index,
The bagpipe-breasted ladies in the deadweed
Blew out the blood gauze through the wound of manwax.

VII

Now stamp the Lord's Prayer on a grain of rice,
A Bible-leaved of all the written woods
Strip to this tree: a rocking alphabet,

Genesis in the root, the scarecrow word,
And one light's language in the book of trees.
Doom on deniers at the wind-turned statement.
Time's tune my ladies with the teats of music,
The scaled sea-sawers, fix in a naked sponge
Who sucks the bell-voiced Adam out of magic,
Time, milk, and magic, from the world beginning.
Time is the tune my ladies lend their heartbreak,
From bald pavilions and the house of bread
Time tracks the sound of shape on man and cloud,
On rose and icicle the ringing handprint.

VIII

This was the crucifixion on the mountain,
Time's nerve in vinegar, the gallow grave
As tarred with blood as the bright thorns I wept;
The world's my wound, God's Mary in her grief,
Bent like three trees and bird-papped through her shift,
With pins for teardrops is the long wound's woman.
This was the sky, Jack Christ, each minstrel angle
Drove in the heaven-driven of the nails
Till the three-coloured rainbow from my nipples
From pole to pole leapt round the snail-waked world.
I by the tree of thieves, all glory's sawbones,
Unsex the skeleton this mountain minute,
And by this blowclock witness of the sun
Suffer the heaven's children through my heartbeat.

IX

From the oracular archives and the parchment,
Prophets and fibre kings in oil and letter,
The lamped calligrapher, the queen in splints,
Buckle to lint and cloth their natron footsteps,
Draw on the glove of prints, dead Cairo's henna
Pour like a halo on the caps and serpents.
This was the resurrection in the desert,
Death from a bandage, rants the mask of scholars
Gold on such features, and the linen spirit
Weds my long gentleman to dusts and furies;

With priest and pharaoh bed my gentle wound,
World in the sand, on the triangle landscape,
With stones of odyssey for ash and garland
And rivers of the dead around my neck.

X

Let the tale's sailor from a Christian voyage
Atlaswise hold half-way off the dummy bay
Time's ship-racked gospel on the globe I balance:
So shall winged harbours through the rockbirds' eyes
Spot the blown word, and on the seas I image
December's thorn screwed in a brow of holly.
Let the first Peter from a rainbow's quayrail
Ask the tall fish swept from the bible east,
What rhubarb man peeled in her foam-blue channel
Has sown a flying garden round that sea-ghost?
Green as beginning, let the garden diving
Soar, with its two bark towers, to that Day
When the worm builds with the gold straws of venom
My nest of mercies in the rude, red tree.

When All My Five and Country Senses See

When all my five and country senses see,
The fingers will forget green thumbs and mark
How, through the halfmoon's vegetable eye,
Husk of young stars and handfull zodiac,
Love in the frost is pared and wintered by,
The whispering ears will watch love drummed away
Down breeze and shell to a discordant beach,
And, lashed to syllables, the lynx tongue cry
That her fond wounds are mended bitterly.
My nostrils see her breath burn like a bush.

My one and noble heart has witnesses
In all love's countries, that will grope awake;
And when blind sleep drops on the spying senses,
The heart is sensual, though five eyes break.

A Refusal to Mourn the Death, by Fire, of a Child in London

Never until the mankind making
Bird beast and flower
Fathering and all humbling darkness
Tells with silence the last light breaking
And the still hour
Is come of the sea tumbling in harness

And I must enter again the round
Zion of the water bead
And the synagogue of the ear of corn
Shall I let pray the shadow of a sound
Or sow my salt seed
In the least valley of sackcloth to mourn

The majesty and burning of the child's death.
I shall not murder
The mankind of her going with a grave truth
Nor blaspheme down the stations of the breath
With any further
Elegy of innocence and youth.

Deep with the first dead lies London's daughter,
Robed in the long friends,
The grains beyond age, the dark veins of her mother,
Secret by the unmourning water
Of the riding Thames.
After the first death, there is no other.

Poem in October

It was my thirtieth year to heaven
Woke to my hearing from harbour and neighbour wood

And the mussel pooled and the heron
                Priested shore
        The morning beckon
With water praying and call of seagull and rook
And the knock of sailing boats on the net webbed wall
        Myself to set foot
                That second
    In the still sleeping town and set forth.

    My birthday began with the water-
Birds and the birds of the winged trees flying my name
    Above the farms and the white horses
                And I rose
            In rainy autumn
And walked abroad in a shower of all my days.
High tide and the heron dived when I took the road
        Over the border
            And the gates
    Of the town closed as the town awoke.

    A springful of larks in a rolling
Cloud and the roadside bushes brimming with whistling
    Blackbirds and the sun of October
                Summery
            On the hill's shoulder,
Here were fond climates and sweet singers suddenly
Come in the morning where I wandered and listened
        To the rain wringing
            Wind blow cold
    In the wood faraway under me.

    Pale rain over the dwindling harbour
And over the sea wet church the size of a snail
    With its horns through mist and the castle
                Brown as owls
            But all the gardens
Of spring and summer were blooming in the tall tales
Beyond the border and under the lark full cloud.

There could I marvel
My birthday
Away but the weather turned around.

It turned away from the blithe country
And down the other air and the blue altered sky
Streamed again a wonder of summer
With apples
Pears and red currants
And I saw in the turning so clearly a child's
Forgotten mornings when he walked with his mother
Through the parables
Of sun light
And the legends of the green chapels

And the twice told fields of infancy
That his tears burned my cheeks and his heart moved in mine.
These were the woods the river and sea
Where a boy
In the listening
Summertime of the dead whispered the truth of his joy
To the trees and the stones and the fish in the tide.
And the mystery
Sang alive
Still in the water and singingbirds.

And there could I marvel my birthday
Away but the weather turned around. And the true
Joy of the long dead child sang burning
In the sun.
It was my thirtieth
Year to heaven stood there then in the summer noon
Though the town below lay leaved with October blood.
O may my heart's truth
Still be sung
On this high hill in a year's turning.

The Hunchback in the Park

The hunchback in the park
A solitary mister
Propped between trees and water
From the opening of the garden lock
That lets the trees and water enter
Until the Sunday sombre bell at dark

Eating bread from a newspaper
Drinking water from the chained cup
That the children filled with gravel
In the fountain basin where I sailed my ship
Slept at night in a dog kennel
But nobody chained him up.

Like the park birds he came early
Like the water he sat down
And Mister they called Hey mister
The truant boys from the town
Running when he had heard them clearly
On out of sound

Past lake and rockery
Laughing when he shook his paper
Hunchbacked in mockery
Through the loud zoo of the willow groves
Dodging the park keeper
With his stick that picked up leaves.

And the old dog sleeper
Alone between nurses and swans
While the boys among willows
Made the tigers jump out of their eyes
To roar on the rockery stones
And the groves were blue with sailors

Made all day until bell time
A woman figure without fault
Straight as a young elm
Straight and tall from his crooked bones
That she might stand in the night
After the locks and chains

All night in the unmade park
After the railings and shrubberies
The birds the grass the trees the lake
And the wild boys innocent as strawberries
Had followed the hunchback
To his kennel in the dark.

Do Not Go Gentle into that Good Night

Do not go gentle into that good night,
Old age should burn and rave at close of day;
Rage, rage against the dying of the light.

Though wise men at their end know dark is right,
Because their words had forked no lightning they
Do not go gentle into that good night.

Good men, the last wave by, crying how bright
Their frail deeds might have danced in a green bay,
Rage, rage against the dying of the light.

Wild men who caught and sang the sun in flight,
And learn, too late, they grieved it on its way,
Do not go gentle into that good night.

Grave men, near death, who see with blinding sight
Blind eyes could blaze like meteors and be gay,
Rage, rage against the dying of the light.
And you, my father, there on the sad height,

Curse, bless, me now with your fierce tears, I pray.
Do not go gentle into that good night.
Rage, rage against the dying of the light.

Fern Hill

Now as I was young and easy under the apple boughs
About the lilting house and happy as the grass was green,
　　The night above the dingle starry,
　　　　Time let me hail and climb
　　Golden in the heydays of his eyes,
And honoured among wagons I was prince of the apple towns
And once below a time I lordly had the trees and leaves
　　　　Trail with daisies and barley
　　Down the rivers of the windfall light.

And as I was green and carefree, famous among the barns
About the happy yard and singing as the farm was home,
　　In the sun that is young once only,
　　　　Time let me play and be
　　Golden in the mercy of his means,
And green and golden I was huntsman and herdsman, the
　　　　　　calves
Sang to my horn, the foxes on the hills barked clear and cold,
　　　　And the sabbath rang slowly
　　In the pebbles of the holy streams.

All the sun long it was running, it was lovely, the hay
Fields high as the house, the tunes from the chimneys, it
　　　　　　was air
　　And playing, lovely and watery
　　　　And fire green as grass.
　　And nightly under the simple stars
As I rode to sleep the owls were bearing the farm away,
All the moon long I heard, blessed among stables, the nightjars
　　Flying with the ricks, and the horses
　　　　Flashing into the dark.

And then to awake, and the farm, like a wanderer white
With the dew, come back, the cock on his shoulder: it was all
    Shining, it was Adam and maiden,
       The sky gathered again
    And the sun grew round that very day.
So it must have been after the birth of the simple light
In the first, spinning place, the spellbound horses walking
       warm
    Out of the whinnying green stable
      On to the fields of praise.

And honoured among foxes and pheasants by the gay house
Under the new made clouds and happy as the heart was long
    In the sun born over and over,
       I ran my heedless ways,
    My wishes raced through the house high hay
And nothing I cared, at my sky blue trades, that time allows
In all his tuneful turning so few and such morning songs
    Before the children green and golden
      Follow him out of grace,

Nothing I cared, in the lamb white days, that time would
       take me
Up to the swallow thronged loft by the shadow of my hand,
    In the moon that is always rising,
       Nor that riding to sleep
    I should hear him fly with the high fields
And wake to the farm forever fled from the childless land.
Oh as I was young and easy in the mercy of his means,
      Time held me green and dying
    Though I sang in my chains like the sea.

In the White Giant's Thigh

    Through throats where many rivers meet, the curlews cry,
    Under the conceiving moon, on the high chalk hill,

And there this night I walk in the white giant's thigh
Where barren as boulders women lie longing still

To labour and love though they lay down long ago.

Through throats where many rivers meet, the women pray,
Pleading in the waded bay for the seed to flow
Though the names on their weed grown stones are rained away,

And alone in the night's eternal, curving act
They yearn with tongues of curlews for the unconceived
And immemorial sons of the cudgelling, hacked

Hill. Who once in gooseskin winter loved all ice leaved
In the courters' lanes, or twined in the ox roasting sun
In the wains tonned so high that the wisps of the hay
Clung to the pitching clouds, or gay with any one
Young as they in the after milking moonlight lay

Under the lighted shapes of faith and their moonshade
Petticoats galed high, or shy with the rough riding boys,
Now clasp me to their grains in the gigantic glade,

Who once, green countries since, were a hedgerow of joys.
Time by, their dust was flesh the swineherd rooted sly,
Flared in the reek of the wiving sty with the rush
Light of his thighs, spreadeagle to the dunghill sky,
Or with their orchard man in the core of the sun's bush
Rough as cows' tongues and thrashed with brambles their buttermilk
Manes, under his quenchless summer barbed gold to the bone,

Or rippling soft in the spinney moon as the silk
And ducked and draked white lake that harps to a hail stone.

Who once were a bloom of wayside brides in the hawed house
And heard the lewd, wooed field flow to the coming frost,
The scurrying, furred small friars squeal, in the dowse
Of day, in the thistle aisles, till the white owl crossed
Their breast, the vaulting does roister, the horned bucks climb

Quick in the wood at love, where a torch of foxes foams,
All birds and beasts of the linked night uproar and chime

And the mole snout blunt under his pilgrimage of domes,
Or, butter fat goosegirls, bounced in a gambo bed,
Their breasts full of honey, under their gander king
Trounced by his wings in the hissing shippen, long dead
And gone that barley dark where their clogs danced in the spring,
And their firefly hairpins flew, and the ricks ran round—

(But nothing bore, no mouthing babe to the veined hives
Hugged, and barren and bare on Mother Goose's ground
They with the simple Jacks were a boulder of wives)—

Now curlew cry me down to kiss the mouths of their dust.

The dust of their kettles and clocks swings to and fro
Where the hay rides now or the bracken kitchens rust
As the arc of the billhooks that flashed the hedges low
And cut the birds' boughs that the minstrel sap ran red.
They from houses where the harvest kneels, hold me hard,
Who heard the tall bell sail down the Sundays of the dead
And the rain wring out its tongues on the faded yard,
Teach me the love that is evergreen after the fall leaved
Grave, after Belovéd on the grass gulfed cross is scrubbed
Off by the sun and Daughters no longer grieved
Save by their long desirers in the fox cubbed
Streets or hungering in the crumbled wood: to these
Hale dead and deathless do the women of the hill
Love for ever meridian through the courters' trees

And the daughters of darkness flame like Fawkes fires still.

CHAD WALSH

(1914–)

Ode to the Finnish Dead

at Hietaniemi Heroes'
Cemetery, Helsinki

In the soft Finnish summer they become
Briefly acres of roses. One hardly sees
The standard stones with name and date and rank,
Nor would a slow addition make the sum
Of all who have their rights here. The very walls
Are eloquent with names that other trees
And flowers hold in trust, who stood and sank
To earth as the gold of a birch tree falls.

There were no roses blooming when they flowered
In winter beauty. Their garden was a dim
Disorder of the frozen lakes, and firs
Lifting with snow. And some the night devoured,
And some the darkness of the crouching east,
Folded petals at the west's utter rim,
Faithful in death against the idolaters
And the stone icons of their blinded beast.

In their far northern tongue they had a name
For Marathon; they held Thermopylae;
No traitor could be bought to sell the way.
Suomussalmi, Tolvajärvi became
The rolling syllables Pheidippides
Spoke dying to the Athens that was free.
Thou stranger, pause, and in Helsinki say
We kept her laws amid these witness trees.

"Remember the Finns," intoned the hierophants
In triple invocation to the beast,
And to the west it turned its sightless eyes.
From reddened squares the univocal chants
Of nameless choirs came to its ears with words
Of antiphon. And when their voices ceased,
It rose by jerks, as wooden puppets rise,
And twittered like a tree of maddened birds.

Walk here amid the superficial beauty
Of roses sprung from loveliness beneath.
Here is renewal of our tattered speech.
Dulce et decorum and honest *duty*
Shine innocent in silver, gold, and red;
A goodness brightens in the world of *death*.
Bloom in the beauty of your giving, each
By each, in mankind's heart, brave Finnish dead.

A Gentleness

A gentleness has sometimes stroked my soul
Till the sweetness like angels' sex has spread
From toes to hair and brain, to warm me whole,
And scent me fragrant as the saintly dead.
This never happens in a double bed

Note: Suomussalmi and Tolvajärvi were two of the crucial battles in the Winter War between Finland and the Soviet Union.—Author.

Nor at the rail where Jesus' flesh is vended.
No herald of the moment rides ahead;
No chaperone warns that the hour is ended.

We are all women in the hands of God
Claiming *jus omnis noctis* when He will;
He enters, and the sun absents its light
Like a subverted servant, and the night
Curtains the earth and heaven out. When God
Rises and goes, the sweet night trembles still.

Rejoice in the Basements of Memory

God was in touch. Stroking the holy
Extent of your arm I adored him,
Sleeping with you in his peace.

God was in sight. Seeing the sumac
That bled in the meadows of eucharist,
Daily I drank the good blood.

Hearing was God. Wind on the ripples
And laughter of girls in the attic
Sang the Commandments of God.

God was in taste. Breasts that I savored,
Dark bread that I baked in the oven
Christened the buds of my tongue.

God was a smell. Musk and the lily
Confused in the rose of a heaven
Cloyed with the fragrance of saints.

Ends of the nerves, perishing senses,
Rejoice in the basements of memory,
Kiss the emptying night.

Ode on a Plastic Stapes

for Dr. Rufus C. Morrow, surgeon

What God hath joined together man has put
Asunder. The stapes of my middle ear
Rests in some surgical kitchen midden.
Good riddance to an otosclerotic pest.
And welcome to the vibrant plastic guest
That shivers at each noise to let me hear.

What would the theologians make of this?
The bone God gave me petered out and failed.
But God made people, too. One of them sawed
A dead bone off and put a new one in.
I hear now through a storebought plastic pin.
Where God's hand shook, his creature's skill availed.

Dig where they bury me and you will find
A skeleton of bone perfected in plastic.
Gleam down the buried years, synthetic bone,
Await the judgment of the Resurrection,
The shining glory or the sharp correction
When calendars and clocks read chiliastic.

Will my old stapes rise, expel my plastic?
Do I own or do I merely borrow?
God is no divorce court judge. What man
Hath joined together, he will not put asunder.
Praise God who made the man who wrought this wonder,
Praise God, give thanks tomorrow and tomorrow.

Ode on the First Ape That Became a Man

Across the cracked savanna, as the sun
Blazed on the highest leaves of scattered trees
He stumbled home, cradling the little rodent

Stiff and dead. His stomach raged in pain,
His thick lips dripped with hungry spit. At last
He saw the nest of stones and broken branches
Where he had left her. The sudden sun set.
The quickening darkness chilled his clutching hands.
And he was cold inside. He ran to feed her.

Lifting a broken branch he made a sound,
Not word or name, a squealing call and summons.
No noise of body answered. The air was colder.
Vaguely he saw her there, chin to knees.
He touched her cheek. His hand sent waves of chill
Up the hair spirals of his arm. Slowly
He dropped the stiffened rodent, seized and shook her.
Her head jerked back and forth, the dead teeth clicked.
He wailed a grunting moan, shook her again.

His hunger ate a path, stomach to mouth.
The rodent lay, fat fleshed, close at his feet.
The hairy hand reached down, drew back, and hovered,
Then rose and masked the seeing of his eyes.
In double darkness he stood there while a life
Of pictures—if there were words they would be thoughts—
There were no thoughts but colors, sounds, and smells—
Tumbled disordered from that primal chaos
Where the bright trophies of two lives were housed.

There was a little cave half up a cliff,
Where they had hidden when the lions raged.
And there, by no decree of herd or custom,
And for no reasons he had images for,
He carried her, and laid her on the ground.
Then one by one he lifted rounded stones
From the dwindled stream and piled them up until
The opening was closed. Some cracks remained.
He gathered mud and filled them one by one.

Then in the darkness of the double night,
He shambled to his nest. The rodent lay there,

Fat and smelling of blood. A hungry stomach
Roared desires. He reached to take and eat.
But before his teeth could rip, he sprang outside,
In an innerness of uncouth images,
Carried the rodent to the cave. He took a stick
And made a hole. He pushed the rodent through.
He sealed the hole with mud. He limped home hungry.

In the double darkness of his nest,
He listened to the sounds of night. The roaring
Of lions, the whir of flying things, the wind
Dry and rough across the tattered grass.
A night bird's song came once, came twice to him,
Two tonic notes, the third a fifth above—
It sounded like Lo-nu-ha. She had been
A singing night. She had a name. "Lo-nu-ha,"
He wailed. In the word was the beginning.

The Archaic Hours

We hear them call,
We see them gambol, stride and wait,
Those frozen centuries, the archaic hours
Of sleep, when the old gods and devils know
That they can come and go at will.

They hide in cluttered cellars during the Christian hours
And rarely call,
Or if they do, it's simple to say No
Or make a mock of deafness. They can wait,
Knowing the peaks and chasms of the will.

Sometimes they strike the poses of the *Noh*
In drama's ritual beyond the easy call
Of the heart's simple, sensate will
Or the gospel's grave and massive weight.
Their play is ours.

The other side of good and evil, they wait,
A Mardi Gras of serious masks, the call
To magic caves, the wind's monsters, the hours
When shamans seek the soul's double, and no
Plato or Moses reins the loosened will.

By the first hairy Adam's will
They are our legacy, on call
And calling us to where the first images wait
In the bright terror of their unbegotten beauty, the hours
That stiffly dance, the thrust lip intoning, "Know, know,
                                        know."
Hours call, wait no will.

Water Lilies

In the cove, shadowed,
Is a ring, lilies,
That descends, falters,
Rises with waves, ripples,
Or the slight breathing
Of a wind blowing.
In the full center
Is a white blossom.

Poverty

A gloss on Luke 6:20–21

The poor are blessed, poverty is not.
It is a nostril sealed with chronic snot.
It is teeth eaten to the gums with rot.

It is the shoddy suit, the hand-me-down,
The vague unease in better parts of town,
The pretty girls that flinch by with a frown.

It is the social worker's clipboard eyes,
The tenement house of urine-seasoned sties,
The charity ward in which the poor man dies.

Poverty, hugged for Christ's sake by the rich,
Is the Lady that made St. Francis itch.
The poor man smells her armpits, that old bitch.

JOHN CIARDI

(1916–)

Elegy

My father was born with a spade in his hand and traded it
for a needle's eye to sit his days cross-legged on tables
till he could sit no more, then sold insurance, reading
the ten-cent-a-week lives like logarithms from
the Tables of Metropolitan to their prepaid tombstones.

Years of the little dimes twinkling on kitchen tables
at Mrs. Fauci's at Mrs. Locatelli's at Mrs. Cataldo's
(*Arrividerla, signora. A la settimana prossima. Mi saluta,
la prego, il marito, Ciao, Anna. Bye-bye.*)
—known as a Debit. And with his ten-year button

he opened a long dream like a piggy bank, spilling the dimes
like mountain water into the moss of himself, and bought
ten piney lots in Wilmington. Sunday by Sunday
he took the train to his woods and walked under the trees
to leave his print on his own land, a patron of seasons.

I have done nothing as perfect as my father's Sundays
on his useless lots. Gardens he dreamed from briar tangle
and the swampy back slope of his ridge rose over him
more flowering than Brazil. Maples transformed to figs,
and briar to blood-blue grapes in his look around

195

when he sat on a stone with his wine-jug and cheese beside him,
his collar and coat on a branch, his shirt open,
his derby back on his head like a standing turtle. A big
man he was. When he sang *Celeste Aida* the woods
filled as if a breeze were swelling through them.

When he stopped, I thought I could hear the sound still moving.
—Well, I have lied. Not so much lied as dreamed it.
I was three when he died. It was someone else—my sister—
went with him under the trees. But if it was her
memory then, it became mine so long since

I will owe nothing on it, having dreamed it from all
the nights I was growing, the wet-pants man of the family.
I have done nothing as perfect as I have dreamed him
from old-wives tales and the running of my blood.
God knows what queer long darks I had no eyes for

followed his stairwell weeks to his Sunday breezeways.
But I will swear the world is not well made that rips
such gardens from the week. Or I should have walked
a saint's way to the cross and nail by nail
hymned out my blood to glory, for one good reason.

To Judith Asleep

My dear, darkened in sleep, turned from the moon
that riots on curtain-stir with every breeze,
leaping in moths of light across your back . . .
far off, then soft and sudden as petals shower
down from wired roses—silently, all at once—
you turn, abandoned and naked, all let down
in ferny streams of sleep and petaled thighs
rippling into my flesh's buzzing garden.

Far and familiar your body's myth-map lights,
traveled by moon and dapple. Sagas were curved
like scimitars to your hips. The raiders' ships

all sailed to your one port. And watchfires burned
your image on the hills. Sweetly you drown
male centuries in your chiaroscuro tide
of breast and breath. And all my memory's shores
you frighten perfectly, washed familiar and far.

Ritual wars have climbed your shadowed flank
where bravos dreaming of fair women tore
rock out of rock to have your cities down
in loot of hearths and trophies of desire.
And desert monks have fought your image back
in a hysteria of mad skeletons.
Bravo and monk (the heads and tails of love)
I stand, a spinning coin of wish and dread,

counting our life, our chairs, our books and walls,
our clock whose radium eye and insect voice
owns all our light and shade, and your white shell
spiraled in moonlight on the bed's white beach;
thinking, I might press you to my ear
and all your coils fall out in sounds of surf
washing a mystery sudden as you are
a light on light in light beyond the light.

Child, child, and making legend of my wish
fastened alive into your naked sprawl—
stir once to stop my fear and miser's panic
that time shall have you last and legendry
undress to old bones from its moon brocade.
Yet sleep and keep our prime of time alive
before that death of legend. My dear of all

saga and century, sleep in familiar-far.
Time still must tick *this is, I am, we are.*

A Thanks That Flesh Is Sad

The sad soft scars, childbitten
      from the rose-dust once of flesh,

I kiss unhailed in my arms and sigh for.
A thanks all lovers come to when they dare.

That you were sunblush lit as the writhen
sprays of orchards in the rush of Spring,
and swelled and softened as ever peach on its bough,
an allegory of plenty on stilled air;

and that I laid my last tears in your breast
like worms' eyes from the long sods of my death,
and sang that sadness over in your arms
till I outlived the white bone in its grave—

I rise past pity in a lust of praise
for every loss that stores us. Scar by scar
the dearest flesh is sad, and spins in man
his rose of fire, the raging of his joys.

Palaver's No Prayer

PALAVER'S no prayer.
There's a nice-ninny priest
at tea in everyone,
all cosy and chatty as auntie,
but a saint comes
and throws rocks through the window.

In Place of a Curse

At the next vacancy for God, if I am elected,
I shall forgive last the delicately wounded
who, having been slugged no harder than anyone else,
never got up again, neither to fight back,
nor to finger their jaws in painful admiration.

They who are wholly broken, and they in whom
mercy is understanding, I shall embrace at once
and lead to pillows in heaven. But they who are

the meek by trade, baiting the best of their betters
with extortions of a mock-helplessness

I shall take last to love, and never wholly.
Let them all into Heaven—I abolish Hell—
but let it be read over them as they enter:
"Beware the calculations of the meek, who gambled nothing,
gave nothing, and could never receive enough."

After Sunday Dinner We Uncles Snooze

Banana-stuffed, the ape behind the brain
scratches his crotch in nature and lies back,
one arm across his eyes, one on his belly.
Thanksgiving afternoon in Africa,
the jungle couches heaped with hairy uncles
between a belch and a snore. All's well that yawns.

Seas in the belly lap a high tide home.
A kind of breathing flip-flop, all arrival,
souses the world full in the sog of time,
lifting slopped apes and uncles from their couches
for the long drift of self to self. Goodbye:
I'm off to idiot heaven in a drowse.

This is a man. This blubbermouth at air
sucking its flaps of breath, grimacing, blowing,
rasping, whistling. Walked through by a zoo
of his own reveries, he changes to it.
His palm's huge dabble over his broken face
rubs out the carnivores. His pixie pout

diddles a butterfly across his lip.
His yeasty smile drools Edens at a spring
where girls from Bali, kneeling to their bath,
cup palms of golden water to their breasts.
His lower lip thrusts back the angry chiefs:
he snarls and clicks his teeth: "Stand back, by God!"

And so, by God, they do, while he descends
to rape those knobs of glory with a sigh,
then clouds, surceased, and drifts away or melts
into another weather of himself
where only a drowned mumble far away
sounds in his throat the frog-pond under time.

O apes and hairy uncles of us all,
I hear the gibberish of a mother tongue
inside this throat. (A prattle from the sea.
A hum in the locked egg. A blather of bloods.)
O angels and attendants past the world,
what shall the sleeps of heaven dream but time?

An Island Galaxy

Once on Saipan at the end of the rains
I came on a flooded tire rut in a field
and found it boiling with a galaxy
of pollywogs, each millionth micro-dot
avid and home in an original swarm.

For twenty yards between the sodden tents
and a coral cliff, a universe ran on
in a forgotten dent of someone's passing.
Clusters and nebulae of whirligigs
whorled and maddened, a burst gas of life

from the night hop of unholdable energy.
Did one frog squatting heavy at the full
of its dark let out this light, these black rapids
inside the heart of light in the light-struck dent
of the accidental and awakened waters?

There on the island of our burning, in man's place
in the fire-swarm of war, and in a sunburst
lens, I stood asking—what? Nothing.

Universes happen. Happen and are come upon.
I stood in the happening of an imagination.

Ten days later, having crossed two seas,
I passed that rut again. The sun had burned
the waters back to order. The rut lay baked.
Twenty upthrust shoreline yards of time
slept in the noon of a finished imagination.

And the bed and the raised faces of the world
lay stippled with the dry seals of the dead,
black wafers with black ribbons, as if affixed
to a last writ, but with such waste of law,
I could not read its reasons for its proofs.

Credibility

Who could believe an ant in theory?
a giraffe in blueprint?
Ten thousand doctors of what's possible
could reason half the jungle out of being.
I speak of love, and something more,
to say we are the thing that proves itself
not against reason, but impossibly true,
and therefore to teach reason reason.

Vodka

Vodka, I hope you will note, is
upwind from all other essences.
Drink it all night and all day
and your aunt's minister could
not track you to perdition, not
even with his nose for it. Vodka
has no breath. Call it the dead-
man's drink. But praise it. As
long as he can stand, a vodka-

drinker is sober, and when he
falls down he is merely sleepy.
Like poetry, vodka informs any-
thing with which it is diluted,
and like poetry, alas, it must be
diluted. Only a Russian can take
it straight, and only after long
conditioning, and just see what
seems to be coming of that!

English A

No paraphrase does
between understanding
and understanding.

You are either
that noun beyond
qualification into

whose round fact
I pass unparsed
and into whose eyes

I speak idioms
beyond construction;
or else get up,

fasten your suffixes
and your hyphenations,
buckle your articles,

spray modifiers
and moods
behind your ears

and take the whole
developed discourse
of your thighs to

          any damned grammarian
          you whatsoever
          wish. Period.

Suburban Homecoming

As far as most of what you call people, my darling, are
concerned, I don't care who or what gets into the phone. I
am not home and not expected and I even, considerably,
        doubt I live here.

I mean this town and its everlasting katzenjammer when-
ever whoever dials again, is going to hell, or to some other
perpetual buffet, in a wheelbarrowful of bad martinis: and
        you, my

legal sweet, forever in the act of putting your hat on
as I come in the door to be told I have exactly five—
or, on good days, ten—minutes to change in because here we
        go

again to some collection of never-quite-the-same-but-
always-no-different faces; you, my moth-brained flutter
from bright cup to cup, no matter what nothing is in them;
        you, my own

brand-named, laboratory-tested, fair-trade-priced, wedded
(as advertised in *Life*) feather-duster, may go jump into
twenty fathoms of Advice to the Lovelorn and pull it in after
        you—

but I have not arrived, am not it, the phone did not ring
and was not answered, we have not really, I believe, met, and
if we do and if I stay to be (I doubt it) introduced, I'm still
        not going.

Was a man

Ted Roethke was a tearing man,
    a slam-bang wham-damn tantrum O
from Saginaw in Michigan
    where the ladies sneeze at ten below
but any man that's half a man
    can keep a sweat up till the freeze
    gets down to ninety-nine degrees.
    For the hair on their chests it hangs down to their knees
        in Saginaw, in Michigan.

Ted Roethke was a drinking man,
    a brandy and a bubbly O.
He wore a roll of fat that ran
    six times around his belly O,
then tucked back in where it began.
    And every ounce of every pound
    of that great lard was built around
    the very best hooch that could be found
        in Saginaw, in Michigan.

Ted Roethke was an ath-a-lete.
    (So it's pronounced in Michigan.)
He played to win and was hard to beat.
    And he'd scream like an orangutan
and claw the air and stamp his feet
    at every shot he couldn't make
    and every point he couldn't take.
    And when he lost he'd hold a wake,
        or damn you for a cheat.

Sometimes he was a friend of mine
    with the empties on the floor O.
And, God, it's fun to be feeling fine

and to pour and pour and pour O.
But just to show we were not swine
    we kept a clock that was stopped at ten,
    and never started before then.
    And just to prove we were gentlemen
        we quit when it got to nine.

Ted Roethke was a roaring man,
    a ring-tailed whing-ding yippee O.
He could outyell all Michigan
    and half the Mississippi O.
But once he sat still and began
    to listen for the lifting word,
    it hovered round him like a bird.
    And oh, sweet Christ, the things he heard
        in Saginaw, in Michigan!

Now Roethke's dead. If there's a man,
    a waking lost and wanting O,
in Saginaw, in Michigan,
    he could hear all his haunting O
in the same wind where it began
    the terrors it could not outface,
    but found the words of, and by grace
    of what words are, found time and place
        in Saginaw, in Michigan.

ROBERT LOWELL

(1917–)

The Holy Innocents

Listen, the hay-bells tinkle as the cart
Wavers on rubber tires along the tar
And cindered ice below the burlap mill
And ale-wife run. The oxen drool and start
In wonder at the fenders of a car,
And blunder hugely up St. Peter's hill.
These are the undefiled by woman—their
Sorrow is not the sorrow of this world:
King Herod shrieking vengeance at the curled
Up knees of Jesus choking in the air,

A king of speechless clods and infants. Still
The world out-Herods Herod; and the year,
The nineteen-hundred forty-fifth of grace,
Lumbers with losses up the clinkered hill
Of our purgation; and the oxen near
The worn foundations of their resting-place,
The holy manger where their bed is corn
And holly torn for Christmas. If they die,
As Jesus, in the harness, who will mourn?
Lamb of the shepherds, Child, how still you lie.

Christmas in Black Rock

Christ God's red shadow hangs upon the wall
The dead leaf's echo on these hours
Whose burden spindles to no breath at all;
Hard at our heels the huntress moonlight towers
And the green needles bristle at the glass
Tiers of defense-plants where the treadmill night
Churns up Long Island Sound with piston-fist.
Tonight, my child, the lifeless leaves will mass,
Heaving and heaping, as the swivelled light
Burns on the bell-spar in the fruitless mist.

Christ Child, your lips are lean and evergreen
Tonight in Black Rock, and the moon
Sidles outside into the needle-screen
And strikes the hand that feeds you with a spoon
Tonight, as drunken Polish night-shifts walk
Over the causeway and their juke-box booms
Hosannah in excelsis Domino.
Tonight, my child, the foot-loose hallows stalk
Us down in the blind alleys of our rooms;
By the mined root the leaves will overflow.

December, old leech, has leafed through Autumn's store
Where Poland has unleashed its dogs
To bay the moon upon the Black Rock shore:
Under our windows, on the rotten logs
The moonbeam, bobbing like an apple, snags
The undertow. O Christ, the spiralling years
Slither with child and manger to a ball
Of ice; and what is man? We tear our rags
To hang the Furies by their itching ears,
And the green needles nail us to the wall.

The Quaker Graveyard in Nantucket

For Warren Winslow, dead at sea

> *Let man have dominion over the fishes of the sea and the fowls of the air and the beasts and the whole earth, and every creeping creature that moveth upon the earth.*

I

A brackish reach of shoal off Madaket,—
The sea was still breaking violently and night
Had steamed into our North Atlantic Fleet,
When the drowned sailor clutched the drag-net. Light
Flashed from his matted head and marble feet,
He grappled at the net
With the coiled, hurdling muscles of his thighs:
The corpse was bloodless, a botch of reds and whites,
Its open, staring eyes
Were lustreless dead-lights
Or cabin-windows on a stranded hulk
Heavy with sand. We weight the body, close
Its eyes and heave it seaward whence it came,
Where the heel-headed dogfish barks its nose
On Ahab's void and forehead; and the name
Is blocked in yellow chalk.
Sailors, who pitch this portent at the sea
Where dreadnaughts shall confess
Its hell-bent deity,
When you are powerless
To sand-bag this Atlantic bulwark, faced
By the earth-shaker, green, unwearied, chaste
In his steel scales: ask for no Orphean lute
To pluck life back. The guns of the steeled fleet
Recoil and then repeat
The hoarse salute.

II

Whenever winds are moving and their breath
Heaves at the roped-in bulwarks of this pier,

The terns and sea-gulls tremble at your death
In these home waters. Sailor, can you hear
The Pequod's sea wings, beating landward, fall
Headlong and break on our Atlantic wall
Off 'Sconset, where the yawing S-boats splash
The bellbuoy, with ballooning spinnakers,
As the entangled, screeching mainsheet clears
The blocks: off Madaket, where lubbers lash
The heavy surf and throw their long lead squids
For blue-fish? Sea-gulls blink their heavy lids
Seaward. The winds' wings beat upon the stones,
Cousin, and scream for you and the claws rush
At the sea's throat and wring it in the slush
Of this old Quaker graveyard where the bones
Cry out in the long night for the hurt beast
Bobbing by Ahab's whaleboats in the East.

III

All you recovered from Poseidon died
With you, my cousin, and the harrowed brine
Is fruitless on the blue beard of the god,
Stretching beyond us to the castles in Spain,
Nantucket's westward haven. To Cape Cod
Guns, cradled on the tide,
Blast the eelgrass about a waterclock
Of bilge and backwash, roil the salt and sand
Lashing earth's scaffold, rock
Our warships in the hand
Of the great God, where time's contrition blues
Whatever it was these Quaker sailors lost
In the mad scramble of their lives. They died
When time was open-eyed,
Wooden and childish; only bones abide
There, in the nowhere, where their boats were tossed
Sky-high, where mariners had fabled news
Of IS, the whited monster. What it cost
Them is their secret. In the sperm-whale's slick
I see the Quakers drown and hear their cry.
"If God himself had not been on our side,

If God himself had not been on our side,
When the Atlantic rose against us, why,
Then it had swallowed us up quick."

IV

This is the end of the whaleroad and the whale
Who spewed Nantucket bones on the thrashed swell
And stirred the troubled waters to whirlpools
To send the Pequod packing off to hell:
This is the end of them, three-quarters fools,
Snatching at straws to sail
Seaward and seaward on the turntail whale,
Spouting out blood and water as it rolls,
Sick as a dog to these Atlantic shoals:
Clamavimus, O depths. Let the sea-gulls wail

For water, for the deep where the high tide
Mutters to its hurt self, mutters and ebbs.
Waves wallow in their wash, go out and out,
Leave only the death-rattle of the crabs,
The beach increasing, its enormous snout
Sucking the ocean's side.
This is the end of running on the waves;
We are poured out like water. Who will dance
The mast-lashed master of Leviathans
Up from this field of Quakers in their unstoned graves?

V

When the whale's viscera go and the roll
Of its corruption overruns this world
Beyond tree-swept Nantucket and Wood's Hole
And Martha's Vineyard, Sailor, will your sword
Whistle and fall and sink into the fat?
In the great ash-pit of Jehoshaphat
The bones cry for the blood of the white whale,
The fat flukes arch and whack about its ears,
The death-lance churns into the sanctuary, tears
The gun-blue swingle, heaving like a flail,

And hacks the coiling life out: it works and drags
And rips the sperm-whale's midriff into rags,
Gobbets of blubber spill to wind and weather,
Sailor, and gulls go round the stoven timbers
Where the morning stars sing out together
And thunder shakes the white surf and dismembers
The red flag hammered in the mast-head. Hide,
Our steel, Jonas Messias, in Thy side.

VI
Our Lady of Walsingham

There once the penitents took off their shoes
And then walked barefoot the remaining mile;
And the small trees, a stream and hedgerows file
Slowly along the munching English lane,
Like cows to the old shrine, until you lose
Track of your dragging pain.
The stream flows down under the druid tree,
Shiloah's whirlpools gurgle and make glad
The castle of God. Sailor, you were glad
And whistled Sion by that stream. But see:

Our Lady, too small for her canopy,
Sits near the altar. There's no comeliness
At all or charm in that expressionless
Face with its heavy eyelids. As before,
This face, for centuries a memory,
Non est species, neque decor,
Expressionless, expresses God: it goes
Past castled Sion. She knows what God knows,
Not Calvary's Cross nor crib at Bethlehem
Now, and the world shall come to Walsingham.

VII

The empty winds are creaking and the oak
Splatters and splatters on the cenotaph,
The boughs are trembling and a gaff
Bobs on the untimely stroke

Of the greased wash exploding on a shoal-bell
In the old mouth of the Atlantic. It's well;
Atlantic, you are fouled with the blue sailors,
Sea-monsters, upward angel, downward fish:
Unmarried and corroding, spare of flesh
Mart once of supercilious, wing'd clippers,
Atlantic, where your bell-trap guts its spoil
You could cut the brackish winds with a knife
Here in Nantucket, and cast up the time
When the Lord God formed man from the sea's slime
And breathed into his face the breath of life,
And blue-lung'd combers lumbered to the kill.
The Lord survives the rainbow of His will.

Winter in Dunbarton

Time smiling on this sundial of a world
Sweltered about the snowman and the worm,
Sacker of painted idols and the peers
Of Europe; but my cat is cold, is curled
Tight as a boulder: she no longer smears
Her catnip mouse from Christmas, for the germ—
Mindless and ice, a world against our world—
Has tamped her round of brains into her ears.

This winter all the snowmen turn to stone,
Or, sick of the long hurly-burly, rise
Like butterflies into Jehovah's eyes
And shift until their crystals must atone

In water. Belle, the cat that used to rat
About my father's books, is dead. All day
The wastes of snow about my house stare in
Through idle windows at the brainless cat;
The coke-barrel in the corner whimpers. May
The snow recede and red clay furrows set
In the grim grin of their erosion, in
The caterpillar tents and roadslides, fat

With muck and winter dropsy, where the tall
Snow-monster wipes the coke-fumes from his eyes
And scatters his corruption and it lies
Gaping until the fungus-eyeballs fall

Into this eldest of the seasons. Cold
Snaps the bronze toes and fingers of the Christ
My father fetched from Florence, and the dead
Chatters to nothing in the thankless ground
His father screwed from Charlie Stark and sold
To the selectmen. Cold has cramped his head
Against his heart: my father's stone is crowned
With snowflakes and the bronze-age shards of Christ.

Salem

In Salem seasick spindrift drifts or skips
To the canvas flapping on the seaward panes
Until the knitting sailor stabs at ships
Nosing like sheep of Morpheus through his brain's
Asylum. Seaman, seaman, how the draft
Lashes the oily slick about your head,
Beating up whitecaps! Seaman, Charon's raft
Dumps its damned goods into the harbor-bed,—
There sewage sickens the rebellious seas.
Remember, seaman, Salem fishermen
Once hung their nimble fleets on the Great Banks.
Where was it that New England bred the men
Who quartered the Leviathan's fat flanks
And fought the British Lion to his knees?

Children of Light

Our fathers wrung their bread from stocks and stones
And fenced their gardens with the Redman's bones;
Embarking from the Nether Land of Holland,
Pilgrims unhouseled by Geneva's night,

They planted here the Serpent's seeds of light;
And here the pivoting searchlights probe to shock
The riotous glass houses built on rock,
And candles gutter by an empty altar,
And light is where the landless blood of Cain
Is burning, burning the unburied grain.

Mr. Edwards and the Spider

I saw the spiders marching through the air,
Swimming from tree to tree that mildewed day
    In latter August when the hay
    Came creaking to the barn. But where
        The wind is westerly,
Where gnarled November makes the spiders fly
Into the apparitions of the sky,
They purpose nothing but their ease and die
Urgently beating east to sunrise and the sea;

What are we in the hands of the great God?
It was in vain you set up thorn and briar
    In battle array against the fire
    And treason crackling in your blood;
        For the wild thorns grow tame
And will do nothing to oppose the flame;
Your lacerations tell the losing game
You play against a sickness past your cure.
How will the hands be strong? How will the heart endure?

A very little thing, a little worm,
Or hourglass-blazoned spider, it is said,
    Can kill a tiger. Will the dead
    Hold up his mirror and affirm
        To the four winds the smell
And flash of his authority? It's well
If God who holds you to the pit of hell,
Much as one holds a spider, will destroy,
Baffle and dissipate your soul. As a small boy

On Windsor Marsh, I saw the spider die
When thrown into the bowels of fierce fire:
   There's no long struggle, no desire
   To get up on its feet and fly—
      It stretches out its feet
And dies. This is the sinner's last retreat;
Yes, and no strength exerted on the heat
Then sinews the abolished will, when sick
And full of burning, it will whistle on a brick.

But who can plumb the sinking of that soul?
Josiah Hawley, picture yourself cast
   Into a brick-kiln where the blast
   Fans your quick vitals to a coal—
      If measured by a glass,
How long would it seem burning! Let there pass
A minute, ten, ten trillion; but the blaze
Is infinite, eternal: this is death,
To die and know it. This is the Black Widow, death.

The Dead in Europe

After the planes unloaded, we fell down
Buried together, unmarried men and women;
Not crown of thorns, not iron, not Lombard crown,
Not grilled and spindle spires pointing to heaven
Could save us. Raise us, Mother, we fell down
Here hugger-mugger in the jellied fire:
Our sacred earth in our day was our curse.

Our Mother, shall we rise on Mary's day
In Maryland, wherever corpses married
Under the rubble, bundled together? Pray
For us whom the blockbusters marred and buried;
When Satan scatters us on Rising-day,
O Mother, snatch our bodies from the fire:
Our sacred earth in our day was our curse.

Mother, my bones are trembling and I hear
The earth's reverberations and the trumpet
Bleating into my shambles. Shall I bear,
(O Mary!) unmarried man and powder-puppet,
Witness to the Devil? Mary, hear,
O Mary, marry earth, sea, air and fire;
Our sacred earth in our day is our curse.

Falling Asleep over the Aeneid

An old man in Concord forgets to go to morning service. He falls asleep, while reading Vergil, and dreams that he is Aeneas at the funeral of Pallas, an Italian prince.

The sun is blue and scarlet on my page,
And *yuck-a, yuck-a, yuck-a, yuck-a,* rage
The yellowhammers mating. Yellow fire
Blankets the captives dancing on their pyre,
And the scorched lictor screams and drops his rod.
Trojans are singing to their drunken God,
Ares. Their helmets catch on fire. Their files
Clank by the body of my comrade—miles
Of filings! Now the scythe-wheeled chariot rolls
Before their lances long as vaulting poles,
And I stand up and heil the thousand men,
Who carry Pallas to the bird-priest. Then
The bird-priest groans, and as his birds foretold,
I greet the body, lip to lip. I hold
The sword that Dido used. It tries to speak,
A bird with Dido's sworded breast. Its beak
Clangs and ejaculates the Punic word
I hear the bird-priest chirping like a bird.
I groan a little. "Who am I, and why?"
It asks, a boy's face, though its arrow-eye
Is working from its socket. "Brother, try,
O Child of Aphrodite, try to die:
To die is life." His harlots hang his bed

With feathers of his long-tailed birds. His head
Is yawning like a person. The plumes blow;
The beard and eyebrows ruffle. Face of snow,
You are the flower that country girls have caught,
A wild bee-pillaged honey-suckle brought
To the returning bridegroom—the design
Has not yet left it, and the petals shine;
The earth, its mother, has, at last, no help:
It is itself. The broken-winded yelp
Of my Phoenician hounds, that fills the brush
With snapping twigs and flying, cannot flush
The ghost of Pallas. But I take his pall,
Stiff with its gold and purple, and recall
How Dido hugged it to her, while she toiled,
Laughing—her golden threads, a serpent coiled
In cypress. Now I lay it like a sheet;
It clinks and settles down upon his feet,
The careless yellow hair that seemed to burn
Beforehand. Left foot, right foot—as they turn,
More pyres are rising: armed horses, bronze,
And gagged Italians, who must file by ones
Across the bitter river, when my thumb
Tightens into their wind-pipes. The beaks drum;
Their headman's cow-horned death's-head bites its tongue,
And stiffens, as it eyes the hero slung
Inside his feathered hammock on the crossed
Staves of the eagles that we winged. Our cost
Is nothing to the lovers, whoring Mars
And Venus, father's lover. Now his car's
Plumage is ready, and my marshals fetch
His squire, Acoetes, white with age, to hitch
Aethon, the hero's charger, and its ears
Prick, and it steps and steps, and stately tears
Lather its teeth; and then the harlots bring
The hero's charms and baton—but the King,
Vain-glorious Turnus, carried off the rest.
"I was myself, but Ares thought it best
The way it happened." At the end of time,
He sets his spear, as my descendants climb
The knees of Father Time, his beard of scalps,

His scythe, the arc of steel that crowns the Alps.
The elephants of Carthage hold those snows,
Turms of Numidian horse unsling their bows,
The flaming turkey-feathered arrows swarm
Beyond the Alps. "Pallas," I raise my arm
And shout, "Brother, eternal health. Farewell
Forever." Church is over, and its bell
Frightens the yellowhammers, as I wake
And watch the whitecaps wrinkle up the lake.
Mother's great-aunt, who died when I was eight,
Stands by our parlor sabre. "Boy, it's late.
Vergil must keep the Sabbath." Eighty years!
It all comes back. My Uncle Charles appears.
Blue-capped and bird-like. Phillips Brooks and Grant
Are frowning at his coffin, and my aunt,
Hearing his colored volunteers parade
Through Concord, laughs, and tells her English maid
To clip his yellow nostril hairs, and fold
His colors on him. . . . It is I, I hold
His sword to keep from falling, for the dust
On the stuffed birds is breathless, for the bust
Of young Augustus weighs on Vergil's shelf:
It scowls into my glasses at itself.

Inauguration Day: January 1953

The snow had buried Stuyvesant.
The subways drummed the vaults. I heard
the El's green girders charge on Third,
Manhattan's truss of adamant,
that groaned in ermine, slummed on want. . . .
Cyclonic zero of the word,
God of our armies, who interred
Cold Harbor's blue immortals, Grant!
Horseman, your sword is in the groove!

Ice, ice. Our wheels no longer move.
Look, the fixed stars, all just alike
as lack-land atoms, split apart,

and the Republic summons Ike,
the mausoleum in her heart.

Grandparents

They're altogether otherworldly now,
those adults champing for their ritual Friday spin
to pharmacist and five-and-ten in Brockton.
Back in my throw-away and shaggy span
of adolescence, Grandpa still waves his stick
like a policeman;
Grandmother, like a Mohammedan, still wears her thick
lavender mourning and touring veil;
the Pierce Arrow clears its throat in a horse-stall.
Then the dry road dust rises to whiten
the fatigued elm leaves—
the nineteenth century, tired of children, is gone.
They're all gone into a world of light; the farm's my own.

The farm's my own!
Back there alone,
I keep indoors, and spoil another season.
I hear the rattley little country gramophone
racking its five foot horn:
"O Summer Time!"
Even at noon here the formidable
Ancien Régime still keeps nature at a distance. Five
green shaded light bulbs spider the billiards-table;
no field is greener than its cloth,
where Grandpa, dipping sugar for us both,
once spilled his demitasse.
His favorite ball, the number three,
still hides the coffee stain.

Never again
to walk there, chalk our cues,
insist on shooting for us both.
Grandpa! Have me, hold me, cherish me!

Tears smut my fingers. There
half my life-lease later,
I hold an *Illustrated London News*—;
disloyal still,
I doodle handlebar
mustaches on the last Russian Czar.

Memories of West Street and Lepke

Only teaching on Tuesdays, book-worming
in pajamas fresh from the washer each morning,
I hog a whole house on Boston's
"hardly passionate Marlborough Street,"
where even the man
scavenging filth in the back alley trash cans,
has two children, a beach wagon, a helpmate,
and is a "young Republican."
I have a nine months' daughter,
young enough to be my granddaughter.
Like the sun she rises in her flame-flamingo infants' wear.

These are the tranquillized *Fifties*,
and I am forty. Ought I to regret my seedtime?
I was a fire-breathing Catholic C.O.,
and made my manic statement,
telling off the state and president, and then
sat waiting sentence in the bull pen
beside a Negro boy with curlicues
of marijuana in his hair.

Given a year,
I walked on the roof of the West Street Jail, a short
enclosure like my school soccer court,
and saw the Hudson River once a day
through sooty clothesline entanglements
and bleaching khaki tenements.
Strolling, I yammered metaphysics with Abramowitz,

a jaundice-yellow ("it's really tan")
and fly-weight pacifist,
so vegetarian,
he wore rope shoes and preferred fallen fruit.
He tried to convert Bioff and Brown,
the Hollywood pimps, to his diet.
Hairy, muscular, suburban,
wearing chocolate double-breasted suits,
they blew their tops and beat him black and blue.

I was so out of things, I'd never heard
of the Jehovah's Witnesses.
"Are you a C.O.?" I asked a fellow jailbird.
"No," he answered, "I'm a J.W."
He taught me the "hospital tuck,"
and pointed out the T shirted back
of *Murder Incorporated's* Czar Lepke,
there piling towels on a rack,
or dawdling off to his little segregated cell full
of things forbidden the common man:
a portable radio, a dresser, two toy American
flags tied together with a ribbon of Easter palm.
Flabby, bald, lobotomized,
he drifted in a sheepish calm,
where no agonizing reappraisal
jarred his concentration on the electric chair—
hanging like an oasis in his air
of lost connections. . . .

Robert Frost

Robert Frost at midnight, the audience gone
to vapor, the great act laid on the shelf in mothballs,
his voice musical, raw and raw—he writes in the flyleaf:
'Robert Lowell from Robert Frost, his friend in the art.'
'Sometimes I feel too full of myself,' I say.
And he, misunderstanding, 'When I am low,
I stray away. My son wasn't your kind. The night

we told him Merrill Moore would come to treat him,
he said, "I'll kill him first." One of my daughters thought things,
knew every male she met was out to make her;
the way she dresses, she couldn't make a whorehouse.'
And I, 'Sometimes I'm so happy I can't stand myself.'
And he, 'When I am too full of joy, I think
how little good my health did anyone near me.'

The Pacification of Columbia

Patches of tan and blood-warm rooftile, azure:
an old jigsawpuzzle Mosque of Omar flung
to vaultless consummation and blue consumption,
exhalation of the desert sand to fire.
I got the message, one the puzzle never sent. . . .
No destructive element emaciates
Columbia this Mayday afternoon;
the thickened buildings look like buildings out
of Raphael, colossal classic, dungeon feudal;
horses, higher artistic types than their grooms,
forage Broadway's median trees, as if
nature were liberated . . . the blue police
lean on the burnished, nervous hides, show they,
at least, have learned to meet and reason together.

May 1, 1968

LAWRENCE FERLINGHETTI
(1919–)

from ''PICTURES OF THE GONE WORLD''

2

        Just as I used to say
                love comes harder to the aged
because they've been running
                on the same old rails too long
  and then when the sly switch comes along
                    they miss the turn
    and burn up the wrong rail while
              the gay caboose goes flying
    and the steamengine driver don't recognize
                  them new electric horns
and the aged run out on the rusty spur
              which ends up in
       the dead grass where
the rusty tincans and bedsprings and old razor
        blades and moldy mattresses
              lie
    and the rail breaks off dead
         right there
   though the ties go on awhile
        and the aged

say to themselves
                    Well
                            this must be the place
                    we were supposed to lie down

  And they do

                        while the bright saloon careens along away
            on a high
                    hilltop
                                its windows full of bluesky and lovers
                    with flowers
                                their long hair streaming
                                        and all of them laughing
                        and waving and
                                        whispering to each other
            and looking out and
                                wondering what that graveyard
                where the rails end
                                    is

from ''A CONEY ISLAND OF THE MIND''
8

        In Golden Gate Park that day
                                    a man and his wife were coming along
            thru the enormous meadow
                                    which was the meadow of the world
    He was wearing green suspenders
                                    and carrying an old beat-up flute
                                            in one hand
            while his wife had a bunch of grapes
                                    which she kept handing out
                                            individually
                            to various squirrels
                                        as if each
                            were a little joke

And then the two of them came on
                    thru the enormous meadow
which was the meadow of the world
                         and then
            at a very still spot where the trees dreamed
            and seemed to have been waiting thru all time
                                   for them
            they sat down together on the grass
                              without looking at each other
              and ate oranges
                    without looking at each other
                              and put the peels
          in a basket which they seemed
                         to have brought for that purpose
            without looking at each other

And then
            he took his shirt and undershirt off
        but kept his hat on
                    sideways
                         and without saying anything
          fell asleep under it
                    And his wife just sat there looking
at the birds which flew about
        calling to each other
                    in the stilly air
        as if they were questioning existence
                    or trying to recall something forgotten

But then finally
            she too lay down flat
                    and just lay there looking up
                              at nothing
          yet fingering the old flute
                         which nobody played
            and finally looking over
                    at him
        without any particular expression

except a certain awful look
of terrible depression

15

Constantly risking absurdity
and death
whenever he performs
above the heads
of his audience
the poet like an acrobat
climbs on rime
to a high wire of his own making
and balancing on eyebeams
above a sea of faces
paces his way
to the other side of day
performing entrechats
and sleight-of-foot tricks
and other high theatrics
and all without mistaking
any thing
for what it may not be

For he's the super realist
who must perforce perceive
taut truth
before the taking of each stance or step
in his supposed advance
toward that still higher perch
where Beauty stands and waits
with gravity
to start her death-defying leap

And he
a little charleychaplin man
who may or may not catch

her fair eternal form
> spreadeagled in the empty air
of existence

28

> Dove sta amore
> Where lies love
> Dove sta amore
> Here lies love
> The ring dove love
> In lyrical delight
> Hear love's hillsong
> Love's true willsong
> Love's low plainsong
> Too sweet painsong
> In passages of night
> Dove sta amore
> Here lies love
> The ring dove love
> Dove sta amore
> Here lies love

from ''ORAL MESSAGES''

Dog *

The dog trots freely in the street
and sees reality
and the things he sees
are bigger than himself
and the things he sees

* "Dog" is one of a group of poems that were "conceived specifically for jazz accompaniment and as such should be considered as spontaneously spoken 'oral messages' rather than as poems written for the printed page. As a result of continued experimental reading with jazz, they are still in a state of change."— Author's note.

are his reality
Drunks in doorways
Moons on trees
The dog trots freely thru the street
and the things he sees
are smaller than himself
Fish on newsprint
Ants in holes
Chickens in Chinatown windows
their heads a block away
The dog trots freely in the street
and the things he smells
smell something like himself
The dog trots freely in the street
past puddles and babies
cats and cigars
poolrooms and policemen
He doesn't hate cops
He merely has no use for them
and he goes past them
and past the dead cows hung up whole
in front of the San Francisco Meat Market
He would rather eat a tender cow
than a tough policeman
though either might do
And he goes past the Romeo Ravioli Factory
and past Coit's Tower
and past Congressman Doyle
He's afraid of Coit's Tower
but he's not afraid of Congressman Doyle
although what he hears is very discouraging
very depressing
very absurd
to a sad young dog like himself
to a serious dog like himself
But he has his own free world to live in
His own fleas to eat
He will not be muzzled

Congressman Doyle is just another
fire hydrant
to him
The dog trots freely in the street
and has his own dog's life to live
and to think about
and to reflect upon
touching and tasting and testing everything
investigating everything
without benefit of perjury
a real realist
with a real tale to tell
and a real tail to tell it with
a real live
      barking
          democratic dog
engaged in real
        free enterprise
with something to say
        about ontology
something to say
      about reality
        and how to see it
          and how to hear it
with his head cocked sideways
        at streetcorners
as if he is just about to have
      his picture taken
         for Victor Records
      listening for
        His Master's Voice
    and looking
      like a living questionmark
        into the
        great gramaphone
       of puzzling existence
   with its wondrous hollow horn
    which always seems

just about to spout forth
                    some Victorious answer
                    to everything

The Great Chinese Dragon

The great Chinese dragon which is the greatest dragon in all the
        world and which once upon a time was towed across
        the Pacific by a crew of coolies rowing in an open boat
        —was the first real live dragon ever actually to reach
        these shores
And the great Chinese dragon passing thru the Golden Gate spouting
        streams of water like a string of fireboats then broke
        loose somewhere near China Camp gulped down a
        hundred Chinese seamen and forthwith ate up all the
        shrimp in San Francisco Bay
And the great Chinese dragon was therefore forever after confined in
        a Chinatown basement and ever since allowed out only
        for Chinese New Year's parades and other Unamerican
        demonstrations paternally watched-over by those be-
        nevolent men in blue who represent our more advanced
        civilization which has reached such a high state of de-
        mocracy as to allow even a few barbarians to carry on
        their quaint native customs in our midst
And thus the great Chinese dragon which is the greatest dragon in all
        the world now can only be seen creeping out of an Adler
        Alley cellar like a worm out of a hole sometime during
        the second week in February every year when it sorties
        out of hibernation in its Chinese storeroom pushed
        from behind by a band of fortythree Chinese elec-
        tricians and technicians who stuff its peristaltic ac-
        cordion-body up thru a sidewalk delivery entrance
And first the swaying snout appears and then the eyes at ground level
        feeling along the curb and then the head itself casting
        about and swaying and heaving finally up to the corner
        of Grant Avenue itself where a huge paper sign pro-
        claims the *World's Largest Chinatown*

And the great Chinese dragon's jaws wired permanently agape as if
by a demented dentist to display the Cadmium teeth
as the hungry head heaves out into Grant Avenue right
under the sign and raising itself with a great snort of
fire suddenly proclaims the official firecracker start of
the Chinese New Year

And the lightbulb eyes lighting up and popping out on coiled wire
springs and the body stretching and rocking further and
further around the corner and down Grant Avenue like
a caterpillar roller-coaster with the eyes sprung out and
waving in the air like the blind feelers of some me-
chanical preying mantis and the eyes blinking on and
off with Chinese red pupils and tiny bamboo-blind eye-
lids going up and down

And still the tail of the dragon in the Adler Alley cellar uncoiling and
unwinding out into the street with the fortythree Chi-
nese technicians still stuffing the dragon out the hole
in the sidewalk and the head of the dragon now three
blocks away in the middle of the parade of fancy floats
presided over by Chinese virgins

And here comes the St. Mary's Chinese Girls' Drum Corps and here
come sixteen white men in pith helmets beating big
bass drums representing the Order of the Moose and
here comes a gang of happy car salesmen disguised as
Islam Shriners and here comes a chapter of the Order
of Improved Red Men and here comes a cordon of
motorcycle cops in crash helmets with radios going fol-
lowed by a small papier-mâché lion fed with Nekko
wafers and run by two guys left over from a Ten-Ten
festival which in turn is followed by the great Chinese
dragon itself gooking over balconies as it comes

And the great Chinese dragon has eaten a hundred humans and their
legs pop out of his underside and are his walking legs
which are not mentioned in the official printed program
in which he is written up as the Great Golden Dragon
made in Hong Kong to the specifications of the Chinese
Chamber of Commerce and he represents the force and
mystery of life and his head sways in the sky between the
balconies as he comes followed by six Chinese boy

And the great Chinese dragon's jaws wired permanently agape as if
by a demented dentist to display the Cadmium teeth
as the hungry head heaves out into Grant Avenue right
under the sign and raising itself with a great snort of
fire suddenly proclaims the official firecracker start of
the Chinese New Year

And the lightbulb eyes lighting up and popping out on coiled wire
springs and the body stretching and rocking further and
further around the corner and down Grant Avenue like
a caterpillar roller-coaster with the eyes sprung out and
waving in the air like the blind feelers of some me-
chanical preying mantis and the eyes blinking on and
off with Chinese red pupils and tiny bamboo-blind eye-
lids going up and down

And still the tail of the dragon in the Adler Alley cellar uncoiling and
unwinding out into the street with the fortythree Chi-
nese technicians still stuffing the dragon out the hole
in the sidewalk and the head of the dragon now three
blocks away in the middle of the parade of fancy floats
presided over by Chinese virgins

And here comes the St. Mary's Chinese Girls' Drum Corps and here
come sixteen white men in pith helmets beating big
bass drums representing the Order of the Moose and
here comes a gang of happy car salesmen disguised as
Islam Shriners and here comes a chapter of the Order
of Improved Red Men and here comes a cordon of
motorcycle cops in crash helmets with radios going fol-
lowed by a small papier-mâché lion fed with Nekko
wafers and run by two guys left over from a Ten-Ten
festival which in turn is followed by the great Chinese
dragon itself gooking over balconies as it comes

And the great Chinese dragon has eaten a hundred humans and their
legs pop out of his underside and are his walking legs
which are not mentioned in the official printed program
in which he is written up as the Great Golden Dragon
made in Hong Kong to the specifications of the Chinese
Chamber of Commerce and he represents the force and
mystery of life and his head sways in the sky between the
balconies as he comes followed by six Chinese boy

how far the great Chinese dragon might really go start-
ing from San Francisco and so they have secretly and
securely tied down the very end of his tail in its hole
                    so that
                            this great pulsing phallus of
life at the very end of its parade at the very end of
Chinatown gives one wild orgasm of a shudder and rolls
over fainting in the bright night street since even for a
dragon every orgasm is a little death
And then the great Chinese dragon starts silently shrinking and
        shriveling up and drawing back and back and back to its
        first cave and the soft silk skin wrinkles up and shrinks
        and shrinks on its sprung bamboo bones and the hand-
        some dejected head hangs down like a defeated prize-
        fighter's and so is stuffed down again at last into its
        private place and the cellar sidewalk doors press down
        again over the great wilted head with one small hole of
        an eye blinking still thru the gratings of the metal doors
        as the great Chinese dragon gives one last convulsive
        earthquake shake and rolls over dead-dog to wait an-
        other white year for the final coming and the final
        sowing of his oats and teeth

stanzas from B A C K   R O A D S   T O
F A R   P L A C E S

            O man in saffron
                    in the Golden Gate
            chanting Hare Krishna
                squatting lotus
                    among the fern-fronds
            At sundown
                    no more Krishna
            The fern-fronds
                    unrolled!

O listen
　to the sound of the sea
　　my son
There is a fish in us
　who hears the ocean's
　　long withdrawing Om
And echoes it

Sunlight casts its leaves
　upon the wall
Wind stirs them
　　even
　in the closed
　　　　room

Time a traveler
　　melting
　　　　in eternity
　(the mind coming and going)
Wash out your ears
　with snow!

Passing by
　　　the roadside image
　　　of some god
　　　I fall
　　　from my
　　　　　sacred cow
　　into
　　　Nothingness

JOHN BENNETT

(1920–)

from THE ZOO MANUSCRIPT

2

Caught up in joy and April and surprise,
sweet Jennifer becomes a magic where:
surrounded by small creatures of her Lord,
she brings the sun to glory in her hair,
and the blue Celtic distance lights her eyes.

Bemused and happy in the Children's Zoo,
she meets with love that can be purely met
amid the gentle seekings young things do:
child, fawn, kid, lamb and tiny leveret
define a force poor Huxley never knew.

4

Broader than boats, deeper than trout brooks are,
the hippo turns submersible at will,
or then bobs up like fatly muscled cork
that heaves his cloudy pond to overspill.

Earthshaking river-creature, miracle
of piggy flesh and long aquatic skill,
his tonnage is the pure amphibious,
not bound like some to fluke and spiracle.

Snoutdeep in hyacinths or deeper yet,
the hippo once possessed the Nile as home:
he was a Grecian joke; or he was Set;
he stood as solid as the church at Rome,
or rolled, transported, through disportive wet,
godlike and fat in hyacinthine foam.

7

Old dragon form *sans* wing and firelung,
and medieval as a corkindrill,
the alligator sleeps amid a spill
of mossy turtles dyed algaic green.
Incredibly heraldic, it is set
gris, mailed, and *couchant* on a field of wet.

It moves.
          A flare of basilisk leaps out
from vitric eye, from slowly yawning snout.

29

Unlike the seals that own a larger lake,
though hardly happier, the otters thrive
within a silver pool;
                    sweet clowns, they make
the April magic deeper;
                      their lithe forms
divide the frolic waters with the spark
of sunlight tossed through sunlight;
                                their eyes mark

a death for any shadow;
                        they contrive
kaleidoscopes from lissome joy;
                        they dive
through antic swirls as if their hearts must raise
the world to matching joy, warmblooded, bright.

Then here see water, flesh, and fire glance
upon and through each other:
                        such acts praise
a God who swims through all evolving worlds
as He creates them out of death and night.

The Paraclete sustains the otter dance
and all the dances in the spheres of light.

Episode:

Father and Small Son

(*In Memory of John Garrigan*)

My father, Irish, good with words and song,
had shoulders like Cuchulain's in his pride,
had arms like steel-and-leather rams, yet he
went gentle as a woman through his world.

One morning while we walked a Berkshire path,
he stopped, bent down, parted the springing grass,
then straightened up and turned and smiled at me,
a slight green ribbon moving in his hand,
a sudden grass-snake held before my eyes
but held away to keep my fear away:
Not now in Ireland. Never there, perhaps.
This kind lives easy. See how shy he is!

So said my father, holding up a snake
as delicate as morning, a green flame
that wrapped itself around his dreaming wrist
and waited there for what the future was.

O! he was gentle with that alien flesh!

They never bite. You cannot make them bite.
Like jewels, see! God's jewels. One of them.

He put the snake down softly on the grass;
it flowed into its anonymity,
and we walked homeward through the shining air,
our love emphatic as the snake was green.

Elegy for Anne Jones

Born in Canada, 1892, Died in Illinois, 1966

In your last autumn, Anne, while efreet winds
mewled through the shrunken fields, through the torn trees
outside your window, alien Illinois
whispered with murderous endings. Harvests burned
in tilt and wither on the ravelled slopes,
hurt fishes wandered through the narrow creeks,
the splintered patterns of a final year
dissolved to starling shadows on dead leaves,
and your grey days went spinning, droning, spinning
through wild, disorient weathers of the flesh.

And there we could not come although we came
through other weathers on sad afternoons.

Forcing ourselves to know your death, we came
from the parched city, north on the strict road
past blowzy suburbs and their scurfy lawns,
past taverns blaring under go-go signs,
past farmland bulldozed raw to six per cent,
past roadside ditches crammed with coils of weed,
along the rest-home driveway limned by elms,
then down the empty hallways to your room.

Grown impotent, grown sick with impotence,
we sat on rigid chairs in the hired room

and watched you where you lay so deeply marred,
so lost in whiteness on the narrow bed,
and all our skill was love, was not enough
to keep you from the cold that sucked you down
through bleak dimensions and increasing night.

Lipped by its edge, the sweat and stale of death,
we sat in terror through long afternoons.
The measured sunlight crumpled into shade,
and though the Crab, expected, stayed apart,
your flesh forgot its offices, forgot
its patterns of renewal while it let
your brain grow skimbleskamble for the blood
that could not rise to loose your memory
nor let your eyes accept their present world.

Your body failed you, then it failed to fail,
and time by that grey treason hurt you still,
half drowned in darkness, half released to light.
We sat and watched you dying and we learned
the quick, disorient weathers of the heart.

We mourned you then. Through droning afternoons,
we mourned your hurt in impotence and hurt.
We mourned you then. We did not mourn when all
the broken years collapsed and you were free.

At a day's ending, Anne, your ending came.
Clichés of twilight flooded through the room
and you were free, made purely regnant in
the long, pure kingdoms of remembered love.

Ah, Anne! Anne! Again in a turning year,
beyond clear windows, swift on April's lawn,
your daughter's children bruit the themes of joy.
Blessed by the year's renewal and green leaves,
they race and tumble through the spheres of day,
singing the song your singing made for them.

You now in Light and they in lesser light
merge, merge in the long unities of love,
and your sweet human seasons turn again
in the quick, golden weathers of the heart.

from THE STRUCK LEVIATHAN

Bulkington: Musing at the Helm, Midnight

From the strict rudder back toward shapeless gloom,
green fire lips and curls along the wake,
then fades to less than starshine on the waves.

Beneath the keel, the gliding Maldive sharks
act out the sea's assertion of the Word—
or partly some assertion of the Word—
while plankton, borne on wandering sea drifts,
act out that fiery pattern of the Word:
here I act out whatever *Yes!* I dare.

Tonight the sea sounds like a massive lung
breathing the sky. Dull thought! Where's chest or brain?
A bodiless lung that eats the wind? *BUT*:

the whale-filled veins of the sea, aye! shark-filled, God-filled,
and I, the fleeting observer, poised for a time
among brief shadows made of oak and flesh,
poised Oh! momently between the beginning and ending
that is my Beginning
                    was the Word
                            in the Beginning
was the Word and the Word was God.
ἐν ἀρχῇ . . . my single tag of Greek translates to use!

Ishmael: The Pod

Under soft sunlight
on the glinting tides
the gentle sea beasts roll
in love or loving play.

Those children of salt time—
those bulls whose greatly muscled sex
would cause the Bull to stare,
those cows whose filling wombs make birth
the absolute of love,
those calves whose innocence hurls them
through tides of hugest joy—
those tons of flesh are gentle as the kiss
that other lovers give.

The halcyon sea and its great beasts are one:
God's holy purpose, single, multiform,
defines a joyous image of itself.

Ahab: His Vision of the Kraken

Where green-skulled whalemen lie, where no tides run,
deep down and dark in that unsculptured gloom,
the great sea squid gropes blindly unaware
of lean Egyptians drowned in spicy rock
or Capricorn knocked hornless in the east,
a blare of goatcry shaking constellations.

Deep down and dark where mudbones gird the world,
by arm and sucking arm and sucking arm,
a polyp blob creeps through the heavy depths
where Satan, homeless, might establish home.

Ahab: At His Cabin Window, Midnight

This shackling cube! caged concentrate of space
borne rigidly above the swirling tides
that suck along the strakes and rudderpost!
Cribbed in this darkly pitching coffin, I
can watch my mind plumb through immensities,
through the chill malice of a universe
that Starbuck might no sooner learn to fear
than he did mother's milk!
                                    Poor mooncalf! grown
brawny as oak, but in his ultimates
as flimsy as some village natural
that cucks and coos over an autumn leaf,
mistaking scarlet for a sign of joy!

I know what he can never dare to know:
by my hurt driven hard, I ram the voids,
denying them by ramming through them, thus!
and chart a godlike course.

                              No single sea
can float the keelson of my great intent:
the winds that rip that wavecurve into spume
are subject to my sail; and all the stars
that crack the firmament with frozen light
are merely points upon the private chart
that leads me circling back to my whole self!

HOWARD NEMEROV

(1920–)

Brainstorm

The house was shaken by a rising wind
That rattled window and door. He sat alone
In an upstairs room and heard these things: a blind
Ran up with a bang, a door slammed, a groan
Came from some hidden joist, a leaky tap,
At any silence of the wind walked like
A blind man through the house. Timber and sap
Revolt, he thought, from washer, baulk and spike.
Bent to his book, continued unafraid
Until the crows came down from their loud flight
To walk along the rooftree overhead.
Their horny feet, so near but out of sight,
Scratched on the slate; when they were blown away
He heard their wings beat till they came again,
While the wind rose, and the house seemed to sway,
And window panes began to blind with rain.
The house was talking, not to him, he thought,
But to the crows; the crows were talking back
In their black voices. The secret might be out:
Houses are only trees stretched on the rack.
And once the crows knew, all nature would know.
Fur, leaf and feather would invade the form,
Nail rust with rain and shingle warp with snow,

Vine tear the wall, till any straw-borne storm
Could rip both roof and rooftree off and show
Naked to nature what they had kept warm.

He came to feel the crows walk on his head
As if he were the house, their crooked feet
Scratched, through the hair, his scalp. He might be **dead,**
It seemed, and all the noises underneath
Be but the cooling of the sinews, veins,
Juices, and sodden sacks suddenly let go;
While in his ruins of wiring, his burst mains,
The rainy wind had been set free to blow
Until the green uprising and mob rule
That ran the world had taken over him,
Split him like seed, and set him in the school
Where any crutch can learn to be a limb.

Inside his head he heard the stormy crows.

Runes

". . . insaniebam salubriter et moriebar vitaliter."

ST. AUGUSTINE

I

This is about the stillness in moving things,
In running water, also in the sleep
Of winter seeds, where time to come has tensed
Itself, enciphering a script so fine
Only the hourglass can magnify it, only
The years unfold its sentence from the root.
I have considered such things often, but
I cannot say I have thought deeply of them:
That is my theme, of thought and the defeat
Of thought before its object, where it turns
As from a mirror, and returns to be
The thought of something and the thought of thought,

A trader doubly burdened, commercing
Out of one stillness and into another.

II

About Ulysses, the learned have reached two
Distinct conclusions. In one, he secretly
Returns to Ithaca, is recognized
By Euryclea, destroys the insolent suitors,
And makes himself known to Penelope,
Describing the bed he built; then, at the last
Dissolve, we see him with Telemachus
Leaving the palace, planning to steal sheep:
The country squire resumes a normal life.
But in the other, out beyond the gates
Of Hercules, gabbling persuasively
About virtue and knowledge, he sails south
To disappear from sight behind the sun;
Drowning near blessed shores he flames in hell.
I do not know which ending is the right one.

III

Sunflowers, traders rounding the horn of time
Into deep afternoons, sleepy with gain,
The fall of silence has begun to storm
Around you where you nod your heavy heads
Whose bare poles, raking out of true, will crack,
Driving your wreckage on the world's lee shore.
Your faces no more will follow the sun,
But bow down to the ground with a heavy truth
That dereliction learns, how charity
Is strangled out of selfishness at last;
When, golden misers in the courts of summer,
You are stripped of gain for coining images
And broken on this quarter of the wheel,
It is on savage ground you spill yourselves,
And spend the tarnished silver of your change.

IV

The seed sleeps in the furnaces of death,
A cock's egg slept till hatching by a serpent
Wound in his wintry coil, a spring so tight
In his radical presence that every tense
Is now. Out of this head the terms of kind,
Distributed in syntax, come to judgment,
Are basilisks who write our sentences
Deep at the scripture's pith, in rooted tongues,
How one shall marry while another dies.
Give us our ignorance, the family tree
Grows upside down and shakes its heavy fruit,
Whose buried stones philosophers have sought.
For each stone bears the living word, each word
Will be made flesh, and all flesh fall to seed:
Such stones from the tree; and from the stones, such blood.

V

The fat time of the year is also time
Of the Atonement; birds to the berry bushes,
Men to the harvest; a time to answer for
Both present plenty and emptiness to come.
When the slain legal deer is salted down,
When apples smell like goodness, cold in the cellar,
You hear the ram's horn sounded in the high
Mount of the Lord, and you lift up your eyes
As though by this observance you might hide
The dry husk of an eaten heart which brings
Nothing to offer up, no sacrifice
Acceptable but the canceled-out desires
And satisfactions of another year's
Abscess, whose zero in His winter's mercy
Still hides the undecipherable seed.

VI

White water now in the snowflake's prison,
A mad king in a skullcap thinks these thoughts

In regular hexagons, each one unlike
Each of the others. The atoms of memory,
Like those that Democritus knew, have hooks
At either end, but these? Insane tycoon,
These are the riches of order snowed without end
In this distracted globe, where is no state
To fingerprint the flakes or number these
Moments melting in flight, seeds mirroring
Substance without position or a speed
And course unsubstanced. What may the spring be,
Deep in the atom, among galactic snows,
But the substance of things hoped for, argument
Of things unseen? White water, fall and fall.

VII

Unstable as water, thou shalt not excel
—Said to the firstborn, the dignity and strength,
And the defiler of his father's bed.
Fit motto for a dehydrated age
Nervously watering whisky and stock,
Quick-freezing dreams into realities.
Brain-surgeons have produced the proustian syndrome,
But patients dunk their tasteless madeleines
In vain, those papers that the Japanese
Amused themselves by watering until
They flowered and became Combray, flower
No more. The plastic and cosmetic arts
Unbreakably record the last word and
The least word, till sometimes even the Muse,
In her transparent raincoat, resembles a condom.

VIII

To go low, to be as nothing, to die,
To sleep in the dark water threading through
The fields of ice, the soapy, frothing water
That slithers under the culvert below the road,
Water of dirt, water of death, dark water,
And through the tangle of the sleeping roots

Under the coppery cold beech woods, the green
Pinewoods, and past the buried hulls of things
To come, and humbly through the breathing dreams
Of all small creatures sleeping in the earth;
To fall with the weight of things down on the one
Still ebbing stream, to go on to the end
With the convict hunted through the swamp all night.
The dog's corpse in the ditch, to come at last
Into the pit where zero's eye is closed.

IX

In this dehydrated time of digests, pills
And condensations, the most expensive presents
Are thought to come in the smallest packages:
In atoms, for example. There are still
To be found, at carnivals, men who engrave
The Lord's Prayer on a grain of wheat for pennies,
But they are a dying race, unlike the men
Now fortunate, who bottle holy water
In plastic tears, and bury mustard seeds
In lucite lockets, and for safety sell
To be planted on the dashboard of your car
The statues, in durable celluloid,
Of Mary and St. Christopher, who both
With humble power in the world's floodwaters
Carried their heavy Savior and their Lord.

X

White water, white water, feather of a form
Between the stones, is the race run to stay
Or pass away? Your utterance is riddled,
Rainbowed and clear and cold, tasting of stone,
Its brilliance blinds me. But still I have seen,
White water, at the breaking of the ice,
When the high places render up the new
Children of water and their tumbling light
Laughter runs down the hills, and the small fist
Of the seed unclenches in the day's dazzle,

How happiness is helpless before your fall,
White water, and history is no more than
The shadows thrown by clouds on mountainsides,
A distant chill, when all is brought to pass
By rain and birth and rising of the dead.

XI

A holy man said to me, "Split the stick
And there is Jesus." When I split the stick
To the dark marrow and the splintery grain
I saw nothing that was not wood, nothing
That was not God, and I began to dream
How from the tree that stood between the rivers
Came Aaron's rod that crawled in front of Pharaoh,
And came the rod of Jesse flowering
In all the generations of the Kings,
And came the timbers of the second tree,
The sticks and yardarms of the holy three-
masted vessel whereon the Son of Man
Hung between thieves, and came the crown of thorns,
The lance and ladder, when was shed that blood
Streamed in the grain of Adam's tainted seed.

XII

Consider how the seed lost by a bird
Will harbor in its branches most remote
Descendants of the bird; while everywhere
And unobserved, the soft green stalks and tubes
Of water are hardening into wood, whose hide,
Gnarled, knotted, flowing, and its hidden grain,
Remember how the water is streaming still.
Now does the seed asleep, as in a dream
Where time is compacted under pressures of
Another order, crack open like stone
From whose division pours a stream, between
The raindrop and the sea, running in one
Direction, down, and gathering in its course
That bitter salt which spices us the food
We sweat for, and the blood and tears we shed.

XIII

There sailed out on the river, Conrad saw,
The dreams of men, the seeds of commonwealths,
The germs of Empire. To the ends of the earth
One many-veined bloodstream swayed the hulls
Of darkness gone, of darkness still to come,
And sent its tendrils steeping through the roots
Of wasted continents. That echoing pulse
Carried the ground swell of all sea-returns
Muttering under history, and its taste,
Saline and cold, was as a mirror of
The taste of human blood. The sailor leaned
To lick the mirror clean, the somber and
Immense mirror that Conrad saw, and saw
The other self, the sacred Cain of blood
Who would seed a commonwealth in the Land of Nod.

XIV

There is a threshold, that meniscus where
The strider walks on drowning waters, or
That tense, curved membrane of the camera's lens
Which darkness holds against the battering light
And the distracted drumming of the world's
Importunate plenty.—Now that threshold,
The water of the eye where the world walks
Delicately, is as a needle threaded
From the reel of a raveling stream, to stitch
Dissolving figures in a watered cloth,
A damask either-sided as the shroud
Of the lord of Ithaca, labored at in light,
Destroyed in darkness, while the spidery oars
Carry his keel across deep mysteries
To harbor in unfathomable mercies.

XV

To watch water, to watch running water
Is to know a secret, seeing the twisted rope

Of runnels on the hillside, the small freshets
Leaping and limping down the tilted field
In April's light, the green, grave and opaque
Swirl in the millpond where the current slides
To be combed and carded silver at the fall;
It is a secret. Or it is not to know
The secret, but to have it in your keeping,
A locked box, Bluebeard's room, the deathless thing
Which it is death to open. Knowing the secret,
Keeping the secret—herringbones of light
Ebbing on beaches, the huge artillery
Of tides—it is not knowing, it is not keeping,
But being the secret hidden from yourself.

A Spell before Winter

After the red leaf and the gold have gone,
Brought down by the wind, then by hammering rain
Bruised and discolored, when October's flame
Goes blue to guttering in the cusp, this land
Sinks deeper into silence, darker into shade.
There is a knowledge in the look of things,
The old hills hunch before the north wind blows.

Now I can see certain simplicities
In the darkening rust and tarnish of the time,
And say over the certain simplicities,
The running water and the standing stone,
The yellow haze of the willow and the black
Smoke of the elm, the silver, silent light
Where suddenly, readying toward nightfall,
The sumac's candelabrum darkly flames.
And I speak to you now with the land's voice,
It is the cold, wild land that says to you
A knowledge glimmers in the sleep of things:
The old hills hunch before the north wind blows.

Human Things

When the sun gets low, in winter,
The lapstreaked side of a red barn
Can put so flat a stop to its light
You'd think everything was finished.

Each dent, fray, scratch, or splinter,
Any gray weathering where the paint
Has scaled off, is a healed scar
Grown harder with the wounds of light.

Only a tree's trembling shadow
Crosses that ruined composure; even
Nail holes look deep enough to swallow
Whatever light has left to give.

And after sundown, when the wall
Slowly surrenders its color, the rest
Remains, its high, obstinate
Hulk more shadowy than the night.

De Anima

Now it is night, now in the brilliant room
A girl stands at the window looking out,
But sees, in the darkness of the frame,
Only her own image.

And there is a young man across the street
Who looks at the girl and into the brilliant room.
They might be in love, might be about to meet,
If this were a romance.

In looking at herself, she tries to look
Beyond herself, and half become another,

Admiring and resenting, maybe dreaming
Her lover might see her so.

The other, the stranger standing in cold and dark,
Looks at the young girl in her crystalline room.
He sees clearly, and hopelessly desires,
A life that is not his.

Given the blindness of her self-possession,
The luminous vision revealed to his despair,
We look to both sides of the glass at once
And see no future in it.

These pure divisions hurt us in some realm
Of parable beyond belief, beyond
The temporal mind. Why is it sorrowful?
Why do we want them together?

Is it the spirit, ransacking through the earth
After its image, its being, its begetting?
The spirit sorrows, for what lovers bring
Into the world is death,

The most exclusive romance, after all,
The sort that lords and ladies listen to
With selfish tears, when she draws down the shade,
When he has turned away,

When the blind embryo with his bow of bees,
His candied arrows tipped with flower heads,
Turns from them too, for mercy or for grief
Refusing to be, refusing to die.

The Dial Tone

A moment of silence, first, then there it is.
But not as though it only now began

Because of my attention; rather, this,
That I begin at one point on its span
Brief kinship with its endless going on.

Between society and self it poses
Neutrality perceptible to sense,
Being a no man's land the lawyer uses
Much as the lover does: charged innocence,
It sits on its own electrified fence,

Is neither pleased nor hurt by race results
Or by the nasty thing John said to Jane;
Is merely interrupted by insults,
Devotions, lecheries; after the sane
And mad hang up at once, it will remain.

Suppose that in God a black bumblebee
Or colorless hummingbird buzzed all night,
Divided the abyss up equally;
And carried its neither sweetness nor its light
Across impossible eternity.

Now take this hummingbird, this bee, away;
And like the Cheshire smile without its cat
The remnant hum continues on its way,
Unwinged, able at once to move and wait,
An endless freight train on an endless flat.

Something like that, some loneliest of powers
That never has confessed its secret name.
I do not doubt that if you gave it hours
And then lost patience, it would be the same
After you left that it was before you came.

Beyond the Pleasure Principle

It comes up out of the darkness, and it returns
Into a further darkness. After the monster,
There is the monster's mother to be dealt with,

Dimly perceived at first, or only speculated on
Between the shadows and reflexions of the tidal cave,
Among the bones and armored emptiness
Of the princes of a former time, who failed.

Our human thought arose at first in myth,
And going far enough became a myth once more;
Its pretty productions in between, those splendid
Tarnhelms and winged sandals, mirroring shields
And swords unbreakable, of guaranteed
Fatality, those endlessly winding labyrinths
In which all minotaurs might find themselves at home,
Deceived us with false views of the end, leaving
Invisible the obstinate residuum, so cloudy, cold,
Archaic, that waits beyond both purpose and fulfilment.

There, toward the end, when the left-handed wish
Is satisfied as it is given up, when the hero
Endures his cancer and more obstinately than ever
Grins at the consolations of religion as at a child's
Frightened pretensions, and when his great courage
Becomes a wish to die, there appears, so obscurely,
Pathetically, out of the wounded torment and the play,
A something primitive and appealing, and still dangerous,
That crawls on bleeding hands and knees over the floor
Toward him, and whispers as if to confess: *again, again*.

RICHARD WILBUR
(1921–)

The Pardon

My dog lay dead five days without a grave
In the thick of summer, hid in a clump of pine
And a jungle of grass and honeysuckle-vine.
I who had loved him while he kept alive

Went only close enough to where he was
To sniff the heavy honeysuckle-smell
Twined with another odor heavier still
And hear the flies' intolerable buzz.

Well, I was ten and very much afraid.
In my kind world the dead were out of range
And I could not forgive the sad or strange
In beast or man. My father took the spade

And buried him. Last night I saw the grass
Slowly divide (it was the same scene
But now it glowed a fierce and mortal green)
And saw the dog emerging. I confess

I felt afraid again, but still he came
In the carnal sun, clothed in a hymn of flies,

And death was breeding in his lively eyes.
I started in to cry and call his name,

Asking forgiveness of his tongueless head.
. . . I dreamt the past was never past redeeming:
But whether this was false or honest dreaming
I beg death's pardon now. And mourn the dead.

Still, Citizen Sparrow

Still, citizen sparrow, this vulture which you call
Unnatural, let him but lumber again to air
Over the rotten office, let him bear
The carrion ballast up, and at the tall

Tip of the sky lie cruising. Then you'll see
That no more beautiful bird is in heaven's height,
No wider more placid wings, no watchfuller flight;
He shoulders nature there, the frightfully free,

The naked-headed one. Pardon him, you
Who dart in the orchard aisles, for it is he
Devours death, mocks mutability,
Has heart to make an end, keeps nature new.

Thinking of Noah, childheart, try to forget
How for so many bedlam hours his saw
Soured the song of birds with its wheezy gnaw,
And the slam of his hammer all the day beset

The people's ears. Forget that he could bear
To see the towns like coral under the keel,
And the fields so dismal deep. Try rather to feel
How high and weary it was, on the waters where

He rocked his only world, and everyone's.
Forgive the hero, you who would have died

Gladly with all you knew; he rode that tide
To Ararat; all men are Noah's sons.

Love Calls Us to the Things of This World

The eyes open to a cry of pulleys,
And spirited from sleep, the astounded soul
Hangs for a moment bodiless and simple
As false dawn.
　　　　　　Outside the open window
The morning air is all awash with angels.

Some are in bed-sheets, some are in blouses,
Some are in smocks: but truly there they are.
Now they are rising together in calm swells
Of halcyon feeling, filling whatever they wear
With the deep joy of their impersonal breathing;

Now they are flying in place, conveying
The terrible speed of their omnipresence, moving
And staying like white water; and now of a sudden
They swoon down into so rapt a quiet
That nobody seems to be there.
　　　　　　　　　　The soul shrinks

From all that it is about to remember,
From the punctual rape of every blessèd day,
And cries,
　　　　　"Oh, let there be nothing on earth but laundry,
Nothing but rosy hands in the rising steam
And clear dances done in the sight of heaven."

Yet, as the sun acknowledges
With a warm look the world's hunks and colors,
The soul descends once more in bitter love
To accept the waking body, saying now
In a changed voice as the man yawns and rises,

"Bring them down from their ruddy gallows;
Let there be clean linen for the backs of thieves;
Let lovers go fresh and sweet to be undone,
And the heaviest nuns walk in a pure floating
Of dark habits,
                    keeping their difficult balance."

A Voice from under the Table

To Robert and Jane Brooks

How shall the wine be drunk, or the woman known?
I take this world for better or for worse,
But seeing rose carafes conceive the sun
My thirst conceives a fierier universe:
And then I toast the birds in the burning trees
That chant their holy lucid drunkenness;
I swallowed all the phosphorus of the seas
Before I fell into this low distress.

You upright people all remember how
Love drove you first to the woods, and there you heard
The loose-mouthed wind complaining *Thou* and *Thou;*
My gawky limbs were shuddered by the word.
Most of it since was nothing but charades
To spell that hankering out and make an end,
But the softest hands against my shoulder-blades
Only increased the crying of the wind.

For this the goddess rose from the midland sea
And stood above the famous wine-dark wave,
To ease our drouth with clearer mystery
And be a South to all our flights of love.
And down by the selfsame water I have seen
A blazing girl with skin like polished stone
Splashing until a far-out breast of green
Arose and with a rose contagion shone.

"A myrtle-shoot in hand, she danced; her hair
Cast on her back and shoulders a moving shade."
Was it some hovering light that showed her fair?
Was it of chafing dark that light was made?
Perhaps it was Archilochus' fantasy,
Or that his saying sublimed the thing he said.
All true enough; and true as well that she
Was beautiful, and danced, and is now dead.

Helen was no such high discarnate thought
As men in dry symposia pursue,
But was as bitterly fugitive, not to be caught
By what men's arms in love or fight could do.
Groan in your cell; rape Troy with sword and flame;
The end of thirst exceeds experience.
A devil told me it was all the same
Whether to fail by spirit or by sense.

God keep me a damned fool, nor charitably
Receive me into his shapely resignations.
I am a sort of martyr, as you see,
A horizontal monument to patience.
The calves of waitresses parade about
My helpless head upon this sodden floor.
Well, I am down again, but not yet out.
O sweet frustrations, I shall be back for more.

Beasts

Beasts in their major freedom
Slumber in peace tonight. The gull on his ledge
Dreams in the guts of himself the moon-plucked waves below,
And the sunfish leans on a stone, slept
By the lyric water,

In which the spotless feet
Of deer make dulcet splashes, and to which
The ripped mouse, safe in the owl's talon, cries

Concordance. Here there is no such harm
And no such darkness

As the selfsame moon observes
Where, warped in window-glass, it sponsors now
The werewolf's painful change. Turning his head away
On the sweaty bolster, he tries to remember
The mood of manhood,

But lies at last, as always,
Letting it happen, the fierce fur soft to his face,
Hearing with sharper ears the wind's exciting minors,
The leaves' panic, and the degradation
Of the heavy streams.

Meantime, at high windows
Far from thicket and pad-fall, suitors of excellence
Sigh and turn from their work to construe again the painful
Beauty of heaven, the lucid moon
And the risen hunter,

Making such dreams for men
As told will break their hearts as always, bringing
Monsters into the city, crows on the public statues,
Navies fed to the fish in the dark
Unbridled waters.

A Baroque Wall-Fountain in the Villa Sciarra

For Dore and Adja

Under the bronze crown
Too big for the head of the stone cherub whose feet
A serpent has begun to eat,
Sweet water brims a cockle and braids down

Past spattered mosses, breaks
On the tipped edge of a second shell, and fills

The massive third below. It spills
In threads then from the scalloped rim, and makes

    A scrim or summery tent
For a faun-ménage and their familiar goose.
    Happy in all that ragged, loose
Collapse of water, its effortless descent

    And flatteries of spray,
The stocky god upholds the shell with ease,
    Watching, about his shaggy knees,
The goatish innocence of his babes at play;

    His fauness all the while
Leans forward, slightly, into a clambering mesh
    Of water-lights, her sparkling flesh
In a saecular ecstasy, her blinded smile

    Bent on the sand floor
Of the trefoil pool, where ripple-shadows come
    And go in swift reticulum,
More addling to the eye than wine, and more

    Interminable to thought
Than pleasure's calculus. Yet since this all
    Is pleasure, flash, and waterfall,
Must it not be too simple? Are we not

    More intricately expressed
In the plain fountains that Maderna set
    Before St. Peter's—the main jet
Struggling aloft until it seems at rest

    In the act of rising, until
The very wish of water is reversed,
    That heaviness borne up to burst
In a clear, high, cavorting head, to fill

With blaze, and then in gauze
Delays, in a gnatlike shimmering, in a fine
    Illumined version of itself, decline,
And patter on the stones its own applause?

    If that is what men are
Or should be, if those water-saints display
    The pattern of our areté,[1]
What of these showered fauns in their bizarre,

    Spangled, and plunging house?
They are at rest in fulness of desire
    For what is given, they do not tire
Of the smart of the sun, the pleasant water-douse

    And riddled pool below,
Reproving our disgust and our ennui
    With humble insatiety.
Francis, perhaps, who lay in sister snow

    Before the wealthy gate
Freezing and praising, might have seen in this
    No trifle, but a shade of bliss—
That land of tolerable flowers, that state

    As near and far as grass
Where eyes become the sunlight, and the hand
    Is worthy of water: the dreamt land
Toward which all hungers leap, all pleasures pass.

Advice to a Prophet *

When you come, as you soon must, to the streets of our city,
    Mad-eyed from stating the obvious,

---

[1] Note: *areté*, a Greek word meaning roughly "virtue."—Author.
* Hephaestus, invoked by Achilles, scalded the river Xanthus (Scamander) in *Iliad* xxi.—Author's note.

Not proclaiming our fall but begging us
In God's name to have self-pity,

Spare us all word of the weapons, their force and range,
The long numbers that rocket the mind;
Our slow, unreckoning hearts will be left behind,
Unable to fear what is too strange.

Nor shall you scare us with talk of the death of the race.
How should we dream of this place without us?—
The sun mere fire, the leaves untroubled about us,
A stone look on the stone's face?

Speak of the world's own change. Though we cannot conceive
Of an undreamt thing, we know to our cost
How the dreamt cloud crumbles, the vines are blackened by frost,
How the view alters. We could believe,

If you told us so, that the white-tailed deer will slip
Into perfect shade, grown perfectly shy,
The lark avoid the reaches of our eye,
The jack-pine lose its knuckled grip

On the cold ledge, and every torrent burn
As Xanthus once, its gliding trout
Stunned in a twinkling. What should we be without
The dolphin's arc, the dove's return,

These things in which we have seen ourselves and spoken?
Ask us, prophet, how we shall call
Our natures forth when that live tongue is all
Dispelled, that glass obscured or broken

In which we have said the rose of our love and the clean
Horse of our courage, in which beheld
The singing locust of the soul unshelled,
And all we mean or wish to mean.

Ask us, ask us whether with the worldless rose
Our hearts shall fail us; come demanding
Whether there shall be lofty or long standing
When the bronze annals of the oak-tree close.

She

What was her beauty in our first estate
When Adam's will was whole, and the least thing
Appeared the gift and creature of his king,
How should we guess? Resemblance had to wait

For separation, and in such a place
She so partook of water, light, and trees
As not to look like any one of these.
He woke and gazed into her naked face.

But then she changed, and coming down amid
The flocks of Abel and the fields of Cain,
Clothed in their wish, her Eden graces hid,
A shape of plenty with a mop of grain,

She broke upon the world, in time took on
The look of every labor and its fruits.
Columnar in a robe of pleated lawn
She cupped her patient hand for attributes,

Was radiant captive of the farthest tower
And shed her honor on the fields of war,
Walked in her garden at the evening hour,
Her shadow like a dark ogival door,

Breasted the seas for all the westward ships
And, come to virgin country, changed again—
A moonlike being truest in eclipse,
And subject goddess of the dreams of men.

Tree, temple, valley, prow, gazelle, machine,
More named and nameless than the morning star,
Lovely in every shape, in all unseen,
We dare not wish to find you as you are,

Whose apparition, biding time until
Desire decay and bring the latter age,
Shall flourish in the ruins of our will
And deck the broken stones like saxifrage.

In the Smoking-Car

The eyelids meet. He'll catch a little nap.
The grizzled, crew-cut head drops to his chest.
It shakes above the briefcase on his lap.
Close voices breathe, "Poor sweet, he did his best."

"Poor sweet, poor sweet," the bird-hushed glades repeat,
Through which in quiet pomp his litter goes,
Carried by native girls with naked feet.
A sighing stream concurs in his repose.

Could he but think, he might recall to mind
The righteous mutiny or sudden gale
That beached him here; the dear ones left behind . . .
So near the ending, he forgets the tale.

Were he to lift his eyelids now, he might
Behold his maiden porters, brown and bare.
But even here he has no appetite.
It is enough to know that they are there.

Enough that now a honeyed music swells,
The gentle, mossed declivities begin,
And the whole air is full of flower-smells.
Failure, the longed-for valley, takes him in.

Fern-Beds in Hampshire County

Although from them
Steep stands of beech and sugar-maple stem,
Varied with birch, or ash, or basswood trees
Which spring will throng with bees,
While intervening thickets grow complex
With flower, seed, and variance of sex,
And the whole wood conspires, by change of kind,
To break the purchase of the gathering mind,
The ferns are as they were.
Let but a trifling stir
Of air traverse their pools or touchy beds
And some will dip their heads,
Some switch a moment like a scribbling quill
And then be still,
Sporadic as in guarded bays
The rockweed slaps a bit, or sways.
Then let the wind grow bluff, and though
The sea lies far to eastward, far below,
These fluent spines, with whipped pale underside,
Will climb through timber as a smoking tide
Through pier-stakes, beat their sprays about the base
Of every boulder, scale its creviced face
And, wave on wave, like some green infantry,
Storm all the slope as high as eye can see.
Whatever at the heart
Of creatures makes them branch and burst apart,
Or at the core of star or tree may burn
At last to turn
And make an end of time,
These airy plants, tenacious of their prime,
Dwell in the swept recurrence of
An ancient conquest, shaken by first love
As when they answered to the boomed command
That the sea's green rise up and take the land.

PHILIP LARKIN

(1922–)

[One Man Walking a Deserted Platform]

One man walking a deserted platform;
Dawn coming, and rain
Driving across a darkening autumn;
One man restlessly waiting a train
While round the streets the wind runs wild,
Beating each shuttered house, that seems
Folded full of the dark silk of dreams,
A shell of sleep cradling a wife or child.

Who can this ambition trace,
To be each dawn perpetually journeying?
To trick this hour when lovers re-embrace
With the unguessed-at heart riding
The winds as gulls do? What lips said
Starset and cockcrow call the dispossessed
On to the next desert, lest
Love sink a grave round the still-sleeping head?

[Heaviest of Flowers, the Head]

Heaviest of flowers, the head
Forever hangs above a stormless bed;

Hands that the heart can govern
Shall be at last by darker hands unwoven;
Every exultant sense
Unstrung to silence—
The sun drift away.

And all the memories that best
Run back beyond this season of unrest
Shall lie upon the earth
That gave them birth.
Like fallen apples, they will lose
Their sweetness at the bruise,
And then decay.

Lines on a Young Lady's Photograph Album

At last you yielded up the album, which,
Once open, sent me distracted. All your ages
Matt and glossy on the thick black pages!
Too much confectionery, too rich:
I choke on such nutritious images.

My swivel eye hungers from pose to pose—
In pigtails, clutching a reluctant cat;
Or furred yourself, a sweet girl-graduate;
Or lifting a heavy-headed rose
Beneath a trellis, or in a trilby hat

(Faintly disturbing, that, in several ways)—
From every side you strike at my control,
Not least through these disquieting chaps who loll
At ease about your earlier days:
Not quite your class, I'd say, dear, on the whole.

But o, photography! as no art is,
Faithful and disappointing! that records
Dull days as dull, and hold-it smiles as frauds,

And will not censor blemishes
Like washing-lines, and Hall's-Distemper boards,

But shows the cat as disinclined, and shades
A chin as doubled when it is, what grace
Your candour thus confers upon her face!
How overwhelmingly persuades
That this is a real girl in a real place,

In every sense empirically true!
Or is it just *the past?* Those flowers, that gate,
These misty parks and motors, lacerate
Simply by being over; you
Contract my heart by looking out of date.

Yes, true; but in the end, surely, we cry
Not only at exclusion, but because
It leaves us free to cry. We know *what was*
Won't call on us to justify
Our grief, however hard we yowl across

The gap from eye to page. So I am left
To mourn (without a chance of consequence)
You, balanced on a bike against a fence;
To wonder if you'd spot the theft
Of this one of you bathing; to condense,

In short, a past that no one now can share,
No matter whose your future; calm and dry,
It holds you like a heaven, and you lie
Unvariably lovely there,
Smaller and clearer as the years go by.

Wedding-Wind

The wind blew all my wedding-day,
And my wedding-night was the night of the high **wind;**

And a stable door was banging, again and again,
That he must go and shut it, leaving me
Stupid in candlelight, hearing rain,
Seeing my face in the twisted candlestick,
Yet seeing nothing. When he came back
He said the horses were restless, and I was sad
That any man or beast that night should lack
The happiness I had.

                   Now in the day
All's ravelled under the sun by the wind's blowing.
He has gone to look at the floods, and I
Carry a chipped pail to the chicken-run,
Set it down, and stare. All is the wind
Hunting through clouds and forests, thrashing
My apron and the hanging cloths on the line.
Can it be borne, this bodying-forth by wind
Of joy my actions turn on, like a thread
Carrying beads? Shall I be let to sleep
Now this perpetual morning shares my bed?
Can even death dry up
These new delighted lakes, conclude
Our kneeling as cattle by all-generous waters?

Reasons for Attendance

The trumpet's voice, loud and authoritative,
Draws me a moment to the lighted glass
To watch the dancers—all under twenty-five—
Shifting intently, face to flushed face,
Solemnly on the beat of happiness.

—Or so I fancy, sensing the smoke and sweat,
The wonderful feel of girls. Why be out here?
But then, why be in there? Sex, yes, but what
Is sex? Surely, to think the lion's share
Of happiness is found by couples—sheer

Inaccuracy, as far as I'm concerned.
What calls me is that lifted, rough-tongued bell
(Art, if you like) whose individual sound
Insists I too am individual.
It speaks; I hear; others may hear as well,

But not for me, nor I for them; and so
With happiness. Therefore I stay outside,
Believing this; and they maul to and fro,
Believing that; and both are satisfied,
If no one has misjudged himself. Or lied.

Going

There is an evening coming in
Across the fields, one never seen before,
That lights no lamps.

Silken it seems at a distance, yet
When it is drawn up over the knees and breast
It brings no comfort.

Where has the tree gone, that locked
Earth to the sky? What is under my hands,
That I cannot feel?

What loads my hands down?

Maiden Name

Marrying left your maiden name disused.
Its five light sounds no longer mean your face,
Your voice, and all your variants of grace;
For since you were so thankfully confused
By law with someone else, you cannot be
Semantically the same as that young beauty:
It was of her that these two words were used.

Now it's a phrase applicable to no one,
Lying just where you left it, scattered through
Old lists, old programmes, a school prize or two,
Packets of letters tied with tartan ribbon—
Then is it scentless, weightless, strengthless, wholly
Untruthful? Try whispering it slowly.
No, it means you. Or, since you're past and gone,

It means what we feel now about you then:
How beautiful you were, and near, and young,
So vivid, you might still be there among
Those first few days, unfingermarked again.
So your old name shelters our faithfulness,
Instead of losing shape and meaning less
With your depreciating luggage laden.

Wires

The widest prairies have electric fences,
For though old cattle know they must not stray
Young steers are always scenting purer water
Not here but anywhere. Beyond the wires

Leads them to blunder up against the wires
Whose muscle-shredding violence gives no quarter.
Young steers become old cattle from that day,
Electric limits to their widest senses.

Church Going

Once I am sure there's nothing going on
I step inside, letting the door thud shut.
Another church: matting, seats, and stone,
And little books; sprawlings of flowers, cut
For Sunday, brownish now; some brass and stuff
Up at the holy end; the small neat organ;

And a tense, musty, unignorable silence,
Brewed God knows how long. Hatless, I take off
My cycle-clips in awkward reverence,

Move forward, run my hand around the font.
From where I stand, the roof looks almost new—
Cleaned, or restored? Someone would know: I don't.
Mounting the lectern, I peruse a few
Hectoring large-scale verses, and pronounce
'Here endeth' much more loudly than I'd meant.
The echoes snigger briefly. Back at the door
I sign the book, donate an Irish sixpence,
Reflect the place was not worth stopping for.

Yet stop I did: in fact I often do,
And always end much at a loss like this,
Wondering what to look for; wondering, too,
When churches fall completely out of use
What we shall turn them into, if we shall keep
A few cathedrals chronically on show,
Their parchment, plate and pyx in locked cases,
And let the rest rent-free to rain and sheep.
Shall we avoid them as unlucky places?

Or, after dark, will dubious women come
To make their children touch a particular stone;
Pick simples for a cancer; or on some
Advised night see walking a dead one?
Power of some sort or other will go on
In games, in riddles, seemingly at random;
But superstition, like belief, must die,
And what remains when disbelief has gone?
Grass, weedy pavement, brambles, buttress, sky,

A shape less recognisable each week,
A purpose more obscure. I wonder who
Will be the last, the very last, to seek
This place for what it was; one of the crew

That tap and jot and know what rood-lofts were?
Some ruin-bibber, randy for antique,
Or Christmas-addict, counting on a whiff
Of gown-and-bands and organ-pipes and myrrh?
Or will he be my representative,

Bored, uninformed, knowing the ghostly silt
Dispersed, yet tending to this cross of ground
Through suburb scrub because it held unspilt
So long and equably what since is found
Only in separation—marriage, and birth,
And death, and thoughts of these—for which was built
This special shell? For, though I've no idea
What this accoutred frowsty barn is worth,
It pleases me to stand in silence here;

A serious house on serious earth it is,
In whose blent air all our compulsions meet,
Are recognised, and robed as destinies.
And that much never can be obsolete,
Since someone will forever be surprising
A hunger in himself to be more serious,
And gravitating with it to this ground,
Which, he once heard, was proper to grow wise in,
If only that so many dead lie round.

Poetry of Departures

Sometimes you hear, fifth-hand,
As epitaph:
*He chucked up everything
And just cleared off,*
And always the voice will sound
Certain you approve
This audacious, purifying,
Elemental move.

And they are right, I think.
We all hate home
And having to be there:
I detest my room,
Its specially-chosen junk,
The good books, the good bed,
And my life, in perfect order:
So to hear it said

He walked out on the whole crowd
Leaves me flushed and stirred,
Like *Then she undid her dress*
Or *Take that you bastard*;
Surely I can, if he did?
And that helps me stay
Sober and industrious.
But I'd go today,

Yes, swagger the nut-strewn roads,
Crouch in the fo'c'sle
Stubbly with goodness, if
It weren't so artificial,
Such a deliberate step backwards
To create an object:
Books; china; a life
Reprehensibly perfect.

If, My Darling

If my darling were once to decide
Not to stop at my eyes,
But to jump, like Alice, with floating skirt into my head,

She would find no tables and chairs,
No mahogany claw-footed sideboards,
No undisturbed embers;

The tantalus would not be filled, nor the fender-seat cosy,
Nor the shelves stuffed with small-printed books for the Sabbath,
Nor the butler bibulous, the housemaids lazy:

She would find herself looped with the creep of varying light,
Monkey-brown, fish-grey, a string of infected circles
Loitering like bullies, about to coagulate;

Delusions that shrink to the size of a woman's glove
Then sicken inclusively outwards. She would also remark
The unwholesome floor, as it might be the skin of a grave,

From which ascends an adhesive sense of betrayal,
A Grecian statue kicked in the privates, money,
A swill-tub of finer feelings. But most of all

She'd be stopping her ears against the incessant recital
Intoned by reality, larded with technical terms,
Each one double-yolked with meaning and meaning's rebuttal:

For the skirl of that bulletin unpicks the world like a knot,
And to hear how the past is past and the future neuter
Might knock my darling off her unpriceable pivot.

Here

Swerving east, from rich industrial shadows
And traffic all night north; swerving through fields
Too thin and thistled to be called meadows,
And now and then a harsh-named halt, that shields
Workmen at dawn; swerving to solitude
Of skies and scarecrows, haystacks, hares and pheasants,
And the widening river's slow presence,
The piled gold clouds, the shining gull-marked mud,

Gathers to the surprise of a large town:
Here domes and statues, spires and cranes cluster
Beside grain-scattered streets, barge-crowded water,

And residents from raw estates, brought down
The dead straight miles by stealing flat-faced trolleys,
Push through plate-glass swing doors to their desires—
Cheap suits, red kitchen-ware, sharp shoes, iced lollies,
Electric mixers, toasters, washers, driers—

A cut-price crowd, urban yet simple, dwelling
Where only salesmen and relations come
Within a terminate and fishy-smelling
Pastoral of ships up streets, the slave museum,
Tattoo-shops, consulates, grim head-scarfed wives;
And out beyond its mortgaged half-built edges
Fast-shadowed wheat-fields, running high as hedges,
Isolate villages, where removed lives

Loneliness clarifies. Here silence stands
Like heat. Here leaves unnoticed thicken,
Hidden weeds flower, neglected waters quicken,
Luminously-peopled air ascends;
And past the poppies bluish neutral distance
Ends the land suddenly beyond a beach
Of shapes and shingle. Here is unfenced existence:
Facing the sun, untalkative, out of reach.

Home is so Sad

Home is so sad. It stays as it was left,
Shaped to the comfort of the last to go
As if to win them back. Instead, bereft
Of anyone to please, it withers so,
Having no heart to put aside the theft

And turn again to what it started as,
A joyous shot at how things ought to be,
Long fallen wide. You can see how it was:
Look at the pictures and the cutlery.
The music in the piano stool. That vase.

JAMES DICKEY

(1923–)

The Heaven of Animals

Here they are. The soft eyes open.
If they have lived in a wood
It is a wood.
If they have lived on plains
It is grass rolling
Under their feet forever.

Having no souls, they have come,
Anyway, beyond their knowing.
Their instincts wholly bloom
And they rise.
The soft eyes open.

To match them, the landscape flowers,
Outdoing, desperately
Outdoing what is required:
The richest wood,
The deepest field.

For some of these,
It could not be the place
It is, without blood.
These hunt, as they have done,
But with claws and teeth grown perfect,

More deadly than they can believe.
They stalk more silently,
And crouch on the limbs of trees,
And their descent
Upon the bright backs of their prey

May take years
In a sovereign floating of joy.
And those that are hunted
Know this as their life,
Their reward: to walk

Under such trees in full knowledge
Of what is in glory above them,
And to feel no fear,
But acceptance, compliance.
Fulfilling themselves without pain

At the cycle's center,
They tremble, they walk
Under the tree,
They fall, they are torn,
They rise, they walk again.

In the Tree House at Night

And now the green household is dark.
The half-moon completely is shining
On the earth-lighted tops of the trees.
To be dead, a house must be still.
The floor and the walls wave me slowly;
I am deep in them over my head.
The needles and pine cones about me

Are full of small birds at their roundest,
Their fists without mercy gripping
Hard down through the tree to the roots
To sing back at light when they feel it.

We lie here like angels in bodies,
My brothers and I, one dead,
The other asleep from much living,

In mid-air huddled beside me.
Dark climbed to us here as we climbed
Up the nails I have hammered all day
Through the sprained, comic rungs of the ladder
Of broom handles, crate slats, and laths
Foot by foot up the trunk to the branches
Where we came out at last over lakes

Of leaves, of fields disencumbered of earth
That move with the moves of the spirit.
Each nail that sustains us I set here;
Each nail in the house is now steadied
By my dead brother's huge, freckled hand.
Through the years, he has pointed his hammer
Up into these limbs, and told us

That we must ascend, and all lie here.
Step after step he has brought me,
Embracing the trunk as his body,
Shaking its limbs with my heartbeat,
Till the pine cones danced without wind
And fell from the branches like apples.
In the arm-slender forks of our dwelling

I breathe my live brother's light hair.
The blanket around us becomes
As solid as stone, and it sways.
With all my heart, I close
The blue, timeless eye of my mind.
Wind springs, as my dead brother smiles
And touches the tree at the root;

A shudder of joy runs up
The trunk; the needles tingle;
One bird uncontrollably cries.

The wind changes round, and I stir
Within another's life. Whose life?
Who is dead? Whose presence is living?
When may I fall strangely to earth,

Who am nailed to this branch by a spirit?
Can two bodies make up a third?
To sing, must I feel the world's light?
My green, graceful bones fill the air
With sleeping birds. Alone, alone
And with them I move gently.
I move at the heart of the world.

In the Lupanar at Pompeii

There are tracks which belong to wheels
Long since turned to air and time.
Those are the powerful chariots
I follow down cobblestones,
Not being dragged, exactly,
But not of my own will, either,
Going past the flower sellers'
And the cindery produce market
And the rich man's home, and the house
Of the man who kept a dog
Set in mosaic.

As tourist, but mostly as lecher,
I seek out the dwelling of women
Who all expect me, still, because
They expect anybody who comes.
I am ready to pay, and I do,
And then go in among them
Where on the dark walls of their home
They hold their eternal postures,
Doing badly drawn, exacting,
Too-willing, wide-eyed things
With dry-eyed art.

I sit down in one of the rooms
Where it happened again and again.
I could be in prison, or dead,
Cast down for my sins in a cell
Still filled with a terrible motion
Like the heaving and sighing of earth
To be free of the heat it restrains.
I feel in my heart how the heart
Of the mountain broke, and the women
Fled onto the damp of the walls
And shaped their embraces

To include whoever would come here
After the stone-cutting chariots.
I think of the marvel of lust
Which can always, at any moment,
Become more than it believed,
And almost always is less:
I think of its possible passing
Beyond, into tender awareness,
Into helplessness, weeping, and death:
It must be like the first
Soft floating of ash,

When, in the world's frankest hands,
Someone lay with his body shaken
Free of the self: that amazement—
For we who must try to explain
Ourselves in the house of this flesh
Never can tell the quick heat
Of our own from another's breathing,
Nor yet from the floating of feathers
That form in our lungs when the mountain
Settles like odd, warm snow against
Our willing limbs.

We never can really tell
Whether nature condemns us or loves us
As we lie here dying of breath

And the painted, unchanging women,
Believing the desperate dead
Where they stripped to the skin of the soul
And whispered to us, as to
Their panting, observing selves:
"Passion. Before we die
Let us hope for no longer
But truly know it."

The Dusk of Horses

Right under their noses, the green
Of the field is paling away
Because of something fallen from the sky.

They see this, and put down
Their long heads deeper in grass
That only just escapes reflecting them

As the dream of a millpond would.
The color green flees over the grass
Like an insect, following the red sun over

The next hill. The grass is white.
There is no cloud so dark and white at once;
There is no pool at dawn that deepens

Their faces and thirsts as this does.
Now they are feeding on solid
Cloud, and one by one,

With nails as silent as stars among the wood
Hewed down years ago and now rotten,
The stalls are put up around them.

Now if they lean, they come
On wood on any side. Not touching it, they sleep.
No beast ever lived who understood

What happened among the sun's fields,
Or cared why the color of grass
Fled over the hill while he stumbled,

Led by the halter to sleep
On his four taxed, worthy legs.
Each thinks he awakens where

The sun is black on the rooftop,
That the green is dancing in the next pasture,
And that the way to sleep

In a cloud, or in a risen lake,
Is to walk as though he were still
In the drained field standing, head down,

To pretend to sleep when led,
And thus to go under the ancient white
Of the meadow, as green goes

And whiteness comes up through his face
Holding stars and rotten rafters,
Quiet, fragrant, and relieved.

The Scarred Girl

All glass may yet be whole
She thinks, it may be put together
From the deep inner flashing of her face.
One moment the windshield held

The countryside, the green
Level fields and the animals,
And these must be restored
To what they were when her brow

Broke into them for nothing, and began
Its sparkling under the gauze.

Though the still, small war for her beauty
Is stitched out of sight and lost,

It is not this field that she thinks of.
It is that her face, buried
And held up inside the slow scars,
Knows how the bright, fractured world

Burns and pulls and weeps
To come together again.
The green meadow lying in fragments
Under the splintered sunlight,

The cattle broken in pieces
By her useless, painful intrusion
Know that her visage contains
The process and hurt of their healing,

The hidden wounds that can
Restore anything, bringing the glass
Of the world together once more,
All as it was when she struck,

All except her. The shattered field
Where they dragged the telescoped car
Off to be pounded to scrap
Waits for her to get up,

For her calm, unimagined face
To emerge from the yards of its wrapping,
Red, raw, mixed-looking but entire,
A new face, an old life,

To confront the pale glass it has dreamed
Made whole and backed with wise silver,
Held in other hands brittle with dread,
A doctor's, a lip-biting nurse's,

Who do not see what she sees
Behind her odd face in the mirror:
The pastures of earth and of heaven
Restored and undamaged, the cattle

Risen out of their jagged graves
To walk in the seamless sunlight
And a newborn countenance
Put upon everything,

Her beauty gone, but to hover
Near for the rest of her life,
And good no nearer, but plainly
In sight, and the only way.

The Poisoned Man

When the rattlesnake bit, I lay
In a dream of the country, and dreamed
Day after day of the river,

Where I sat with a jackknife and quickly
Opened my sole to the water.
Blood shed for the sake of one's life

Takes on the hid shape of the channel,
Disappearing under logs and through boulders.
The freezing river poured on

And as it took hold of my blood,
Leapt up round the rocks and boiled over.
I felt that my heart's blood could flow

Unendingly out of the mountain,
Splitting bedrock apart upon redness,
And the current of life at my instep

Give deathlessly as a spring.
Some leaves fell from trees and whirled under.
I saw my struck bloodstream assume,

Inside the cold path of the river,
The inmost routes of a serpent
Through grass, through branches and leaves.

When I rose, the live-oaks were ashen
And the wild grass was dead without flame.
Through the blasted corn field I hobbled,

My foot tied up in my shirt,
And met my old wife in the garden,
Where she reached for a withering apple.

I lay in the country and dreamed
Of the substance and course of the river
While the different colors of fever

Like quilt patches flickered upon me.
At last I arose, with the poison
Gone out of the seam of the scar,

And brought my wife eastward and weeping,
Through the copper fields springing alive
With the promise of harvest for no one.

from ''MESSAGES''

II
Giving a Son to the Sea

Gentle blondness and the moray eel go at the same time
On in my mind as you grow, who fired at me at the age
Of six, a Christmas toy for child
Spies: a bullet with a Special Secret
Message Compartment. My hands undid the bullet meant

For my heart, and it read aloud
"I love you." That message hits me most
When I watch you swim, that being your only talent.
The sea obsesses you, and your room is full of it:

Your room is full
of flippers and snorkels and books
On spearfishing.
O the depths,
My gentle son. Out of that room and into the real
Wonder and weightless horror
Of water   into the shifts of vastness
You will probably go, for someone must lead
Mankind, your father and your sons,
Down there to live, or we all die
Of crowding. Many of yóu
Will die, in the cold roll
Of the bottom currents, and the life lost
More totally than anywhere, there in the dark
Of no breath at all.
And I must let you go, out of your gentle
Childhood into your own man suspended
In its body, slowly waving its feet
Deeper and deeper, while the dark grows, the cold
Grows careless, the sun is put
Out by the weight of the planet
As it sinks to the bottom. Maybe you will find us there
An agonizing new life, much like the life
Of the drowned, where we will farm eat sleep and bear children
Who dream of birds.
Switch on your sea-lamp, then,
And go downward, son, with your only message
Echoing. Your message to the world, remember,
Came to your father
At Christmas like a bullet. When the great fish roll
With you, herded deep in the deepest dance,
When the shark cuts through your invisible
Trail, I will send back

That message, though nothing that lives
Underwater will ever receive it.
That does not matter, my gentle blond
Son. That does not matter.

In the Pocket
NFL

Going backward
All of me and some
Of my friends are forming a shell   my arm is looking
Everywhere and some are breaking
In   breaking down
And out   breaking
Across, and one is going deep   deeper
Than my arm. Where is Number One hooking
Into the violent green alive
With linebackers? I cannot find him he cannot beat
His man   I fall back more
Into the pocket   it is raging and breaking
Number Two has disappeared into the chalk
Of the sideline   Number Three is cutting with half
A step of grace   my friends are crumbling
Around me the wrong color
Is looming   hands are coming
Up and over between
My arm and Number Three: throw it hit him in the middle
Of his enemies   hit move scramble
Before death and the ground
Come up   LEAP STAND KILL DIE STRIKE

Now.

DENISE LEVERTOV

(1923–)

The Gypsy's Window

It seems a stage
backed by imaginations of velvet,
cotton, satin, loops and stripes—

A lovely unconcern
scattered the trivial plates, the rosaries
and centered
a narrownecked dark vase,
unopened yellow and pink
paper roses, a luxury of open red
paper roses—

Watching the trucks go by, from stiff chairs
behind the window show, an old
bandanna'd brutal dignified
woman, a young beautiful woman
her mouth a huge contemptuous rose—

The courage
of natural rhetoric tosses to dusty
Hudson St. the chance of poetry, a chance
poetry gives passion to the roses,
the roses in the gypsy's window in a blue

vase, look real, as unreal
as real roses.

Laying the Dust

What a sweet smell rises
            when you lay the dust—
bucket after bucket of water thrown
on the yellow grass.
                        The water
flashes
each time you
make it leap—
            arching its glittering back.
The sound of
                more water
pouring into the pail
almost quenches my thirst.
Surely when flowers
grow here, they'll not
smell sweeter than this
            wet ground, suddenly black.

Merritt Parkway

        As if it were
forever that they move, that we
        keep moving—

                Under a wan sky where
                as the lights went on a star
                        pierced the haze & now
                follows steadily
                        a constant
                above our six lanes
                the dreamlike continuum . . .

And the people—ourselves!
   the humans from inside the
   cars, apparent
   only at gasoline stops
                    unsure,
    eyeing each other

                 drink coffee hastily at the
          slot machines & hurry
    back to the cars
      vanish
      into them forever, to
      keep moving—

Houses now & then beyond the
sealed road, the trees / trees, bushes
passing by, passing
    the cars that
        keep moving ahead of
    us, past us, pressing behind us
                 and
        over left, those that come
      toward us shining too brightly
moving relentlessly

    in six lanes, gliding
    north & south, speeding with
    a slurred sound—

Illustrious Ancestors

The Rav
of Northern White Russia declined,
in his youth, to learn the
language of birds, because
the extraneous did not interest him; nevertheless
when he grew old it was found
he understood them anyway, having

listened well, and as it is said, 'prayed
                          with the bench and the floor.' He used
what was at hand—as did
Angel Jones of Mold, whose meditations
were sewn into coats and britches.
                          Well, I would like to make,
thinking some line still taut between me and them,
poems direct as what the birds said,
hard as a floor, sound as a bench,
mysterious as the silence when the tailor
would pause with his needle in the air.

With Eyes at the Back of Our Heads

With eyes at the back of our heads
we see a mountain
not obstructed with woods but laced
here and there with feathery groves.

The doors before us in a facade
that perhaps has no house in back of it
are too narrow, and one is set high
with no doorsill. The architect sees

the imperfect proposition and
turns eagerly to the knitter.
Set it to rights!
The knitter begins to knit.

For we want
to enter the house, if there is a house,
to pass through the doors at least
into whatever lies beyond them,

we want to enter the arms
of the knitted garment. As one
is re-formed, so the other,
in proportion.

When the doors widen
when the sleeves admit us
the way to the mountain will clear,
the mountain we see with
eyes at the back of our heads, mountain
green, mountain
cut of limestone, echoing
with hidden rivers, mountain
of short grass and subtle shadows.

The Quarry Pool

Between town and the
old house, an inn—
the Half-Way House.
So far one could ride, I remember,

the rest was an uphill walk,
a mountain lane with
steep banks and sweet
hedges, half walls of

gray rock. Looking
again at this looking-glass face
unaccountably changed in a week,
three weeks, a month,

I think without thinking of
Half-Way House. Is it
the thought that this far
I've driven at ease, as in a bus,

a country bus where one could talk to the driver?
Now on foot towards the village;
the dust clears, silence
draws in around one. I hear
the rustle and hum of the fields: alone.

It must be the sense
of essential solitude that chills me
looking into my eyes.
I should remember

the old house at the walk's ending,
a square place with a courtyard,
granaries, netted strawberry-beds,
a garden that was many

gardens, each one
a world hidden from the
next by leaves, enlaced trees,
fern-hairy walls, gilly-flowers.

I should see, making
a strange face at myself,
nothing to fear in the thought of
Half-Way House—

the place one got down
to walk—. What is
this shudder, this
dry mouth?

Think, please, of the quarry pool,
the garden's furthest
garden, of your childhood's
joy in its solitude.

To the Snake

Green Snake, when I hung you round my neck
and stroked your cold, pulsing throat
            as you hissed to me, glinting
arrowy gold scales, and I felt
            the weight of you on my shoulders,

and the whispering silver of your dryness
      sounded close at my ears—

Green Snake—I swore to my companions that certainly
      you were harmless! But truly
I had no certainty, and no hope, only desiring
      to hold you, for that joy,
               which left
a long wake of pleasure, as the leaves moved
and you faded into the pattern
of grass and shadows, and I returned
smiling and haunted, to a dark morning.

A Map of the Western Part of the County of Essex in England

Something forgotten for twenty years: though my fathers
and mothers came from Cordova and Vitepsk and Caernarvon,
and though I am a citizen of the United States and less a
stranger here than anywhere else, perhaps,
I am Essex-born:
Cranbrook Wash called me into its dark tunnel,
the little streams of Valentines heard my resolves,
Roding held my head above water when I thought it was
drowning me; in Hainault only a haze of thin trees
stood between the red doubledecker buses and the boar-hunt,
the spirit of merciful Phillipa glimmered there.
Pergo Park knew me, and Clavering, and Havering-atte-Bower,
Stanford Rivers lost me in osier beds, Stapleford Abbots
sent me safe home on the dark road after Simeon-quiet evensong,
Wanstead drew me over and over into its basic poetry,
in its serpentine lake I saw bass-viols among the golden dead leaves,
through its trees the ghost of a great house. In
Ilford High Road I saw the multitudes passing pale under the
light of flaring sundown, seven kings
in somber starry robes gathered at Seven Kings
the place of law

where my birth and marriage are recorded
and the death of my father. Woodford Wells
where an old house was called The Naked Beauty (a white
statue forlorn in its garden)
saw the meeting and parting of two sisters,
(forgotten? and further away
the hill before Thaxted? where peace befell us? not once
but many times?).
All the Ivans dreaming of their villages
all the Marias dreaming of their walled cities,
picking up fragments of New World slowly,
not knowing how to put them together nor how to join
image with image, now I know how it was with you, an old map
made long before I was born shows ancient
rights of way where I walked when I was ten burning with desire
for the world's great splendors, a child who traced voyages
indelibly all over the atlas, who now in a far country
remembers the first river, the first
field, bricks and lumber dumped in it ready for building,
that new smell, and remembers
the walls of the garden, the first light.

Resting Figure

The head Byzantine or from
Fayyum, the shoulders naked,
a little of the
dark-haired breast visible
above the sheet,

from deep in the dark head
his smile glowing
outward into the
room's severe twilight,

he lies, a dark-shadowed
mellow gold against

the flattened white pillow,
a gentle man—

strength and despair
quiet there in the bed,
the line of his limbs
half-shown, as under stone
or bronze folds.

The Jacob's Ladder

The stairway is not
a thing of gleaming strands
a radiant evanescence
for angels' feet that only glance in their tread, and need not
touch the stone.

It is of stone.
A rosy stone that takes
a glowing tone of softness
only because behind it the sky is a doubtful, a doubting
night gray.

A stairway of sharp
angles, solidly built.
One sees that the angels must spring
down from one step to the next, giving a little
lift of the wings:

and a man climbing
must scrape his knees, and bring
the grip of his hands into play. The cut stone
consoles his groping feet. Wings brush past him.
The poem ascends.

Matins

I

The authentic! Shadows of it
sweep past in dreams, one could say imprecisely,
evoking the almost-silent
ripping apart of giant
sheets of cellophane. No.
It thrusts up close. Exactly in dreams
it has you off-guard, you
recognize it before you have time.
For a second before waking
the alarm bell is a red conical hat, it
takes form.

II

The authentic! I said
rising from the toilet seat.
The radiator in rhythmic knockings
spoke of the rising steam.
The authentic, I said
breaking the handle of my hairbrush as I
brushed my hair in
rhythmic strokes: That's it,
that's joy, it's always
a recognition, the known
appearing fully itself, and
more itself than one knew.

III

The new day rises
as heat rises,
knocking in the pipes
with rhythms it seizes for its own
to speak of its invention—
the real, the new-laid
egg whose speckled shell
the poet fondles and must break
if he will be nourished.

IV

A shadow painted where
yes, a shadow must fall.
The cow's breath
not forgotten in the mist, in the
words. Yes,
verisimilitude draws up
heat in us, zest
to follow through,
follow through,
follow
transformations of day
in its turning, in its becoming.

V

Stir the holy grains, set
the bowls on the table and
call the child to eat.

While we eat we think,
as we think an undercurrent
of dream runs through us
faster than thought
towards recognition.

Call the child to eat,
send him off, his mouth
tasting of toothpaste, to go down
into the ground, into a roaring train
and to school.

His cheeks are pink
his black eyes hold his dreams, he has left
forgetting his glasses.

Follow down the stairs at a clatter
to give them to him and save
his clear sight.

Cold air
comes in at the street door.

VI

The authentic! It rolls
just out of reach, beyond
running feet and
stretching fingers, down
the green slope and into
the black waves of the sea.
Speak to me, little horse, beloved,
tell me
how to follow the iron ball,
how to follow through to the country
beneath the waves
to the place where I must kill you and you step out
of your bones and flystrewn meat
tall, smiling, renewed,
formed in your own likeness.

VII

Marvelous Truth, confront us
at every turn,
in every guise, iron ball,
egg, dark horse, shadow,
cloud
of breath on the air,

dwell
in our crowded hearts
our steaming bathrooms, kitchens full of
things to be done, the
ordinary streets.

Thrust close your smile
that we know you, terrible joy.

The Heart

At any moment the heart
breaks for nothing—

poor folk got up in their best,
rich ones trying, trying to please—

each touch and a new fissure appears,
such a network, I think of an old
china pie-plate
left too long in the oven.

If on the bloody muscle its namesake
  patiently pumping in the thoracic cavity

each flick of fate incised itself,
who'd live long?—but this beats on

in the habit of minute response,
with no gift for the absolute.

Disasters
of history weigh on it, anguish

of mortality presses
in on its sides

but neither crush it to dust nor
split it apart. What

is under the cracked glaze?

PATRICIA BEER

(1924–)

Ghost

He died a year ago
And months of quiet have made
Him tall as air

Whose speech was like a root
Groping and grey. Each sun
Tolls him awake.

He was enclosed in wood,
Hushed into crumbling; smooth
Graining of ribs

Showed where the life had lain.
The sawing light caught no more
On knotted blood.

But he escaped through paths
Of soil and worm and stone
To fidget like a tree

Over this house, and all
The leaves that flew are tamed
On to his hand.

Rome Twelve O'clock

Out of the hazardous morning this hour opens
Like a parachute; the sky that was as flat
As Jericho is now shored up with the hooters
Of mid-day.   Trees humped like snails
Draw in their sensitive last inch of shadow
As noon halloos and hunts over the roofs.

The lover, left outdistanced by the cool
Early striding of the sun, now glances up
At his fifth-storey room and feels the day
Turn towards him once again.   And his girl moves
Up there, noon swaying in her waist
And glowing through the lantern of her bones.

We all look up as mid-day, whose roots walk
Deep in the buried streets of the old city,
Flowers into an entire Rome above the air,
Where we are momentary issue of the timeless
Man who made the clock, and of the god
Who pushed the sun higher than we could reach.

Love Song

Never be fool enough to think
The wrecking sea will cast up
Anything worth the salvaging,
A gold plate or a cup,
Silk or a piece of furniture,
Any vestige you can save,
Now your cargo, shining like a fish,
Is baled up in a wave.

Neither believe there is only shore,
That you can stamp your foot
And shut the door in the cliff side
To keep the ocean out,
For you cannot stop the sea mist
From fingering things, nor rub
The seagulls from your tumbling sky
Now land is at an ebb.

Let them swallow each other, soil
And water, and fish and bait.
In vertigo lies your only hope
For if you can admit
No difference between sea and land
You may find your love again,
Changed but with greater scope,
Re-born an amphibian.

Lemmings

Lemmings die every year. Over the cliff
They pour, hot blood into cold sea,
So that you half imagine steam
Will rise. They do not part company
At first, but spread out, a brown team
Like seaweed, undulant and tough.

Light changes, and the wind may veer
As they swim out and on. The sea
May become sleek or shrewish. Foam
May blind them or may let them see
The wet horizon. It takes time.
They do not die within an hour.

One by one they leave the air
And drown as individuals.

From minute to minute they blink out
Like aeroplanes or stars or gulls
Whose vanishing is never caught.
All in time will disappear.

And though their vitality
Does not look morbid enough
People call it suicide
Which it has some appearance of.
But it may well be that the mood
In which each year these lemmings die

Is nothing worse than restlessness,
The need to change and nothing else.
They have learnt this piece of strand
So thoroughly it now seems false.
They jump, thinking there is land
Beyond them, as indeed there is.

Brunhild

My father laid me in a ring
Of fire, and then like thunder rolled
Away, though I had been more close
To him than in his arms. He told
Me I should never see his face
Now he had voiced me like a song,

Made me a separate thing, no more
His warrior daughter but a woman.
But I do see his face, I see
It all the time. Though I am human
He can still rule. He promised me
That a brave man should break the fire,

A man he would approve of, no
Tentative weakling. He will have

My father's dominant beard and mighty
Shoulders, and instead of love
This obligation to be doughty.
I wait for the entrance of the hero

Dressed up in my father's fashion.
If I were free to love I would
Decide on someone thin and shaven.
But in the ring I lie like wood
Or soil, that cannot yield or even
Be raped except with his permission.

Head of a Snowdrop

After the north-east wind I carried
A snowdrop indoors. Taut as a bead
And bright, it lay in a bottle-top,
Nothing but petal from the wound up.

Its roots, stem, were still out of doors; strange
That away from them it could so change,
Normally opening into flower,
Wide as a primrose in one warm hour.

Human fingernails and hair move less
After death and lack naturalness.
Births after death—young Macduff—have such
Horror they can be used by a witch.

Anti-vivisectionists show men
Keeping dogs' heads alive, yapping even.
Schoolboys studying the Stuarts laugh
About Charles talking with his head off.

And I have this freak on my own hearth
Making me think about roots and birth
By false analogies and ignore
Its fulfilled purpose: an open flower.

Young Widow

It is a luxury at my age
To say 'I am too old' when asked to marry.
Autumn leaves, fading coals and sunset
Are metaphors to state that I am weary

But no more than that; sunset does not
Become darkness, nor a live coal a dead one.
Perhaps I should have called in the stars
And proved that no one born under Scorpion

Can take up with a Crab. Class or race
Might have been good excuses, or heart scared
By sorrow. It is deft and polite to tell lies
To a suitor. The truth is, I am dead tired.

On Saturday evening I said no,
But on Sunday morning walked in bad weather,
My own mistress, around the churchyard
Where people older than I lay together.

A Dream of Hanging

He rang me up
In a dream,
My brother did.
He had been hanged
That morning,
Innocent,
And I had slept
Through the striking
Of the clock
While it had taken place,
Eight,
Just about time enough

For it to happen.
He spoke to me
On the telephone
That afternoon
To reassure me,
My dear brother
Who had killed nobody,
And I asked him,
Long distance,
What it had felt like
To be hanged.
'Oh, don't worry, lovey', he said,
'When your time comes.
It tickled rather.'

A Visit to Little Gidding

This is a place of departure
Not of arrival. Even the signpost
Saying Little Gidding, a shock
To any poetry-lover, seems
Meant to be read retrospectively
By tourists on their way back.

As we rise from the fens to where
The hills begin, the flatlands
Give the impression of leaving
Us rather than being left
And they carry the sun away on them,
Warmth going not cold coming.

The pilgrims have gone; they have been
Here this afternoon with flowers
For Ferrar's tomb, so large a wreath
They were either rich or numerous,
We do not know which, they have gone
And their flowers are bright and dying.

The Scouts camping in the next field
Are lugging tea-urns and dismantling
Trestle tables. It has been visitors'
Day, but the parents have gone
Now, leaving their stalwart sons
Jesting shakily like survivors.

And we must go, if we want to be home
Before dark, for home is not here,
Less here, in fact, than in most places.
We are visiting a famous poet
Who followed a famous king
Who sought out a famous good man

And so on back to the beginning,
Which is the end, where the line vanishes,
Where the mirrors stop reflecting.
And the prayers, the escape-route
And the poem were perhaps
Not light coming but darkness going.

VASSAR MILLER

(1924–)

Adam's Footprint

Once as a child I loved to hop
On round plump bugs and make them stop
Before they crossed a certain crack.
My bantam brawn could turn them back,
My crooked step wrenched straight to kill
Live pods that then screwed tight and still.

Small sinner, stripping boughs of pears,
Shinnied past sweet and wholesome airs,
How could a tree be so unclean?
Nobody knows but Augustine.
He nuzzled pears for dam-sin's dugs—
And I scrunched roly-poly bugs.

No wolf's imprint or tiger's trace
Does Christ hunt down to catch with grace
In nets of love the devious preys
Whose feet go softly all their days:
The foot of Adam leaves the mark
Of some child scrabbling in the dark.

Fantasy on the Resurrection

Flaws cling to flesh as dews cling to a rose:
The cripples limp as though they would prolong,
Walking, a waltz; the deaf ears, opened, close
As if their convolutions hoard all song;
The blind eyes keep half shut as if to fold
A vision fast men never glimpse by staring;
Against their will the mute lips move that hold
A language which was never tongue's for sharing.
Shocked shag of earth and everything thereunder
Turned inside out—the nail-gnarled have caught Heaven
Like a bright ball. Not in their reknit wonder,
But in their wounds lies Christ's sprung grace engraven—
Not in the body lighter than word spoken,
But in the side still breached, the hands still broken.

The Final Hunger

Hurl down the nerve-gnarled body hurtling head-
Long into sworls of shade-hush. Plummeting, keep
The latch of eyelids shut to so outleap
Care's claws. Arms, legs, abandon grace and spread
Your spent sprawl—glutton ravening to be fed
With fats, creams, fruits, meats, spice that heavy-heap
The hands, that golden-gloss the flesh, of sleep,
Sleep, the sole lover that I take to bed.

But they couch crouching in the darkness, city
Of wakefulness uncaptured by assaulting—
Senses by sleep unravished and unwon.
Sun-sword night-sheathed, lie never between (have pity!)
Between me and my love, between me and the vaulting
Down the dense sweetness of oblivion.

No Return

Once over summer streams the ice-crusts harden,
No one can wade therein to wash his feet
Thence to go flying after nymphs that fleet
Naked and nimble through the woods. Time's warden
Has locked them all (or is it us?) past pardon.
Yet freed, we could not find the path that beat
Toward—call it any name—fauns, home, retreat;
For there is no returning to that garden.

No, not to Adam's. We must keep our own,
Remembering. In Eden's greenery
God walked. While in our garden rocks are brown
With His dried blood where He has crouched to groan.
Our apples rotted, only His crosstree
Bears crimson fruit. But no hand plucks it down.

Ballad of the Unmiraculous Miracle

Sit under a pine on Christmas Eve,
Heart bruised like a fallen nestling,
And the angels will sing you—no song save
The wind in the branches wrestling.

Peer down a mystical well and see
Far down in its waters mirrored—
The only sign there imaged for me,
My own face mournful and harrowed.

Seek out a stable known of old
And see the oxen kneel—
With me crouched here before the cold
And hunger sharp as steel.

Go wander through the winter snows
And spy the Christmas bud
Unfold itself—the only rose
The brambles bear, my blood.

Like wingless birds are wind and wood,
Well, oxen, flowering bush
Till Christmas Day when I see God
Plumaged in my plucked flesh.

Song for a Marriage

Housed in each other's arms,
Thatched with each other's grace,
Your bodies, flint on steel
Striking out fire to fend
The cold away awhile;
With sweat for mortar, brace
Your walls against the sleet
And the rib-riddling wind.

A house, you house yourselves,
Housed, you will house another,
Scaled to a subtler blueprint
Than architects can draw—
A triple function yours
In this world's winter weather,
Oh, breathing brick and stone,
I look on you with awe.

A fig for praise that calls
Flesh a bundle of sticks,
Kindling for flame that feels
Like swallowing the sun!
Yet luxury turned labor's
No old maid's rancid mix,
But how bone-masonry
Outweighs the skeleton.

In Consolation

Do I love you? The question might be well
Rephrased, What do I love? Your face?
Suppose it twisted to a charred grimace.
Your mind? But if it turned hospital cell,
Though pity for its inmate might compel
Sick calls from time to time, I should embrace
A staring stranger whom I could not place.
So, cease demanding what I cannot tell

Till He who made you shows me where He keeps you,
And not some shadow of you I pursue
And, having found, have only flushed a wraith.
Nor am I Christ to cleave the dark that steeps you.
He loves you then, not I—Or if I do,
I love you only by an act of faith.

Return

From what I am, to be what I am not,
To be what once I was, from plan and plot
To learn to take no thought,
I go, my God, to Thee.

With act of faith whose throes and throbs convulse
My heart as if all other acts were else
Than dyings, prayer than pulse,
I go, my God, to Thee.

On feet thread through by seams of blood and fire,
Dancing the narrow pathway, strictest wire,
As butterflies a briar,
I go, my God, to Thee.

To balance like a bird with wings aflare,
Pinned to the cross as though I merely were

Stenciled by light on air,
I go, my God, to Thee.

My spirit, trim, uncorseted from stress,
Stripping to wind and sunlight, to the grace
Of Eden's nakedness
Will go, my God, to Thee.

For Instruction

Teach me some prayer
tender as you are tender when
one of my shadows mingles with one of yours and makes
an intricate weave we walk on for a moment,
gentle as you are gentle when
you humble yourself to take my kiss,
wordless as we are wordless when
a pause has fallen between us like a petal.

From an Old Maid

You come and say that it is restful here
to speak your pain into my silences,
wafting your words across them like the hair
of drowning sailors lost in churning seas.

And if I ever told you, you would laugh
to think I made your moment's reef of calm
by holding up your listless body, half
submerged in water, lightly on my palm.

Digging into my flesh with terror's claws
until the times you hope you hear the oar
of your salvation, do you never pause
to wonder when or where I drift to shore?

Protest

Where the air in this room warms by the fire like a cat,
where music no one can touch swaddles the ear in satin,
where one may hear words as though he were tasting them,
where wine curls over the tongue, sliding down like a lover's kiss,
where the merest shadow of love bears the odor of roses
in whose heart I am flayed as by fire,
here I lie naked, spitted upon my senses
like a plucked bird caught upon thorns.

Love's Eschatology

I touch you all over
as if every part were a petal
when now you are away.

Never has your body
before so budded to my senses
as to my empty fingers.

Love, may we in Heaven
view all for the first time forever
through the lens of the last.

Sloth

Sloth is the summer sin
when the soul is smug
as a sunning cat
and hides herself beneath
the green docility
of shade, where growing fat,
smirking her innocence,
she makes my shadow seem her habitat.

Remembering Aunt Helen

Dimly remembering how your life made
pious abstractions dance in flesh and blood
and stern negation gentle to a child—
my heart breaks into rainbows of hosannas
hovering around the memory of your head.
Remembering how somebody said, "Why, Helen
could ask me anything. I wouldn't mind."
I see that even timid hearts take courage
Under the uncondemning gaze of kindness.
Remembering how you told a little boy
who asked to buy your cat, "Honey, we don't
sell what we love," I think how most old maids'
affection for their pets is loneliness,
while yours was charity. The daily dust
your footstep stirred became a cloud of glory.
The dust I kick up irritates the nose.
What shall I do then? Shun strong drink as you did?
Read Scripture every night? Keep Sunday strictly?
Or practice with a different set of gimmicks?
Eat fish on Friday? Go to Mass each morning?
Or else fall into trances? Speak in tongues?
Remembering you, I think not. Although poets
grow beards, get drunk, and go to bed unmarried,
their imitators pull the selfsame antics
and never make it, because poems never
spring out of opium. So sanctity
changes its wardrobe at the wearer's will
not to be copied by poor little oddballs
playing their games of holy-holy-holy.
Remembering you, I weep because I find
the skirts discarded but the dancer vanished.

JOHN WAIN

(1925–)

Reason for not Writing Orthodox Nature Poetry

The January sky is deep and calm.
The mountain sprawls in comfort, and the sea
Sleeps in the crook of that enormous arm.

And Nature from a simple recipe—
Rocks, water, mist, a sunlit winter's day—
Has brewed a cup whose strength has dizzied me.

So little beauty is enough to pay;
The heart so soon yields up its store of love,
And where you love you cannot break away.

So sages never found it hard to prove
Nor prophets to declare in metaphor
That God and Nature must be hand in glove.

And this became the basis of their lore.
Then later poets found it easy going
To give the public what they bargained for,

And like a spectacled curator showing
The wares of his museum to the crowd,
They yearly waxed more eloquent and knowing

More slick, more photographic, and more proud:
From Tennyson with notebook in his hand
(His truth to Nature fits him like a shroud)

To moderns who devoutly hymn the land.
So be it: each is welcome to his voice;
They are a gentle, if a useless, band.

But leave me free to make a sterner choice;
Content, without embellishment, to note
How little beauty bids the heart rejoice,

How little beauty catches at the throat,
Simply, I love this mountain and this bay
With love that I can never speak by rote,

And where you love you cannot break away.

This Above All Is Precious and Remarkable

This above all is precious and remarkable,
How we put ourselves in one another's care,
How in spite of everything we trust each other.

Fishermen at whatever point they are dipping and lifting
On the dark green swell they partly think of as home
Hear the gale warnings that fly to them like gulls.

The scientists study the weather for love of studying it,
And not specially for love of the fishermen,
And the wireless engineers do the transmission for love of
        wireless,

But how it adds up is that when the terrible white malice
Of the waves high as cliffs is let loose to seek a victim,
The fishermen are somewhere else and so not drowned.

And why should this chain of miracles be easier to believe
Than that my darling should come to me as naturally
As she trusts a restaurant not to poison her?

They are simply examples of well-known types of miracle,
The two of them,
That can happen at any time of the day or night.

Anniversary

These are my thoughts on realizing
That I am the same age as my father was
On the day I was born.

As a little scarlet howling mammal,
Crumpled and unformed, I depended entirely on someone
Not very different from what I am to-day.

When I think this over,
I feel more crumpled and unformed than ever:
I ask myself what I have done to compare with *that*.

It also makes me aware, inescapably,
Of having entered upon the high table-land,
The broad flat life of a mature man.

Where everything is seen from its actual distance,
E.g. childhood not so remote as to seem a boring myth,
Nor senility as something that awaits other people.

But deeper than that,
It is like entering a dark cone,
The shadow thrown across my life by the life it derives from.

And deeper than that still,
It is the knowledge that life is the one communicable thing.
It called. I heard it from where I slept in seed and liquid.

The patterns of seed and brine coalesced in a solemn dance,
Whence my life arose in the form of a crest,
And has carried itself blindly forward until now.

In ignorance of its uniqueness until now,
Until I stumbled over these thoughts solid as bricks,
And like bricks fearsome in their everyday squareness.

Apology for Understatement

Forgive me that I pitch your praise too low.
Such reticence my reverence demands,
For silence falls with laying on of hands.

Forgive me that my words come thin and slow.
This could not be a time for eloquence,
For silence falls with healing of the sense.

We only utter what we lightly know.
And it is rather that my love knows me.
It is that your perfection set me free.

Verse is dressed up that has nowhere to go.
You took away my glibness with my fear.
Forgive me that I stand in silence here.

It is not words could pay you what I owe.

Brooklyn Heights

This is the gay cliff of the nineteenth century,
Drenched in the hopeful ozone of a new day.

Erect and brown, like retired sea-captains,
The houses gaze vigorously at the ocean.

With the hospitable eyes of retired captains
They preside over the meeting of sea and river.

On Sunday mornings the citizens revisit their beginnings.
Whose families walk in the fresh air of the past.

Their children tricycle down the nineteenth century:
America comes smiling towards them like a neighbour.

While the past on three wheels unrolls beneath them,
They hammer in the blazing forge of the future.

Brooklyn Bridge flies through the air on feathers.
The children do not know the weight of its girders.

It is the citizens carry the bridge on their shoulders:
Its overhead lights crackle in their blood vessels.

But now it is Sunday morning, and a sky swept clean.
The citizens put down the bridge and stroll at ease.

They jingle the hopeful change in their pockets.
They forget the tripping dance of the profit motive.

The big ships glide in under the high statue,
The towers cluster like spear-grass on the famous island.

And the citizens dream themselves back in a sparkle of morning.
They ride with their children under a sky swept clean.

Dream on, citizens! Dream the true America, the healer,
Drawing the hot blood from throbbing Europe!

Dream the dark-eyed immigrants from the narrow cities:
Dream the iron steamers loaded with prayers and bundles:

Breathe the ozone older than the name of commerce:
Be the citizens of the true survival!

A Song about Major Eatherly

The book (Fernard Gigon's *Formula for Death—The Atom Bombs and After*) also describes how Major Claude R. Eatherly, pilot of the aircraft which carried the second bomb to Nagasaki, later started having nightmares. His wife is quoted as saying: 'He often jumps up in the middle of the night and screams out in an inhuman voice which makes me feel ill: "Release it, release it." '

Major Eatherly began to suffer brief periods of madness, says Gigon. The doctors diagnosed extreme nervous depression, and Eatherly was awarded a pension of 237 dollars a month.

This he appears to have regarded 'as a premium for murder, as a payment for what had been done to the two Japanese cities'. He never touched the money, and took to petty thievery, for which he was committed to Fort Worth prison.

Report in *The Observer*, August 1958.

I

Good news. It seems he loved them after all.
His orders were to fry their bones to ash.
He carried up the bomb and let it fall.
And then his orders were to take the cash,

A hero's pension. But he let it lie.
It was in vain to ask him for the cause.
Simply that if he touched it he would die.
He fought his own, and not his country's wars.

His orders told him he was not a man:
An instrument, fine-tempered, clear of stain,
All fears and passions closed up like a fan:
No more volition than his aeroplane.

But now he fought to win his manhood back.
Steep from the sunset of his pain he flew
Against the darkness in that last attack.
It was for love he fought, to make that true.

11

To take life is always to die a little: to stop
any feeling and moving contrivance, however ugly,
unnecesary, or hateful, is to reduce by so much the total
of life there is. And that is to die a little.

To take the life of an enemy is to help him,
a little, towards destroying your own. Indeed, that is why
we hate our enemies: because they force us to kill them.
A murderer hides the dead man in the ground:
but his crime rears up and topples on to the living,
for it is they who now must hunt the murderer,
murder him, and hide him in the ground: it is they
who now feel the touch of death cold in their bones.

Animals hate death. A trapped fox will gnaw
through his own leg: it is so important to live
that he forgives himself the agony,
consenting, for life's sake, to the desperate teeth
grating through bone and pulp, the gasping yelps.

That is the reason the trapper hates the fox.
You think the trapper doesn't hate the fox?
But he does, and the fox can tell how much.
It is not the fox's teeth that grind his bones,
It is the trapper's. It is the trapper, there,
Who keeps his head down, gnawing, hour after hour.

And the people the trapper works for, they are there too,
heads down beside the trap, gnawing away.
Why shouldn't they hate the fox? Their cheeks are smeared
with his rank blood, and on their tongues his bone
being splintered, feels uncomfortably sharp.

So once Major Eatherly hated the Japanese.

III

Hell is a furnace, so the wise men taught.
The punishment for sin is to be broiled.
A glowing coal for every sinful thought.

The heat of God's great furnace ate up sin,
Which whispered up in smoke or fell in ash:
So that each hour a new hour could begin.

So fire was holy, though it tortured souls,
The sinners' anguish never ceased, but still
Their sin was burnt from them by shining coals.

Hell fried the criminal but burnt the crime,
Purged where it punished, healed where it destroyed:
It was a stove that warmed the rooms of time.

No man begrudged the flames their appetite.
All were afraid of fire, yet none rebelled.
The wise men taught that hell was just and right.

'The soul desires its necessary dread:
Only among the thorns can patience weave
A bower where the mind can make its bed.'

Even the holy saints whose patient jaws
Chewed bitter rind and hands raised up the dead
Were chestnuts roasted at God's furnace doors.

The wise men passed. The clever men appeared.
They ruled that hell be called a pumpkin face.
They robbed the soul of what it justly feared.

Coal after coal the fires of hell went out.
Their heat no longer warmed the rooms of time,
Which glistened now with fluorescent doubt.

The chilly saints went striding up and down
To warm their blood with useful exercise.
They rolled like conkers through the draughty town.

Those emblematic flames sank down to rest,
But metaphysical fire can not go out:
Men ran from devils they had dispossessed,

And felt within their skulls the dancing heat
No longer stored in God's deep boiler-room.
Fire scorched their temples, frostbite chewed their feet.

That parasitic fire could race and climb
More swiftly than the stately flames of hell.
Its fuel gone, it licked the beams of time.

So time dried out and youngest hearts grew old.
The smoky minutes cracked and broke apart.
The world was roasting but the men were cold.

Now from this pain worse pain was brought to birth,
More hate, more anguish, till at last they cried,
'Release this fire to gnaw the crusty earth:

Make it a flame that's obvious to sight
And let us say we kindled it ourselves,
To split the skulls of men and let in light.

Since death is camped among us, wish him joy,
Invite him to our table and our games.
We cannot judge, but we can still destroy'.

And so the curtains of the mind were drawn.
Men conjured hell a first, a second time:
And Major Eatherly took off at dawn.

IV

Suppose a sea-bird,
its wings stuck down with oil, riding the waves
in no direction, under the storm-clouds, helpless,
lifted for an instant by each moving billow
to scan the meaningless horizon, helpless,
helpless, and the storms coming, and its wings dead,
its bird-nature dead:
                        Imagine this castaway,
loved, perhaps, by the Creator, and yet abandoned,
mocked by the flashing scales of the fish beneath it,
who leap, twist, dive, as free of the wide sea
as formerly the bird of the wide sky,
now helpless, starving, a prisoner of the surface,
unable to dive or rise:
                        this is your emblem.
Take away the bird, let it be drowned
in the steep black waves of the storm, let it be broken
against rocks in the morning light, too faint to swim:
take away the bird, but keep the emblem.

It is the emblem of Major Eatherly,
who looked round quickly from the height of each wave,
but saw no land, only the rim of the sky
into which he was not free to rise, or the silver
gleam of the mocking scales of the fish diving
where he was not free to dive.

Men have clung always to emblems,
to tokens of absolution from their sins.
Once it was the scapegoat driven out, bearing
its load of guilt under the empty sky
until its shape was lost, merged in the scrub.

Now we are civilized, there is no wild heath.
Instead of the nimble scapegoat running out
to be lost under the wild and empty sky,

the load of guilt is packed into prison walls,
and men file inward through the heavy doors.

But now that image, too, is obsolete.
The Major entering prison is no scapegoat.
His penitence will not take away our guilt,
nor sort with any consoling ritual:
this is penitence for its own sake, beautiful,
uncomprehending, inconsolable, unforeseen.
He is not in prison for his penitence:
it is no outrage to our law that he wakes
with cries of pity on his parching lips.
We do not punish him for cries or nightmares.
We punish him for stealing things from stores.

O, give his pension to the storekeeper.
Tell him it is the price of all our souls.
But do not trouble to unlock the door
and bring the Major out into the sun.
Leave him: it is all one: perhaps his nightmares
grow cooler in the twilight of the prison.
Leave him; if he is sleeping, come away.
But lay a folded paper by his head,
nothing official or embossed, a page
torn from your notebook, and the words in pencil.
Say nothing of love, or thanks, or penitence:
say only 'Eatherly, we have your message.'

from WILDTRACK

Sestina for Khasan Israelov

The Chechen-Ingush, a mountain people in the northern Caucasus, resisted
domination by Catherine the Great of Russia, and were not finally subdued
till 1859; they revolted against the Czars in 1867, 1877 and 1905, and
after the Soviets came to power they continued to resist absorption and col-
lectivization. They rebelled in 1930, and were crushed. In 1941, the Chechen-
Ingush struck for their freedom one last time, under the leadership of a
young poet, Khasan Israelov. Stalin's answer was to obliterate the entire
nation by execution and mass deportation on February 23, 1944. Under the
direction of General Serov, the entire operation, whereby 500,000 people
were swept off to death or slavery, took just twenty-four hours.

1.

All those who knew you are dispersed or dead
five hundred thousand people wiped away
corpses or prisoners to the last one.
But listen, Khasan Israelov, where you lie.
I speak in a voice that wishes it were yours.
Listen, Khasan, with your mud-stopped ear.

2.

I saw your mountains once, not far away.
In the cold Caucasus I saw them lie
as the eagle sees them, high-shining, one by one.
They know you, Khasan, still, though you are dead.
The wind whose tunes put magic in your ear
whirls in the crannies where the wild goats lie.

3.

Eryri or Wicklow, half a world away
I tread on hill-paths that were never yours
and pluck the fragrant heather where I lie.
Mountains are many, but their voice is one,
still crying freedom! into the world's ear,
though by each bluff stiffen the defiant dead.

4.

Climb with me, Khasan, till bitterness is dead.
I have not the strength to face an end like yours.
But take this homage, do not turn away.
I hear your mountain music, though my ear
is dulled with cowardice: you are the one
to guide me where the quiet heroes lie.

5.

Khasan, your written chronicle is a brief one.
Such sagas are banned from the captive ear.
Soldiers have killed, now bureaucrats must lie.
Five hundred thousand truths to sponge away.
If your name lives, the victory will be yours.
Your strength cannot be tamed now you are dead.

6.

The wild chamois is your symbol, if you need one:
Who, chased to the final edge where the hunt stops dead,
Leaps down, with a delicate madness much like yours.
May its gentle ghost be welcome where your bones lie,
Who thought rather to throw life steeply away
than make a story pleasant to the huntsman's ear!

Khasan, only courage like yours can burn hatred away.
Unstop your ear: pity me from where you lie:
Climb with me, turbulent one, till bitterness is dead!

ROBERT CREELEY

(1926–)

The Immoral Proposition

If you never do anything for anyone else
you are spared the tragedy of human relation-

ships. If quietly and like another time
there is the passage of an unexpected thing:

to look at it is more
than it was. God knows

nothing is competent nothing is
all there is. The unsure

egoist is not
good for himself.

The Operation

By Saturday I said you would be better on Sunday.
The insistence was a part of a reconciliation.

Your eyes bulged, the grey
light hung on you, you were hideous.

My involvement is just an old
habitual relationship.

Cruel, cruel to describe
what there is no reason to describe.

The Whip

I spent a night turning in bed,
my love was a feather, a flat

sleeping thing. She was
very white

and quiet, and above us on
the roof, there was another woman I

also loved, had
addressed myself to in

a fit she
returned. That

encompasses it. But now I was
lonely, I yelled,

but what is that? Ugh,
she said, beside me, she put

her hand on
my back, for which act

I think to say this
wrongly.

A Wicker Basket

Comes the time when it's later
and onto your table the headwaiter

puts the bill, and very soon after
rings out the sound of lively laughter—

Picking up change, hands like a walrus,
and a face like a barndoor's,
and a head without an apparent size,
nothing but two eyes—

So that's you, man,
or me. I make it as I can,
I pick up, I go
faster than they know—

Out the door, the street like a night,
any night, and no one in sight,
but then, well, there she is,
old friend Liz—

And she opens the door of her cadillac,
I step in back,
and we're gone.
She turns me on—

There are very huge stars, man, in the sky,
and from somewhere very far off someone hands me a slice of
        apple pie,
with a gob of white, white ice cream on top of it,
and I eat it—

Slowly. And while certainly
they are laughing at me, and all around me is racket
of these cats not making it, I make it

in my wicker basket.

She Went to Stay

Trying to chop mother down is like
hunting deer inside Russia
with phalangists for hat-pins.
I couldn't.

Ballad of the Despairing Husband

My wife and I lived all alone,
contention was our only bone.
I fought with her, she fought with me,
and things went on right merrily.

But now I live here by myself
with hardly a damn thing on the shelf,
and pass my days with little cheer
since I have parted from my dear.

Oh come home soon, I write to her.
Go screw yourself, is her answer.
Now what is that, for Christian word?
I hope she feeds on dried goose turd.

But still I love her, yes I do.
I love her and the children too.
I only think it fit that she
should quickly come right back to me.

Ah no, she says, and she is tough,
and smacks me down with her rebuff.
Ah no, she says, I will not come
after the bloody things you've done.

Oh wife, oh wife—I tell you true,
I never loved no one but you.

I never will, it cannot be
another woman is for me.

That may be right, she will say then,
but as for me, there's other men.
And I will tell you I propose
to catch them firmly by the nose.

And I will wear what dresses I choose!
And I will dance, and what's to lose!
I'm free of you, you little prick,
and I'm the one can make it stick.

Was this the darling I did love?
Was this that mercy from above
did open violets in the spring—
and made my own worn self to sing?

She was. I know. And she is still,
and if I love her? then so I will.
And I will tell her, and tell her right . . .

Oh lovely lady, morning or evening or afternoon.
Oh lovely lady, eating with or without a spoon.
Oh most lovely lady, whether dressed or undressed or partly.
Oh most lovely lady, getting up or going to bed or sitting only.

Oh loveliest of ladies, than whom none is more fair, more
        gracious, more beautiful.
Oh loveliest of ladies, whether you are just or unjust,
        merciful, indifferent, or cruel.
Oh most loveliest of ladies, doing whatever, seeing whatever,
        being whatever.
Oh most loveliest of ladies, in rain, in shine, in any weather.

Oh lady, grant me time,
please, to finish my rhyme.

The Door

for Robert Duncan

It is hard going to the door
cut so small in the wall where
the vision which echoes loneliness
brings a scent of wild flowers in a wood.

What I understood, I understand.
My mind is sometime torment,
sometimes good and filled with livelihood,
and feels the ground.

But I see the door,
and knew the wall, and wanted the wood,
and would get there if I could
with my feet and hands and mind.

Lady, do not banish me
for digressions. My nature
is a quagmire of unresolved
confessions. Lady, I follow.

I walked away from myself,
I left the room, I found the garden,
I knew the woman
in it, together we lay down.

Dead night remembers. In December
we change, not multiplied but dispersed,
sneaked out of childhood,
the ritual of dismemberment.

Mighty magic is a mother,
in her there is another issue
of fixture, repeated form, the race renewal,
the charge of the command.

The garden echoes across the room.
It is fixed in the wall like a mirror
that faces a window behind you
and reflects the shadows.

May I go now?
Am I allowed to bow myself down
in the ridiculous posture of renewal,
of the insistence of which I am the virtue?

Nothing for You is untoward.
Inside You would also be tall,
more tall, more beautiful.
Come toward me from the wall, I want to be with You.

So I screamed to You,
who hears as the wind, and changes
multiply, invariably,
changes in the mind.

Running to the door, I ran down
as a clock runs down. Walked backwards,
stumbled, sat down
hard on the floor near the wall.

Where were You.
How absurd, how vicious.
There is nothing to do but get up.
My knees were iron, I rusted in worship, of You.

For that one sings, one
writes the spring poem, one goes on walking.
The Lady has always moved to the next town
and you stumble on after Her.

The door in the wall leads to the garden
where in the sunlight sit

the Graces in long Victorian dresses,
of which my grandmother had spoken.

History sings in their faces.
They are young, they are obtainable,
and you follow after them also
in the service of God and Truth.

But the Lady is indefinable,
she will be the door in the wall
to the garden in sunlight.
I will go on talking forever.

I will never get there.
Oh Lady, remember me
who in Your service grows older
not wiser, no more than before.

How can I die alone.
Where will I be then who am now alone,
what groans so pathetically
in this room where I am alone?

I will go to the garden.
I will be a romantic. I will sell
myself in hell,
in heaven also I will be.

In my mind I see the door,
I see the sunlight before me across the floor
beckon to me, as the Lady's skirt
moves small beyond it.

Jack's Blues

I'm going to roll up
a monkey and smoke it, put

an elephant in the pot. I'm going out
and never come back.

What's better than that.
Lying on your back, flat
on your back with your
eyes to the view.

Oh the view is blue, I saw that
too, yesterday and you,
red eyes and blue,
funked.

I'm going to roll up
a rug and smoke it, put
the car in the garage and I'm
gone, like a sad old candle.

The Name

Be natural,
wise
as you can be,
my daughter,

let my name
be in you flesh
I gave you
in the act of

loving your mother,
all your days
her ways,
the woman in you

brought from
sensuality's measure,

no other,
there was no thought

of it but such
pleasure all women
must be in her,
as you. But not wiser,

not more of nature
than her hair,
the eyes
she gives you.

There will not be another
woman such as you
are. Remember
your mother,

the way you came,
the days of waiting.
Be natural,
daughter, wise

as you can be,
all my daughters,
be women
for men

when that time comes.
Let the rhetoric
stay with me
your father. Let

me talk about it,
saving you such
vicious self-
exposure, let you

pass it on
in you. I cannot
be more than the man
who watches.

The Rose

for Bobbie

Up and down
she walks, listless
form, a movement
quietly misled.

Now, speak to her.
"Did you want
to go, then why
don't you."

She went. There were
things she left
in the room
as a form of it.

He follows, walking.
Where do they walk now?
Do they talk now
where they are

in that other place
grown monstrous,
quiet quiet air
as breath.

And all about a rosy
mark discloses
her nature
to him, vague and unsure.

There roses, here roses,
flowers, a pose of
nature, her
nature has disclosed to him.

Yet breathing, crouched
in the dark,
he is there
also, recovers,

to bring her back
to herself, himself.
The room wavers,
wavers.

And as if,
as if a cloud had
broken at last
open

and all the rain
from that,
from that had fallen
on them,

on them there is a mark
of her nature, her flowers,
and his room, his nature,
to come home to.

The Wife

I know two women
and the one
is tangible substance,
flesh and bone.

The other in my mind
   occurs.
She keeps her strict
   proportion there.

But how should I
   propose to live
with two such creatures
   in my bed—

or how shall he
   who has a wife
yield two to one
   and watch the other die.

The Moon

Earlier in the evening the moon
was clear to the east,
over the snow of the yard
and fields—a lovely

bright clarity and perfect
roundness, isolate,
riding as they say the
black sky. Then we went

about our businesses of the
evening, eating supper, talking,
watching television, then
going to bed, making love,

and then to sleep. But before
we did I asked her to look
out the window at the moon
now straight up, so that

she bent her head and looked
sharply up, to see it.
Through the night it must
have shone on, in that

fact of things—another
moon, another night—a
full moon in the winter's
space, a white loneliness.

I came awake to the blue
white light in the darkness,
and felt as if someone
were there, waiting, alone.

The Boy

Push yourself in on others
hard enough, they beat you
with sticks and whips—the birth

of love. E.g., affection aroused,
it moves to be close, touch, and
feel the warm livingness of an-

other, any other, sucked, stroked,
the club itself possibly a symbol of
the obvious. My mother had hair,

and when I grew older, so did
I, all over my face, which I wanted
to be there, and grew a beard henceforth.

ALLEN GINSBERG

(1926–)

In the Baggage Room at Greyhound

I

In the depths of the Greyhound Terminal

sitting dumbly on a baggage truck looking at the sky waiting for
the Los Angeles Express to depart

worrying about eternity over the Post Office roof in the night-time
red downtown heaven,

staring through my eyeglasses I realized shuddering these thoughts
were not eternity, nor the poverty of our lives, irritable
baggage clerks,

nor the millions of weeping relatives surrounding the buses waving
goodbye,

nor other millions of the poor rushing around from city to city to
see their loved ones,

nor an indian dead with fright talking to a huge cop by the Coke
machine,

nor this trembling old lady with a cane taking the last trip of her
life,

nor the red capped cynical porter collecting his quarters and smiling
over the smashed baggage,

nor me looking around at the horrible dream,

nor mustached negro Operating Clerk named Spade, dealing out with his marvelous long hand the fate of thousands of express packages,

nor fairy Sam in the basement limping from leaden trunk to trunk,

nor Joe at the counter with his nervous breakdown smiling cowardly at the customers,

nor the grayish-green whale's stomach interior loft where we keep the baggage in hideous racks,

hundreds of suitcases full of tragedy rocking back and forth waiting to be opened,

nor the baggage that's lost, nor damaged handles, nameplates vanished, busted wires & broken ropes, whole trunks exploding on the concrete floor,

nor seabags emptied into the night in the final warehouse.

II

Yet Spade reminded me of Angel, unloading a bus,

dressed in blue overalls black face official Angel's workman cap,

pushing with his belly a huge tin horse piled high with black baggage,

looking up as he passed the yellow light bulb of the loft

and holding high on his arm an iron shepherd's crook.

III

It was the racks, I realized, sitting myself on top of them now as is my wont at lunchtime to rest my tired foot,

it was the racks, great wooden shelves and stanchions posts and beams assembled floor to roof jumbled with baggage,

—the Japanese white metal postwar trunk gaudily flowered & headed for Fort Bragg,

one Mexican green paper package in purple rope adorned with names for Nogales,

hundreds of radiators all at once for Eureka,

crates of Hawaiian underwear,

rolls of posters scattered over the Peninsula, nuts to Sacramento,

one human eye for Napa,

an aluminum box of human blood for Stockton

and a little red package of teeth for Calistoga—

it was the racks and these on the racks I saw naked in electric light
    the night before I quit,
the racks were created to hang our possessions, to keep us together,
    a temporary shift in space,
God's only way of building the rickety structure of Time,
to hold the bags to send on the roads, to carry our luggage from place
    to place
looking for a bus to ride us back home to Eternity where the heart
    was left and farewell tears began.

    I V

A swarm of baggage sitting by the counter as the transcontinental
    bus pulls in.
The clock registering 12.15 A.M., May 9, 1956, the second hand
    moving forward, red.
Getting ready to load my last bus.—Farewell, Walnut Creek
    Richmond Vallejo Portland Pacific Highway
Fleet-footed Quicksilver, God of transience.
One last package sits lone at midnight sticking up out of the Coast
    rack high as the dusty fluorescent light.

The wage they pay us is too low to live on. Tragedy reduced to
    numbers.
This for the poor shepherds. I am a communist.

Farewell ye Greyhound where I suffered so much,
hurt my knee and scraped my hand and built my pectoral muscles
    big as vagina.

from KADDISH

    I V
O mother
what have I left out
O mother
what have I forgotten
O mother
farewell
with a long black shoe
farewell

with Communist Party and a broken stocking
farewell
with six dark hairs on the wen of your breast
farewell
with your old dress and a long black beard around the vagina
farewell
with your sagging belly
with your fear of Hitler
with your mouth of bad short stories
with your fingers of rotten mandolines
with your arms of fat Paterson porches
with your belly of strikes and smokestacks
with your chin of Trotsky and the Spanish War
with your voice singing for the decaying overbroken workers
with your nose of bad lay with your nose of the smell of the pickles
    of Newark
with your eyes
with your eyes of Russia
with your eyes of no money
with your eyes of false China
with your eyes of Aunt Elanor
with your eyes of starving India
with your eyes pissing in the park
with your eyes of America taking a fall
with your eyes of your failure at the piano
with your eyes of your relatives in California
with your eyes of Ma Rainey dying in an ambulance
with your eyes of Czechoslovakia attacked by robots
with your eyes going to painting class at night in the Bronx
with your eyes of the killer Grandma you see on the horizon from
    the Fire-Escape
with your eyes running naked out of the apartment screaming into
    the hall
with your eyes being led away by policemen to an ambulance
with your eyes strapped down on the operating table
with your eyes with the pancreas removed
with your eyes of appendix operation
with your eyes of abortion
with your eyes of ovaries removed

with your eyes of shock
with your eyes of lobotomy
with your eyes of divorce
with your eyes of stroke
with your eyes alone
with your eyes
with your eyes
with your Death full of Flowers

Kral Majales

And the Communists have nothing to offer but fat cheeks and
    eyeglasses and lying policemen
and the Capitalists proffer Napalm and money in green suitcases
    to the Naked,
and the Communists create heavy industry but the heart is also
    heavy
and the beautiful engineers are all dead, the secret technicians
    conspire for their own glamor
in the Future, in the Future, but now drink vodka and lament
    the Security Forces,
and the Capitalists drink gin and whiskey on airplanes but let
    Indian brown millions starve
and when Communist and Capitalist assholes tangle the Just man
    is arrested or robbed or had his head cut off,
but not like Kabir, and the cigarette cough of the Just man
    above the clouds
in the bright sunshine is a salute to the health of the blue sky.
For I was arrested thrice in Prague, once for singing drunk on
    Narodni street,
once knocked down on the midnight pavement by a mustached
    agent who screamed out BOUZERANT,
once for losing my notebooks of unusual sex politics dream opinions,
and I was sent from Havana by plane by detectives in green
    uniform,
and I was sent from Prague by plane by detectives in Czechoslo-
    vakian business suits,
Cardplayers out of Cezanne, the two strange dolls that entered

Joseph K's room at morn
also entered mine, and ate at my table, and examined my scribbles,
and followed me night and morn from the houses of lovers to the
    cafés of Centrum—
And I am the King of May, which is the power of sexual youth,
and I am the King of May, which is industry in eloquence and
    action in amour,
and I am the King of May, which is long hair of Adam and the
    Beard of my own body
and I am the King of May, which is Kral Majales in the Czecho-
    slovakian tongue,
and I am the King of May, which is old Human poesy, and
    100,000 people chose my name,
and I am the King of May, and in a few minutes I will land at
    London Airport,
and I am the King of May, naturally, for I am of Slavic parentage
    and a Buddhist Jew
who worships the Sacred Heart of Christ the blue body of Krishna
    the straight back of Ram
the beads of Chango the Nigerian singing Shiva Shiva in a manner
    which I have invented,
and the King of May is a middleeuropean honor, mine in the
    XX century
despite space and the Time Machine, because I heard the voice
    of Blake in a vision,
and repeat that voice. And I am King of May that sleeps with
    teenagers laughing.
And I am the King of May, that I may be expelled from my
    Kingdom with Honor, as of old,
To shew the difference between Caesar's Kingdom and the King-
    dom of the May of Man—
and I am the King of May, tho paranoid, for the Kingdom of
    May is too beautiful to last for more than a month—
and I am the King of May because I touched my finger to my
    forehead saluting
a luminous heavy girl trembling hands who said "one moment
    Mr. Ginsberg"
before a fat young Plainclothesman stepped between our bodies
    —I was going to England—

and I am the King of May, returning to see Bunhill Fields and walk on Hampstead Heath,

and I am the King of May, in a giant jetplane touching Albion's airfield trembling in fear

as the plane roars to a landing on the grey concrete, shakes & expells air,

and rolls slowly to a stop under the clouds with part of blue heaven still visible.

And *tho* I am the King of May, the Marxists have beat me upon the street, kept me up all night in Police Station, followed me thru Springtime Prague, detained me in secret and deported me from our kingdom by airplane.

Thus I have written this poem on a jet seat in mid Heaven.

May 7, 1965

Wales Visitation

White fog lifting & falling on mountain-brow
   Trees moving in rivers of wind
       The clouds arise
 as on a wave, gigantic eddy lifting mist
   above teeming ferns exquisitely swayed
         along a green crag
  glimpsed thru mullioned glass in valley raine—

Bardic, O Self, Visitacione, tell naught
 but what seen by one man in a vale in Albion,
  of the folk, whose physical sciences end in Ecology,
     the wisdom of earthly relations,
  of mouths & eyes interknit ten centuries visible
    orchards of mind language manifest human,
 of the satanic thistle that raises its horned symmetry
  flowering above sister grass-daisies' pink tiny
     bloomlets angelic as lightbulbs—

Remember 160 miles from London's symmetrical thorned tower & network of TV pictures flashing bearded your Self

the lambs on the tree-nooked hillside this day bleating
heard in Blake's old ear, & the silent thought of Wordsworth in
eld Stillness
clouds passing through skeleton arches of Tintern Abbey—
Bard Nameless as the Vast, babble to Vastness!

All the Valley quivered, one extended motion, wind
undulating on mossy hills
a giant wash that sank white fog delicately down red runnels
on the mountainside
whose leaf-branch tendrils moved asway
in granitic undertow down—
and lifted the floating Nebulous upward, and lifted the arms of the
trees

and lifted the grasses an instant in balance
and lifted the lambs to hold still
and lifted the green of the hill, in one solemn wave

A solid mass of Heaven, mist-infused, ebbs thru the vale,
a wavelet of Immensity, lapping gigantic through Llanthony
Valley,
the length of all England, valley upon valley under Heaven's ocean
tonned with cloud-hang,
—Heaven balanced on a grassblade.
Roar of the mountain wind slow, sigh of the body,
One Being on the mountainside stirring gently
Exquisite scales trembling everywhere in balance,
one motion thru the cloudy sky-floor shifting on the million
feet of daisies,
one Majesty the motion that stirred wet grass quivering
to the farthest tendril of white fog poured down
through shivering flowers on the mountain's
head—

No imperfection in the budded mountain,
Valleys breathe, heaven and earth move together,
daisies push inches of yellow air, vegetables tremble,
green atoms shimmer in grassy mandalas,
sheep speckle the mountainside, revolving their jaws with empty
eyes,

horses dance in the warm rain,
tree-lined canals network through live farmland,
blueberries fringe stone walls
on hill breasts nippled with hawthorn,
pheasants croak up meadow-bellies haired with fern—

Out, out on the hillside, into the ocean sound, into delicate
gusts of wet air,
Fall on the ground, O great Wetness, O Mother, No harm on
thy body!
Stare close, no imperfection in the grass,
each flower Buddha-eye, repeating the story,
the myriad-formed soul
Kneel before the foxglove raising green buds, mauve bells drooped
doubled down the stem trembling antennae,
& look in the eyes of the branded lambs that stare
breathing stockstill under dripping hawthorn—
I lay down mixing my beard with the wet hair of the mountainside,
smelling the brown vagina-moist ground, harmless,
tasting the violet thistle-hair, sweetness—
One being so balanced, so vast, that its softest breath
moves every floweret in the stillness on the valley floor,
trembles lamb-hair hung gossamer rain-beaded in the grass,
lifts trees on their roots, birds in the great draught
hiding their strength in the rain, bearing same weight,

Groan thru breast and neck, a great Oh! to earth heart
Calling our Presence together
The great secret is no secret
Senses fit the winds,
Visible is visible,
rain-mist curtains wave through the bearded vale,
grey atoms wet the wind's Kaballah
Crosslegged on a rock in dusk rain,
rubber booted in soft grass, mind moveless,
breath trembles in white daisies by the roadside,
Heaven breath and my own symmetric
Airs wavering thru antlered green fern
drawn in my navel, same breath as breathes thru Capel-Y-Ffn,
Sounds of Aleph and Aum

> through forests of gristle,
> my skull and Lord Hereford's Knob equal,
> All Albion one.

What did I notice? Particulars! The
    vision of the great One is myriad—
smoke curls upward from ash tray,
    house fire burned low,
The night, still wet & moody black heaven
    starless
upward in motion with wet wind.

July 29, 1967 (LSD)—August 3, 1967 (London)

Rain-Wet Asphalt Heat, Garbage Curbed Cans Overflowing

I hauled down lifeless mattresses to sidewalk refuse-piles,
old rugs stept on from Paterson to Lower East Side filled with
    bedbugs,
grey pillows, couch seats treasured from the street laid back on the
    street
—out, to hear Murder-tale, 3rd Street cyclists attacked tonite—
Bopping along in rain, Chaos fallen over City roofs,
shrouds of chemical vapour drifting over building-tops—
Get the *Times*, Nixon says peace reflected from the Moon,
but I found no boy body to sleep with all night on pavements till
    3 AM home in sweating drizzle—
Those mattresses soggy lying by full five garbagepails—
Barbara, Maretta, Peter Steven Rosebud slept on these Pillows years
    ago,
forgotten names, also made love to me, I had these mattresses four
    years on my floor—
Gerard, Jimmy many months, even blond Gordon later,
Paul with the beautiful big cock, that teenage boy that lived in
    Pennsylvania,
forgotten numbers, young dream loves and lovers, earthly bellies—
many strong youths with eyes closed, come sighing and helping me
    come—

Desires already forgotten, tender persons used and kissed goodbye
and all the times I came to myself alone in the dark dreaming of
   Neal or Billy Budd
—nameless angels of half-life—heart beating & eyes weeping for
   lovely phantoms—
Back from the Gem Spa, and into the hallway, a glance behind
and sudden farewell to the bedbug-ridden mattresses piled soggy in
   dark rain.

August 2, 1969

W. D. SNODGRASS

(1926–)

Orpheus

Stone lips to the unspoken cave;
Fingering the nervous strings, alone,
I crossed that gray sill, raised my head
To lift my song into the grave
Meanders of unfolding stone,
Following where the echo led
Down blind alleys of our dead.

Down the forbidden, backward street
To the lower town, condemned, asleep
In blank remembering mazes where
Smoke rose, the ashes hid my feet
And slow walls crumpled, settling deep
In rubble of the central square.
All ruin I could sound was there.

At the charred rail and windowsill,
Widows hunched in fusty shawls,
This only once the Furies wept;
The watchdog turned to hear me till
Head by head forgot its howls,
Loosed the torn images it kept,
Let sag its sore jaws and slept.

Then to my singing's radius
Seethed faces like a pauper's crowd
Or flies of an old injury.
The piteous dead who lived on us
Whined in my air, anarchic, loud
Till my soft voice that set them free,
Lost in this grievous enemy,

Rose up and laid them in low slumbers;
I meant to see in them what dark
Powers be, what eminent plotters.
Midmost those hushed, downcast numbers
Starved Tantalus stood upright, stark,
Waistdeep where the declining waters
Swelled their tides, where Danaus' daughters

Dropped in full surf their unfilled tub;
Now leaned against his rolling stone
Slept Sisyphus beneath the hill;
That screaming half-beast, strapped at the hub,
Whom Juno's animal mist had known,
Ixion's wheel creaked and was still.
I held all hell to hear my will.

"Powers of the Underworld, who rule
All higher powers by graft or debt,
Within whose mortgage all men live:
No spy, no shining power's fool,
I think in the unthought worlds to get
The light you only freely give
Who are all bright worlds' negative

You gave wink in an undue crime
To love—strong even here, they say.
I sing, as the blind beggars sing,
To ask of you this little time
—All lives foreclose in their due day—
That flowered bride cut down in Spring,
Struck by the snake, your underling."

In one long avenue she was
Wandering toward me, vague, uncertain,
Limping a little still, the hair
And garments tenuous as gauze
And drifting loose like a white curtain
Vacillating in black night air
That holds white lilacs, God knows where.

"Close your eyes," said the inner ear;
"As night lookouts learn not to see
Ahead but only off one side,
As the eye's sight is never clear
But blind, dead center, you must be
Content; look not upon your bride
Till day's light lifts her eyelids wide."

I turned my back to her, set out
My own way back and let her follow
Like some curious albino beast
That prowls in areas of drought,
Lured past the town's slack doors, the hollow
Walls, the stream-bed lost in mist,
That breathless long climb, with no least

Doubt she must track me close behind;
As the actual scent of flesh, she must
Trail my voice unquestioning where.
Yet where the dawn first edged my mind
In one white flashing of mistrust
I turned and she, she was not there.
My hands closed on the high, thin air.

It was the nature of the thing:
No moon outlives its leaving night,
No sun its day. And I went on
Rich in the loss of all I sing
To the threshold of waking light,
To larksong and the live, gray dawn.
So night by night, my life has gone.

The Marsh

Swampstrife and spatterdock
    lull in the heavy waters;
some thirty little frogs
    spring with each step you walk;
a fish's belly glitters
    tangled near rotting logs.

Over by the gray rocks
    muskrats dip and circle.
Out of his rim of ooze
    a silt-black pond snail walks
inverted on the surface
    toward what food he may choose.

You look up; while you walk
    the sun bobs and is snarled
in the enclosing weir
    of trees, in their dead stalks.
Stick in the mud, old heart,
    what are you doing here?

September in the Park

This pinched face of the moon
    all afternoon
spies through the hanging smoke
that glows where maples, turning,
    recall for one
more hour the tarnished sun
in rust of their last burning.

Still, those who are out walking
    will hear the laughter
of drab blue-chevroned ducks;
the drunkard echo mocking

where they carouse
on minnow ponds still flowing.
Beyond the bare oak's
    reach of boughs,
as black as some charred rafter,
are slow and waiting flocks,
    but they are going.

    This world is going
to leave the furnitures
of its unsheltering house
    in snow's dustcovers.
This old moon on its rounds
of the estate and grounds
    can well make sure
that no trespasser stirs
the fireplace or uncovers
    the burned out bed
of ashes. The young lovers
will not be coming here
    to give the bear
the offer of their bread.
This watchful face of age
    set pale and stern
over the gray iron cage
where his old habits turn
    and pace again
must mind his days to turn
him back in single, deep,
    cold-blooded sleep.

The hurrying, gray squirrels
    gather together
their hoard of the rich acorns
to their tall, windblown nest.
    And I, dear girl,
remember I have gathered
my hand upon your breast.

The Operation

From stainless steel basins of water
They brought warm cloths and they washed me,
From spun aluminum bowls, cold Zephiran sponges, fuming;
Gripped in the dead yellow glove, a bright straight razor
Inched on my stomach, down my groin,
Paring the brown hair off. They left me
White as a child, not frightened. I was not
Ashamed. They clothed me, then,
In the thin, loose, light, white garments,
The delicate sandals of poor Pierrot,
A schoolgirl first offering her sacrament.

I was drifting, inexorably, on toward sleep.
In skullcaps, masked, in blue-green gowns, attendants
Towed my cart, afloat in its white cloths,
The body with its tributary poisons borne
Down corridors of the diseased, thronging:
The scrofulous faces, contagious grim boys,
The huddled families, weeping, a staring woman
Arched to her gnarled stick,—a child was somewhere
Screaming, screaming—then, blind silence, the elevator rising
To the arena, humming, vast with lights; blank hero,
Shackled and spellbound, to enact my deed.

Into flowers, into women, I have awakened.
Too weak to think of strength, I have thought all day,
Or dozed among standing friends. I lie in night, now,
A small mound under linen like the drifted snow.
Only by nurses visited, in radiance, saying, Rest.
Opposite, ranked office windows glare; headlamps, below,
Trace out our highways; their cargoes under dark
        tarpaulins,
Trucks climb, thundering, and sirens may
Wail for the fugitive. It is very still. In my brandy bowl
Of sweet peas at the window, the crystal world
Is inverted, slow and gay.

The Campus on the Hill

Up the reputable walks of old established trees
They stalk, children of the *nouveaux riches*; chimes
Of the tall Clock Tower drench their heads in blessing:
"I don't wanna play at your house;
I don't like you any more."
My house stands opposite, on the other hill,
Among meadows, with the orchard fences down and falling;
Deer come almost to the door.
You cannot see it, even in this clearest morning.
White birds hang in the air between
Over the garbage landfill and those homes thereto adjacent,
Hovering slowly, turning, settling down
Like the flakes sifting imperceptibly onto the little town
In a waterball of glass.
And yet, this morning, beyond this quiet scene,
The floating birds, the backyards of the poor,
Beyond the shopping plaza, the dead canal, the hillside lying tilted
    in the air,
Tomorrow has broken out today:
Riot in Algeria, in Cyprus, in Alabama;
Aged in wrong, the empires are declining,
And China gathers, soundlessly, like evidence.
What shall I say to the young on such a morning?—
Mind is the one salvation?—also grammar?—
No; my little ones lean not toward revolt. They
Are the Whites, the vaguely furiously driven, who resist
Their souls with such passivity
As would make Quakers swear. All day, dear Lord, all day
They wear their godhead lightly.
They look out from their hill and say,
To themselves, "We have nowhere to go but down;
The great destination is to stay."
Surely the nations will be reasonable;
They look at the world—don't they?—the world's way?
The clock just now has nothing more to say.

These Trees Stand . . .

These trees stand very tall under the heavens.
While *they* stand, if I walk, all stars traverse
This steep celestial gulf their branches chart.
Though lovers stand at sixes and at sevens
While civilizations come down with the curse,
Snodgrass is walking through the universe.

I can't make any world go around *your* house.
But note this moon. Recall how the night nurse
Goes ward-rounds, by the mild, reflective art
Of focusing her flashlight on her blouse.
Your name's safe conduct into love or verse;
Snodgrass is walking through the universe.

Your name's absurd, miraculous as sperm
And as decisive. If you can't coerce
One thing outside yourself, why you're the poet!

What irrefrangible atoms whirl, affirm
Their destiny and form Lucinda's skirts!
She can't make up your mind. Soon as you know it,
Your firmament grows touchable and firm.
If all this world runs battlefield or worse,
Come, let us wipe our glasses on our shirts:
Snodgrass is walking through the universe.

Vampire's Aubade

Why so drawn, so worn,
        My dearest;
    Should this sun-drenched morn
Find you so burned out and so pale?
Until now I've had no fear lest
    You'd be quick to fail.

Just last night, your glowing
    Cheek and breast
Entranced me, overflowing
With their young love, warm and strong.
Not to freely give your best,
  Dear—you'd think that wrong.

Then rise; shine; let your laughter
    Fill the air.
When I do need looking after
And there's so much to be done,
Dear, it surely isn't fair
  So to hang on everyone.

        Or don't you care?

RICHARD MURPHY

(1927–)

Droit de Seigneur

1820

In a grey rectory a clergyman was reading
Fortunate by firelight the *Connaught Journal*.
The shutters were closed, for famine was spreading
Among the people. The portrait of Cromwell,
One hand on the Bible, the other on a sword,
Had been stowed that evening under a haystack.
The air was crackling with the whips of rhetoric.

A groom was saddling his mare in the stable
While a redcoat stumbled down the loft ladder
Buttoning his tunic, followed by a girl
Who ran to the kitchen. The yard lantern
Yellowed the stirrups and the buckled leather
On the mare's girth as he combed her down.
The master was for hunting the Ribbonmen:

A secret band, swearing oaths by moonlight,
Refusing to pay tithes or rent to the landlord,
Who battered on lonely doors after midnight,
And wore round their sleeves a white riband.
He called it his duty to commit these rogues
To the jury of gentlemen at Galway Assizes.
Saving of property went with saving of souls.

So he galloped out with a few soldiers
On to the gravelled road under the lime-trees
With his father's pistol in a handsome holster.
They ambushed a wedding from the next parish.
All escaped except a young simpleton
In whose pocket they found a white bandage.
Twenty miles to Galway he was marched in chains.

In the pigeon park the heifers were grazing
Under the beech-trees. The soldiers had gone.
Behind the frown of the windows, browsing
On the price of cattle in the *Connaught Journal,*
The rector looked out on the frost and the sun.
The girl ran across the yard with a bucket
'Tomorrow', he read, 'the boy will be executed.'

from ''THE BATTLE OF AUGHRIM''

[*After the Noose, and the Black Diary Deeds*]

After the noose, and the black diary deeds
Gossiped, his fame roots in prison lime:
The hanged bones burn, a revolution seeds.
Now Casement's skeleton is flying home.

A gun salutes, the troops slow-march, our new
Nation atones for her shawled motherland
Whose welcome gaoled him when a U-boat threw
This rebel quixote soaked on Banna Strand.

Soldiers in green guard the draped catafalque
With chalk remains of once ambiguous bone
Which fathered nothing till the traitor's dock
Hurt him to tower in legend like Wolfe Tone.

From gaol yard to the Liberator's tomb,
Pillared in frost, they carry the freed ash,
Transmuted relic of a death-cell flame
Which purged for martyrdom the diarist's flesh.

On the small screen I watch the packed cortège
Pace from High Mass. Rebels in silk hats now
Exploit the grave with an old comrade's speech:
White hair tossed, a black cape flecked with snow.

The God Who Eats Corn*

William Lindsay Murphy
1887–1965

1

In his loyal garden, like Horace's farm,
He asks his visitors to plant a tree.
The black shadow of the African msasa
Squats among the lawn's colonial company.

In honour among watersprays that spin
Rainbows over cool English rose-beds
Hand-weeded by a pink-soled piccanin
The Queen Mother's cypress nods in a straw hood.

---

* At the end of the nineteeth century there was no word in the language of the Matabele to describe the white man who came to settle in central Africa, so he was called 'the god who eats corn,' meaning that although he had god-like powers, he had to eat, and to die. My father, who was born in an Irish rectory, retired from the British Colonial Service as Governor of the Bahamas, and settled in Southern Rhodesia in 1950 on virgin land, where he established a farm and later a school for African children. The time is the last year of Federation—and the myth of 'partnership'—1963.—Author's note.

The trees are labelled: a chairman of mines
Gave this copper beech, that silver oak
Was trowelled by a Governor: great names
Written on tags, Llewellin and Tredgold.

Livingstone's heir presented this wild fig
From the burnt-out forest of Africa:
On its branches by moonlight a boomslang swings.
This Cape creeper has a cold blue flower.

As a son I choose the native candelabra:
Perched on an ant-hill, after years of drought,
From its cut spines a milky sap flows:
To my father I give this tree as a tribute.

His own plane-tree, brought by seed from Cos,
From shade where Hippocrates swore his oath,
Wilts in the voodoo climate, while gums
The trekkers imported have sapped the earth.

Under these trees, he believes that indaba [1]
Could heal the blood-feud. Bull-frogs crackle
In the lily-pond. Tolerant water
Eases roots, and cools the racial fever.

2

From his green study half-door he looks out
On the young plantation of his old age:
An ibis is perched on a cone hut,
Rain-birds croak in the citrus orchard.

Boys are sharpening pangas at the wood-pile:
Trailers approach, filling barns from the field
With limp tobacco to be dried by steam.
A Union Jack droops on the school flag-pole.

[1] In tribal society, the chieftain decided his policy after hearing advice from his counsellors in the shade of a large tree. This counsel was called the indaba. The tree could be any kind of large African tree, a mopani, a fig, or, most likely, a msasa, a lovely deciduous tree of the bush.—Author's note.

Hunkered on dust in kaffir quarters
With rickety babies, the sewing-club meets
My mother bringing gifts through trellis doors
Frail as a lily in her straw sun-hat.

Such tinkle of bangles, such ivory teeth
Clacking, they gossip of clothes and clinics.
A child rolls a pram-wheel over the earth,
A cat is stalking the cooped-up chickens.

He drives to the store to collect his *Times*
And letters from home, tulip-trees in flower,
Road-grit on his tongue, tobacco booms
A memory, hot wind raising a dust-choked roar.

He swims before breakfast in a blue pool
Sometimes recalling Atlantic light
Splashed on to hymn-books in a pitch-pine hall
Where his father preached. He prays at night.

At the carol service in the grading-shed
He reads the lesson, joining trade with truth.
My knees remember his coconut mats,
The mesh of our duty to improve the earth.

3
'To do some good for this poor Africa'
Was Livingstone's prayer, but not the Founder's dream.
Towards gold and diamonds, the Pioneer Column
Trekked at the bidding of a childless millionaire.

They came with ox-wagons, claiming a treaty,
To the king's kraal, his great indaba tree,
With charming letters from Queen Victoria:
There the chameleon swallowed the black fly.

In dusty dorps they slept with slave-girls,
On farms they divided the royal herd.

In stifling mine-shafts the disarmed warriors
Were flogged to work, their grazing-grounds wired.

So now at white homesteads, the coffee steams
On creepered verandahs. Racial partners
Do not mix in wedlock sons and daughters.
The white man rides: the black man is his horse.

Brown bare feet slide softly over the tiles
Soothing the master, scrubbing his bath,
Folding his towels, timidly with smiles
Smoothing his pillow, and wincing at his wrath.

To each black, his ten acres for millet;
To each white, his three thousand of grass.
The gospel of peace preached from the pulpit;
From the hungry fields the gospel of force.

4
In a paradise for white gods he grows old
Cutting rafters out of the felled wood,
Baking bricks from the clay of ant-hills:
He plants the first rose on the burnt sandveld.

Thirteen years ago his books were unpacked
In the path of mambas, where nomads' fires
Lit stone-age sketches on the walls of caves
And the sand was printed by lion spoor.

His Governor's helmet stowed in a teak chest,
He called back Homer after forty years'
Damp decay in the West of Ireland:
He retired into sunlight on a thousand acres.

Trapped from tribes in their idle forest
Negroes gathered to work for meal and poll-tax,
Their teeming women overcrawled by bony kids,
Calling him 'Baas,' grinning, hungry, diseased.

They wove wicker-and-mud hovels to sleep in.
Tractors invaded the elephant road.
A bore-hole was sunk. Cicadas at his fly-screen
Halted and shrilled. The kudu retreated.

He fed corn to his gang and cured fever.
Cigarettes sold in a London shop
Kept people stooped on his kopje alive.
Each year he felled more trees to plant a crop.

Between the auction floors and seed-bed sowing
First in a thatched hut he began a school.
The market rose and fell, drought followed flooding,
When the leaves ripened there were showers of hail.

Daily at dawn, they clang the plough-disc gong
That winds a chain of men through vleis and veld.
No boss-boy drives them with a sjambok's thong.
At dusk they come to class-rooms to be schooled.

Children are chanting hymns, their lean bodies
Tropically sensual behind puritan desks,
From mealie plot and swamp of tsetse flies
Lured by the witchcraft of the god's mechanics.

A red-hot poker flowers in the playground,
A viper sleeps on the sand. The dry slate
Under the sweating palm is rubbed and scrawled.
They wait like logs, ready for fire and wind.

5
Tall in his garden, shaded and brick-walled,
He upholds the manners of a lost empire.
Time has confused dead honour with dead guilt
But lets a sunbird sip at a gold creeper.

His scholar's head, disguised in a bush hat,
Spectacled eyes, that watch the weaver's nest

Woven, have helped a high dam to be built
Where once the Zambesi was worshipped and wasted.

Sometimes he dreams of a rogue elephant
That smashed the discharged rifle in his hand:
Or reading, remembers the horns of buffalo,
The leopards he shipped to the Dublin zoo.

On the game-cleared plateau the settlers say
'This is our home: this is white man's country.'
Dust-storms gather to hide their traces
Under boulders balanced in a smouldering sky.

6

They say, when the god goes, the rain falls,
Contour ridges burst, sweeping off crops,
The rafters crumble, trees shoot through floors,
And wind carves the fields into smooth dust-heaps.

The concrete cracks and the brown rivers bleed,
Cattle die of rinderpest, dogs with rabies
Bite their masters, the half-freed slaves are freed
But not into a garden that anyone remembers.

Now the old mopani forest is felled.
The settlers try to cling to their laagers,
Wire for a gun-boat, profit in gold-shares,
Dream of silk flags and showers of assegais.

The trees that fail are soon devoured by ants.
Sundowners bind together a white crowd:
Some preach of partners, more sneer at the Munts
Getting cheeky, lazier than ever. He's bored.

While he prepares to fly to Ithaca
The B.S.A. police hold rifle drill,
Pyres kindle under *Pax Britannica*.
He stays to build a club-room for the school.

At dusk on the stoep he greets ambassadors
From Kenya and Ceylon. The silver trays
Are lit by candles cupped in the flower borders.
Husks hang on his dry indaba trees.

Last thing at night he checks the rain-gauge
Remembering his father on a rectory lawn
Thunder is pent in the drums of the compound.
He feels too old to love the rising moon.

BINK NOLL

(1927–)

The Picador Bit

Inside that figure rides opaque malice
who by drilling makes the great heart lift
its fountain and waste the lake of blood.
His lance strikes, holds. Longer, the don's full weight.

Men for this circumstance of sport have made
laws that order place, gear, conduct and four tries
but the bull learns rage instead. He erupts
through headlong pain and strikes wrath back again.

Today's malice, part horse saved by blindfold
and morphine from panic at horns, stands,
its legal right side out, and standing so
tempts this, the next enlargement of the hole

—and part brawny don, mechanic who finds
and fits his point to drain the immense will.
Again the spot. The centaur shocks sideward
till the hole is important, like a whale's spout.

The crowd feels the lance in its own ripe hole,
in its hump knows the monster with two heads,

the blackness of its law, this letting of force
and the pump emptying the tongue of red.

Blood foams down. The head is dropped forever now.
Justice is satisfied. Its constable trots
darkly off. Left to his killers, the bull—
danger's substance, lure, huge hate itself—

thrills every male groin while he swings there
and, helpless, spills the fire of his urine.

"All My Pretty Ones? Did You Say All?"

Sleep stands off to watch me brood the curse
That ripens even while hope—the star
That once adorned my eye—pales.
The hag Anguish keeps cave in my back.

These days in broad day harpies peck
While my three children swell into heirs
Of my disorder, plaiting garlands
From nettles and crazy buds and weeds

Bred in wild churchyards across Europe
And new forced from this other soil
Where moisture thrives the dead, gives them source,
Lifts their corollas to the flaming light.

As greenery threatens to parch and drop
The rich summer that fulfills all greens
So these heads I dream are beset
By like loveliness that prowls its parent.

Poised in Eden moments, they are ravished
With delight in mirrors, combing of hair.
Their songs will wake the morning doors
And float, still innocent, through this used air.

I their father wear the bethorned head,
The web knotted from every Noll's error,
The body wracked from every Noll's wife
And perfected in this adult fright.

For innocence takes its father for lens,
For very ear to garner up the mind.
I am the dream of their correctness.
The hero! The safety! I! The right!

I once thought to orphan them from this love,
Leave them to the wide world and change of names—
Thought to be of error and misery,
Imperfection and fever not the genitor

But last inheritor. As if a father
Might nip the booming miracle of his yeast!
Harpies warmed the egg of that disaster
But despair glared in the night of my mind:

A sour delicacy of stomach,
Congenital rage, shared tropisms, odd tics
And deeper intimacies of our blood
Had made their signs in each pretty one.

They are doomed beyond my bravery
To save them. The lesson tells of cause,
How the passion of the flesh for pain
Matures, how my seeds are cast and blasted

In the dread of time, how the law is waste
And glories, waste and glories, waste and glories.
The lesson instructs me to recall
A season of joy, an endless round noon

Of which I am the fat debris.
The noon is happening to virgins
While my thrilled nerves, having cast these seeds,
Die back into the dark humus.

Air Tunnel, Monticello

On Palladio's rural theme, a farmhouse
Flanked by sheds—because on that he'd improvise
A villa basic to his well-examined life

Mr. Jefferson contrived this tube—
Wheels, chain, pulley, mason's work, hooks, and crocks—
And had it buried to spirit out of view

The wilt, the waste, the metabolic slops,
An arch of stone hidden in the ground,
A modest device to purify the mansion.

Then on he planned, organizing light and space
Along the bellevues from his mountaintop,
Shaping the clean air with axioms.

The sun stopped to glare down on his marvel,
On dome, portico, skylights and marble,
On paths, plantings, lawns that prove still

The elegance of County Albemarle
And of the mind that crystallized it
Along these axes of his sane eye,

The mind that made it stand as simile
For the whole known world, felicitous and lucid.
What a lord's schedule this design meant!

Time planned, time valued, time husbanded,
Time kept fresh like fish in the brick pool,
The hours swimming brightly till his demand.

His tube required one field hand at the down end
To carry off and dump the smelly crocks,
One ignorant field hand lucky to get this near

The palazzo of his master's intellect,
Mr. Jefferson's order of elaborate balances—
The fulcrum for which is this discreet stone arch,

This nook of effluvium wedged
Where all planes of light intersect,
The orifice smoking in the county of hope.

Lunch on Omaha Beach

The killers are killed, their violent rinds
Conveyed, and the beach is back to summer.
I eat sausage with bread. Full of ease, the sea
Makes the sound of cows chewing through high grass.

They're deposited in government lawn
Set with nine thousand decencies of stone
To wet the eye, shake the heart, and lose
Each name in a catalog of graven names.

They are wasted in the blank of herohood.
They are dead to fondness and paradox.
They're all the same. In the field of lawn
Above the beach, they're put away the same.

They should be left exactly here below where
Death's great bronze mares shook earth and bloodied them,
Where violence of noise isolated each boy
In the body of his scream, and dropped him.

No worn Norman hill should be scarred and smoothed
To suit officials' tidy thoughts for graveyards
But the wreckage left, shrinking in rust and rags
And carrion to dust or tumuli.

To honor my thoughts against shrines, to find
The beast who naked wakes in us and walks

In flags, to watch the color of his day
I spill my last Bordeaux into the sand.

Watching, I wonder at the white quiet,
The fields of butter cows, my countrymen
Come to study battle maps, blue peasants
Still moving back and forth, the day's soft sea.

For Jane Kane, Whom We Knew in Our Young Marriages

Tall Jane is dark who was burnished bright,
Who walked her fine long bones through rooms
And fixed her striding in my eye's vigor.

Extravagance of cells broke the balance
Where Jane thrived and in her waste morality
Has made its blind ironic grave.

She is blind and night-eyed who drank our light,
Who thirsted back through the sleep of weeks.
News of her darkness darkens my bravery.

Among us the idea of her has been elevated.
She is the sign of our generation. She is sealed:
The first scattering from our number.

For her the filament of hunger has dried away.
Her mind's store is put in a cave.
Her movement is turned to salt. She is straight.

She is our edge, our pioneer and spy,
Our steeple at the curve where land stops.
For her we're paid back this warning of trumpets;

For tall Jane, lurking through the scrub of time,
Found for us the serpent stopped
Upon a slab of sunlight, letting out its long hiss.

The Rented Garden

We Sunday strode—I in leather,
My kids in red—through pure October.
We smelled a country gone bright
From decay, but I went to delight
In such burning
                until we stood
In our garden across Lyme Road,
A rectangle hired at minor cost
To grow our greens on. I saw: cornstalks
Rattled white against blue, the squash vine
Had sprawled down in softness, and slime
Cracked from bleached tomato skins. Just thus
Our richness went, by three quick frosts.
The youngsters sang along the packed earth.
I listened. As if for some birth
The fool crickets whirred for this cloudless
Relic of summer. Deaf and dauntless,
My girl ran to a bonfire the wind
Had readied gaily, at the end
Of the garden. My boy followed; he
Ran right through the blighted broccoli.

The Hunchback's Bath

She seems to have forgot the hump there
forcing her head forward from the porcelain.
Now she's finished with her feet and stands.
I suppose she feels fresh as anyone.

In the medicine-chest mirror she views
her head with pride, turning it side to side
while she twists that torso and dries
the hump, familiar as an elbow,

mere bone that children are not supposed
to stare at, but do. The mother did,
stared and stared. Didn't she hate the bone
like a curse? yet guard her child from that view?

Nevertheless, that elongated head
raves against us, grown one of those gnomes,
papier-mâché, that run side to side in parades
on tiny legs stuck out underneath.

No! I am unfair, wrong. I confess
ignorance. I exaggerate.
Yet should she make an advance, the way
beauty permits, I would be ashamed.

She has a husband, but once or twice
she must have found his taste grotesque
and love between them so. Still, I failed to guess
such handsome breasts crowded on these ribs.

She might consider herself a sign,
proof that we're all more or less victims
but she's a scandal of the chromosomes,
lonelier than a boy just found out he's a Jew.

I don't know. I don't understand
how her heart shoulders the birthright
swollen from her waist and—bared like this—
enough to make children screaming run.

When her vanity hides it best she can
and enters among men, her sweet defense
makes men seem to ignore that powerful shape
and compress their knees to hide the flinch.

To the God Morpheus

What I've learned since thirty of self-deceit
and deceit found common among my friends
so I can detect craft and self-seeking
and loss of dignity in everyone.

Tonight let me not wake into the black
and hear lists of accusation
where my loves, miscalculated, end
but hide me in the deaf and dumb obscure.

O Dream-shaper, lay me deeper down
than dreams begin, into the blindest dark.
Supply me specifics, the silver pill,
capsule and ampule, the mouthful of Lethe.

Not the cave where needs and dream confuse
in the filthy dark and force failure up,
back to its home, this room where it wakes me
into wide self-horror. But blindest dark!

I lie here making a diagram of day
guessed from the parts that hurt and men's reports.
Like the map of beef the butcher learns from
before he starts in business for himself.

On the pillow I listen to my heart—
afraid that it may or may not stop.
Don't wake me to daylight, god, till your drug
has repaired my black heart and left it blank

and helps me sneak into the first routines
when briefly fresh-mouthed, still stunned with sleep, I
tolerate my own industry and my friends'
while youngsters whistle on their way to knowledge.

Angel

The dusk we bring the spruce in is like
last year's or the year-before's, many
darkening backward to one obscure
when a man hammered the first stand on
and tilted the tree up this stairwell
so its top showed on the second floor
and secured it like this, with packthread.

While we help holiness show herself,
carols play—albums once more dug out
for this hour, or hour and a half.
The strings of lights first, then on which branch
which ornament hangs best, then tinsel
until the angel, the same creature,
substantiates on time but sings not
nor plays her harp nor preens. The carols sing.

While they sing words we don't even hear,
we repeat "This is the prettiest yet."
Can we recall? Not one innocent
is left whose wish has come true tonight.
We sit in a circle on the floor
as before. Our grown-up faces glow
in the pink redundant radiance

spilling generously from our guest,
whom we've coaxed back because we're afraid
to admit what has happened to what
we once were or at least to say so
or quite let go, though each one's eyes show
that the shelter the house was, when first
we moved, is not what the house is now.

JAMES WRIGHT
(1927–)

On Minding One's Own Business

Ignorant two, we glide
On ripples near the shore.
The rainbows leap no more,
And men in boats alight
To see the day subside.

All evening fins have drowned
Back in the summer dark.
Above us, up the bank,
Obscure on lonely ground,
A shack receives the night.

I hold the lefthand oar
Out of the wash, and guide
The skiff away so wide
We wander out of sight
As soundless as before.

We will not land to bear
Our will upon that house,
Nor force on any place
Our dull offensive weight.

Somebody may be there,
Peering at us outside
Across the even lake,
Wondering why we take
Our time and stay so late.

Long may the lovers hide
In viny shacks from those
Who thrash among the trees,
Who curse, who have no peace,
Who pitch and moan all night
For fear of someone's joys,
Deploring the human face.

From prudes and muddying fools,
Kind Aphrodite, spare
All hunted criminals,
Hoboes, and whip-poor-wills,
And girls with rumpled hair,
All, all of whom might hide
Within that darkening shack.
Lovers may live, and abide.
Wherefore, I turn my back,
And trawl our boat away,
Lest someone fear to call
A girl's name till we go
Over the lake so slow
We hear the darkness fall.

A Blessing

Just off the highway to Rochester, Minnesota,
Twilight bounds softly forth on the grass.
And the eyes of those two Indian ponies
Darken with kindness.
They have come gladly out of the willows
To welcome my friend and me.

We step over the barbed wire into the pasture
Where they have been grazing all day, alone.
They ripple tensely, they can hardly contain their happiness
That we have come.
They bow shyly as wet swans. They love each other.
There is no loneliness like theirs.
At home once more,
They begin munching the young tufts of spring in the darkness.
I would like to hold the slenderer one in my arms,
For she has walked over to me
And nuzzled my left hand.
She is black and white,
Her mane falls wild on her forehead,
And the light breeze moves me to caress her long ear
That is delicate as the skin over a girl's wrist.
Suddenly I realize
That if I stepped out of my body I would break
Into blossom.

The Minneapolis Poem

1 .

I wonder how many old men last winter
Hungry and frightened by namelessness prowled
The Mississippi shore
Lashed blind by the wind, dreaming
Of suicide in the river.
The police remove their cadavers by daybreak
And turn them in somewhere.
Where?
How does the city keep lists of its fathers
Who have no names?
By Nicollet Island I gaze down at the dark water
So beautifully slow.
And I wish my brothers good luck
And a warm grave.

2 .
The Chippewa young men
Stab one another shrieking
Jesus Christ.
Split-lipped homosexuals limp in terror of assault.
High school backfields search under benches
Near the Post Office. Their faces are the rich
Raw bacon without eyes.
The Walker Art Center crowd stare
At the Guthrie Theater.

3.
Tall Negro girls from Chicago
Listen to light songs.
They know when the supposed patron
Is a plainclothesman.
A cop's palm
Is a roach dangling down the scorched fangs
Of a light bulb.
The soul of a cop's eyes
Is an eternity of Sunday daybreak in the suburbs
Of Juárez, Mexico.

4 .
The legless beggars are gone, carried away
By white birds.
The Artificial Limbs Exchange is gutted
And sown with lime.
The whalebone crutches and hand-me-down trusses
Huddle together dreaming in a desolation
Of dry groins.
I think of poor men astonished to waken
Exposed in broad daylight by the blade
Of a strange plough.

5 .
All over the walls of comb cells
Automobiles perfumed and blindered
Consent with a mutter of high good humor
To take their two naps a day.

Without sound windows glide back
Into dusk.
The sockets of a thousand blind bee graves tier upon tier
Tower not quite toppling.
There are men in this city who labor dawn after dawn
To sell me my death.

6.
But I could not bear
To allow my poor brother my body to die
In Minneapolis.
The old man Walt Whitman our countryman
Is now in America our country
Dead.
But he was not buried in Minneapolis
At least.
And no more may I be
Please God.

7.
I want to be lifted up
By some great white bird unknown to the police,
And soar for a thousand miles and be carefully hidden
Modest and golden as one last corn grain,
Stored with the secrets of the wheat and the mysterious lives
Of the unnamed poor.

In Terror of Hospital Bills

I still have some money
To eat with, alone
And frightened, knowing how soon
I will waken a poor man.

It snows freely and freely hardens
On the lawns of my hope, my secret
Hounded and flayed. I wonder
What words to beg money with.

Pardon me, sir, could you?
Which way is St. Paul?
I thirst.
I am a full-blooded Sioux Indian.

Soon I am sure to become so hungry
I will have to leap barefoot through gas-fire veils of shame,
I will have to stalk timid strangers
On the whorehouse corners.

Oh moon, sow leaves on my hands,
On my seared face, oh I love you.
My throat is open, insane,
Tempting pneumonia.

But my life was never so precious
To me as now.
I will have to beg coins
After dark.

I will learn to scent the police,
And sit or go blind, stay mute, be taken for dead
For your sake, oh my secret,
My life.

Outside Fargo, North Dakota

Along the sprawled body of the derailed
    Great Northern freight car,
I strike a match slowly and lift it slowly.
No wind.

Beyond town, three heavy white horses
Wade all the way to their shoulders
In a silo shadow.

Suddenly the freight car lurches.
The door slams back, a man with a flashlight

Calls me good evening.
I nod as I write good evening, lonely
And sick for home.

The Frontier

The man on the radio mourns
That another endless American winter
Daybreak is beginning to fall
On Idaho, on the mountains.

How many scrawny children
Lie dead and half-hidden among frozen ruts
In my body, along my dark roads.
Lean coyotes pass among clouds
On mountain trails, and smile,
And pass on in snow.

A girl stands in a doorway.
Her arms are bare to the elbows,
Her face gray, she stares coldly
At the daybreak.
When the howl goes up, her eyes
Flare white, like a mare's.

The Lights in the Hallway

The lights in the hallway
Have been out a long time.
I clasp her,
Terrified by the roundness of the earth
And its apples and the voluptuous rings
Of poplar trees, the secret Africas,
The children they give us.
She is slim enough.
Her knee feels like the face
Of a surprised lioness

Nursing the lost children
Of a gazelle by pure accident.
In that body I long for,
The Gabon poets gaze for hours
Between boughs toward heaven, their noble faces
Too secret to weep.
How do I know what color her hair is? I float among
Lonely animals, longing
For the red spider who is God.

Two Postures Beside a Fire

1.

Tonight I watch my father's hair,
As he sits dreaming near his stove.
Knowing my feather of despair,
He sent me an owl's plume for love,
Lest I not know, so I've come home.
Tonight Ohio, where I once
Hounded and cursed my loneliness,
Shows me my father, who broke stones,
Wrestled and mastered great machines,
And rests, shadowing his lovely face.

2.

Nobly his hands fold together in his repose.
He is proud of me, believing
I have done strong things among men and become a man
Of place among men of place in the large cities.
I will not waken him.
I have come home alone, without wife or child
To delight him. Awake, solitary and welcome,
I too sit near his stove, the lines
Of an ugly age scarring my face, and my hands
Twitch nervously about.

In Response to a Rumor That the Oldest Whorehouse in Wheeling, West Virginia, Has Been Condemned

I will grieve alone,
As I strolled alone, years ago, down along
The Ohio shore.
I hid in the hobo jungle weeds
Upstream from the sewer main,
Pondering, gazing.

I saw, down river,
At Twenty-third and Water Streets
By the vinegar works,
The doors open in early evening.
Swinging their purses, the women
Poured down the long street to the river
And into the river.

I do not know how it was
They could drown every evening.
What time near dawn did they climb up the other shore,
Drying their wings?

For the river at Wheeling, West Virginia
Has only two shores:
The one in hell, the other
In Bridgeport, Ohio.

And nobody would commit suicide, only
To find beyond death
Bridgeport, Ohio.

ANNE SEXTON

(1928–)

Some Foreign Letters

I knew you forever and you were always old,
soft white lady of my heart. Surely you would scold
me for sitting up late, reading your letters,
as if these foreign postmarks were meant for me.
You posted them first in London, wearing furs
and a new dress in the winter of eighteen-ninety.
I read how London is dull on Lord Mayor's Day,
where you guided past groups of robbers, the sad holes
of Whitechapel, clutching your pocketbook, on the way
to Jack the Ripper dissecting his famous bones.
This Wednesday in Berlin, you say, you will
go to a bazaar at Bismarck's house. And I
see you as a young girl in a good world still,
writing three generations before mine. I try
to reach into your page and breathe it back . . .
but life is a trick, life is a kitten in a sack.

This is the sack of time your death vacates.
How distant you are on your nickel-plated skates
in the skating park in Berlin, gliding past
me with your Count, while a military band
plays a Strauss waltz. I loved you last,
a pleated old lady with a crooked hand.

Once you read *Lohengrin* and every goose
hung high while you practiced castle life
in Hanover. Tonight your letters reduce
history to a guess. The Count had a wife.
You were the old maid aunt who lived with us.
Tonight I read how the winter howled around
the towers of Schloss Schwöbber, how the tedious
language grew in your jaw, how you loved the sound
of the music of the rats tapping on the stone
floors. When you were mine you wore an earphone.

This is Wednesday, May 9th, near Lucerne,
Switzerland, sixty-nine years ago. I learn
your first climb up Mount San Salvatore;
this is the rocky path, the hole in your shoes,
the yankee girl, the iron interior
of her sweet body. You let the Count choose
your next climb. You went together, armed
with alpine stocks, with ham sandwiches
and *seltzer wasser*. You were not alarmed
by the thick woods of briars and bushes,
nor the rugged cliff, nor the first vertigo
up over Lake Lucerne. The Count sweated
with his coat off as you waded through top snow.
He held your hand and kissed you. You rattled
down on the train to catch a steamboat for home;
or other postmarks: Paris, Verona, Rome.

This is Italy. You learn its mother tongue.
I read how you walked on the Palatine among
the ruins of the palaces of the Caesars;
alone in the Roman autumn, alone since July.
When you were mine they wrapped you out of here
with your best hat over your face. I cried
because I was seventeen. I am older now.
I read how your student ticket admitted you
into the private chapel of the Vatican and how
you cheered with the others, as we used to do

on the Fourth of July. One Wednesday in November
you watched a balloon, painted like a silver ball,
float up over the Forum, up over the lost emperors,
to shiver its little modern cage in an occasional
breeze. You worked your New England conscience out
beside artisans, chestnut vendors and the devout.

Tonight I will learn to love you twice;
learn your first days, your mid-Victorian face.
Tonight I will speak up and interrupt
your letters, warning you that wars are coming,
that the Count will die, that you will accept
your America back to live like a prim thing
on the farm in Maine. I tell you, you will come
here, to the suburbs of Boston, to see the blue-nose
world go drunk each night, to see the handsome
children jitterbug, to feel your left ear close
one Friday at Symphony. And I tell you,
you will tip your boot feet out of that hall,
rocking from its sour sound, out onto
the crowded street, letting your spectacles fall
and your hair net tangle as you stop passers-by
to mumble your guilty love while your ears die.

The Truth the Dead Know

*For my mother, born March 1902, died March 1959
and my father, born February 1900, died June 1959*

Gone, I say and walk from church,
refusing the stiff procession to the grave,
letting the dead ride alone in the hearse.
It is June. I am tired of being brave.

We drive to the Cape. I cultivate
myself where the sun gutters from the sky,
where the sea swings in like an iron gate
and we touch. In another country people die.

My darling, the wind falls in like stones
from the whitehearted water and when we touch
we enter touch entirely. No one's alone.
Men kill for this, or for as much.

And what of the dead? They lie without shoes
in their stone boats. They are more like stone
than the sea would be if it stopped. They refuse
to be blessed, throat, eye and knucklebone.

In the Deep Museum

My God, my God, what queer corner am I in?
Didn't I die, blood running down the post,
lungs gagging for air, die there for the sin
of anyone, my sour mouth giving up the ghost?
Surely my body is done? Surely I died?
And yet, I know, I'm here. What place is this?
Cold and queer, I sting with life. I lied.
Yes, I lied. Or else in some damned cowardice
my body would not give me up. I touch
fine cloth with my hands and my cheeks are cold.
If this is hell, then hell could not be much,
neither as special nor as ugly as I was told.

What's that I hear, snuffling and pawing its way
toward me? Its tongue knocks a pebble out of place
as it slides in, a sovereign. How can I pray?
It is panting; it is an odor with a face
like the skin of a donkey. It laps my sores.
It is hurt, I think, as I touch its little head.
It bleeds. I have forgiven murderers and whores
and now I must wait like old Jonah, not dead
nor alive, stroking a clumsy animal. A rat.
His teeth test me; he waits like a good cook,
knowing his own ground. I forgive him that,
as I forgave my Judas the money he took.

Now I hold his soft red sore to my lips
as his brothers crowd in, hairy angels who take
my gift. My ankles are a flute. I lose hips
and wrists. For three days, for love's sake,
I bless this other death. Oh, not in air—
in dirt. Under the rotting veins of its roots,
under the markets, under the sheep bed where
the hill is food, under the slippery fruits
of the vineyard, I go. Unto the bellies and jaws
of rats I commit my prophecy and fear.
Far below The Cross, I correct its flaws.
We have kept the miracle. I will not be here.

The Fortress

while taking a nap with Linda

Under the pink quilted covers
I hold the pulse that counts your blood.
I think the woods outdoors
are half asleep,
left over from summer
like a stack of books after a flood,
left over like those promises I never keep.
On the right, the scrub pine tree
waits like a fruit store
holding up bunches of tufted broccoli.

We watch the wind from our square bed.
I press down my index finger—
half in jest, half in dread—
on the brown mole
under your left eye, inherited
from my right cheek: a spot of danger
where a bewitched worm ate its way through our soul
in search of beauty. My child, since July
the leaves have been fed
secretly from a pool of beet-red dye.

And sometimes they are battle green
with trunks as wet as hunters' boots,
smacked hard by the wind, clean
as oilskins. No,
the wind's not off the ocean.
Yes, it cried in your room like a wolf
and your pony tail hurt you. That was a long time ago.
The wind rolled the tide like a dying
woman. She wouldn't sleep,
she rolled there all night, grunting and sighing.

Darling, life is not in my hands;
life with its terrible changes
will take you, bombs or glands,
your own child at
your breast, your own house on your own land.
Outside the bittersweet turns orange.
Before she died, my mother and I picked those fat
branches, finding orange nipples
on the gray wire strands.
We weeded the forest, curing trees like cripples.

Your feet thump-thump against my back
and you whisper to yourself. Child,
what are you wishing? What pact
are you making?
What mouse runs between your eyes? What ark
can I fill for you when the world goes wild?
The woods are underwater, their weeds are shaking
in the tide; birches like zebra fish
flash by in a pack.
Child, I cannot promise that you will get your wish.

I cannot promise very much.
I give you the images I know.
Lie still with me and watch.
A pheasant moves
by like a seal, pulled through the mulch
by his thick white collar. He's on show

like a clown. He drags a beige feather that he removed,
one time, from on old lady's hat.
We laugh and we touch.
I promise you love. Time will not take away that.

For My Lover,
Returning to His Wife

She is all there.
She was melted carefully down for you
and cast up from your childhood,
cast up from your one hundred favorite aggies.

She has always been there, my darling.
She is, in fact, exquisite.
Fireworks in the dull middle of February
and as real as a cast-iron pot.

Let's face it, I have been momentary.
A luxury. A bright red sloop in the harbor.
My hair rising like smoke from the car window.
Littleneck clams out of season.

She is more than· that. She is your have to have,
has grown you your practical your tropical growth.
This is not an experiment. She is all harmony.
She sees to oars and oarlocks for the dinghy,

has placed wild flowers at the window at breakfast,
sat by the potter's wheel at midday,
set forth three children under the moon,
three cherubs drawn by Michelangelo,

done this with her legs spread out
in the terrible months in the chapel.
If you glance up, the children are there
like delicate balloons resting on the ceiling.

She has also carried each one down the hall
after supper, their heads privately bent,
two legs protesting, person to person,
her face flushed with a song and their little sleep.

I give you back your heart.
I give you permission—

for the fuse inside her, throbbing
angrily in the dirt, for the bitch in her
and the burying of her wound—
for the burying of her small red wound alive—

for the pale flickering flare under her ribs,
for the drunken sailor who waits in her left pulse,
for the mother's knee, for the stockings,
for the garter belt, for the call—

the curious call
when you will burrow in arms and breasts
and tug at the orange ribbon in her hair
and answer the call, the curious call.

She is so naked and singular.
She is the sum of yourself and your dream.
Climb her like a monument, step after step.
She is solid.

As for me, I am a watercolor.
I wash off.

You All Know the Story
of the Other Woman

It's a little Walden.
She is private in her breathbed
as his body takes off and flies,
flies straight as an arrow.

But it's a bad translation.
Daylight is nobody's friend.
God comes in like a landlord
and flashes on his brassy lamp.
Now she is just so-so.
He puts his bones back on,
turning the clock back an hour.
She knows flesh, that skin balloon,
the unbound limbs, the boards,
the roof, the removable roof.
She is his selection, part time.
You know the story too! Look,
when it is over he places her,
like a phone, back on the hook.

THOM GUNN

(1929–)

The Beach Head

Now that a letter gives me ground at last
For starting from, I see my enterprise
Is more than application by a blast
Upon a trumpet slung beside a gate,
Security a fraud, and how unwise
Was disembarking on your Welfare State.

What should they see in you but what I see,
These friends you mention whom I do not know?
—You unsuspecting that a refugee
Might want the land complete, write in a tone
Too matter-of-fact, of small affairs below
Some minister's seduction of the Crown.

And even if they could be innocent,
They still applaud you, keep you satisfied
And occupy your time, which I resent.
Their werewolf lust and cunning are afraid
Of night-exposure in the hair, so hide
Distant as possible from my palisade.

I have my ground. A brain-sick enemy
Pacing the beach head he so plotted for

Which now seems trivial to his jealousy
And ignorance of the great important part,
I almost wish I had no narrow shore.
I seek a pathway to the country's heart.

Shall I be John a Gaunt and with my band
Of mad bloods pass in one spectacular dash,
Fighting before and after, through your land,
To issue out unharmed the farther side,
With little object other than panache
And showing what great odds may be defied?

That way achievement would at once be history:
Living inside, I would not know, the danger:
Hurry is blind and so does not brave mystery;
I should be led to underrate, by haste,
Your natural beauties: while I, hare-brained stranger,
Would not be much distinguished from the rest.

Or shall I wait and calculate my chances,
Consolidating this my inch-square base,
Picking off rival spies that tread your glances:
Then plan when you have least supplies or clothing
A pincer-move to end in an embrace,
And risk that your mild liking turn to loathing?

On the Move

'Man, you gotta Go.'

The blue jay scuffling in the bushes follows
Some hidden purpose, and the gust of birds
That spurts across the field, the wheeling swallows,
Have nested in the trees and undergrowth.
Seeking their instinct, or their poise, or both,
One moves with an uncertain violence
Under the dust thrown by a baffled sense
Or the dull thunder of approximate words.

On motorcycles, up the road, they come:
Small, black, as flies hanging in heat, the Boys,
Until the distance throws them forth, their hum
Bulges to thunder held by calf and thigh.
In goggles, donned impersonality,
In gleaming jackets trophied with the dust,
They strap in doubt—by hiding it, robust—
And almost hear a meaning in their noise.

Exact conclusion of their hardiness
Has no shape yet, but from known whereabouts
They ride, direction where the tires press.
They scare a flight of birds across the field:
Much that is natural, to the will must yield.
Men manufacture both machine and soul,
And use what they imperfectly control
To dare a future from the taken routes.

It is a part solution, after all.
One is not necessarily discord
On earth; or damned because, half animal,
One lacks direct instinct, because one wakes
Afloat on movement that divides and breaks.
One joins the movement in a valueless world,
Choosing it, till, both hurler and the hurled,
One moves as well, always toward, toward.

A minute holds them, who have come to go:
The self-defined, astride the created will
They burst away; the towns they travel through
Are home for neither bird nor holiness,
For birds and saints complete their purposes.
At worst, one is in motion; and at best,
Reaching no absolute, in which to rest,
One is always nearer by not keeping still.

California

The Silver Age

Do not enquire from the centurion nodding
At the corner, with his head gentle over
The swelling breastplate, where true Rome is found.
Even of Livy there are volumes lost.
All he can do is guide you through the moonlight.

When he moves, mark how his eager striding,
To which we know the darkness is a river
Sullen with mud, is easy as on ground.
We know it is a river never crossed
By any but some few who hate the moonlight.

And when he speaks, mark how his ancient wording
Is hard with indignation of a lover.
'I do not think our new Emperor likes the sound
Of turning squadrons or the last post.
Consorts with Christians, I think he lives in moonlight.'

Hurrying to show you his companions guarding,
He grips your arm like a cold strap of leather,
Then halts, earthpale, as he stares round and round.
What made this one fragment of a sunken coast
Remain, far out, to be beaten by the moonlight?

The Corridor

A separate place between the thought and felt
The empty hotel corridor was dark.
But here the keyhole shone, a meaning spark.
What fires were latent in it! So he knelt.

Now, at the corridor's much lighter end,
A pierglass hung upon the wall and showed,

As by an easily deciphered code,
Dark, door, and man, hooped by a single band.

He squinted through the keyhole, and within
Surveyed an act of love that frank as air
He was too ugly for, or could not dare,
Or at a crucial moment thought a sin.

Pleasure was simple thus: he mastered it.
If once he acted as participant
He would be mastered, the inhabitant
Of someone else's world, mere shred to fit.

He moved himself to get a better look
And then it was he noticed in the glass
Two strange eyes in a fascinated face
That watched him like a picture in a book.

The instant drove simplicity away—
The scene was altered, it depended on
His kneeling, when he rose they were clean gone
The couple in the keyhole; this would stay.

For if the watcher of the watcher shown
There in the distant glass, should be watched too,
Who can be master, free of others; who
Can look around and say he is alone?

Moreover, who can know that what he sees
Is not distorted, that he is not seen
Distorted by a pierglass, curved and lean?
Those curious eyes, through him, were linked to these—

These lovers altered in the cornea's bend.
What could he do but leave the keyhole, rise,
Holding those eyes as equal in his eyes,
And go, one hand held out, to meet a friend?

Innocence

for Tony White

He ran the course and as he ran he grew,
And smelt his fragrance in the field. Already,
Running he knew the most he ever knew,
The egotism of a healthy body.

Ran into manhood, ignorant of the past:
Culture of guilt and guilt's vague heritage,
Self-pity and the soul; what he possessed
Was rich, potential, like the bud's tipped rage.

The Corps developed, it was plain to see,
Courage, endurance, loyalty and skill
To a morale firm as morality,
Hardening him to an instrument, until

The finitude of virtues that were there
Bodied within the swarthy uniform
A compact innocence, child-like and clear,
No doubt could penetrate, no act could harm.

When he stood near the Russian partisan
Being burned alive, he therefore could behold
The ribs wear gently through the darkening skin
And sicken only at the Northern cold,

Could watch the fat burn with a violet flame
And feel disgusted only at the smell,
And judge that all pain finishes the same
As melting quietly by his boots it fell.

Flying Above California

Spread beneath me it lies—lean upland
sinewed and tawny in the sun, and

valley cool with mustard, or sweet with
loquat. I repeat under my breath

names of places I have not been to:
Crescent City, San Bernardino

—Mediterranean and Northern names.
Such richness can make you drunk. Sometimes

on fogless days by the Pacific,
there is a cold hard light without break

that reveals merely what is—no more
and no less. That limiting candor,

that accuracy of the beaches,
is part of the ultimate richness.

My Sad Captains

One by one they appear in
the darkness: a few friends, and
a few with historical
names. How late they start to shine!
but before they fade they stand
perfectly embodied, all

the past lapping them like a
cloak of chaos. They were men
who, I thought, lived only to
renew the wasteful force they
spent with each hot convulsion.
They remind me, distant now.

True, they are not at rest yet,
but now that they are indeed
apart, winnowed from failures,
they withdraw to an orbit

and turn with disinterested
hard energy, like the stars.

The Goddess

When eyeless fish meet her on
her way upward, they gently
turn together in the dark
brooks. But naked and searching
as a wind, she will allow
no hindrance, none, and bursts up

through potholes and narrow flues
seeking an outlet. Unslowed
by fire, rock, water or clay,
she after a time reaches
the soft abundant soil, which
still does not dissipate her

force—for look! sinewy thyme
reeking in the sunlight; rats
breeding, breeding, in their nests;
and the soldier by a park
bench with his greatcoat collar
up, waiting all evening for

a woman, any woman
whose dress is tight across her ass
as bark in moonlight. Goddess,
Proserpina: it is we,
vulnerable, quivering,
who stay you to abundance.

Touch

You are already
asleep. I lower

myself in next to
you, my skin slightly
numb with the restraint
of habits, the patina of
self, the black frost
of outsideness, so that even
unclothed it is
a resilient chilly
hardness, a superficially
malleable, dead
rubbery texture.

You are a mound
of bedclothes, where the cat
in sleep braces
its paws against your
calf through the blankets,
and kneads each paw in turn.

Meanwhile and slowly
I feel a is it
my own warmth surfacing or
the ferment of your whole
body that in darkness beneath
the cover is stealing
bit by bit to break
down that chill.

        You turn and
hold me tightly, do
you know who
I am or am I
your mother or
the nearest human being to
hold on to in a
dreamed pogrom.

What I, now loosened,
sink into is an old

              big place, it is
              there already, for
              you are already
              there, and the cat
              got there before you, yet
              it is hard to locate.
              What is more, the place is
              not found but seeps
              from our touch in
              continuous creation, dark
              enclosing cocoon round
              ourselves alone, dark
              wide realm where we
              walk with everyone.

The glassy grain of water looking upward I see the bed
Of the river above me upside down very clear
What am I doing here in mid-air? Why do I find

TED HUGHES
(1930–)

The Hawk in the Rain

I drown in the drumming ploughland, I drag up
Heel after heel from the swallowing of the earth's mouth,
From clay that clutches my each step to the ankle
With the habit of the dogged grave, but the hawk

Effortlessly at height hangs his still eye.
His wings hold all creation in a weightless quiet,
Steady as a hallucination in the streaming air.
While banging wind kills these stubborn hedges,

Thumbs my eyes, throws my breath, tackles my heart,
And rain hacks my head to the bone, the hawk hangs
The diamond point of will that polestars
The sea drowner's endurance: and I,

Bloodily grabbed dazed last-moment-counting
Morsel in the earth's mouth, strain towards the master-
Fulcrum of violence where the hawk hangs still.
That maybe in his own time meets the weather

Coming the wrong way, suffers the air, hurled upside down,
Fall from his eye, the ponderous shires crash on him,
The horizon trap him; the round angelic eye
Smashed, mix his heart's blood with the mire of the land.

Secretary

If I should touch her she would shriek and weeping
Crawl off to nurse the terrible wound: all
Day like a starling under the bellies of bulls
She hurries among men, ducking, peeping,

Off in a whirl at the first move of a horn.
At dusk she scuttles down the gauntlet of lust
Like a clockwork mouse. Safe home at last
She mends socks with holes, shirts that are torn

For father and brother, and a delicate supper cooks:
Goes to bed early, shuts out with the light
Her thirty years, and lies with buttocks tight,
Hiding her lovely eyes until day break.

The Jaguar

The apes yawn and adore their fleas in the sun.
The parrots shriek as if they were on fire, or strut
Like cheap tarts to attract the stroller with the nut.
Fatigued with indolence, tiger and lion

Lie still as the sun. The boa-constrictor's coil
Is a fossil. Cage after cage seems empty, or
Stinks of sleepers from the breathing straw.
It might be painted on a nursery wall.

But who runs like the rest past these arrives
At a cage where the crowd stands, stares, mesmerized,
As a child at a dream, at a jaguar hurrying enraged
Through prison darkness after the drills of his eyes

On a short fierce fuse. Not in boredom—
The eye satisfied to be blind in fire,

By the bang of blood in the brain deaf the ear—
He spins from the bars, but there's no cage to him

More than to the visionary his cell:
His stride is wildernesses of freedom:
The world rolls under the long thrust of his heel.
Over the cage floor the horizons come.

Childbirth

When, on the bearing mother, death's
Door opened its furious inch,
Instant of struggling and blood,
The commonplace became so strange

There was not looking at table or chair:
Miracle struck out the brain
Of order and ordinary: bare
Onto the heart the earth dropped then

With whirling quarters, the axle cracked,
Through that miracle-breached bed
All the dead could have got back;
With shriek and heave and spout of blood

The huge-eyed looming horde from
Under the floor of the heart, that run
To the madman's eye-corner came
Deafening towards light, whereon

A child whimpered upon the bed,
Frowning ten-toed ten-fingered birth
Put the skull back about the head
Righted the stagger of the earth.

Law in the Country of the Cats

When two men meet for the first time in all
Eternity and outright hate each other,
Not as a beggar-man and a rich man,
Not as cuckold-maker and cuckold,
Not as bully and delicate boy, but
As dog and wolf because their blood before
They are aware has bristled into their hackles,
Because one has clubbed the other to death
With the bottle first broached to toast their transaction
And swears to God he went helpless black-out
While they were mixing smiles, facts have sacked
The oath of the pious witness who judged all men
As a one humble brotherhood of man.

When two men at first meeting hate each other
Even in passing, without words, in the street,
They are not likely to halt as if remembering
They once met somewhere, where in fact they met,
And discuss "universal brotherhood,"
"Love of humanity and each fellow-man,"
Or "the growing likelihood of perpetual peace,"
But if, by chance, they do meet, so mistaking,
There will be that moment's horrible pause
As each looks into the gulf in the eye of the other,
Then a flash of violent incredible action,
Then one man letting his brains gently to the gutter,
And one man bursting into the police station
Crying: "Let Justice be done. I did it. I."

Dick Straightup

Past eighty, but never in eighty years—
Eighty winters on the windy ridge
Of England—has he buttoned his shirt or his jacket.

He sits in the bar-room seat he·has been
Polishing with his backside sixty-odd years
Where nobody else sits. White is his head,
But his cheek high, hale as when he emptied
Every Saturday the twelve-pint tankard at a tilt,
Swallowed the whole serving of thirty eggs,
And banged the big bass drum for Heptonstall—
With a hundred other great works, still talked of.
Age has stiffened him, but not dazed or bent,
The blue eye has come clear of time:
At a single pint, now, his memory sips slowly,
His belly strong as a tree bole.

He survives among hills, nourished by stone and height.
The dust of Achilles and Cuchulain
Itches in the palms of scholars; thin clerks exercise
In their bed-sitters at midnight, and the meat salesman can
Loft fully four hundred pounds. But this one,
With no more application than sitting,
And drinking, and singing, fell in the sleet, late,
Dammed the pouring gutter; and slept there; and, throughout
A night searched by shouts and lamps, froze,
Grew to the road with welts of ice. He was chipped out at dawn
Warm as a pie and snoring.

The gossip of men younger by forty years—
Loud in his company since he no longer says much—
Empties, refills and empties their glasses.
Or their strenuous silence places the dominoes
(That are old as the house) into patterns
Gone with the game; the darts that glint to the dartboard
Pin no remarkable instant. The young men sitting
Taste their beer as by imitation,
Borrow their words as by impertinence
Because he sits there so full of legend and life
Quiet as a man alone.

He lives with sixty and seventy years ago,
And of everything he knows three quarters is in the grave,

Or tumbled down, or vanished. To be understood
His words must tug up the bottom-most stones of this village,
This clutter of blackstone gulleys, peeping curtains,
And a graveyard bigger and deeper than the village
That sways in the tide of wind and rain some fifty
Miles off the Irish sea.
                      The lamp above the pub-door
Wept yellow when he went out and the street
Of spinning darkness roared like a machine
As the wind applied itself. His upright walk,
His strong back, I commemorate now,
And his white blown head going out between a sky and an
    earth
That were bundled into placeless blackness, the one
Company of his mind.

Obit.

Now, you are strong as the earth you have entered.

This is a birthplace picture. Green into blue
The hills run deep and limpid. The weasel's
Berry-eyed red lock-head, gripping the dream
That holds good, goes lost in the heaved calm

Of the earth you have entered.

Dark Women

My neighbour moves less and less, attempts less.
If his right hand still moves, it is a farewell
Already days posthumous.

But the left hand seems to freeze,
And the left leg with its crude plumbing,
And the left half jaw and the left eyelid and the words,
    all the huge cries

Frozen in his brain his tongue cannot unfreeze—
While somewhere through a dark heaven
The dark bloodclot moves in.

I watch it approaching, but I cannot fear it.
The punctual evening star,
Worse, the warm hawthorn blossoms, their foam,

Their palls of deathly perfume,
Worst of all the beanflower
Badged with jet like the ear of the tiger

Unmake and remake me. That star
And that flower and that flower
And living mouth and living mouth all

One flaring annihilation
Of old brains, old bowels, old bodies
In the scarves of dew, the wet hair of nightfall.

New Moon in January

A splinter, flicked
Into the wide eyeball,
Severs its warnings.

The head, severed while staring,
Felt nothing, only
Tilted slightly.

O lone
Eyelash on the darkening
Stripe of blood, O sail of death!

Frozen
In ether
Unearthly

Shelley's faint-shriek
Trying to thaw while zero
Itself loses consciousness.

Encounter

A cool small evening shrunk to a dog bark and the clank of a bucket—

And you listening.
A spider's web, tense for the dew's touch,
A pail lifted still and brimming—mirror
To tempt a first star to a tremor.

Cows are going home in the lane there, looping the hedges with
    their warm wreaths of breath—
A dark river of blood, many boulders,
Balancing unspilled milk.

Moon, you cry suddenly, Moon! Moon!

The moon has stepped back like an artist gazing amazed at a work

That points at him amazed.

The cows submerge.
The moon has opened you wide and bright like a pond.

The moon lifts you off the grass—
A cat's cradle of spider's web, where the stars are trembling
    into place.

The brimming moon looks through you and you cannot move.

Any minute
A bat will fly out of a cat's ear.

Wodwo

What am I? nosing here, turning leaves over
following a faint stain on the air to the river's edge
I enter water. What am I to split
the glassy grain of water looking upward I see the bed
of the river above me upside down very clear
what am I doing here in mid-air? Why do I find
this frog so interesting as I inspect its most secret
interior and make it my own? Do these weeds
know me and name me to each other have they
seen me before, do I fit in their world? I seem
separate from the ground and not rooted but dropped
out of nothing casually I've no threads
fastening me to anything I can go anywhere
I seem to have been given the freedom
of this place what am I then? And picking
bits of bark off this rotten stump gives me
no pleasure and it's no use so why do I do it
me and doing that have coincided very queerly
But what shall I be called am I the first
have I an owner what shape am I what
shape am I am I huge if I go
to the end on this way past these trees and past these trees
till I get tired that's touching one wall of me
for the moment if I sit still how everything
stops to watch me I suppose I am the exact centre
but there's all this what is it roots
roots roots roots and here's the water
again very queer but I'll go on looking

Lineage

In the beginning was Scream
Who begat Blood
Who begat Eye
Who begat Fear

Who begat Wing
Who begat Bone
Who begat Granite
Who begat Violet
Who begat Guitar
Who begat Sweat
Who begat Adam
Who begat Mary
Who begat God
Who begat Nothing
Who begat Never
Never Never Never

Who begat Crow

Screaming for Blood
Grubs, crusts
Anything

Trembling featherless elbows in the nest's filth

Examination at the Womb-Door

Who owns these scrawny little feet?   *Death.*
Who owns this bristly scorched-looking face?   *Death.*
Who owns these still-working lungs?   *Death.*
Who owns this utility coat of muscles?   *Death.*
Who owns these unspeakable guts?   *Death.*
Who owns these questionable brains?   *Death.*
All this messy blood?   *Death.*
These minimum-efficiency eyes?   *Death.*
This wicked little tongue?   *Death.*
This occasional wakefulness?   *Death.*

Given, stolen, or held pending trial?
Held.

Who owns the whole rainy, stony earth?   *Death.*
Who owns all of space?   *Death.*

Who is stronger than hope?   *Death.*
Who is stronger than the will?   *Death.*
Stronger than love?   *Death.*
Stronger than life?   *Death.*

But who is stronger than death?

Me, evidently.

Pass, Crow.

Crow and Mama

When Crow cried his mother's ear
Scorched to a stump.

When he laughed she wept
Blood her breasts her palms her brow all wept blood.

He tried a step, then a step, and again a step—
Every one scarred her face forever.

When he burst out in rage
She fell back with an awful gash and a fearful cry.

When he stopped she closed on him like a book
On a bookmark, he had to get going.

He jumped into the car the towrope
Was around her neck he jumped out.

He jumped into the plane but her body was jammed in the jet—
There was a great row, the flight was cancelled.

He jumped into the rocket and its trajectory
Drilled clean through her heart he kept on

And it was cosy in the rocket, he could not see much
But he peered out through the portholes at Creation

And saw the stars millions of miles away
And saw the future and the universe

Opening and opening
And kept on and slept and at last

Crashed on the moon awoke and crawled out

Under his mother's buttocks.

GARY SNYDER

(1930–)

[*The Ancient Forests of China Logged*]

But ye shall destroy their altars,
break their images, and cut down their groves.
—EXODUS 34:13

The ancient forests of China logged
    and the hills slipped into the Yellow Sea.
Squared beams, log dogs,
    on a tamped-earth sill.
San Francisco 2×4s
    were the woods around Seattle:
Someone killed and someone built, a house,
    a forest, wrecked or raised
All America hung on a hook
    & burned by men, in their own praise.

Snow on fresh stumps and brush-piles.
The generator starts and rumbles
               in the frosty dawn
I wake from bitter dreams,

Rise and build a fire,
Pull on and lace the stiff cold boots
Eat huge flapjacks by a gloomy Swede
In splintery cookhouse light
                    grab my tin pisspot hat
Ride off to the show in a crummy-truck
And start the Cat.

"Pines grasp the clouds with iron claws
like dragons rising from sleep"
250,000 board feet a day
If both Cats keep working
& nobody gets hurt

Maudgalyâyana saw hell

Under the shuddering eyelid
Dreams gnawing the nerve-strings,
The mind grabs and the shut eye sees:
Down dimensions floating below sunlight,
Worlds of the dead, Bardo, mind-worlds
& horror of sunless cave-ritual
Meeting conscious monk bums
Blown on winds of karma from hell
To endless changing hell,
Life and death whipped
On this froth of reality (wind & rain
Realms human and full of desire) over the cold
Hanging enormous unknown, below
Art and History and all mankind living thoughts,
Occult & witchcraft evils each all true.
The thin edge of nature rising fragile
And helpless with its love and sentient stone
And flesh, above dark drug-death dreams.

Clouds I cannot lose, we cannot leave.
We learn to love, horror accepted.
Beyond, within, all normal beauties

Of the science-conscious sex and love-receiving
Day-to-day got vision of this sick
Sparkling person at the inturned dreaming
Blooming human mind
Dropping it all, and opening the eyes.

from ''SIX YEARS''

January

          the pine tree is perfect

Walking in the snowhills the trail goes just right
Eat snow off pine needles
        the city's not so big, the
           hills surround it.
Hieizan wrapped in his own cloud—
Back there no big houses, only a little farm shack
        crows cawing back and forth
        over the valley of grass-bamboo
          and small pine.

If I had a peaceful heart it would look like this.
        the train down in the city

        was once a snowy hill

Beneath My Hand and Eye the Distant Hills,
Your Body

What my hand follows on your body
Is the line. A stream of love
   of heat, of light,   what my
   eye   lascivious
      licks
  over, watching
  far snow-dappled Uintah mountains

Is that stream.
Of power.   what my
   hand curves over, following the line.
    "hip" and "groin"
Where "I"
   follow by hand and eye
   the swimming limit of your body.
As when vision idly dallies on the hills
Loving what it feeds on.
   soft cinder cones and craters;
    —Drum Hadley in the Pinacate
     took ten minutes more to look again—
A leap of power unfurling:
    left,   right—right—
My heart beat faster looking
   at the snowy Uintah mountains.

As my hand feeds on you
   runs down your side and curls beneath your hip.
   oil pool; stratum; water—

What "is" within   not known
   but feel it
   sinking with a breath
   pusht ruthless, surely, down.

Beneath this long caress of hand and eye
   "we" learn the flower burning,
    outward, from "below".

Wave

Grooving clam shell,
    streakt through marble,
   sweeping down ponderosa pine bark-scale
    rip-cut tree grain
       sand-dunes, lava
       flow

Wave   wife.
              woman—wyfman—
"veiled; vibrating; vague"
   sawtooth ranges pulsing;
                veins on the back of the hand.

Forkt out: birdsfoot-alluvium
              wash

         great dunes rolling
Each inch rippld, every grain a wave.

Leaning against sand cornices til they blow away

   —wind, shake
   stiff thorns of cholla, ocotillo
   sometimes I get stuck in thickets—

Ah, trembling spreading radiating wyf
             racing zebra
  catch me and fling me wide
To the dancing grain of things
             of my mind!

Kyoto Born in Spring Song

   Beautiful little children
      found in melons,
      in bamboo,
    in a "strangely glowing warbler egg"
      a perfect baby girl—

  baby, baby,
    tiny precious
      mice and worms:

   Great majesty of Dharma turning
   Great dance of Vajra power

lizard baby by the fern
centipede baby scrambling toward the wall
cat baby left to mew for milk alone
mouse baby too afraid to run

O sing   born in spring
the weavers swallows babies in Nishijin
nests below the eaves

glinting mothers wings
swoop to the sound of looms

and three fat babies
with three human mothers
every morning doing laundry
"good
morning how's your baby?"
Tomoharu, Itsuko, and Kenji—

Mouse, begin again.

Bushmen are laughing
at the coyote-tricking
that made us think machines

wild babies
in the ferns and plums and weeds.

Burning Island

O Wave God   who broke through me today
Sea Bream
massive pink and silver
cool swimming down with me watching
staying away from the spear

Volcano belly Keeper who lifted this island
    for our own beaded bodies adornment
    and sprinkles us all with his laugh—
                ash in the eye
    mist, or smoke,
    on the bare high limits—
            underwater lava flows easing to coral
                holes filled with striped feeding swimmers

O Sky Gods   cartwheeling
    out of   Pacific
    turning rainsqualls over like lids on us
    then shine on our sodden—
         (scanned out a rainbow today at the
            cow drinking trough
              sluicing off
        LAKHS of crystal Buddha Fields
        right on the hair of the arm!)

Who wavers right now in the bamboo:
  a half-gone waning moon.
         drank down a bowlful of shochu
           in praise of Antares
         gazing far up the lanes of Sagittarius
           richest stream of our sky—
  a cup to the center of the galaxy!

        and let the eyes stray
right-angling the pitch of the Milky Way:
      horse-heads   rings
      clouds   too distant to *be*
      slide free.
         on the crest of the wave.

  Each night
  O Earth Mother
    I have wrappt my hand

over the jut of your cobra-hood
                          sleeping;
    left my ear
All night long by your mouth.

O   All
Gods   tides   capes   currents
Flows and spirals of
        pool and powers—

As we hoe the field
    let sweet potato grow.
And as sit us all down when we may
To consider the Dharma
    bring with a flower and a glimmer.
Let us all sleep in peace   together.

Bless Masa and me as we marry
    at new moon   on the crater
This summer.

Revolution in the Revolution
in the Revolution

The country surrounds the city
The back country surrounds the country

"From the masses to the masses" the most
Revolutionary consciousness is to be found
Among the most ruthlessly exploited classes:
Animals, trees, water, air, grasses

We must pass through the stage of the
"Dictatorship of the Unconscious" before we can
Hope for the withering-away of the states
And finally arrive at true Communionism.

If the capitalists and imperialists
     are the exploiters, the masses are the workers.
        and the party
        is the communist.

If civilization
     is the exploiter, the masses is nature.
        and the party
        is the poets.

If the abstract rational intellect
     is the exploiter, the masses is the unconscious.
        and the party
        is the yogins.

& POWER
comes out of the seed-syllables of mantras.

What You Should Know to Be a Poet

all you can about animals as persons.
the names of trees and flowers and weeds.
names of stars, and the movements of the planets
        and the moon.

your own six senses, with a watchful and elegant mind.

at least one kind of traditional magic:
divination, astrology, the *book of changes,* the tarot;

dreams.
the illusory demons and illusory shining gods;

kiss the ass of the devil and eat shit;
fuck his horny barbed cock,
fuck the hag,
and all the celestial angels
        and maidens perfum'd and golden—

& then love the human: wives   husbands   and friends.

childrens' games, comic books, bubble-gum,
the weirdness of television and advertising.

work, long dry hours of dull work swallowed and accepted
and livd with and finally lovd.   exhaustion,
                          hunger, rest.

the wild freedom of the dance, *extasy*
silent solitary illumination, *enstasy*

real danger.   gambles.   and the edge of death.

DEREK WALCOTT

(1930–)

A Far Cry from Africa

A wind is ruffling the tawny pelt
Of Africa. Kikuyu, quick as flies
Batten upon the bloodstreams of the veldt.
Corpses are scattered through a paradise.
But still the worm, colonel of carrion, cries:
'Waste no compassion on these separate dead'
Statistics justify and scholars seize
The salients of colonial policy.
What is that to the white child hacked in bed?
To savages, expendable as Jews?

Threshed out by beaters, the long rushes break
In a white dust of ibises whose cries
Have wheeled since civilization's dawn
From the parched river or beast-teeming plain;
The violence of beast on beast is read
As natural law, but upright man
Seeks his divinity with inflicting pain.
Delirious as these worried beasts, his wars
Dance to the tightened carcass of a drum,
While he calls courage still, that native dread
Of the white peace contracted by the dead.

448   DEREK WALCOTT

Again brutish necessity wipes its hands
Upon the napkin of a dirty cause, again
A waste of our compassion, as with Spain.
The gorilla wrestles with the superman.

I who am poisoned with the blood of both,
Where shall I turn, divided to the vein?
I who have cursed
The drunken officer of British rule, how choose
Between this Africa and the English tongue I love?
Betray them both, or give back what they give?
How can I face such slaughter and be cool?
How can I turn from Africa and live?

Ruins of a Great House

> though our longest sun sets at right declensions and makes but winter
> arches, it cannot be long before we lie down in darkness, and have our light
> in ashes . . .
>
> BROWNE: *Urn Burial*

Stones only, the *disjecta membra* of this Great House,
Whose moth-like girls are mixed with candledust,
Remain to file the lizard's dragonish claws;
The mouths of those gate cherubs streaked with stain.
Axle and coachwheel silted under the muck
Of cattle droppings.

        Three crows flap for the trees,
And settle, creaking the eucalyptus boughs.
A smell of dead limes quickens in the nose
The leprosy of Empire.

        'Farewell, green fields'
        'Farewell, ye happy groves!'

Marble as Greece, like Faulkner's south in stone,
Deciduous beauty prospered and is gone;

But where the lawn breaks in a rash of trees
A spade below dead leaves will ring the bone
Of some dead animal or human thing
Fallen from evil days, from evil times.

It seems that the original crops were limes
Grown in that silt that clogs the river's skirt;
The imperious rakes are gone, their bright girls gone,
The river flows, obliterating hurt.

I climbed a wall with the grill ironwork
Of exiled craftsmen, protecting that great house
From guilt, perhaps, but not from the worm's rent,
Nor from the padded cavalry of the mouse.
And when a wind shook in the limes I heard
What Kipling heard; the death of a great empire, the abuse
Of ignorance by Bible and by sword.

A green lawn, broken by low walls of stone
Dipped to the rivulet, and pacing, I thought next
Of men like Hawkins, Walter Raleigh, Drake,
Ancestral murderers and poets, more perplexed
In memory now by every ulcerous crime.
The world's green age then was a rotting lime
Whose stench became the charnel galleon's text.
The rot remains with us, the men are gone.
But, as dead ash is lifted in a wind,
That fans the blackening ember of the mind,
My eyes burned from the ashen prose of Donne.

Ablaze with rage, I thought
Some slave is rotting in this manorial lake,
And still the coal of my compassion fought:
That Albion too, was once
A colony like ours, 'Part of the continent, piece of the main'
Nook-shotten, rook o'er blown, deranged
By foaming channels, and the vain expense
Of bitter faction.

All in compassion ends
So differently from what the heart arranged:
'as well as if a manor of thy friend's . . .'

Parang

. . . the second cuatroman sings.

Man, I suck me tooth when I hear
How dem croptime fiddlers lie,
And de wailing, kiss-me-arse flutes
That bring water to me eye!
O, when I t'ink how from young
I wasted time at de fêtes,
I could bawl in a red-eyed rage
For desire turned to regret,
Not knowing the truth that I sang
At parang and la comette.
Boy, every damned tune them tune
Of love that will last forever
Is the wax and the wane of the moon
Since Adam catch body-fever.

I old, so the young crop won't
Have these claws to reap their waist,
But I know 'do more' from 'don't'
Since the grave cry out 'Make haste!'
This banjo world have one string
And all man does dance to that tune:
That love is a place in the bush
With music grieving from far,
As you look past her shoulder and see
Like her one tear afterwards
The falling of a fixed star.
Young men does bring love to disgrace
With remorseful, regretful words,
When flesh upon flesh was the tune

Since the first cloud raise up to disclose
The breast of the naked moon.

A Letter from Brooklyn

An old lady writes me in a spidery style,
Each character trembling, and I see a veined hand
Pellucid as paper, travelling on a skein
Of such frail thoughts its thread is often broken;
Or else the filament from which a phrase is hung
Dims to my sense, but caught, it shines like steel,
As touch a line, and the whole web will feel.
She describes my father, yet I forget her face
More easily than my father's yearly dying;
Of her I remember small, buttoned boots and the place
She kept in our wooden church on those Sundays
Whenever her strength allowed;
Grey haired, thin voiced, perpetually bowed.

'I am Mable Rawlins,' she writes, 'and know both your parents;'
He is dead, Miss Rawlins, but God bless your tense:
'Your father was a dutiful, honest,
Faithful and useful person.'
For such plain praise what fame is recompense?
'A horn-painter, he painted delicately on horn,
He used to sit around the table and paint pictures.'
The peace of God needs nothing to adorn
It, nor glory nor ambition.
'He is twenty-eight years buried,' she writes, 'he was called home,
And is, I am sure, doing greater work.'

The strength of one frail hand in a dim room
Somewhere in Brooklyn, patient and assured,
Restores my sacred duty to the Word.
'Home, home,' she can write, with such short time to live,
Alone as she spins the blessings of her years;
Not withered of beauty if she can bring such tears,
Nor withdrawn from the world that breaks its lovers so;

Heaven is to her the place where painters go,
All who bring beauty on frail shell or horn,
There was all made, thence their lux-mundi drawn,
Drawn, drawn, till the thread is resilient steel,
Lost though it seems in darkening periods,
And there they return to do work that is God's.

So this old lady writes, and again I believe,
I believe it all, and for no man's death I grieve.

The Polish Rider

The grey horse, Death, in profile bears the young Titus
To dark woods by the dying coal of day;
The father, with worn vision portrays the son
Like Dürer's knight astride a Rozinante;
The horse disturbs more than the youth delights us.
The warrior turns his sure gaze for a second,
Assurance looks its father in the eye,
The inherited, bony hack heads accurately
Towards the symbolical forests that have beckoned
Such knights, squired by the scyther, where to lie.
But skill dispassionately praises the rider,
Despair details the grey, cadaverous steed,
The immortal image holds its murderer
In a clear gaze for the next age to read.

Bronze

Hammered to the serenity of copper,
Her drowsing mask with slitted eyes,
Cupped in a palm and quiet as a plaque,
By tears unrunnelled, guiltless of surprise,
Bathes in dawn's wind, the wild night hair blown back.

Those mottled marbles I admired,
Bone-coloured in their pagan calm,

Sea-flowering Aphrodite borne on shells,
That blunt, androgynous Venus with one arm,
Male-thighed Dianas in their hunting dells,
And Ledas lost in blizzards of the swan,
Not one of those in such fierce sex was fired
Or holds its cunning secret as this one
Of lasting bronze, art of a savage race,
Marble, bronze, ebonwood, white, creole, black.

The elongated eyes look Arawak,
Arawak or Carib, but nakedness unsurprised
By armoured men dividing jungle leaves,
The sun ablaze on helmet, breastplate, greaves;
They close in groaning irony at their rape,
For that earth-colored flesh buries all men
In immolations mocked by the wild ape,
At that brute cry all civilizations crack.

The high-boned ridges of the drowsing cheek
Are Amerindian by West African,
And is there any Egypt in that head?

Though, by the books, it seems impossible;
Still, those flinched nostrils have smelt the dead
And in my book that's sibylline; our sibyl
Has seen worse death in our Egyptian past
Than ritualistic slaughter to a faith;
That metal peace was hammered in a blast
Of burning heaps of pyramidical dead. Those veins
Are coloured rivers of the violent slain,
Cooled by dawn's wind, like sea-wind over canes
Which the East Indian heaps with burning back.

The hair is night, its skeins are the night's winds,
Out of such savage, tangled roots was born
This monolithic, unforgiving face
Wrought in a furious kiln, in which each race
Expects its hundredth dawn.

The Gulf

for Jack and Barbara Harrison

I

The airport coffee tastes less of America.
Sour, unshaven, dreading the exertion
of tightening, racked nerves fuelled with liquor,

some smoky, resinous Bourbon,
the body, buckling at its casket hole,
a roar like last night's blast racing its engines,

watches the fumes of the exhausted soul
as the trans-Texas jet, screeching, begins
its flight and friends diminish. So, to be aware

of the divine union the soul detaches
itself from created things. 'We're in the air,'
the Texan near me grins. All things: these matches

from LBJ's campaign hotel, this rose
given me at dawn in Austin by a child,
this book of fables by Borges, its prose

a stalking, moonlit tiger. What was willed
on innocent, sun-streaked Dallas, the beast's claw
curled round that hairspring rifle is revealed

on every page as lunacy or feral law;
circling that wound we leave Love Field.
Fondled, these objects conjure hotels,

quarrels, new friendships, brown limbs
nakedly moulded as these autumn hills
memory penetrates as the jet climbs

the new clouds over Texas; their home means
an island suburb, forest, mountain water;
they are the simple properties for scenes

whose joy exhausts like grief, scenes where we learn,
exchanging the least gifts, this rose, this napkin,
that those we love are objects we return,

that this lens on the desert's wrinkled skin
has priced our flesh, all that we love in pawn
to that brass ball, that the gifts, multiplying

clutter and choke the heart, and that I shall
watch love reclaim its things as I lie dying.
My very flesh and blood! Each seems a petal

shrivelling from its core. I watch them burn,
by the nerves' flare I catch their skeletal
candour! Best never to be born

the great dead cry. Their works shine on our shelves,
by twilight tour their gilded gravestone spines,
and read until the lamplit page revolves

to a white stasis whose detachment shines
like a propeller's rainbowed radiance.
Circling like us; no comfort for their loves!

II

The cold glass darkens. Elizabeth wrote once
that we make glass the image of our pain;
I watch clouds boil past the cold, sweating pane

above the Gulf. All styles yearn to be plain
as life. The face of the loved object under glass
is plainer still. Yet, somehow, at this height,

above this cauldron boiling with its wars,
our old earth, breaking to familiar light,
that cloud-bound mummy with self-healing scars

peeled of her cerements again looks new;
some cratered valley heals itself with sage,
through that grey, fading massacre a blue

light-hearted creek flutes of some siege
to the amnesia of drumming water.
Their cause is crystalline: the divine union

of these detached, divided States, whose slaughter
darkens each summer now, as one by one,
the smoke of bursting ghettos clouds the glass

down every coast where filling-station signs
proclaim the Gulf, an air, heavy with gas,
sickens the state, from Newark to New Orleans.

III

Yet the South felt like home. Wrought balconies,
the sluggish river with its tidal drawl,
the tropic air charged with the extremities

of patience, a heat heavy with oil,
canebrakes, that legendary jazz. But fear
thickened my voice, that strange, familiar soil

prickled and barbed the texture of my hair,
my status as a secondary soul.
The Gulf, your gulf, is daily widening,

each blood-red rose warns of that coming night
when there's no rock cleft to go hidin' in
and all the rocks catch fire, when that black might,

their stalking, moonless panthers turn from Him
whose voice they can no more believe, when the black X's
mark their passover with slain seraphim.

IV

   The Gulf shines, dull as lead. The coast of Texas
glints like a metal rim. I have no home
as long as summer bubbling to its head

   boils for that day when in the Lord God's name
the coals of fire are heaped upon the head
of all whose gospel is the whip and flame,

   age after age, the uninstructing dead.

GEORGE MAC BETH

(1932–)

Report to the Director

I'd say their marble cubicles were a shade
Too small for the taller men, but they all appeared
To be standing at ease. O the usual postures—hands
In their pockets, hands on their hips, hands on the wall.
A few touched themselves. A few were saying prayers
Perhaps. I expect a few were feeling the cold
From that bare cement floor in those bedroom slippers.
I did, in my shoes; but still, I suppose one allows
A little latitude in the provinces. No money
To do it all in style. However, it worked
And we did get going. One man was reluctant
To co-operate about buttons—a big fellow
With a lot of weight to throw around: it's always
Annoying that sort of thing: a nasty business
It can be on those tiles. So we gave a hand,
Igor and I. The locals didn't mind,
They rarely do. From there it was plain sailing
To the main business. The five attendants came
All according to the book, well-turned-out men

In their new aprons, with the usual hoses, and a good
Flexible pump. (I gave them marks for that. You know
There's a lot of friction on those grids if they scuffle
When you fit the neck-plates.
It might be worthwhile specifying cable,
Steel-strapped stuff; it would save in the long run.)
Fortunately, we didn't need it: they were all so docile,
Queued and shuffled out with no trouble at all.
Though the line-up was tricky—they'd done the count wrong
So we had to use the shoe-horn on a couple.
But after that it was fine: taps on,
Mask fitted, the legs well held, the right grip
And a nice simple injection—I always think
Those gas-cylinders are all wrong. The infusion
Was one of the smoothest I've seen. Evacuation
Very decent. An infinity of freshness
In a little diffusion of bitter carbolic. Rather sweet.
It took about fifteen minutes to get the stories,
And not much mess: they had to scrub the channel
To clear some vomit, otherwise all O.K.
No frills: but at least the operation was completed
With all proper precautions, the doors closed,
The men screened: and, O yes, the windows open
To clean the air. I doubt if anyone smelled
A rat in the whole building, or heard as much
As a squeak from a plimsoll. They moved like professionals
From start to finish. I'd say it was all good work.
They certainly do things with the minimum fuss.
I'd recommend we exonerate the whole depot.

The Blood-Woman *

I
    She is coming. In the low wooden room
    by the Wedgwood light at the window

* The Blood-Woman: In the moment of composition, a poet believes he
is waiting for a Muse whose embraces will drain his blood. He relates the
vampire-act of poetry to the sacrificial rites of the Aztecs, the conquests of the
Norsemen, and the movements of his own body.—Author's note.

with the spring fire hissing below
its paper logs, the questing sharpness
moves on the wood. It feels the infection, the needle.

II

The first movement is one of clouds.
Under my elbows I feel the American walnut, its
nippled bronze in my palms. The
Indies have lent their tree to adjust my
hip. It is air here, the frames and the

eagles' feathers, the world of wood.
The poisoned body moves through the light
and is still. In the arm, through the wrist,
through the blunt fingers, the blood-kingdoms
run. Out of the torn heart, the sun

drinks like a hind. I feel the great snake
of the arteries hang and twist through
my neck, the Mexican coin on its chain.
The priests are alive in the light. They
feel the ships come in the sun.

III

The second movement is one of leaves.
There are signs in shields, pierced, dripping,
hung in firs. Blood is alive
in the soil: cold, ready, the snow-drop
waits with its ice-axe. The North moves

in the grain of apple-trees. It speaks out of nine centuries,
through rocks and worms. In the slither of polished
black over white the starved musk-ox and the
thinning polar bear step down into
light. There are calendars in the bones of whales.

IV

The third movement is one of flames.
As the blood gathers, floods into words,

the black signals carved in the wood
scorch in the fire. I am in its arms,
it rocks me against the cold. And

music comes from the fire: it burns in
a world of wires. I hear the organ
paw through the mass, the Christian death
of Socrates. The man of wisdom stepped
in the blood-flow. He drinks the poison.

v

The last movement is one of liquids.
I hear the blood hiss in the grate; rain
on the roof. The North is here
in the room. Fluid is under my knuckles,
over my pencil. The foreign alliance

of heat and wetness that blood makes
rocks me in darkness. The
walnut slips away. The Indian tree
is gone into air. I am naked, stripped
of the sheep and the bull. There is nothing

but whiteness. The clean room is
the clean page is the cleared theatre
where the nun intoning her requiem wilts
into light. My pencil is broken.
Here is the needle, the blood-woman.

Marshall

It occurred to Marshall
that if he were a vegetable, he'd
be a bean. Not
one of your thin, stringy
green beans, or your

dry, marbly
Burlotti beans. No, he'd be
a broad bean,
a rich, nutritious,
meaningful bean,

alert for advantages,
inquisitive with potatoes,
mixing with every kind
and condition of vegetable,
and a good friend

to meat and lager. Yes, he'd
leap from his huge
rough pod with a loud
popping sound
into the pot: always

in hot water
and out of it with a soft
heart inside
his horny carapace. He'd
carry the whole

world's hunger on
his broad shoulders, green
with best butter
or brown with gravy. And if
some starving Indian saw his

flesh bleeding
when the gas was turned on
or the knife went in
he'd accept the homage and prayers,
and become a god, and die like a man,

which, as things were, wasn't so easy.

Ode on a Grecian Urn *

after Keats

I

You're not
more than a fresh girl
in a cool church,
                    now are
you?
            Cross of a few
thousand centuries, and
not much noise,
                    you
got your bland touch
with the country stuff
                        (I grant
you, lusher than mine)
through lasting
                    simply,
frocked with tree-myths
in ghost-fashion,
                    gods
and us,
            and a garnish
of coy girls, lechers,
rape, riot, and
                    the final
big O.

II

It's always
easier on the ear
not to have the
                    music

* These "distortions" are an attempt to extend the method of Lowell's *Imitations* to poems in one's own language. Readers wishing to make a comparison of texts may be helped to know that each section corresponds to one stanza of the Keats original.—Author's note.

actually *playing*.

I

mean, if the oboe
tickles the fine roots
of the metaphysical

man, not
the material one, you
draw a bonus.

As,
for example, that
fine boy there

in the clearing, he
won't ever get
what he's after, or

see
(for that matter) the
leaves fall,

but she'll
be as Camay-fresh
and desirable

tomorrow, that
cool bint with
the Jimi Hendrix.

III

Once you have
the consummation, it's
your swollen eyes, your

morning
sickness and your Alka-
Seltzer.

Whereas here,
I grant you, they're
all swinging, even
the vocalist,

and
the trees.

As for
those kids, warm

in each other's
                    expectations,
aren't they just
having a ball,
                    static
in glazed love,
and with all the new tunes!

IV

          Take the religious
piece, too.
                    I agree
it's far better
from the cow's point
                    of view,
not to be having
that funny boy with
                    the dog-collar
really getting down
to his carve-up
                    in the grove.
So she goes on
all smooth and flowery, and

                    mooing, too.
Then there's the bare city
beside the water,
                    with the lynch-mob
all gone off to
their blood-letting,
                    and not a soul
left with a bad story
to tell the sheriff
                    about
where they are, and who with.
It helps, it
          helps.

V

     Yes, you have
us all voting
for Miss Timeless,
           the Greek
bird with the
curvy look.
        She
has it all made,
the cold-as-marble look,
           the few
twigs in her hair,
the down-trodden stance.
            When we're
all grey, and fucked up,
(and it's coming)
           you'll be there,
still charming, a mite cool
maybe, to our minds
          in our troubles
but (and here's good news)
bearing the same message:
          life's a bowl
of cherries, if you believe it,
if you believe it, life's
          a bowl of cherries. That's
the big secret, man,
the only secret.

SYLVIA PLATH

(1932–63)

Two Views
of a Cadaver Room

1

The day she visited the dissecting room
They had four men laid out, black as burnt turkey,
Already half unstrung. A vinegary fume
of the death vats clung to them;
The white-smocked boys started working.
The head of his cadaver had caved in,
And she could scarcely make out anything
In that rubble of skull plates and old leather.
A sallow piece of string held it together.

In their jars the snail-nosed babies moon and glow.
He hands her the cut-out heart like a cracked heirloom.

2

In Brueghel's panorama of smoke and slaughter
Two people only are blind to the carrion army:
He, afloat in the sea of her blue satin
Skirts, sings in the direction
Of her bare shoulder, while she bends,

Fingering a leaflet of music, over him,
Both of them deaf to the fiddle in the hands
Of the death's-head shadowing their song.
These Flemish lovers flourish; not for long.

Yet desolation, stalled in paint, spares the little country
Foolish, delicate, in the lower right-hand corner.

The Colossus

I shall never get you put together entirely,
Pieced, glued, and properly jointed.
Mule-bray, pig-grunt and bawdy cackles
Proceed from your great lips.
It's worse than a barnyard.

Perhaps you consider yourself an oracle,
Mouthpiece of the dead, or of some god or other.
Thirty years now I have labored
To dredge the silt from your throat.
I am none the wiser.

Scaling little ladders with gluepots and pails of lysol
I crawl like an ant in mourning
Over the weedy acres of your brow
To mend the immense skull plates and clear
The bald, white tumuli of your eyes.

A blue sky out of the Oresteia
Arches above us. O father, all by yourself
You are pithy and historical as the Roman Forum.
I open my lunch on a hill of black cypress.
Your fluted bones and acanthine hair are littered

In their old anarchy to the horizon-line.
It would take more than a lightning-stroke
To create such a ruin.

Nights, I squat in the cornucopia
Of your left ear, out of the wind,

Counting the red stars and those of plum-color.
The sun rises under the pillar of your tongue.
My hours are married to shadow.
No longer do I listen for the scrape of a keel
On the blank stones of the landing.

Lady Lazarus

I have done it again.
One year in every ten
I manage it—

A sort of walking miracle, my skin
Bright as a Nazi lampshade,
My right foot

A paperweight,
My face a featureless, fine
Jew linen.

Peel off the napkin
O my enemy.
Do I terrify?—

The nose, the eye pits, the full set of teeth?
The sour breath
Will vanish in a day.

Soon, soon the flesh
The grave cave ate will be
At home on me

And I a smiling woman.
I am only thirty.
And like the cat I have nine times to die.

This is Number Three.
What a trash
To annihilate each decade.

What a million filaments.
The peanut-crunching crowd
Shoves in to see

Them unwrap me hand and foot—
The big strip tease.
Gentleman, ladies,

These are my hands,
My knees.
I may be skin and bone,

Nevertheless, I am the same, identical woman.
The first time it happened I was ten.
It was an accident.

The second time I meant
To last it out and not come back at all.
I rocked shut

As a seashell.
They had to call and call
And pick the worms off me like sticky pearls.

Dying
Is an art, like everything else.
I do it exceptionally well.

I do it so it feels like hell.
I do it so it feels real.
I guess you could say I've a call.

It's easy enough to do it in a cell.
It's easy enough to do it and stay put.
It's the theatrical

Comeback in broad day
To the same place, the same face, the same brute
Amused shout:

"A miracle!"
That knocks me out.
There is a charge

For the eyeing of my scars, there is a charge
For the hearing of my heart—
It really goes.

And there is a charge, a very large charge,
For a word or a touch
Or a bit of blood

Or a piece of my hair or my clothes.
So, so, Herr Doktor.
So, Herr Enemy.

I am your opus,
I am your valuable,
The pure gold baby

That melts to a shriek.
I turn and burn.
Do not think I underestimate your great concern.

Ash, ash—
You poke and stir.
Flesh, bone, there is nothing there—

A cake of soap,
A wedding ring,
A gold filling.

Herr God, Herr Lucifer,
Beware
Beware.

Out of the ash
I rise with my red hair
And I eat men like air.

Daddy

You do not do, you do not do
Any more, black shoe
In which I have lived like a foot
For thirty years, poor and white,
Barely daring to breathe or Achoo.

Daddy, I have had to kill you.
You died before I had time—
Marble-heavy, a bag full of God,
Ghastly statue with one grey toe
Big as a Frisco seal

And a head in the freakish Atlantic
Where it pours bean green over blue
In the waters off beautiful Nauset.
I used to pray to recover you.
Ach, du.

In the German tongue, in the Polish town
Scraped flat by the roller
Of wars, wars, wars.
But the name of the town is common.
My Polack friend

Says there are a dozen or two.
So I never could tell where you
Put your foot, your root,
I never could talk to you.
The tongue stuck in my jaw.

It stuck in a barb wire snare.
Ich, ich, ich, ich,

I could hardly speak.
I thought every German was you.
And the language obscene

An engine, an engine
Chuffing me off like a Jew.
A Jew to Dachau, Auschwitz, Belsen.
I began to talk like a Jew.
I think I may well be a Jew.

The snows of the Tyrol, the clear beer of Vienna
Are not very pure or true.
With my gypsy ancestress and my weird luck
And my Taroc pack and my Taroc pack
I may be a bit of a Jew.

I have always been scared of *you*,
With your Luftwaffe, your gobbledygoo.
And your neat moustache
And your Aryan eye, bright blue.
Panzer-man, panzer-man, O You—

Not God but a swastika
So black no sky could squeak through.
Every woman adores a Fascist,
The boot in the face, the brute
Brute heart of a brute like you.

You stand at the blackboard, daddy,
In the picture I have of you,
A cleft in your chin instead of your foot
But no less a devil for that, no not
Any less the black man who

Bit my pretty red heart in two.
I was ten when they buried you.
At twenty I tried to die
And get back, back, back to you.
I thought even the bones would do.

But they pulled me out of the sack,
And they stuck me together with glue.
And then I knew what to do.
I made a model of you,
A man in black with a Meinkampf look

And a love of the rack and the screw.
And I said I do, I do.
So daddy, I'm finally through.
The black telephone's off at the root,
The voices just can't worm through.

If I've killed one man, I've killed two—
The vampire who said he was you
And drank my blood for a year,
Seven years, if you want to know.
Daddy, you can lie back now.

There's a stake in your fat black heart
And the villagers never liked you.
They are dancing and stamping on you.
They always *knew* it was you.
Daddy, daddy, you bastard, I'm through.

Contusion

Colour floods to the spot, dull purple.
The rest of the body is all washed out,
The colour of pearl.

In a pit of rock
The sea sucks obsessively,
One hollow the whole sea's pivot.

The size of a fly,
The doom mark
Crawls down the wall.

The heart shuts,
The sea slides back,
The mirrors are sheeted.

DIANE WAKOSKI

(1937–)

Sleep

The mole
lifting snouts-
full of strained black dirt

     —his perfect tunnel
      sculptured
      to fit
      the fat
      body. Sleep
fits tight
—must keep bringing out
the fine grit
to keep size
for even one day.

Winter Apples

Lady, you are walking in your sleep.
You are stealing my apples
and even though I know
you are walking
while you sleep

I cannot forgive the theft. I fear even more
what forces you out of bed;
makes you walk by
and steal apples from my bowl.

The Night a Sailor Came to Me in a Dream

At the point of shining feathers,
that moment when dawn
ran her finger along the knife edge sky;
at the point when chickens come out of the living room rug
to peck for corn and the grains like
old yellow eyes
roll as marbles across the floor;
at that sweet sprouting point when the seed of day
rests on your tongue,
and you haven't swallowed reality yet. Then,
then, yes, at that instant of shimmering new pine needles
came a dream, a blister from a new burn,
and you walked in,
old times,
no player piano or beer,
reality held my toes,
the silver ball of sleep was on my stomach,
the structure of dream,
like a harness
lowered over my head, around me,
and I cannot remember what you said, though the harbor was foggy,
and your pea coat seemed to drip with moisture.

Thirty years of travelling this ocean.

Perhaps you told me
you were not
dead.

from ''FROM THE TAROT DECK''

The Hermit

With gravel glued together for arms and legs,
charcoal-blackened wood for feet,
hands,
the body a leather bolster,
head a hard ball—
                    the withered dried up man who had
                    eaten nothing but sweetened dew for 30 years
                    knelt by the roadside.
                    A robber attacked him from behind
                    cutting down the old man with his knife.
                    He put on the old man's ragged robe
                    and himself began to pray.
                    "Lord, Lord, I have killed a good man
                    gratuitously. What shall I do?"
                    But nothing happened.
                    The old man's body began to rot.
                    The robber sang and chanted.
                    He forgot
                    after some time
                    his origins.

In Place of a Phone Call to Arabia

                    an empty ashtray
                    because I don't smoke
                    is the mark
                    of something missing

the hollow
in my throat
when you can see one blue vein
like a protruding nail in a pine board
is empty too

a woman is one half of a siamese twin.
My other half/ the part
that fills the socket
of my throat
that whispers in my ear with a warm tongue
and turns my body
like an hour glass
is running empty guns in Arabia.

Sand in my mouth;
they burn it into sapphires.
You are a missing scar on my arm.
A smoked cigarette
an empty Gauloise Bleu package
I am the silver
paper
lining
it.

The Magician

Your wand,
the flowering stalk of the radish,
hot,
not spicy but sharp;

I touch
with my teeth
the root,
that white bulb;

Vegetables
remind me I love you,
your transformations;

The magician works in silence.
There is no music around him, the only rhythm
a pulse in the frightened rabbit's ear.

When he folds his silks
and hangs up his suit,
he slips his baton
into his elbow.

That naked magician walks up to my doorbell
which doesn't ring.
I hear him,
the magic being now
in my ears.

He leaves his eyes on my shoulders and powdering my knees.

The Magellanic Clouds

(for Eleanor who likes to see her name in print)

The photographic plate is blurred.
That blurry area
is where you laughed and
breathed on the plate; lizard skinned
prickly pears roll out of your mouth; a purple bird
twists your tongue with his beak
and crazy cactus leaves of love pin you luckily to
one man;
you have a mouthful of stars when you laugh
and you fall over the milky way at your feet.
Next door the Magellanic Clouds swirl
and try to force themselves into your paintings

but you are too happy painting
little hearts and big hearts and sticking them
all over your husband
who is a river washing silver fish over you in the dark.

Look carefully.
My scream makes a silver line on the graph.
The photographic plate is blurred.
That blurry area
is the Magellanic Clouds
from another galaxy.
Inside me swirls something like the Magellanic
Clouds.
All the animals I ride are found in the Magellanic Clouds.
My life is destined to be a cloud,
galaxies, light years,
removed. The dust storm on the desert. The fog over the river.
A handful of dust with tiny shell fragments.
A gold outline against the sky.

How can I explain it to you and all the succulent women I know.
Wives, mothers, loved, protected,
by men they love,
having the shoulder to curl their heads into at night.
How can I explain to myself this dust cloud that is my life?
I talk in my sleep, just as I talk when I'm awake.
No one listens to me but strangers.
Once a blue vein of electricity came to me in the Magellanic
                                        Clouds

and said there is a price
on everyone's life.
Uncurling my ears like new leaves,
I looked at my world,
my scarred body,
my missing children,
separation from the men who spoke my language.
The price is to walk
alone
up the stairs,

alone
every night with your candle,
and alone
down the stairs
alone
every morning with white footsteps
and teacups of tears.
In your day dreams you must carry the bodies of your children
wrapped in white and strapped to stiff boards;
people will chase you and accuse you of murder.
The children will sing in your ears and cut you with the
sharp corners of their smiles.
Your songs will be bled out
of you
every day, as you are cut with different tools,
razor blades, knives, scissors, grass, paper, glass.
One day the words will come out of your elbows and one day
out of your knees. Scars and holes and craters will cover you.
When people look at you they will run away
but words,
the words you've bought will creep out of holes
like beautiful skeins of thread.
Some day I will vanish in the Magellanic Clouds
but will wait in rooms to get inside of paintings.
Even the electricity, the fire
tells me I will
not have to spend all my
time
in the sky.
Someday it will be my breath blurring the photographic plates
and the astronomers will say
"See that cloudy spot on the plate?
We once thought it was the Magellanic Clouds, but they have
moved
farther out
into space.
It is something new, another enormous cloud made up of strange
gases and foreign particles. It is something new
and we have no name for it yet,"

and I will breathe harder,
will blow harder,
will blur more of the plate,
will pass through rooms and rooms and rooms of memories in
                                        the shape

of apples, birds, iron wheels.

The clouds, the clouds, the Magellanic Clouds, the clouds in my
heart, the clouds I ride on, the clouds under my bed,
the clouds of my life, the clouds always in
the next room seeping under the door.

I am a cloud,
dust on the desert,
fog over the waters,
gases in the sky,

Can there be any
sadness
once I am named.

DON L. LEE

(1942–)

The Self-Hatred of Don L. Lee

(9/22/63)
        i,
        at one time,
        loved
        my
        color—
        it
        opened sMall
        doors of
        tokenism
        &
        acceptance.
                (doors called, "the only one" & "our negro")
        after painfully
        struggling
        thru Du Bois,
        Roger, Locke,
        Wright & others,
        my blindness

was vanquished
by pitchblack
paragraphs of
"us, we, me, i"
awareness.

i
began
to love
only a
part of
me—
my inner
self which
is all
black—
&
developed a
vehement
hatred of
my light
brown
outer.

But He Was Cool
or: he even stopped for green lights

super-cool
ultrablack
a tan/purple
had a beautiful shade.

he had a double-natural
that wd put the sisters to shame.
his dashikis were tailor made
& his beads were imported sea shells
        (from some blk/country i never heard of)
he was triple-hip.

his tikis were hand carved
out of ivory
& came express from the motherland.
he would greet u in swahili
& say good-by in yoruba.
woooooooooooo-jim he bes so cool & ill tel li gent

cool-cool is so cool he was un-cooled by
other niggers' cool
cool-cool ultracool was bop-cool/ice box
cool so cool cold cool
his wine didn't have to be cooled, him was
air conditioned cool
cool-cool/real cool made me cool—now
ain't that cool
cool-cool so cool him nick-named refrig-
erator.

cool-cool so cool
he didn't know,
after detroit, newark, chicago &c.,
we had to hip
cool-cool/ super-cool/ real cool
that
to be black
is
to be
very-hot.

communication in whi-te

dee dee dee dee dee wee weee eeeeee wee we
deweeeeeeee ee ee ee nig
nig nig nig niggggggggg gggggggg cleek cleek cleek
cleeeeee cleekcleek
rip rip rip rip rip/rip/rip/rip/rip/riprripripripripripriprip
pi pi pi pi pip
bom bom bom bom bom/bom/bom/bombombombom

bombbombbombbombbombbomb
deathtocleekdeathtocleekdeathtocleekdeathtocleek
    deathtocleekdeathtodeathto
alllllllllllalllllllllll allll lllllllll deathtoallllllll l allllllllll
    allllllleeeeeeee
te te te te te te   te/te/te/te/te/te/tetetetetetetetetete
    tetetetetetetete:
the paris peace talks, 1968.

Malcolm Spoke/ who listened?
(this poem is for my consciousness too)

he didn't say
wear yr/blackness in
outer garments
& blk/slogans fr/the top 10.

he was fr a long
line of super-cools,
    doo-rag lovers &
    revolutionary pimps.
u are playing that
high-yellow game in blackface
minus the straighthair.
now
it's nappy-black
& air conditioned volkswagens
with undercover whi
te girls who studied faulkner at
smith
& are authorities on "militant"
knee/grows
selling u at jew town rates:
    niggers with wornout tongues
    three for a quarter/ or will consider a trade

the double-breasted hipster
has been replaced with a
dashiki wearing rip-off
who went to city college
majoring in physical education.

animals come in all colors.
dark meat will roast as fast as whi-te meat
especially in
the unitedstatesofamerica's
new
self-cleaning ovens.

if we don't listen.

Black Sketches

1

i
was five
when
mom & dad got married
& i
didn't realize that
i
was illegitimate
until i started
school.

2

i was at
the airport
& had
to use the
men's room
real bad
& didn't have a
dime.

3

somebody
made a
mistake (they said)
&
sent the
peace corps to
europe.

4

went to cash
my
1968 tax refund
&
the check bounced;
insufficient funds.

5

i
read the
newspapers today
&
thought that
everything
was
all right.

6

nat turner
returned
&
killed
william styron
&
his momma too.

7

ed brooke
sat at his

desk
crying & slashing
his wrist
because somebody
called him
black.

8

general westmoreland
was transferred
to the
westside of chicago
&
he lost
there too.

9

in 1959
my mom
was dead at the
age of
35
& nobody thought it unusual;
not even
me.

10

in 1963
i
became black
& everyone thought it unusual;
even me.

11

the american dream:
  nigger bible in
  every hotel;
  iceberg slim (pimp) getting

next to julia;
& roy wilkins on
the mod squad.

A Message All Blackpeople Can Dig
(& a few negroes too)

we are going to do it.
US: blackpeople, beautiful people; the sons and daughters of
    beautiful people.
bring it back to
US: the unimpossibility.
now is
the time, the test
while there is something to save (other than our lives).

we'll move together
hands on weapons & families
blending into the sun,
into each/other.
we'll love,
we've always loved.
just be cool & help one/another.
go ahead.
walk a righteous direction
under the moon,
in the night
bring new meanings to
the north star,
the blackness,
to US.

discover new stars:
street-light stars that will explode into evil-eyes,
light-bulb stars visible only to the realpeople,
clean stars, african & asian stars,
black aesthetic stars that will damage the whi-temind;

killer stars that will move against
the unpeople.

came
brothers/fathers/sisters/mothers/sons/daughters
dance as one
walk slow & hip.
hip to what life is
and can be.
& remember we are not hippies,
WE WERE BORN HIP.
walk on. smile a little
yeah, that's it beautiful people
move on in, take over. take over, take over take/over
    takeovertakeovertakeover
  takeovertakeover   overtakeovertakeovertake over/take over take,
    over take,
  over take, over take.
blackpeople
are moving, moving to return
  this earth into the hands of

human beings.

BRIAN PATTEN

(1946–)

Little Johnny's Confession

This morning
          being rather young and foolish
          I borrowed a machinegun my father
          had left hidden since the war, went out,
          and eliminated a number of small enemies.
          Since then I have not returned home.

This morning
          swarms of police with trackerdogs
          wander about the city
          with my description printed
          on their minds, asking:
          'Have you seen him?
          He is seven years old,
          likes Pluto, Mighty Mouse
          and Biffo the Bear,
          have you seen him, anywhere?'

This morning
          sitting alone in a strange playground

muttering you've blundered, you've blundered
over and over to myself
I work out my next move
but cannot move.
The trackerdogs will sniff me out,
they have my lollypops.

Little Johnny Takes a Trip to Another Planet

Through his bedroom window, later they confirmed
Johnny drifted one Monday evening
Up above the sleeping world.

He left this message:

I've taken a trip to another planet
And I'll be away for a while,
so don't send the Escaped Children Squad after me
the Universe is too wild.

Now among black glass trees
he weaves intricate shapes
in a world an inch away from ours,
and from behind his eyes
he sees into a waiting room of light
and maps out the route dawn takes through
the nurseries of night.

He has switched on a world and walked inside;
and as silence blooms among the flowers
he wonders at people groping
through transparent hours.
He's found the perfect loophole:
sits on the other side,
a child with eyes as big as planets
whose dreams do not collide
with any forms of teaching
with any form of lies.

So don't send the Escaped Children Squad after him
he'll be away for a while,
he's taken a trip to another planet
and the Universe is too wild
for him to make it back
in the same state of mind.

Now We Will Either Sleep, Lie Still, or Dress Again

Evening and the sun warming the bird
in her cupped hands.
Over the room's silence other voices and sounds.
My love, the world is a distant planet

. . . and bending here you are naked,
wind from the half open skylight hardens breasts,
your blonde hair falling is spread across me.
The bird in your cupped hands rising.

Let our touchings be open;
We do not belong to a race of pale children
whose bodies are hardly born
nor among the virgins hung still inside their sadness,
but waking in strange beds we are screwed and perfect.

Littered about the room still
are the clothes we wore while meeting.
Evening and the sun has moved across the room.
Now we will either sleep, lie still, or dress again.

The Prophet's Good Idea

A new prophet appeared recently; was first seen
walking out an ocean. Which? We've forgotten.

He said

to the hushed crowds that had gathered, to
the journalists, the radio and television newscasters,
the Look at Life team and the politicians:
                    'Stay in Bed.'
That was his message. 'Bring each other
cups of coffee;
lie naked as near as possible without touching,
think of governments, chewing-gum, wars,
Queen Elizabeth coronation cups, anything—
you're bound finally to burst out laughing.
Draw peace maps across each others bodies.
Climb into bed. Imagine if everyone did.
Returning astronauts would hear
only the sound of dreaming.'

   Well the hushed crowds, the journalists, the
radio and television newscasters,
the Look at Life team and the politicians
thought it sounded a good message; a clear message,
the kind they could pass on
quite harmlessly to children.
Bed manufacturers were informed.
They loved the idea, loved it. Made beds big enough
to hold several hundred people
thinking of chewing-gum, Queen Elizabeth coronation cups,
                                                anything—

   'It sounds so good a message,' said the people,
'that something's bound to be wrong. . . .'
              So philosophers, house-hold names and a
                                    TV personality
gathered to discuss the message. There were
a few flaws to be ironed out—
Robots were to be invented for the menial task
of running the planet—otherwise, a fine message.

And so now the whole planet's sleeping;
East and West snores, Hansel and Gretel personified.
Moss and moonwort burst out from bank-vaults;

all manner of creatures make themselves at home in houses;
from bed to bed spiders spin their webs, dream-catchers.
And there are sleep-walkers and sleep-lovers
in nightgowns or pyjamas, in underwear or nothing,
wandering through fields or suburbs, all so quietly.
And some woken from nightmares sit and comfort one another
whispering, *and o it's all madness!*

               And occasionally
the prophet rising from his ocean
drifts down the inland currents, watches whatever moves.
Occasionally drags himself up into radio-ships
where earphones to his brain he listens,
makes sure it is all still silent.
And o it's all madness and he has little else to do
him suffering from insomnia,
adrift in his faery-tale silence.

Through the Tall Grass in Your Head

Through the tall grass in your head
a grasshopper made out of stars is leaping;
It moves through those planets of information
Then leaves them behind it.
They'll soon explode.

You no longer bother watching how
Time and age leak down your mirror disfiguring it
Nor how that animal the centuries have tamed
Roams less restless now inside you.

You have reached that state
Where so much has ceased to matter
And outside your window you see that the garden too
Has grown weary of sunlight
And time has whittled down the cabbage leaves to thin white wings.
All you did finally was to ask whether it was good.

Sad Adam

Sad Adam
Uncurling from a concrete wall
Woken at dawn by rain and sudden light
You will move out now
Watching how the trees retreat down avenues of themselves
In your concrete century
Holding some vague idea of the sight you saw
When your eyes first clicked open into paradise

Here it seems
Even the stars are temporary
And the lives that spin beneath them
Rotate without memory.
Of the waiting world.
New Adam
In the markets touching apples
Huge exploding seeds!
Pink mirrors of the barrows!
You come in the brain
when market women offer you warm flowers

Or in rainpark cafés
Your teacup full of leaves
Escaping onto the open lawns
Afraid of the chained pathways
The green notice boards warning against sunset
Sorry for the frightened intruders
The mad dawners escaped from cities
Who pin notes to their bodies then disappear. . . .

Eveless Adam, touching yourself through blue shirts;
Your pale face reflecting in the rain
As the wind blows it passed and shatters it against leaves—

Twenty centuries are nothing here
The sickest headlines disintegrate
The selfish public world is cancelled out.

Yet for all your huge garden
From your own sad body
You cannot escape—
Let it make its own way out then,
Out across parks
And back into cities.
You'll return there coughing up bricks of dust,
Yet from that island you call a soul
Still slow birds will fly out and be evidence
And on the walls of city banks
The memory of a leaf will sing.

NOTES ON THE POETS

For more detailed information on most of the poets represented in *Today's Poets*, by far the most useful reference work is Rosalie Murphy (ed.), *Contemporary Poets of the English Language*, St. James Press, Chicago and London. Other useful works are *Contemporary Authors; Current Biography; Who's Who* (British); *Who's Who in America*.

Many of the poets have recorded their work on records, tapes, or cassettes. Certain companies, such as Caedmon and Spoken Arts, specialize in poetry recordings, and their catalogues should be consulted. Another very useful source of information is *Schwann Supplementary Record and Tape Guide* (W. Schwann, 137 Newbury St., Boston, Mass. 02116). The U.S. Library of Congress publishes *The National Union Catalog: Music and Phono-records* (semiannual with annual and five-year cumulation); also *Literary Recordings: A Checklist of the Archive of Recorded Poetry and Literature in the Library of Congress* (1966). Other useful works: *Audio Visual Market Place: A Multimedia Guide* (R. R. Bowker, New York, 1970) and Helen Pauline Roach, *Spoken Records* (3rd ed., Scarecrow, New York, 1970).

The brief comments that follow on the work of individual poets are not intended as formal, critical judgments; they merely serve to point out certain qualities that make the poetry interesting and worth reading.

George Barker

When George Barker's *Collected Poems: 1930–1955* appeared in 1957, a curious note was printed at the front: "One long poem, *The True Confession of George Barker*, which Mr. Barker wished to include in this volume, has been omitted at the publishers' request." *The True Confession* had earlier been broadcast in the Home Service of the BBC, and its plain treatment of sex had outraged so many listeners that the Director-General of the BBC had been obliged to make an official apology.

Critical opinion is divided down the middle on Barker. Some see him as a poet with impressive force and vision; others find him chaotic, uneven, and frequently tasteless. In an England still somewhat dominated by the well-behaved "Movement," his poetry seems brash and strident to many.

Barker was born in 1913, educated at Marlborough Road London County Council School, Chelsea. In 1939 he was professor of English literature at Imperial Tohoku University, Japan, and in 1965–66 was Visiting Professor at State University of New York at Buffalo. Despite the anti-privilege tone of his poems, he is a fellow of the Society for the Preservation of Ancient Monuments; and in "Stanzas on a Visit to Longleat House in Wiltshire, October 1953" he shows himself as hostile to the complacent proletariat as he has always been to the merely rich.

Thirty Preliminary Poems appeared in 1933 and has been followed by a dozen volumes of poetry. His tone and style are in constant evolution; and he remains, as from the beginning, a poet hard to put into any neat category.

Patricia Beer

In contemporary England where poetry remains something of a man's world, Patricia Beer (born 1924 in Exmouth, Devon) is one of the most distinctive women poets. She studied at Exeter University and Oxford, was a lecturer for seven years at various Italian universities and institutes, more recently at London University. She is married to the architect Damien Parsons.

Her growing reputation is based on three books of verse: *Loss of the Magyar* (1959), *The Survivors* (1963), and *Just Like the Resurrection* (1967). She has also published a prose autobiography, *Mrs. Beer's House* (1968). Discussing the latter in *Contemporary Poets*, she commented: "The writing of my autobiography has influenced my work in two ways: the intense use of prose has made me try for greater precision in my poetry; and since the publication of the autobiography I have felt able to deal poetically with subjects of a more overtly personal nature."

"Neatly elegant," Anthony Thwaite characterized her poetry. In recent years her style, like that of many contemporary poets, has been moving toward looser forms and rhythms, and a greater tone of informality.

John Bennett

A late bloomer or at least a late publisher, John Bennett first became widely known in his late forties when *The Zoo Manuscript* (1968) was published. This was closely followed by *Griefs and Exultations* (1970) and *The Struck Leviathan* (1970), the latter winning the Devin's Memorial Poetry Award out of more than three hundred manuscripts in competition.

Bennett was born in 1920 in Pittsfield, Massachusetts, and grew up in New Hampshire. His studies at Oberlin College were interrupted by four years in the U.S. Army, where he was commissioned in the field artillery. He served in the European theater as a member of the Office of Strategic Services doing liaison work with the Free French Underground. Returning to Oberlin, he received his B.A. in 1947. In 1956 he was awarded the Ph.D. in English at the University of Wisconsin, writing his dissertation on Melville. He now holds a special chair in English at St. Norbert College.

Of his three books, *The Zoo Manuscript* is a modern bestiary, infused by a sacramental sense of the ultimate radiance revealed by visible creatures of the world. *The Struck Leviathan* is a series of dramatic monologues spoken by characters from *Moby Dick*. *Griefs and Exultations*, a miscellaneous collection, received the Midland Poetry Award.

In many ways, Bennett runs counter to current poetic trends. His poetry tends to a kind of contemplation in which the poet withdraws his own personality, concentrating instead on the object beheld. He has a highly versatile mastery of poetic forms, and an angle of vision both implicitly and explicitly Christian.

John Berryman

"Something can (has) been said for sobriety," John Berryman once stated in a poem, adding, "but very little." This autobiographical confession could characterize his poetry—staggering with the impulses of imagination, dizzy with vitality, unpredictable from one book to the next, but always controlled by a powerful poetic sensibility, adept at manipulating everything from the Petrarchan sonnet to echoes of minstrel show banter.

Born in McAlester, Oklahoma, in 1914, and educated at Columbia and Oxford, Berryman has taught on countless campuses, his present base being the University of Minnesota. He first came to critical attention in 1940 when he appeared in *Five Young American Poets.* Several individual volumes followed, including a book-length tribute to America's first woman poet, *Homage to Mistress Bradstreet* (1956). An adulterous liaison in the 1940's produced *Berryman's Sonnets,* not published until 1967. The *Dream Songs,* collectively compared by some to Pound's *Cantos,* have appeared in several installments. His most recent collection of verse, *Love & Fame* (1970), culminates in "Eleven Addresses to the Lord," the result of a conversion experience.

In his early fifties he became the belated recipient of many major honors, among them a Pulitzer Prize, National Book Award, Bollingen Prize, and a Fellowship of the Academy of American Poets.

Often loosely grouped with the "confessional poets" (see Introduction), Berryman is so distinctively and bewilderingly himself that he fits awkwardly in any critical pigeonhole. Few poets can maul and distort the language as thoroughly as he does and—most of the time— create poetry in the process. His raging and sometimes antic ego is the central subject of his recent work, with God now recognized as one other ego worthy of respect and poetic recognition.

Carl Bode

One of the most distinguished scholars in the field of American literature, Carl Bode is also a highly gifted poet, though so far better known in England—where he was cultural attaché 1957–59 and was elected to the Royal Society of Literature—than in America. In his three published volumes of verse, *The Sacred Seasons* (1953), *The Calendar of Love* (1959), and *The Man Behind You* (1959), he reveals an easy mastery of traditional forms, the sonnet in particular, which he uses to celebrate both the sacred and secular moments of life. Underlying his poetry is the tension between his candid sensuousness and his preoccupation with God.

He has been Professor of English at the University of Maryland since 1947, receiving a Guggenheim Fellowship, 1954–55. He writes both literary and cultural history. His books include *The American Lyceum* (1956, 1968), *The Half-World of American Culture* (1965,

1967), and *Mencken* (1969), and he is finishing work on a new volume of poems to be called *Love in Three Lessons*.

Bode was born in 1911 in Milwaukee and received his under-graduate degree at the University of Chicago and his graduate degrees at Northwestern. He is married to Margaret Lutze; they have three daughters.

John Ciardi

John Ciardi was born in 1916 in Boston of Italian parents, Carmin and Concetta di Benedictus Ciardi. It is easy to speculate that something of that heritage is revealed in his poetry, which has a direct, sensuous rich-ness rare today—a wide-eyed openness to the delights of the world without any excessive illusions about its reliability.

Ciardi was educated at Bates College and Tufts (magna cum laude, 1938). In 1939 he went to the University of Michigan and studied for his M.A. under the famous teacher of writing, Professor Cowden, who in his long career launched many poets on a successful career. Winning the Hopwood Award in poetry, Ciardi went on to a succession of teaching positions—University of Kansas City, Harvard, Rutgers—with a Salzburg Seminar along the way in 1951. Since 1955 he has been director of the Bread Loaf Writers Conference, and since 1956 he has served as poetry editor of the *Saturday Review*, where his witty and sometimes mordant articles on contemporary poets have provoked countless letters to the editor. In 1961 he resigned from Rutgers to free lance.

A member of the Army Air Forces during the war, Ciardi married in 1946 the Judith who figures in many of his poems. They have three chil-dren and live in Metuchen, N.J.

Ciardi's first book, *Homeward to America* (1940) was followed by frequent others, the most recent being the autobiographical *Lives of X* (1971). He has produced the best poetic translation of Dante's *Divine Comedy*, several books of poetry for children, and a college textbook, *How Does a Poem Mean?*

Robert Creeley

Born in 1926 in Arlington, Massachusetts, Robert Creeley attended Harvard but took his B.A. at Black Mountain College. (The experi-mental North Carolina school, now defunct, was a center of poetic experimentation while it lasted.) His master's degree was at the University of New Mexico. He has taught on many campuses, currently at the State University of New York at Buffalo.

Along the way, Creeley has spent much of his life in distant places, including India and Burma, where he was with the American Field Service. Usually grouped with Charles Olson and Robert Duncan as "the Black Mountain school" of poetry, he has had an enormous influence, in his anti-academic and anti-symbolist attitude and especially by the positive example of his poetry, on many of the younger poets coming along in the 'fifties and 'sixties.

Creeley's first book of verse, *Le Fou*, was published in 1952; it was followed by a rapid succession, mostly issued by small presses. *For Love: Poems 1950–1960*, published in 1962, revealed the growing scope of his work. *Words: Poems* (1967) and *Pieces* (1969) show him wrestling with longer poems. He is also author of a collection of short stories, *The Gold Diggers* (1954), and a novel, *The Island* (1963). Widely in demand for poetry readings, he has received such honors as a Guggenheim Fellowship and a Rockefeller Foundation grant.

James Dickey

"I am trying to find a way to make poetry (or my poetry, anyway) the kind of thing that means something to people in their life-situations, and get away from the notion of the poem as a sort of display of literary virtues," James Dickey writes. His poetry, coming out of a deep Southern background (he was born in Atlanta, in 1923, on Groundhog Day, he is careful to point out), reveals a deep sense of ordinary experience, but goes beyond the mere chronicling of happenings.

His first appearance in book form, *Into the Stone and Other Poems* (published in *Poets of Today*, VII, 1960), introduced a highly distinctive talent. A strong sense of the continuity of man and nature pervades his poetry as revealed in subsequent volumes, the latest being *The Eye-Beaters, Blood, Victory, Madness, Bulkhead and Mercy* (1970). He is also author of a best-selling novel, *Deliverance* (1970), and several books of literary criticism. He held the Chair of Poetry at the Library of Congress, 1967–69.

Dickey attended Clemson College, graduated from Vanderbilt University, Phi Beta Kappa, magna cum laude, and had the distinction of winning the Cotton Carnival High Hurdles at Memphis. He also took a master's degree at Vanderbilt. He is passionately devoted to hunting and archery ("I am an absolute nut, spending all my money on arrows") and plays the guitar in the style of "three-finger picking." His numerous honors have included a Guggenheim Fellowship, a *Sewanee*

Review Creative Writing Fellowship, and a National Book Award. He has taught on many campuses and since 1969 has been Professor of English and Writer in Residence at the University of South Carolina.

Lawrence Durrell

Of Irish ancestry, Lawrence Durrell spent his life in a large part of the far-flung British Commonwealth and its interests. He was born in Julunda in the Himalayas in 1912, educated first in the college of St. Joseph, Darjeeling, and then in St. Edmund's School, Canterbury. At one time or another he was Foreign Service press officer in Athens and Cairo, press attaché in Alexandria, and director of the British Council institutes of Kalamata, Greece, and Córdoba, Argentina. More recently he was director of public relations for the Government of Cyprus. Meanwhile, he has been a fantastically productive writer, famous most of all for the four novels constituting the "Alexandria Quartet." His poetry, though he began to publish it in the 1930's, is still to be appreciated at its full worth. More than half a dozen volumes of verse have appeared in recent years, including the *Selected Poems* (1956), *Collected Poems* (1960), and most recently, *The Ikons* (1966).

Durrell is a poet who stands apart from most of the fashionable movements and trends. A deeply experienced observer of the human scene, elegant and meditative, he captures the moments and impressions of a life spent far away from the British Isles.

William Everson (Brother Antoninus)

From William Everson to Brother Antoninus back to plain William Everson—this summarizes the life history of the poet who has been called by the *Evergreen Review* "probably the most profoundly moving and durable of the poets of the San Francisco Renaissance."

Born 1912 in Sacramento, Calif., William Everson grew up in Selma. Earning his living as a laborer and farmer, he came under the influence of Robinson Jeffers, which he says "opened my soul to the constitutive religious reality sustaining the cosmos." Everson dropped out of Fresno State College and set out to be a poet. During World War II he was drafted to do alternative service as a conscientious objector. Later he settled in the San Francisco area and was active in the anarcho-pacifist group that gathered around Kenneth Rexroth. Entering the Catholic Church in 1949, he was drawn to the Catholic Worker movement, but in 1951 became a lay brother of the Dominican Order. When the San Francisco Renaissance burst upon public attention in 1957, he was one of its most prominent figures and soon found himself doing poetry readings all over the country. In 1969 he returned to lay life and married; he is now the father of a daughter.

In his early career Everson published several books of poetry privately. He first came to more general attention when New Directions brought out *The Residual Years* (1948), which led to a Guggenheim Fellowship. Books have followed in rapid succession, of which the best known are *The Crooked Lines of God* (1959), *The Hazards of Holiness* (1962), and *The Rose of Solitude* (1967).

Lawrence Ferlinghetti

Publisher of many lively poets and an outstanding San Francisco poet himself, Lawrence Ferlinghetti is known for a rapid succession of books from *Pictures of the Gone World* (1955) to *Back Roads to Far Places* (1971). He is particularly interested in the oral aspects of poetry and frequently goes on the poetry-reading circuit, where he is a favorite of college audiences, who unfailingly identify with him and his poetry. In addition to poetry, Ferlinghetti has published several plays and a novel, *Her* (1960).

Ferlinghetti was born in Yonkers, New York, in 1919. He received an A.B. from the University of North Carolina, M.A. from Columbia, and *Doctorat de l'Université* from the Sorbonne. Returning to the United States, he and Peter D. Martin founded the first all-paperbound bookstore in the country, City Lights, which soon became a publishing house and issued, among many other notable books, Allen Ginsberg's *Howl*. The flat-footed attempt of the San Francisco authorities to suppress the book as obscene greatly redounded to the fame and prestige of the poet and the publisher.

Insisting from the beginning that the poet must be *engagé*, Ferlinghetti says: "The wiggy nihilism of the Beat hipster, if carried to its natural conclusion actually means the death of the creative artist himself" (from *The New American Poetry*, ed. Donald M. Allen, 1960). He is convinced that poets spend too much time concentrating on sheer technique, and that a social concern, akin to that of the 1930's, must inspire contemporary poetry, a prophecy that has subsequently, to a large extent, come true.

Roy Fuller

"Only Roy Fuller has carried over into the nineteen-fifties and early nineteen-sixties the kind of concern with social values, the blend of Marxist historicism and Freudian analysis, which lent the verse of Auden and his coevals so pungent and curious a flavour," the British critic John Press writes in *Rule and Energy* (1963).

Born in 1912 in Failsworth, England, Roy Fuller was educated at private schools and qualified as a solicitor in 1933. He served in the Royal Navy, 1941–46, an experience reflected in many of his poems. For years he was solicitor to the Woolwich Equitable Building Society; and among his publications is *The Building Societies Acts, 1874–1960, with Extracts from Associated Legislation*, which he edited. He is now director of a building society.

Fuller's *Poems* (1939) were followed by more than half a dozen volumes, including *Collected Poems* (1961), *Buff* (1965), and *New Poems* (1968), the last reflecting an increased preoccupation with direct experience and freer in form than his earlier work. He is the author of a number of novels, the latest being *The Carnal Island* (1970). In 1968 he was elected Professor of Poetry at Oxford.

Though often compared to the early Auden, Fuller has gone his own way, deeply concerned about mankind and its public and private fate, but too wary of easy answers to give himself completely to any ideology.

Allen Ginsberg

Allen Ginsberg (born 1926 in Newark, New Jersey) has provoked more controversy than any other poet of his generation. Describing his school of verse as "Beat-Hip-Gnostic-Imagist," Ginsberg has powerfully revived the tradition of the "barbaric yawp" and, like Whitman, has taken himself, mankind, God, and the universe as subject matter, celebrated or lamented in lines composed more for chanting than interment in books. As a practicing and outspoken homosexual, drug-taker, anti-war activist and Zen meditator, he has been a godsend to the mass media looking for newsworthy figures from the literary world.

A graduate of Columbia, Ginsberg during the 1950's moved from one job to another and traveled widely in the United States. He and Jack Kerouac are considered the prime inspiration for the Beat Movement, which constituted a psychological as well as literary watershed in the mid 'fifties. His subsequent travels in foreign countries seem associated with a deepening commitment to Oriental manifestations of religion. He received a Guggenheim Fellowship in 1963–64 but otherwise appears to have attracted the notice of few honor-bestowing organizations. His numerous books, many hardly larger than pamphlets, range from *Howl* (1956) to *Airplane Dreams* (1969).

Again like Whitman, Ginsberg—who acknowledges also such influences as Blake, the Bible, Rimbaud, Shakespeare, Pound, and W. C. Williams—is an extremely uneven poet, alternating between stretches of stridently flat verse and whole sections that can scarcely be matched by any living poet. He has been immensely influential on younger poets and has been one of the leaders in the development of poetry as an oral art.

Thom Gunn

American universities have been importing young English poets on an increasing scale; one of the most notable is Thom Gunn, who appears in the "Movement" anthology *New Lines* but has since developed in a distinctly individual direction. His American experience, which began when he came to the United States on a Fulbright Award, has included time at Stanford and San Antonio State College; from 1958–66 he was a member of the English Department at the University of California, since then a free-lance writer.

Gunn was born in 1929, educated at University College School, Hampstead, and Trinity College, Cambridge. He served in the British Army, 1948–50, and lived in Paris for a large part of 1950 and in Rome during 1953–54 before coming to the United States.

An early bloomer, while still at Cambridge Gunn wrote the poems included in his first book, *Fighting Terms* (1954), a work he has subsequently revised several times. He first came to general attention on John Lehmann's BBC program, "New Soundings." His later books include *Positives* (1966) and *Touch* (1967).

In his earlier poetry there is a tough-minded celebration of black-jacketed motorcycle boys; Gunn himself wrecked his motorcycle while in San Antonio. The emphasis on ruthlessness and will is less evident in his later and more varied work. He writes of himself: "I don't deliberately belong to any school, but I suppose I am part of the National Service generation and have a few of its characteristics: i.e. lack of concern with religion, lack of class, a rather undirected impatience." He lists "reading, drinking, going to films" as his preferred activities.

Robert Hayden

Born in Detroit, Michigan (1913), Robert Hayden was educated at
Wayne State University and the University of Michigan. Beginning
in 1946 he taught for more than two decades at Fisk University,
moving in 1968 to the University of Michigan, where he is now
Professor of English. His first book of verse, *Heartshape in the Dust*,
came out in 1940, followed by *The Lion and the Archer* (1948) and
A Ballad of Remembrance (1962), the latter winning in 1966 the Grand
Prize for Poetry at the First World Festival of Negro Arts held in
Dakar, Senegal. His latest books, *Selected Poems* (1966) and *Words
in the Mourning Time* (1970) have established him as one of the
major poets of his age group. His commitment to the Bahá'í faith
quietly infuses a great deal of his poetry, which can be by turn lyrical,
meditative, and dramatic.

Recipient of the Russell Loines Award (American Academy of
Arts and Letters) in 1970, he is widely known for his poetry readings
on campuses. He is editor of the anthology *Kaleidoscope: Poems by
American Negro Poets* (1967) and edits the poetry section of the
Bahá'í magazine, *World Order*.

Ted Hughes

A poet, like a prophet, frequently is first honored in another country.
Robert Frost's first book was published and acclaimed in England.
Ted Hughes—born in 1930 in Mytholmroyd (West Riding of York-
shire)—came to public attention during a long stay in America, when
his book *The Hawk in the Rain* (1957), won the first publication
award of the Poetry Center of the New York City YM-YWHA. This
was followed by *Lupercal* (1960), *Meet My Folks* (verse for children,
1961), and *Selected Poems* (with Thom Gunn, 1962). He quickly be-
came recognized in both countries as one of the most interesting poets
since the "Movement." His more recent books include *Wodwo* (1967)
and *Crow* (1971). In the latter, his preoccupation with violence and
animal symbolism, which has stirred up lively critical discussion and
controversy, reaches its ultimate intensity, with a vision of man, a
savage, in a world of brutal nature and confronted by a hostile and
mocking God.

A ground wireless mechanic in the Royal Air Force after the War,
Hughes subsequently studied at Cambridge, where he met and married

the distinguished American poet Sylvia Plath (*q.v.*), who was on a Fulbright Fellowship.

Among the honors Hughes has received are first place in the Guinness Poetry Awards, 1958, a Guggenheim Fellowship, 1959–60, and the Hawthornden Prize, 1961.

Philip Larkin

In many ways the most representative of the "Movement" poets is Philip Larkin, who was born in 1922 in Coventry (Warwickshire). Educated at King Henry VIII School, Coventry, and St. John's College, Oxford, he earns his living as librarian of the University of Hull. Larkin lists "listening to jazz" as his favorite recreation, and is author of *All What Jazz: A Record Diary 1961–68*. He has published two novels, *Jill* (1946), and *A Girl in Winter* (1947). The three volumes of verse on which his reputation mainly rests are *The North Ship* (1945), *The Less Deceived* (1955), and *The Whitsun Weddings* (1964).

Larkin's poetry has little in common with the jazz that he listens to. The American poetic appetite, accustomed to the bloody meat offered by the wild men and the exotically spiced dishes of the more academic poets, may at first find Larkin's verse flat, unexciting. He writes about ordinary events and experiences and emotions in a world of suburbs and unheroic days. It is, however, a poetry with great accuracy of observation and an almost unfailing sense for the low-keyed but completely right word and phrase. If he scales no Dantean or Miltonic heights, he is the laureate of the flat plain on which most of life is lived.

Don L. Lee

In the Introduction to his first book, *Think Black!* (1967), Don L. Lee states: "I was born into slavery in Feb. of 1942. In the spring of that same year 110,000 persons of Japanese descent were placed in protective custody by the white people of the United States." He continues: "Black. Poet. Black poet am I. . . . Black art will elevate and enlighten our people and lead them toward an awareness of self, i.e., their blackness. It will show them mirrors. Beautiful symbols. And will aid in the destruction of anything nasty and detrimental to our advancement as a people."

Born in Little Rock, Arkansas, Lee grew up in Detroit, served in the Army 1960–63, and went to college in Chicago. He has taught in various colleges, and is widely known for his poetry readings. His later books include *Black Pride* (1968), *Don't Cry, Scream* (1969), *We Walk the Way of the New World* (1970), and *Selected and New Poems* (1971).

In *Dynamite Voices: New Black Poets of the 1960's* (1970) Lee undertakes to evaluate the rising generation of black poets. In his totally *engagé* stance, he is one of the writers who have made poetry into a weapon of militancy as well as an art.

Laurie Lee

A lyric poet with an exquisitely accurate sense of language is Laurie Lee, who was born in 1914 in the Cotswolds, one of a family of eight. At the age of nineteen he ran away to London and from there went to Spain, playing the fiddle in the streets and taverns, and sleeping where he could. The Spanish Civil War began; he was hustled out of the country but later smuggled himself back in and began broadcasting from Madrid. Subsequently he traveled in Italy, Greece, and Cyprus.

With the onset of World War II he was back in London, where he began to publish poetry. He made documentary films, continuing with this work some time after the end of the war, and visiting Cyprus and India. He was caption writer-in-chief for the Festival of Britain, 1950–51, and was decorated by the Queen. During this time he married Catherine Francesca Polge, the daughter of a French fisherman.

His varied background is reflected in several of his prose books: *We Made a Film in Cyprus* (with Ralph Keene, 1947), *The Voyage of Magellan: A Dramatic Chronicle for Radio* (1948), and *Epstein: A Camera Study of the Sculptor at Work* (1957). He is also the author of *A Rose for Winter: Travels in Andalusia* (1955) and an autobiography, *Cider with Rosie* (1959)—published as *The Edge of Day* in the United States—and continued in *As I Walked Out One Midsummer Morning* (1969).

It is, however, his poetry on which Lee's literary reputation is most firmly based. His first book of verse was *The Sun My Monument* (1944), followed by *The Bloom of Candles* (1947), *My Many-Coated Man* (1955), and *Poems* (1960).

Denise Levertov

Metaphorically speaking, Denise Levertov is the meeting of the poetic east and the poetic west. She was the only poet who appeared both in the predominantly academic *New Poets of England and America: Second Selection* (ed. Donald Hall and Robert Pack, 1962) and the more experimental *The New American Poetry 1945–1960* (ed. Donald M. Allen, 1960). In still other ways, she is a bridge between differing worlds. Her father was related to a famous Hasid philosopher, Schneour Zalman, and, after leaving Russia, eventually became an Anglican priest in England. Her mother was a descendant of the Welsh tailor and mystic, Angel Jones of Mold. Denise Levertov was born in 1923 in England, and educated at home except for ballet school. She met her future husband, the American novelist Mitchell Goodman in 1947 at Geneva, and since 1948 has been mainly in America. She has become an American citizen.

Denise Levertov is the author of nearly a dozen books of poetry, beginning with *The Double Image* (1946), and including *The Sorrow Dance* (1967) with its memorable series of poems on the Viet Nam War, and *Relearning the Alphabet* (1970).

Well known for her poetry readings, Miss Levertov has been—with her husband—an active supporter of draft resistance.

Robert Lowell

By ancestry, Robert Traill Spence Lowell, born in 1917 in Boston, is a Brahmin of the Brahmins—related to James Russell Lowell, Amy Lowell, and President Lowell of Harvard. The stubborn and rebellious New England conscience is part of his heritage. In 1943 he tried twice to enlist but was rejected. Then when he was drafted he refused to serve, maintaining that America was now out of danger and that the mass air raids against enemy civilians could not be defended. He spent five months in federal prison, an experience reflected in some of his poems. Meanwhile he became for a time a Roman Catholic, and his early poetry mirrors a Catholic sensibility superimposed over the Puritan heritage.

Lowell's education was first at Harvard, then at Kenyon (summa cum laude, 1940), where he studied with John Crowe Ransom. He has since been an occasional teacher at various colleges and universities, most recently at Harvard. He was married in 1940 to Jean Stafford.

After their divorce in 1948, he married Elizabeth Hardwick. They have one daughter and live in New York City. Active in protesting the Indo-Chinese War, Lowell, in much of his later poetry, reflects his political and social commitments.

Lowell was first recognized as an important poet with the publication of *Lord Weary's Castle* (1946), a work of formal majesty and agonized power. His *The Mills of the Kavanaughs* (1951) is a more uneven achievement. *Life Studies* (1959) represents a startling departure: poems much more directly personal and written in a relaxed rhythm. The insights gained from psychotherapy plus the experience of reading poetry aloud may account for the increasing immediacy and directness of style. Of his other books, *For the Union Dead* (1964) contains an impressive title poem, whereas *Near the Ocean* (1967) seems to reflect a decline in poetic vitality. His latest collection, *Notebooks, 1967–68* (1969)—reissued in a revised and expanded edition (1970)—is the subject of violent critical controversy, some seeing it as another peak achievement, others as a falling off. Lowell has also published poems freely rendered from, or merely inspired by, foreign poems—*Imitations* (1961). He has adapted American short stories and plays by Racine and Aeschylus for the stage. Among the honors he has received are the Pulitzer Prize, National Book Award, and the Bollingen Translation Prize.

In many ways the central figure in contemporary American poetry, Lowell also reflects some poetic trends in his own highly individual career: in particular the move toward freer forms, the confessional tone, and political engagement.

George MacBeth

Born in the mining village of Shotts in Lanarkshire, Scotland, in 1932, George MacBeth was educated at King Edward VII School (Sheffield, Yorkshire) and New College, Oxford. Since 1955 he has held a key role in British cultural life, producing programs about the arts and literature for the BBC.

MacBeth's first book, *A Form of Words* (1954) was followed by half a dozen others, including *The Broken Places* (1963), *The Colour of Blood* (1967), *The Night of Stones* (1968), and *The Burning Cone* (1970). He has edited *The Penguin Book of Sick Verse* (1963) and several other anthologies.

Almost as versatile in his command of poetic forms as Auden, MacBeth reveals a mordant humor and at times a ghoulishly Gothic sensibility in his poetry. His eye is extremely observant and unfailingly accurate in catching the nuances of everyday life. At times his play of wit and a certain dancing-in-the-graveyard high spirits blind the reader to the underlying seriousness of his poetry and his ability to treat with insight such traditional themes as life, death, love, war. During a period when British poetry tends to be understated and restrained, MacBeth's work stands out for its vitality and variety.

Vassar Miller

Louis Untermeyer quotes Vassar Miller as saying: "Poetry, like all art, has a trinitarian function: creative, redemptive, and sanctifying. It is creative because it takes the raw materials of fact and feeling and makes them into that which is neither fact nor feeling. It is redemptive because it can transform the pain and ugliness of life into joy and beauty. It is sanctifying because it thus gives the transitory at least a relative form and meaning. Hence poetry, whether avowedly so or not, is always religious; it is akin to prayer, an act of love."

In Vassar Miller's first two books of poetry there is the marriage of strict forms strictly written—the sonnet has been a favorite of hers—with a religious intensity seldom encountered since Gerard Manley Hopkins. Her more recent work has represented a movement toward freer forms and a greater variety of subject matter, though the religious themes are still central.

Born in 1924 in Houston, Texas, Vassar Miller received her B.S. and M.A. at the University of Houston and lives in Houston. Afflicted with cerebral palsy from birth, she has dedicated herself single-mindedly to poetry and has demonstrated—if demonstration were needed—that craftsmanship, religious fervor, and personal joy and agony can produce significant poetry. Her books: *Adam's Footprint* (1956), *Wage War on Silence* (1960), *My Bones Being Wiser* (1963), *Onions and Roses* (1968).

Richard Murphy

In many ways an odd man out, Richard Murphy has spent most of his life far from the centers of poetic ferment and intrigue and has developed a style—leisurely, elegiac, meditative—that seems at times old-fashioned but is peculiarly suited for the long narrative or reflective poems in which he specializes.

Born on a farm belonging to his grandparents in County Galway,

Ireland, in 1927, Murphy found his early childhood divided between Ireland and Ceylon, where his father was a civil servant. The poet took a degree at Magdalen College, Oxford, and later studied at the Sorbonne. More at home in the countryside than the cities, he has at various periods been a watchman on a salmon river, a sheep-farmer, and skipper of a Galway hooker sailing off the west coast of Ireland. In 1964 he made his first coast-to-coast reading tour of the United States and has subsequently taught at the University of Virginia and Colgate University.

Murphy's books are *The Archaeology of Love* (1955), *Sailing to an Island* (1963), and *The Battle of Aughrim* (1968). The last was dramatized over the BBC, and recordings are available from Claddagh Records, Dublin.

Howard Nemerov

Born 1920 in New York City, Howard Nemerov published his first book of poetry, *The Image and the Law*, in 1947. This has been followed by numerous other volumes, including *Mirrors and Windows* (1958), *New and Selected Poems* (1960), *The Next Room of the Dream: Poems and Two Plays* (1962), and *The Blue Swallows* (1967). He is also the author of several novels and a collection of short stories, as well as works in literary criticism. Nemerov, a Harvard graduate, served as a pilot with the RCAF and USAF during World War II. Married to an Englishwoman, Margaret Russell, he is the father of three children. He has taught at many schools, currently at Washington University, and during 1963–64 was Consultant in Poetry to the Library of Congress. Among his honors: National Institute of Arts and Letters grant, first Theodore Roethke Memorial Award, Guggenheim Fellowship, Fellow of the Academy of American Poets.

"Howard Nemerov's poems are, on the one hand, often about bugs, birds, trees, and running water," Julia Randall Sawyer writes in *Contemporary Poets*. "On the other, they are about the Great American Society and its works, e.g. the loyalty oath, the committee, the Indian-head nickel, and the packaged meat in the super-market." The poet's career has been one of steadily widening and deepening talent, so that he now ranks as one of the most solidly established poets of his generation. He is here represented by several short poems as well as the fifteen-part "Runes," which illustrates his command of the architecture of long poems.

Bink Noll

Bink Noll (born 1927) grew up in South Orange, N.J. He received his A.B. at Princeton, M.A. in writing at Johns Hopkins, and Ph.D. in English at the University of Colorado. A member of the English Department at Dartmouth for a number of years, he went to Beloit College in 1961 where he is now Professor of English and Poet in Residence, and reputedly the most accomplished gourmet cook in town.

The Center of the Circle (1962) is the traditional "slender first volume" but reveals a highly developed and unusual talent. The author proposed at first to call it "Elegies and Other Pieces," and the elegiac tone—half wry, half resigned—is strong throughout the book. Many of the poems grow from intensely personal experiences of family or friendship, but the experience becomes the starting point for poems more than merely personal. These extremely civilized poems show an extraordinary sense of language and the formal aspects of poetry, and beneath their urbane surface lurks a savage intensity.

His second book, The Feast (1967), reveals again Noll's ability to extract from language its full richness, while pointing at the same time toward the simpler style that characterizes many of his recent poems.

During 1960–61 Noll was Fulbright lecturer in American Literature at Zaragoza, Spain, and in 1967–68 Writer in Residence at Princeton. He has read his poetry on numerous campuses and is a director of the Wisconsin-Minnesota Poetry Circuit.

Kenneth Patchen

"Patchen seems to me more like Blake than any other contemporary poet," Frederick Eckman wrote in Poetry (September, 1958). "There is the same sense of deep isolation, partly self-willed, from the mass of humanity; of choking rage at shoddy secularity, orthodoxy, and materialism; of a tender, child-like wonder for the beautiful, pure, and innocent; of a desire for joy and freedom that leads at last into mystic contemplation."

The son of a steelmill worker, Patchen was born in 1911 in Niles, Ohio. At seventeen he went to work in the steelmill. For a year he studied at Alexander Meiklejohn's Experimental College, then functioning at the University of Wisconsin. Several years of drifting about the country followed. He was married in 1934 to Miriam Oikemus. He received a Guggenheim Fellowship in 1936, the same year in which his first book of poetry, *Before the Brave*, was published. He has since written several dozen books, mostly poetry or combinations of poetry and prose or poetry and drawings; and despite a severe spinal injury which has long limited his activities, he has been one of the most productive and provocative American poets. In 1967 Patchen received one of the first grants made by the National Endowment for the Arts. His *Collected Poems* appeared in 1968.

A pioneer in reading poetry with jazz, Patchen (like Blake) is notably successful in combining poetry with the visual arts. Many of his more recent books illustrate this marriage of the arts. The "Painted Edition Patchen Books" are volumes created individually by the author.

Discussed in detail by Amos N. Wilder in *Spiritual Aspects of the New Poetry* Patchen's poetry is out of all conventional modern poetic grooves and is full of both violent and tender surprises for the perceptive reader.

Brian Patten

Born in Liverpool (1946), a city that has since become one of the poetry centers of England, Brian Patten has the distinction of earning most of his living from poetry readings. He has been described by Allen Ginsberg as "an atomic Adam"; Edward Lucie-Smith remarks with more restraint: "The poetry has a song-like quality, plaintive and nostalgic, yet is sufficiently dense and sufficiently abrupt in its transitions to avoid looking like words in search of a tune."

Patten dropped out of school at fourteen to work on a local newspaper and subsequently traveled to Paris, Spain, Tangier, and Dublin. At one time he was editor of *Underdog*, a magazine of the so-called poetic underground. He has received the Eric Gregory Award for poetry.

Portraits (1962) was privately printed. It was followed by his two best-known books, *Little Johnny's Confession* (1967) and *Notes to the Hurrying Man* (1969). Patten refuses to identify himself with any school of poetry and says of his work: "Outside poetry I feel there are too many ways of saying things for me to be able to speak clearly. So the poems are their own statements. A translation into words of a world beyond worlds is the best I can say about them."

Sylvia Plath

Of German and Austrian descent, Sylvia Plath was born in Boston (1932), the daughter of a professor of biology and scientific German, the "daddy" who figures prominently in a number of love-hate poems. After graduating from Smith College, she went to Cambridge as a Fulbright scholar and received her M.A. in 1957. Meanwhile she had met and married the British poet Ted Hughes. After a brief return to America, the two settled permanently in England. Her first book, *The Colossus*, was published in 1960. Along the way two children were born. In 1963 her autobiographical novel, *The Bell Jar*, was brought out in England under a pseudonym and in 1966 under her real name; American publication did not occur until 1971.

Toward the end of her life Sylvia Plath wrote at a frenzied rate, sometimes three poems a day, as though she were racing death, which came by her own hand in 1963. The poems published posthumously in 1965 under the title of *Ariel* revealed a depth of anguish and clear-eyed madness hardly rivaled by any other poets of the "confessional" school. Robert Penn Warren says of the book: "It scarcely seems a book at all, rather a keen, cold gust of reality as though somebody had knocked out a window pane on a brilliant night."

Theodore Roethke

A poet so versatile in technique and subject matter that the critics find in him not a single "voice" but a whole choir of singers is Theodore Roethke. Born in 1908 in Saginaw, Michigan, he studied at the University of Michigan and Harvard. After teaching at Lafayette College, Pennsylvania State University, and Bennington College, he went to the University of Washington in 1947 and was Professor of English until his death in 1963. His widow is the former Beatrice Heath O'Connell, whom he married in 1953.

Roethke's first book appeared in 1941, *Open House and Other Poems*. It was followed by several others, which were later included in *The Waking: Poems 1933–1953*, published in 1953 and winner of the Pulitzer Prize. More recent works are *Words for the Wind* (1958), *I am! Says the Lamb* (verse for children, 1961), and *The Far Field*, published posthumously.

A succession of poetic honors came to Roethke—among others, two Guggenheim Fellowships, and the Bollingen Prize for poetry (1958). During 1955 he was a Fulbright lecturer in American literature, in Italy.

Moving easily from meditations in a greenhouse to tender love songs and vast portraits of wild countryside, Roethke is a poet of singularly varied moods and poetic forms. In his most recent poetry the mystic came more to the fore. He never boxed himself in by premature success.

His poetry continued to grow and change to the end of his life. His work remains a key influence in the evolution of contemporary poetry.

Anne Sexton

Anne Sexton—*née* Harvey—has lived a thoroughly New England life. She was born in 1928 in Newton, Mass., grew up in Wellesley, and lives now in Newton Lower Falls, frequently summering in Gloucester, on Cape Ann, and in Maine. She is the mother of two daughters who often figure in her intensely personal and frequently stark poetry. While in high school she wrote poetry but lost interest until later, when she resumed under the stimulation of Robert Lowell at Boston University. Along the way she was a fashion model and a librarian. Her first book, *To Bedlam and Part Way Back* (1960), revealed a classical severity of technique combined with a probing examination of the author's mental breakdown and recovery. The second book, *All My Pretty Ones* (1962), continues the same autobiographical strain, but with greater breadth and freedom of style. Her more recent books include *Love Poems* (1969) —a torrid and frequently tortured series of confessions in verse—and *Transformations* (1971).

Anne Sexton has received a series of awards. She was Robert Frost Fellow at Bread Loaf and was one of the first persons selected for the recently created Radcliffe New Institute for Independent Study. When the American Academy of Arts and Letters came to a parting of the ways with the American Academy in Rome and abolished its Prix de Rome Award, she was chosen to receive the first traveling Literary Fellowship, which had been established to take the place of the former Prix. In 1967 she was awarded the Pulitzer Prize.

In the poetry of Anne Sexton one finds combined an exquisite and precise sense of technique and the agonizing compulsion to explore psychological experiences to their roots, without pity for the poet or the reader. The themes of death and love weave in and out of her poetry, and the reality of the present moment is constantly seen against the backdrop of extinction.

Karl Shapiro

Karl Shapiro was born in 1913 in Baltimore and educated at the University of Virginia and at Johns Hopkins. Drafted into the Army in March 1941, he served in the South Pacific until 1945. During 1946–47 he was Consultant in Poetry at the Library of Congress. He taught at Johns

Hopkins 1947–50 and was editor of *Poetry* magazine 1950–56. Subsequently he taught at the University of Nebraska and the Chicago Circle campus of the University of Illinois. He is now Professor of English, University of California at Davis.

Shapiro's first book, *Poems*, appeared—privately printed—in 1935. His reputation dates from *Person, Place and Thing* (1942). In this and in several other wartime books, notably *V-Letter and Other Poems* (1944), the War generation seemed to find its voice, despite the poet's insistence that he was not a "war poet." These early poems of Shapiro's are disillusioned, in the sense that they offer no ready-made ideologies and solutions, but there is in them a feeling and sometimes a real tenderness beneath the realistic and hard-bitten surface. In 1953 his previous poetry was brought together in *Poems, 1940–1953*, followed in 1958 by *Poems of a Jew* and in 1964 by *The Bourgeois Poet*.

Shapiro has twice been awarded a Guggenheim Fellowship. He won the Pulitzer Prize in 1945. In his critical thinking, he has been moving away from the "school of Eliot" and has become a defender of the contemporary wild men of poetry—see his *Beyond Criticism* (1953) and *In Defense of Ignorance* (1960).

At the time of *The Bourgeois Poet* Shapiro was violently moving away from polished, intellectual verse, and toward the style of the Beats and other poetic nonconformists. *White-Haired Lover* (1968) represents yet another swing, this time to the sonnet and lyricism.

W. D. Snodgrass

That remarkable training ground for young writers, the University of Iowa, could claim another success in 1960 when William DeWitt Snodgrass' *Heart's Needle* (1959) won the Pulitzer Prize. Snodgrass was born in 1926 in Wilkinsburg, Pa. He attended Geneva College one year, then joined the Navy. Upon his discharge he returned to Geneva College for a year, subsequently transferred to the State University of Iowa for his B.A., M.A., and M.F.A. degrees. He has taught on various campuses and since 1968 has been Professor of English and Speech at Syracuse University.

Married in 1946 and the father of a daughter, Snodgrass was divorced in 1953, remarried in 1954, widowed in 1966 and remarried again in 1967. The details of his family life, together with his experiences under psychoanalysis are highly relevant to his poetry, much of which is extremely personal. The title poem of his first book is a ten-part sequence, built around the pathos of his relationship with his little daughter at the time of the divorce. Few modern poets have laid their hearts as directly bare, and few have done it with a surer touch or greater technical skill.

His later book, *After Experience* (1968), contains some "confessional" poems, but moves toward a greater preoccupation with social and philosophic questions; the poetic form also tends to be looser and more experimental.

Gary Snyder

"The phenomenal world experienced at certain pitches," Gary Snyder says, "is totally living, exciting, mysterious, filling one with a trembling awe, leaving one grateful and humble. The wonder of the mystery returns direct to one's own senses and consciousness: inside and outside; the voice breathes, 'Ah!' "

Born in San Francisco in 1930, Snyder grew up in the Pacific Northwest where he worked as a logger and forest ranger. At Reed College he specialized in anthropology and literature, and at Berkeley he studied Japanese and Chinese civilization. A Bollingen research grant enabled him to spend 1966–67 in Japan studying Zen Buddhism under the master Oda Sessō Rōshi. While there he met his future wife, Masa, whom he has celebrated in later poems.

Snyder's long list of books extends from *Riprip* (1959) to *Regarding Wave* (1970). In them he proclaims and celebrates "the most archaic values on earth. They go back to the late paleolithic; the fertility of the soil, the magic of animals, the power-vision in solitude, the terrifying initiation and rebirth, the love and ecstasy of the dance, the common work of the tribe." Profoundly influenced by the American Indians, Zen, and his own knowledge of nature, Snyder has long been deeply aware of ecology and involved in the movement to reverse man's exploitative attitude toward the planet that sustains him.

Dylan Thomas

A legend long before his death (1953) at the age of thirty-nine, Thomas captured the imagination of the general public which alternatively clucked disapprovingly and chuckled with delight as it read of his buffooneries on his lecture tours in America and his undisputed ability to outdrink any of his poetic companions.

Thomas may have drunk himself to an early grave; he did not drink when he wrote. Despite what at first seems a barbaric splendor of chaos in his poems, they show a highly disciplined poetic intelligence back of the kaleidoscopic surface. Few poets have been as conscious of sheer technique or worked at it more unrelentingly.

Born in 1914 in Swansea (Wales) and sketchily educated at the local school, Thomas, at the age of twenty, published his first volume, 18 Poems (1934), a work utterly out of key with the dominant Auden-Spender school of socially conscious poetry. It was followed by a steady stream of books—stories, autobiography, plays, and verse. Collected Poems came out the year before his death and was followed by various posthumous works, including the wholly delightful radio play, Under Milk Wood (1954). Many of his poems are available on records.

A vast and increasing amount of scholarship has already been devoted to Thomas. The legendary events of his poetry tours are recounted by John Malcolm Brinnin, Dylan Thomas in America: An Intimate Journal (1955). Thomas' wife, Caitlin Thomas, has told her side of their relationship in Leftover Life to Kill (1957). Important as a poet, Thomas—probably more than any other one man—created the market for poetry readings and prepared the way for countless other poets who have followed his example.

R. S. Thomas

A long line of country parsons—Herbert, Herrick, Crabbe, Andrew Young, to mention a few—has enriched British verse with accurate and frequently hard-bitten observations of rural life. The latest is the Welshman R. S. Thomas (no relation to Dylan Thomas), who emerged in 1955 when his privately published volumes, plus some new poems, appeared in Song at the Year's Turning, with a long, laudatory introduction by John Betjeman. This won the Heinemann Award of the Royal Society of Literature. It was followed by Poetry for Supper (1958), Tares (1961), The Bread of Truth (1963), Pietà (1966), and Not That He Brought Flowers (1968).

Born in 1913 at Cardiff, Thomas studied at the University of Wales and St. Michael's College (Llandaff). Ordained deacon in 1936 and priest in 1937, he has served a number of country churches, teaching himself Welsh meanwhile. His poetry contains no easy piety and consolation. He is said to be a dour and taciturn man; certainly his poetry has an angular quality as he pictures the stark life of the Welsh small farmers. At times he broadens out to consider the condition of twentieth-century mankind as a whole, and occasionally he deals with an explicitly religious theme. Living in Wales, he has been shielded from the literary coteries that flourish in London and has developed his own style. Within his somewhat limited scope of subject matter he is one of the most interesting poets now writing in Great Britain, though still little known in America.

John Wain

One of the most interesting and promising of the "Movement" poets, John Wain has evolved from the deliberate understatement and *terza rima* fixation of his first book, *A Word Carved on a Sill* (1956), toward a freer use of form and an outspoken social conscience. His willingness to pull out all the stops when appropriate, as in *Weep Before God* (1961), resulted in one of the few successful poems about the atomic bomb, "A Song about Major Eatherly." His book-length poem, *Wildtrack* (1965), and *Letters to Five Artists* (1969) reveal a still further departure from the tidy doctrines of the "Movement" and demonstrates that Wain is now completely following his own strong and individual poetic impulses.

John Wain was born in 1925 at Stoke-on-Trent, and received his degree from St. John's College, Oxford. During 1947–55 he was lecturer in English literature at the University of Reading, a position he resigned to become a free-lance author and critic, occasionally serving as a visiting professor on various campuses. Supporting himself by lectures "on three continents," film and dramatic criticism, radio and TV work, etc., he has found time to write numerous novels in addition to the poetry and is the author of several works of literary criticism, including *Essays on Literature and Ideas* (1963). *Sprightly Running* (1962) is his autobiography.

Diane Wakoski

"My external life is dull," Diane Wakoski writes. "Anything interesting about me is in my poems." Indeed, the plain biographical facts lack the high drama that some poets can boast. Born 1937 in Whittier, California, she was educated at the University of California (Berkeley), worked for several years in a bookstore, taught junior high school 1963–69, and since then has been a teacher at the New School for Social Research, New York City. She has been the recipient of a National Council on the Arts Prize and a Robert Frost Fellowship (Bread Loaf Writers Conference).

If Miss Wakoski's external life has been dull it may be partly because her inner life as a poet is full. Widely recognized as one of the most promising poets of her generation, she is author of almost a dozen volumes, including *Coins and Coffins* (1962), *Discrepancies and Apparitions* (1966), *Inside the Blood Factory* (1968), *The Magellanic Clouds* (1969), and *The Motorcycle Betrayal Poems* (1971).

Derek Walcott

The most interesting voice to come from the West Indies in recent years is Derek Walcott. Born in 1930 in Castries, St. Lucia, he was educated at St. Mary's College and the University of the West Indies. He has at various times been a teacher, journalist, and theatrical director and is the author of more than half a dozen plays. Among the honors he has received for his poetry are a Guinness Prize, a Royal Society of Literature Award, and the Cholmondeley Award.

As early as 1948 Walcott published a first volume of verse, *Twenty-five Poems*, but he first came to general attention in 1962 when one of the leading British houses brought out *In a Green Night: Poems 1948–1960*. This book revealed an impressively rich command of the magic and majesty of language, and a point of view rarely represented in English poetry. Many of the poems reflect the poet's double racial heritage: European and Negro. From this inner dialogue arise some of his most moving poems.

His latest books, *The Castaway* (1965) and *The Gulf* (1969), have revealed a steady development of scope and command. The title poem of the latter has a Miltonic quality of resonance and marks the author as one of the living poets most likely to achieve major status.

Chad Walsh

Born in South Boston, Virginia (1914), Chad Walsh grew up in Marion, Virginia, where during high school and junior college he worked for Sherwood Anderson's two weeklies. He received his A.B. in French from the University of Virginia and Ph.D. in English from the University of Michigan. Since 1945 he has been a member of the English faculty at Beloit College. During this time he has twice served as a Fulbright lecturer in American literature (Turku, Finland, 1957–58, and Rome, 1962).

Walsh has published a number of prose books in literary criticism, religion (he is a part-time Episcopal priest), and social theory, as well as five volumes of verse, the most recent being *The Psalm of Christ*

(1964), *The Unknowing Dance* (1964), and *The End of Nature* (1969). He has twice received Society of Midland Authors Awards and Yaddo Fellowships and was the first Protestant to be accorded the annual Spirit Award of the Catholic Poetry Society. As a result of giving poetry readings on various campuses, he has become especially interested in the oral aspects of poetry, and has recently been involved in writing experimental radio dramas. He is married to Eva Tuttle, a member of the English faculty at Rockford College, and they have four daughters.

Richard Wilbur

Endowed with a superb command of poetic technique and an observant eye, Richard Wilbur (born in 1921 in New York City) established himself with his first book of poetry, *The Beautiful Changes* (1947), followed by *Ceremony and Other Poems* (1950), *Things of This World* (1956), *Advice to a Prophet* (1961), *The Poems of Richard Wilbur* (1963), and *Walking to Sleep* (1969). His versatility is revealed by his other books: *A Bestiary*, which he edited (1955), translations of Molière's *Misanthrope* (1955), *Tartuffe* (1963), *School for Wives* (1971), and his edition of Poe's poems (1959).

Among the honors he has received are two Guggenheim Awards, the Prix de Rome, 1954 (where he wrote "A Baroque Wall-Fountain in the Villa Sciarra," included in this anthology), the Pulitzer Prize, 1957, and an extended trip to Russia in 1961 as State Department cultural representative, under the cultural exchange program. In 1971 he was awarded the Bollingen Prize in Poetry.

Wilbur received his A.B. and an honorary A.M. at Amherst, an A.M. at Harvard, and an honorary L.H.D. at Lawrence College. He has taught at Harvard and Wellesley and since 1957 has been Professor of English at Wesleyan University.

It is often remarked that the universities and foundations have replaced the traditional patrons of the arts. Wilbur is one of the most gifted of the poets who demonstrate that the new system of "patronage" can sometimes discern and encourage talent when it first becomes evident. If the word "esthete" may be used nonpejoratively, Wilbur is the outstanding example in contemporary American poetry.

James Wright

James Wright was born, 1927, at Martin's Ferry, Ohio, received his B.A. at Kenyon College (where he studied with John Crowe Ransom) and his Ph.D. at the University of Washington (where he studied with Theodore Roethke). He has taught on various campuses and is currently a member of the English faculty at Hunter College.

Wright's first book, *The Green Wall* (1957), won the annual Yale Series of Younger Poets contest. It was followed two years later by *Saint Judas*. In these two books the poet showed a strong preference for traditional stanza forms and an attitude toward subject matter sometimes compared to that of Frost, Robinson, and Hardy. His later poetry, *The Branch Will Not Break* (1963) and *Shall We Gather at the River* (1968), is much freer in form, and more inwardly turned.

Describing himself as a "bookish man" whose life has been uneventful, Wright has been the recipient of numerous honors, among them a Fulbright Fellowship at the University of Vienna, a Guggenheim Fellowship, a grant from the National Institute of Arts and Letters, and a Kenyon Review Fellowship. He has done verse translations of Theodor Storm, George Trakl, Cesar Vallejo, and Pablo Neruda.

INDEX

INDEX

of Authors and Titles

Names of the authors are in CAPITALS. The first page reference after each name refers to the poems, the second to the biographical note.

Titles, listed under author's name, are in *italics*. When there is no title, the first line, bracketed, is used. The initial words *a*, *an*, and *the*, are disregarded in the alphabetical arrangement.